Britain Since 1945

EDITED BY
TERRY GOURVISH
and
ALAN O'DAY

MACMILLAN

First published 1991 by
THE MACMILLAN PRESS LTD
Houndmills, Basingstoke, Hampshire RG21 2XS
and London
Companies and representatives
throughout the world

ISBN 0–333–49157–2 hardcover
ISBN 0–333–49158–0 paperback

A catalogue record for this book is available
from the British Library.

Reprinted 1992, 1994

Printed in Hong Kong

Contents

Preface

Britain Since 1945 is similar to companion volumes in the 'Problems in Focus' series in assessing a limited number of important themes. The book does not pretend to treat all the issues of the period or to offer a unified view of the time. Each contributor has stressed essential aspects of the age but the articles are the product of individual perspectives and do not attempt to present an identical or even consistent outlook.

The editors are grateful to the contributors who accepted our nagging, particularly about length, with grace and responded in a helpful way to criticism. Several generously offered construc-tive comment on other articles in the collection. We are pleased to acknowledge the totality of what is a joint effort to produce a book useful to students, teachers and scholars. We benefited from the support of Vanessa Graham who encouraged us to develop the book and as our editor at Macmillan showed a tolerant attitude to occasional difficulties.

T. R. G.
A. O'D.

1. Decline or Resurgence? Post-War Britain

TERRY GOURVISH and ALAN O'DAY

ALTHOUGH battered and bruised by the war, Britain looked to the future with considerable optimism in 1945. There were strong expectations that victory could be translated into broader social and economic achievements, that a 'new Jerusalem' could be created. To ensure that it was not still-born, as the 'land fit for heroes' had been in 1918, the nation turned its war leader, Churchill, out of office and elected a Labour government. Soon it became apparent that paradise could not be achieved quickly. As in John Mortimer's *Paradise Postponed*, the new world proved elusive, in fact, indefinitely postponed.

Britain's failure to live up to the expectations of many among the wartime generation encouraged disillusionment, but it also opened a lively debate on causes and possible remedies. Was there an absence of commitment to change? Did Britain simply lack sufficient resources? Was the attempt to maintain 'Great Power' status a mistake? Or, as a number of writers have asserted recently, was the very quest for a new society the root of the difficulty? Did the reforms intended to create the rebirth of Britain contribute to its perceived decline? 'Failure', or at least a widespread sense of 'decline', set in train a long-term discussion about objectives and the means to achieve them in the post-war environment.

Consideration of the options available to post-war governments has hinged on the matter of the country's economic performance, which has often proved to be a direct influence on rates of change generally and the enthusiasm for reform. Britain's economic condition has been a key political issue since the war. Both Labour and the Conservatives have appealed to the electorate on the basis of the perceived health of the economy. Governments have triumphed or fallen with the voters' interpretation of the economic record. The dominance of economic

1

concerns has not been unique to the post-1945 period nor has it been an exclusively British feature, of course. Between the wars, economic issues and notably the high levels of unemployment raised strong emotions, but there was also a belief that economics was a science functioning independently of government tinkering. In contrast, from 1945 to the late 1970s there was fairly general agreement that the state, armed with Keynesian macroeconomic theory, should be the strategic manager of the economy.

Evaluation of Britain's economic progress involves three separate strands. First, it means an analysis of absolute growth rates and the distribution of wealth, with necessary subdivisions by sector and period. Second, the domestic experience has to be placed alongside that of other advanced economies, again giving due weight to subperiods and special factors. Finally, there is a 'psychological' dimension – how the state of the economy has been perceived by people at grass roots level. Though the strands are linked each has separate implications and ramifications. This book, as one would expect, gives due attention to an assessment of economic trends, examining the structures in which the economy operated, the constraints on growth, and the consequences of both. But it is not a volume dealing exclusively with economic analysis but rather one which seeks to assess the relevance of economics in the provision of social services, education, housing and planning, the demands of women for equal pay, the relative position of racial minorities and problems on the country's periphery, notably the violence in Northern Ireland. Within the debate on political economy there is an underlying attempt to determine the extent to which Britain has declined or experienced a resurgence in the four decades since the end of the war.

Clearly, to speak of Britain as an entity or of the years since 1945 as a unity would be foolish. There was no single Britain at any time. While over the period much changed for the whole country, individual sections and distinct geographical regions had differing experiences. It would be more accurate to refer to several 'Britains'. The divisions of Scotland, Wales and Northern Ireland come obviously to mind, as does the so-called 'north-south divide', all features which pre-date 1945, of course. Other necessary distinctions include class, occupation, gender, race and generation. Not surprisingly, visions of post-war Britain depend on the standpoint that is taken from a broad range of experiences. And yet, despite these differing perspectives, and the numerous shocks to the system created by war and economic crisis (Korea, Suez, the 1967 devaluation, the 1973 oil crisis, etc.), British institutions of all kinds have remained fairly stable, and in some instances rigidly conservative. Notwithstanding talk in the 1980s of 'breaking the mould', there has been a high degree of consensus about the forms for conducting national disputes, the right of dissent and the desire to continue the basic social fabric. Reform has proceeded by consent and has been gradual. Only in Northern Ireland has the essential agreement on the survival of the present State been challenged. Here, and only here, has the acceptance of the elementary rules for society and politics been rejected by a sufficiently sizeable section of the community to undermine the legitimacy of government.

Institutional stability should not be taken for tranquillity and an absence of change. In fact, post-war Britain has experienced marked changes, and not a few contradictions. In the economy, for example, manufacturing industry has contracted sharply, while the financial sector, and the prestige of occupations associated with it, has blossomed. Within specific sectors progress has differed markedly also. Since the mid-1960s Britain's position as a producer of mass-market automobiles has deteriorated, but the demand for high-value, quality cars such as Jaguar and Rolls Royce has grown. Curiously, at the same time as its domestic textile industry contracted, Britain emerged as a fashion centre capable of mounting a serious challenge to France and Italy. Education, too, has reflected the full range of diverse experience. From the 1970s privileged institutions at all levels have enhanced their already impressive reputations, attracting rising numbers of overseas students. However, over the same period public sector education has suffered financially and fallen in esteem. The same economic changes have also inspired totally divergent interpretations. Thus, the change of direction produced by governments since 1979 has inspired Cassandras bewailing the end of Keynesianism, the assault on the public sector, and the collapse of manufacturing, while enthusiastic disciples preach the virtues of monetarism, a low borrowing requirement, and the 'economic miracle' produced by an 'enterprise society'. It is too early, perhaps, for a considered perspective on the economic achievements of the 1980s, but as shown in this book the record has been equivocal, to say the least. The resignation of Margaret Thatcher, following arguments about the strength of Britain's commitment to a unified Europe, opposition to the poll tax, and concern about the quality of education and other vital services, points towards a more critical conclusion than was popular five years ago.

Politics, while operating within institutions that appear stable, has also changed significantly since the 1940s as successive generations of party leaders have come and gone. Before the early 1960s the leading figures were drawn from a generation whose formative experiences pre-dated 1945, and sometimes went back to the period before 1914: Churchill, Eden, Attlee and Macmillan. In the 1960s and 70s a new group emerged. They also had pre-1945 antecedents but tended to have reached maturity and more particularly acquired responsibility in the years following the war. They shared their predecessors' concerns but frequently gave older visions a fresh focus. By the 1980s a third generation was politically dominant. This had few pre-war memories, no direct experience of the spectres of the 1930s such as fascism and mass unemployment, little regard for old international alignments, and expressed a profound distrust of orthodox economic ideas and business methods. Many of them were keen to reverse the supposed enervating effects of the welfarist reforms of the 1940s. Thus, beneath the veneer of continuity and stability there lay essential differences of temperament, outlook, and choice of the means to create a revitalised Britain.

The idea of reconstruction has also changed with these political trends. In the late 1940s, the term meant both the rebuilding of destroyed cities and industry and the reconversion of the country to civilian life. For many, as indicated already, it also meant a commitment to the restructuring of British society in ways which would ensure universalism of social provision, equality of opportunity, and the destruction of barriers inhibiting the flow of talent. The next generation of politicians did not challenge these goals but gave certain of them distinctive meanings and set fresh priorities. By the 1970s, however, the prospect of a reconstructed Britain seemed much more remote. Social inequality persisted, the economy had faltered badly, and considerable dissatisfaction was being expressed at the periphery, in Scotland, but more especially in Northern Ireland. By the 1970s reconstruction had diverse meanings. For some the traditional aims remained paramount, but for others, and in particular the 'New Right', it represented a challenge to the very assumptions and aspirations of the post-war consensus.

This volume assesses and re-examines a number of the principal issues of the post-1945 period. Its object is to highlight in a concise manner specific problems and remedies though the chapters adopt distinct and individual perspectives. The book begins with Maurice Kirby's investigation of the performance of the economy. His piece neatly illuminates the equivocal nature of the record, showing that although the country achieved historically respectable growth rates, it compared badly with other advanced societies, particularly in manufacturing. He also notes that the Thatcher programme of the 1980s has been less novel and made a smaller impact than has been maintained by political propagandists. Kirby's account has two other valuable features: it provides insights into the economic constraints upon social planning; and, indirectly, explains why comparatively poor growth rates have not led to public disruption or even disillusionment. Despite the many weaknesses identified at a national level, the standard of living in Britain, including Scotland and Northern Ireland, has risen substantially since 1945, if at an uneven pace.

Jose Harris, like Kirby, presents her topic – the Welfare State – in both a domestic and an international context. In outlining the extent and quality of social provision in Britain, she contests the popular argument of Corelli Barnett in *The Audit of War* that Britain's 'decline' should be blamed upon wartime aspirations and the pursuance of social policies which the country could not afford. Her contention is that Britain spent less on welfare than other major economies even in the 1950s. Moreover, she seeks to exonerate William Beveridge from the charge that he tried to impose principles and programmes irrespective of the fiscal implications. The post-war reforms were never intended to be more than a limited programme. The deep-rooted belief in self-help, the notion of the 'deserving poor', and due regard to the cost to central government of reform – all remained entrenched features of social policy. The 'Welfare State' was intended to provide a safety net which allowed people sufficient security to expand their potential. Far from undermining responsibility, the Beveridge reforms were designed to reinforce individualism. Thus, Harris provides a useful reappraisal of welfare provision while pointing out how such provision has been interpreted in the political debates of the 1980s. For many students her analysis will serve as an apt example of the shifting sands of historical interpretation, and the use of the past by political polemicists.

Critics of the post-war economic record often attribute Britain's shortcomings to the undue influence of trade unions and the frequency of industrial action. Chris Wrigley's chapter provides a detailed examination of the government's involvement in the pay bargaining process. Concentrating in particular on prices and incomes policies he shows that until the late 1970s much of the strategy revolved around negotiations designed to satisfy workers' demands without pressing too severely on prices and industrial competitiveness. At the core of the relationship was the much firmer manipulation of public sector pay and prices. While it is difficult to assess the effectiveness of government policies, it is clear that both formal and informal interventions have tended to be fragile. Yet, as Wrigley demonstrates, the fraught triangle of government, employers and labour has not generated an exceptionally high level of industrial stoppages over the period. From the late 1970s a shift in outlook coupled with a fall in union membership has enabled governments to ignore or even confront the labour movement, though it is unclear whether the new approach has made a significant impact upon the economic situation. Wrigley's essay offers an important caveat to those who seek easy generalisations about the roots of Britain's less than impressive economic performance.

John Stevenson changes the direction of the argument some-what. Focusing upon housing, he points out that an initial faith in planning was from the 1960s followed by considerable sus-picion and disillusionment. This loss of confidence was part of a declining support for the view that 'experts' or 'managers' were capable of building the new Jerusalem. Stevenson's succinct account of post-war housing policy reflects the intimate connec-tion between the economy, social ideals and the implementation of specific programmes. His analysis is supported from another vantage-point in Terry Gourvish's examination of the changing fortunes of state-owned enterprise. Nationalisation, as he sug-gests, had several origins: ideological commitment, the run-down condition of certain post-war industries, and a perceived need to bring parts of the economy under coordinated direction as part of the reconstruction effort. To an extent, nationalisation was part of the prevalent belief in organisation, efficiency, expert direction and planning generally, although the programme itself was a product of earlier government-industry relations and Labour Party thinking in the inter-war years. The operation of the new state enterprises was then constrained by an initial uncertainty about the way they should be organised, and by political hostility. Above all, the difficulty of clarifying the relationship with government under the 'public corporation' model led to confusion about goals and the assessment of performance. All too often, the 'efficiency' of state industries was sacrificed upon the altar of macroeconomic policy, or was subordinated to private sector needs. Privatisation in the 1980s, also examined by Gourvish, was one way of addressing this confusion.

The first five chapters, then, are directed towards the economy and arguments about the best way to secure and utilise improved economic growth. The essays by Michael Dockrill, Michael Sanderson, Pat Thane and Colin Holmes focus attention on major difficulties or constraints in the system. Dockrill's discussion of defence policy is not exclusively about the economic implications of military spending. At one level he provides an assessment of the main contours of defence thinking under the shadow of the Cold War, referring to imperial, European and American commitments. But he also gives particular emphasis to the escalating cost of defence in the atomic and nuclear age. All post-war governments have been preoccupied with striking a balance between a sufficiently high level of military preparedness and the financing of modern weaponry in a period of rapid technological change. Britain has had to dance on the tightrope of military requirements and the expense of major power status. Her defence budget since the 1940s has absorbed a high proportion of GNP compared with her major competitors, including the United States. Whether the Cold War should be blamed for the relative decline of the industrial sector is a matter for debate, but there can be little doubt that military burdens have placed a greater strain on Britain than they have upon, for example, Germany or Japan. Dockrill shows that although the rhetoric of Thatcherism on defence has been more aggressive, the actual options available to the government since 1979 have been familiar, and the policy followed has been broadly similar to that pursued since 1945.

Whereas many of the contributions in this volume stress continuity of outlook or reveal equivocal verdicts on the causes of Britain's relative economic decline, Michael Sanderson's provocative piece argues strongly that education policy has been a significant factor in the process. He maintains that successive governments have adopted education policies based on social rather than economic considerations. At all levels, he contends, the social objective of equality of opportunity has outweighed training for industrial employment. Hence, comparatively cheap educational provision in the arts and social sciences has been favoured at the expense of training in applied and industrial subjects. Sanderson suggests that the economic and industrial cost of giving such a priority to social aspiration has been enormous and provides a potent explanation for Britain's economic weakness internationally.

Pat Thane looks at the interaction of economic performance and the situation of women, mainly as seen through the struggle for equal pay. She explains the slow progress towards equality under both Labour and Conservative governments. Leaders were hesitant to implement equal pay despite post-war labour shortages because they feared its effect upon general wage rates and the cost of production. Her argument forms an original contribution to the economic theme but also marks a vital limitation to the acceptance of the need for greater equality of opportunity in post-war society. Essentially, governments were concerned to secure a labour market which was compliant and cheap – a feature of both the 1980s and the 1940s. The labour market is a concern of Colin Holmes as well. In his analysis of immigration he explores two main issues – the immigrant's place in the economy and the political commitment to the securing of greater equality of opportunity. His conclusion parallels that of Pat Thane. Post-war governments were anxious to secure the supply of inexpensive labour but loath to open up avenues of equality. Holmes identifies a pattern of official indifference or hostility to immigrants from an early date, an attitude which gained momentum from the later 1950s.

Contributions by Anthony Seldon, Martin Ceadel and Alan O'Day take up more traditional political themes. Seldon and Ceadel examine the functions and achievements of the Conservative and Labour parties, while O'Day deals with the construction of British policy towards Northern Ireland as the province tottered into a prolonged crisis. Seldon's wide-ranging chapter gives attention to the electoral record, policies and phases, ideologies and factions, organisation, composition and finance, and the personalities which have animated Conservatism. He points out that the Conservatives, in many ways a non-ideological grouping, shifted away from the post-war consensus under Margaret Thatcher, though how permanently remains to be seen. He rejects the views of those who argue that the post-war consensus was a myth or assert that the Thatcherite position represented continuity of approach on crucial issues. In the context of this volume, his argument that the Conservatives have prospered or languished according to the state of the economy has obvious relevance. Seldon shows that party alignment and electoral results depended on the key issue of economic vitality or decline, or at least, on perceptions of both. Ceadel's examination of the fortunes of the Labour Party follows a different format. He focuses on the disputes within the party, identifying six phases in the struggle for internal dominance between the left and the right wings. The contest, needless to say, always hinged on the party's electoral position and prospects. Since the main political debate since 1945 has centred on reform and the economy, his account reveals the contours of opinion on these issues. Labour has been beset by problems in identifying precisely what kind of society it wished to establish. Ceadel's chapter, when taken with those of Harris and Stevenson, shows the deep divisions within the moderate left over the shape, pace and character of economic and social reform.

Northern Ireland received but slight attention from British governments prior to the 'troubles' of 1968. Consequent unrest has tended to exasperate successive administrations anxious to tackle more pressing economic problems. However, in investigating the development of official policy since 1945, O'Day notes the remarkable unanimity which has characterised the attitudes of both Conservative and Labour cabinets. This is significant not only because earlier Irish disputes provoked intense party warfare, but also because this solidarity remained intact even though the policy itself underwent considerable change. This consensus, he suggests, was built upon the fundamental desire to keep Irish affairs out of the give and take of British political debate and party competition.

This volume cannot hope to address all the problems which have confronted Britain since 1945. The issue of Britain's place in Europe, which may well dominate the political agenda of the 1990s, is not included here; it probably deserves a volume to itself. As an indication of the possibilities which remain, we conclude with a quite different contribution. John Street provides an entertaining discussion of the role of popular music since the war, focusing in particular upon its entry, in the 1980s, into the political arena. As the State has withdrawn from sectors of social provision, including aid to the Third World, private initiatives have assumed greater prominence, as exemplified in a spectacular fashion by the recent vogue for charity-oriented rock concerts. There is clearly scope for another book on consumerism, leisure, and the political content of both.

Historians, more than anyone else, should require no reminding of the perils of generalisation without adequate perspective. It is a necessary cliché to state that the judgements in this book, particularly those which deal with the events of the last decade or so, must remain tentative. But important general themes *have* emerged: the primacy of the debate about relative economic decline; the options available to a society whose economy is perceived to be under-performing; the economic and social implications for a country whose economic preoccupations and policies have often been skewed to match the desire to retain (an illusory?) great power status. These themes will no doubt continue to attract attention from scholars.

2. The Economic Record since 1945

M. W. KIRBY

SINCE the end of the Second World War Britain's economic performance has been highly respectable in historical terms. In the period 1950–73 gross domestic product (GDP) was rising at the rate of 3.0 per cent per annum, compared with only 1.3 per cent in the years 1913–50. Taking the same period, output-per-man-hour in manufacturing industry increased by well over 200 per cent with gross fixed investment (other than in dwellings) running at a rate of 15 per cent of Gross National Product accelerating to more than 17 per cent from 1965 to the mid-1970s. As for the standard of living, between 1945 and 1974 the real weekly earnings of manual workers doubled, as did total consumers' expenditure at constant prices. Between 1968–9 and 1974–5 – a period notable for the growing burden of personal taxation – average real incomes still rose by a substantial 17 per cent after tax. No wonder then that despite the extent to which consumption levels were periodically sustained by overseas borrowing, so notable a critic of Britain's economic achievements as Sir Henry Phelps Brown could conclude in the later 1970s that 'the British people today are far better supplied with the necessities and amenities of life and more fully provided with remedial and supportive services than ever in their history before'.[1]

There is, however, an alternative perspective on these years, and one which is rooted firmly in the reality of Britain's international economic performance. Unprecedented levels of consumer affluence notwithstanding, the post-war decades from 1950 to the end of the 1970s were an era of unremitting national economic decline, the inevitable consequence of the progressive weakening in Britain's status as an advanced industrial and trading nation. No matter which index of economic performance is taken – the rate of growth of GDP, of industrial production, of labour productivity, and Britain's share of world trade in manufactured goods – all of these statistics make depressing reading when compared with the achievements of other countries, notably the founder members of the EEC, Britain's partners in EFTA, and Japan. Only the USA has a comparable record of relative failure, but that could be no source of comfort to Britain in view of the higher absolute level of the American standard of living.

Reinforcing the perception of relative decline has been the pervasive sense of crisis which has afflicted the record of economic management. The attempts by Conservative and Labour administrations to grapple with balance of payments and exchange rate problems in the later 1950s and 1960s were followed

TABLE 2.1   Phases of GDP growth, 1870–1984 (average annual compound growth rates)

	I 1870–1913	II 1913–50	III 1950–73	IV 1973–84
United Kingdom	1.9	1.3	3.0	1.1
France	1.7	1.1	5.1	2.2
West Germany	2.8	1.3	5.9	1.7
Japan	2.5	2.2	9.4	3.8
Netherlands	2.1	2.4	4.7	1.6
Five country average	2.2	1.7	5.6	2.1
USA	4.2	2.8	3.7	2.3

SOURCE: Angus Maddison, 'Growth and Slowdown in Advanced Capitalist Economics': Techniques of Quantitative Assessment', *Journal of Economic Literature*, XXXV (June 1987), Table 1, 650.

TABLE 2.2   Phases of growth in labour productivity (GDP per hour worked), 1870–1984 (average annual compound growth rates)

	I 1870–13	II 1913–50	III 1950–73	IV 1973–84
United Kingdom	1.2	1.6	3.2	2.4
France	1.7	2.0	5.1	3.4
West Germany	1.9	1.0	6.0	3.0
Japan	1.8	1.7	7.7	3.2
Netherlands	1.2	1.7	4.4	1.9
Five country average	1.6	1.6	5.3	2.8
USA	2.0	2.4	2.5	1.0

SOURCE: Maddison, 'Growth and Slowdown in Advanced Capitalist Economics', Table 2, 650.

TABLE 2.3   Growth of industrial production (average annual percentage changes)

	1960–73	1973–85	1960–85
United Kingdom	3.0	0.6	1.9
France	5.9	1.0	3.5
West Germany	5.5	1.1	3.4
United States	4.9	2.3	3.6
Japan	12.6	3.4	8.2
OECD countries	5.7	1.9	3.8

SOURCE: *National Institute Economic Review* (various issues).

TABLE 2.4 UK share in world trade in manufactures (percentages)

1950	25.4	1969	11.2
1954	20.5	1974	8.8
1959	17.7	1979	9.1
1964	14.2	1984	7.6

SOURCE: Table 3.1 in House of Lords, *Report from the Select Committee on Overseas Trade*, vol. 1 (Session 1984–5), p. 23.

in the 1970s by a growing preoccupation with inflation and unemployment. In these novel circumstances of 'stagflation' the Keynesian consensus on economic policy, which had seemed to be established so firmly in the two post-war decades, was eroded steadily. The growing incompatibility of the key policy objectives – full employment, minimal price inflation, balance of payments and exchange rate equilibrium, and the pursuit of economic growth – meant that the goals of successful economic management were increasingly elusive. On the political plane, the disillusion of the electorate was reflected in a new volatility in voting patterns which periodically seemed to threaten the stability of the two-party system. Indeed, it was in the political arena that the term 'deindustrialisation' was first coined in the early 1970s to highlight the problem of mounting unemployment in the industrial sector of the economy. An ugly if emotive term, it conjured up images of economic decadence similar to those encapsulated in the contemporary notion of the 'British disease'.

Thus, in assessing Britain's post-war economic performance

there are two phenomena which require explanation: first the reasons for the absolute improvement in growth performance as compared with the pre-war decades, and second the reasons for the relative failure to match the growth rates of competing economies in the period since 1950. The former can be readily explained in general terms by the fortuitous combination of several factors conducive to rapid economic progress and high levels of economic activity among all of the western industrialised economies, at least until the later 1960s. In the first instance, post-war reconstruction programmes, in so far as they entailed modernisation and renewal of technical equipment and other fixed plant, acted in conjunction with a cumulative backlog of profitable investment opportunities outside North America to enhance productivity levels in Western Europe and Japan. After 1945, moreover, social and political forces gave rise to historic-ally high levels of public expenditure by democratic govern-ments, with a new emphasis on welfare and income maintenance payments after 1960 in particular. These autonomous sources of expansion were in turn complemented by the general post-war economic policy and institutional environment which provided a further major contrast to the inter-war period. Not only was there a lack of coincidence in inter-country trade cycles, and a general absence of serious balance of payments and exchange rate problems, but the 'expectational climate' was transformed due to American underwriting of the world economy via the Bretton Woods institutions (the International Monetary Fund and the World Bank) and the general commitment of the governments of OECD countries to the pursuit of Keynesian-style full employ-ment policies. In these circumstances 'the weapons of policy were not really tested in adversity' since business and investor con-fidence were sustained at high levels in the context of a booming world economy which redounded to the advantage of the UK.[2] The techniques of demand management were therefore applied only lightly by governments in the 1950s and 1960s. Indeed, it has been pointed out that UK fiscal policy was 'quite deflation-ary' in this period.[3] Thus the general acceleration in economic growth was largely the product of favourable cyclical forces both domestic and international, leading to an upward movement in the investment supply function in the UK, the product of a major change in the climate of investor expectations, grounded in the belief that OECD governments in general, and the British government in particular, would not permit a slump to develop.

In analysing the causes of Britain's relative growth failure there is a broad consensus, fully reflected in the literature on deindustrialisation, that attention should be concentrated on the industrial, mainly manufacturing, sector for it is here that Britain's competitive failure has been most strikingly demonstrated (see Tables 2.3 and 2.4).[4] The absolute level of employment in manufacturing industry peaked in the UK in 1966 at 9.2 million: by 1981 it had fallen to just over 6 million – a loss in manufacturing employment of 34 per cent in fifteen years and representing the greatest decline in any OECD economy. The share of manufacturing employment peaked rather earlier at 36 per cent of the total workforce in 1955, and stayed close to that level until 1966 (when it was 35 per cent) but then declined significantly to reach 31 per cent by 1979 and 23 per cent in 1988.

As for the share of manufacturing in total economic activity this too was steadily shrinking. Between 1966 and 1979 GDP increased by 29 per cent whilst manufacturing output grew by only 11 per cent. After a 17 per cent fall in production between 1979 and 1981 the rate of growth of manufacturing output averaged less than 1 per cent per annum during the 1980s – comparable to the record of the 1970s, but much below that of the 1960s. After 1979, moreover, manufacturing output was not only falling faster than GDP in volume terms, but was also diminishing as a proportion of GDP at constant prices. It is hardly surprising, therefore, that from 1983 onwards the balance of trade in manufactures exhibited a mounting deficit large enough by the end of the decade to dominate the current account balance of payments as a whole.

Profound structural change was reflected not only in the absolute decline in the contribution of manufacturing industry to total output, but also in the expansion of the tertiary, or service sector of the economy. If service sector employment is taken to exclude transport and communications it increased from 40.6 per cent of total employment in 1961 to 50.9 per cent in 1976. The most impressive expansion took place in professional and scientific services (dominated by the health and education services) where the share of total employment rose from 9.6 per cent in 1961 to 15.7 per cent in 1976, representing an addition of 1.5 million workers in this subsector alone. Significant increases were also recorded in public administration and defence, miscellaneous services, insurance, banking, and financial and business services, but the total increase here was less than in professional and scientific services alone.[5]

The expansion in service sector employment was by no means confined to the UK, and from the 1960s onwards a number of studies have appeared seeking to interpret the phenomenon in a long-term perspective.[6] Much of this literature has accepted both the inevitability and the desirability of the so-called 'service revolution' as a necessary stage of transition towards a 'post-industrial' society analogous to the 'deruralisation' which accompanied the ongoing process of industrialisation in the nineteenth century. In the case of the UK – the pioneering industrial country – it might be argued that the onset of deindustrialisation was a prime manifestation of the service revolution and that the contraction of the industrial sector was in accordance with long-established trends. In addition, the UK arguably has been uniquely placed to take advantage of the continued growth of the service economy as a result of the country's long-standing comparative advantage in the provision of international financial and business services, primarily through the banking and insurance companies located in the City of London. Thus, in relation to the balance of payments, for example, as foreign real incomes grow any deterioration in the visible trade account could be offset by a growing surplus from invisible trade.[7]

At first sight this reasoning is plausible – all the more so since the comparative advantage in the production of manufactures was moving away from the established manufacturing countries from the mid-1970s. It is, however, flawed in a number of respects. If international business services are examined at a disaggregated level it appears that the bulk of Britain's invisible surplus has been derived not from credits on sea transport, civil aviation and tourism (where there are matching debits), but almost wholly from the category of 'other services' dominated by the overseas earnings of City financial institutions. If, for example, in 1976 UK exports of manufactures had declined by 1 per cent the current account balance of payments would have deteriorated to the extent of £3.1 billion. For service exports to have compensated for this sum would have required a rise in the UK's share of the world market for service exports by a third (from 9.9 per cent to 13.0 per cent), a Herculean task in view of the fact that Britain already possessed a relatively large share of a comparatively small market – a market, moreover, which was destined to become increasingly competitive in the 1980s in response to the increasing globalisation of financial markets.[8] It can also be argued that to portray the financial services sector as the saviour of the balance of payments is perverse in view of the modest productivity record of the relevant institutions for much of the post-war period. Britain's share of the world market for services may have declined far less than that for manufactures but this was counterbalanced by a rate of productivity growth well below that of domestic manufacturing industry, and even further beneath that attained by overseas manufacturing competitors. Britain's comparative advantage, therefore, lay in a sector with a poor productivity record and in these circumstances 'it may well have paid other industrial economies to allow the UK to take in their financial washing'.[9]

The argument that the external account could be safeguarded by service income seemed to be so much stronger at a time when North Sea oil had yet to exert its maximum impact on the balance of payments. But in the light of trends in the British economy since 1981 it seems legitimate to conclude that given the finite contribution of North Sea oil to the current account, large balance of payments deficits, even at less-than-full employment, can only be avoided if the traditional exporting sectors, dominated by manufacturing industry, achieve a substantial increase in exports. Whether this can be accomplished after years of deindustrialisation is an open question.

Whilst it is possible to draw attention to deindustrialisation as a process which has resulted in profound structural changes with serious implications for the stability of the UK external accounts, the business of explanation is far more complex in view of the myriad influences which have been at work. In order to provide clarity of exposition, therefore, the following discussion of causal factors has been divided into those which economists and economic historians have identified as operating in the short, medium and longer terms.

I

Academic respectability was conferred upon deindustrialisation as a meaningful concept as a result of the work of two Oxford University economists, Robert Bacon and Walter Eltis, who advanced the view that Britain's relatively poor economic performance up to the mid-1970s was due to the progressive

shrinkage in size of the country's manufacturing base, a development which had gathered pace in the 1960s as a result of the
growing pre-emption of resources of both capital and labour by
the non-productive sector of the economy.[10] By 'non-productive'
Bacon and Eltis wre referring to the service sector, in particular
that part which is controlled by central and local government
and which does not produce 'marketable output' with a direct
salable value (unlike, say, the banking and insurance institutions
of the City of London).

The thesis that industry was 'crowded out' by the expansion of
public services has been the subject of intense academic scrutiny,
almost all of which has been critical. In the first instance, on the
issue of labour utilisation, it seems inappropriate to speak of the
industrial sector being starved of labour at a time when British
industry was noted for overmanning and comparatively low
levels of productivity, and when the trend rate of unemployment
had been rising over successive cycles since the mid-1950s.[11]
More specifically, if the 1966 level of manufacturing output had
been maintained industrial output in 1974 would have been 8.6
per cent higher. But if the industrial sector had ben able to match
the productivity record of France and West Germany after 1950
(an annual rate of growth of output-per-man-hour of 5.5 per cent
instead of the actual 3.2 per cent achieved) then the level of
output in 1974 would have been 70 per cent higher. As one
authority has observed, it was the cumulative effects of the post-
war productivity failure (see Table 2, p. 00) which rendered the
UK economy so vulnerable to the loss of industrial employment
after 1966.[12] It should also be borne in mind that the expansion
in service sector employment from the early 1960s resulted in
extra employment for females in the workforce, whereas the bulk
of registered unemployed were males.[13]

On the subject of the availability of finance for productive
investment it is similarly difficult to argue that industry was
'crowded out' by the demands of the public sector. Although the
pre-tax profitability of UK industry declined steadily after 1960
there is little evidence to suggest that the expansion of private
industry was constrained by lack of access to external funding.
As the Treasury pointed out in its evidence to the Wilson
Committee on the functioning of financial institutions in 1977:

all the signs are that industrial borrowing has been determined
by the level of demand. In the year to mid-February 1977

sterling lending to manufacturing industry increased by about £1,350 million or 24 per cent, while sterling lending to the personal sector increased by only about £200 million, or 5 per cent – a fall in real terms.[14]

– and all of this at a time when interest rates had reached unprecedentedly high levels. These observations are in accord with the long-standing view, based upon much empirical evidence, that investment decisions are determined by expectations of demand and profitability rather than by the cost of borrowing alone.[15]

As for the burden of taxation imposed on industry, the available evidence is hardly consistent with the Bacon and Eltis thesis since it indicates that there was a significant decline in the effective company tax rate after 1950 and that 'the slow growth of demand, shortages of liquidity and a declining real rate of return on capital have presented a much greater threat to investment than increases in corporate tax'.[16] In fact, the record of *post-tax* profit shares for the period 1950–73 suggests that there was no long-run tendency for the share of profits to decline.[17] On the issue of personal taxation it is certainly difficult to refute the argument that the expansion of public sector services contributed powerfully towards cost-push inflation to the detriment of profits in manufacturing industry, notably in the period after 1969. But even here a note of warning should be sounded. In international terms, and especially in comparison with some of the more buoyant European economies, the British people were not excessively penalised at the hands of the state during the period covered by the Bacon and Eltis thesis.[18]

A final criticism of the 'crowding out' hypothesis is that it is both unhistorical and unrealistically monocausal. Bacon and Eltis dated Britain's economic difficulties from the mid-1960s following the upsurge in public expenditure in the first half of the decade. Yet in so far as Britain's relative economic decline has its origins in the past – to be precise, a century ago in the final quarter of the nineteenth century when UK industry began to lose foreign and domestic markets to overseas competitors – one of the dangers of the Bacon and Eltis thesis was that its very plausibility could be used to justify economic policy prescriptions which were inappropriate, or alternatively of limited effectiveness. This is certainly not to suggest that historical argument alone is the way to understand contemporary problems or that the extreme complexity of the process of economic decline dictates that history is the most appropriate means to understanding, merely that analysis of the causes of deindustrialisation must be approached in such a way as to take account not only of the post-1960 weakness of the UK economy, but also its longer term causes.

II

If the 'crowding out' hypothesis has given rise to substantial criticisms it might be thought that an explanation of deindustrialisation founded on the growing contribution to the economy of North Sea oil after 1975 – the short-term factor *par excellence* – would be far less contentious. This is not, however, the case. It might, for example, be argued that in so far as part of the fall in manufacturing production as a proportion of GDP could be attributed to rising oil production the decline in the relative contribution of manufacturing industry to the economy was nothing more than a temporary adjustment to the expansion of the primary sector which would be reversed when oil production begins to fall. As noted already, however, it is an open question whether a manufacturing sector which is also in *long-term* decline will be able to fill the growing void in the balance of payments consequent upon falling oil production and revenues. Furthermore, it is all too easy to accept the view that the accelerating decline in the manufacturing sector which set in after 1979 was the sole product of the oil-induced appreciation of the exchange rate leading to a reduction in the competitiveness of UK industry. Quite apart from the fact that industry had already experienced substantial contraction before the arrival of North Sea oil, the dramatic appreciation of sterling after 1979, coinciding with a sharp rise in oil prices, was far more the effect of the Conservative government's macroeconomic policy which accorded primacy to reducing the rate of inflation by means of high interest rates and a restrictive monetary policy. In these circumstances the post-1979 improvement in the UK balance of payments was a direct consequence of deepening slump in the domestic economy: as experience in the later 1980s has suggested, a higher level of economic activity in response to a relaxation of monetary constraints would have led to a deterioration in the UK international accounts in spite of the rise in oil production.[19]

III

The fact that deindustrialisation was well under way before North Sea oil began to exert a significant impact on the economy, together with the inadequacies of the Bacon and Eltis thesis, inevitably focuses attention on the medium and longer term causes of the contraction in manufacturing industry. One definition of the *process* of deindustrialisation which encompasses many of these causes has been advanced by Ajit Singh. In a penetrating study published in 1977 Singh argued that in view of the historical evolution of the UK industrial structure (a net importer of food and raw materials paid for largely, but not exclusively by manufactured exports) 'an efficient manufacturing sector . . . may be defined as one which given the normal levels of other components of the balance of payments, yields sufficient net exports (both currently, but more importantly, potentially) to pay for import requirements at sociably acceptable levels of output, employment and the exchange rate'.[20] The latter qualifications are important because in their absence almost any manufacturing sector might be able to meet the criteria for efficiency. Hence the UK has experienced deindustrialisation to the extent that the economy, in failing to maintain its share of world trade in manufactures, and in the light of the growing import penetration of the domestic market, is 'becoming increasingly unable to pay for its current [full employment] import requirements by means of exports of goods and services and property income from abroad'.[21] The UK has therefore been unable to combine full employment with balance of payments equilibrium. This problem arises primarily from the fact that the world income elasticity of demand for UK exports of manufactures has been lower than the UK's income elasticity of demand for manufactured imports. As world income rises, therefore, these unfavourable elasticities dictate that the UK has a permanent tendency towards balance of payments deficit. One important study traced this phenomenon back to the early 1950s and although the relevant data have been criticised, subsequent investigations have served to confirm the fact of disequilibrium in the current account balance of payments – despite improvements in the UK's price competitiveness in the 1960s and, since 1970, a substantial labour cost advantage over the country's major overseas competitors.[22] It is thus difficult to resist the conclusion that Britain's industrial decline has been the product of an increasingly poor trading performance by the UK manufacturing sector as a result of unfavourable price and income elasticities.

It is important, therefore, to consider the reasons for the comparatively weak market performance of UK industry. Why did significant parts of the UK manufacturing sector, from television and audio equipment, to motor cycles and cars, succumb to foreign competition after 1960? The answer is complex and constraints on space permit only a cursory examination of the contributory factors which have been of greatest importance in the medium and longer term setting.

IV

One aspect of Britain's economic history which has received much attention in the debate on industrial decline concerns the allocation of investment resources. In 1955 total research and development expenditure in the UK amounted to £187 million, the highest figure for any country in Western Europe, yet 63 per cent of this total was spent on defence and less than one-third was funded by private industry. Clearly, the UK was not neglecting R and D, but the resources available were being allocated in a way which was inimical to the long-term growth prospects of the industrial sector. There were in fact two distinctive aspects of the pattern of R and D expenditures in the three post-war decades: first, the high concentration on the aircraft industry, especially in comparison with West Germany and Japan, and secondly, the great preponderance of government-sponsored expenditures which were directed to a few areas of high technology, notably in the field of defence equipment.[23] In the 1940s and 1950s, for example, there was the nuclear power programme in both its civil and military aspects. It may be that under the prospective conditions of energy supply in the late twentieth century nuclear power will have an enhanced role to play, but for the UK in the circumstances of the 1950s, to be operating at the frontiers of technology in a high-risk multimillion pound industry appears in retrospect to have been a mistake. Prestige was a luxury that post-war Britain could ill afford: despite its early lead in electricity generation by nuclear power the UK has been unable to exploit overseas markets for nuclear power plants, and such activities were arguably best left to the USA which possessed the requisite expertise, financial resources, and market size capable of generating scale economies. A further illustration of this point dating from the 1960s, is located in the aircraft industry. Again, the UK, admittedly in cooperation with France, was operating at the limits of known technology in the race to produce a supersonic jet airliner. All that needs to be said on the issue of the Concorde project is that in spite of its escalating cost, and the extreme uncertainty as to the aircraft's financial viability, many hundreds of millions of pounds were swallowed up in an exercise which proved to be a lamentable commercial disaster. It may well be said in mitigation that the undoubted scientific and engineering excellence of such endeavours brought valuable prestige and some technological spin-offs to Britain, but both of the quoted examples are exquisite illustrations of the fact that governments are motivated by criteria other than the strictly economic in arriving at investment decisions.[24] Although the UK achieved some outstanding technological successes in military aviation, especially in the light of the immense competitive and financial advantages enjoyed by the USA, the counterpart of the British effort was the relatively low proportion of R and D expenditures devoted to the more mundane areas of machinery, vehicles and chemicals, precisely those sectors of manufacturing industry experiencing the most rapid market growth, and in which West Germany and Japan were to have their earliest and most important successes.[25] Despite the impressive British performance in areas such as radar and aero-engines, the overall returns were low, and to make matters worse such high-prestige activities made serious inroads into the supply of scarce scientific and engineering manpower which, from the strictly commercial standpoint, would have been better employed in conventional manufacturing industry – in machinery, vehicles, and metal products.[26]

V

Throughout the post-war period up to the mid-1970s the UK experienced a sequence of alternate booms and slumps – the so-called 'stop-go cycle'. Most of them were initiated by a balance of payments deficit (1947, 1949, 1951, 1955, 1957, 1961, 1964–7 and 1973–6). According to Sidney Pollard the origins of the stop-go cycle can be traced back to the legacy of Britain's military victory in 1945.[27] In the devastated countries of continental Europe there was a general consensus that industrial reconstruction should receive the highest priority at the expense of private consumption. In the UK, however, where real incomes had been sustained at surprisingly high levels after 1939, the spoils of victory were expected in the form of high and rising standards of consumption. Hence:

> The pressures characterised as inflationary in the early [post-war] years were in reality pressures to keep up personal incomes, and successive governments were easily tempted to give in and squeeze investment and exports instead. The squeeze on exports took rapid revenge in balance of payments crises which had to be rectified one way or another, but there was no one to defend investment programmes. To cut investment was the easy touch and thus were taken the first steps on the slippery downwards slope.[28]

In short, the periodic curtailment of investment retarded the growth of industrial productivity, thus leading to a cumulative weakness in the UK's competitive position in world markets. By 1976 the stop-go cycle had so damaged the productive capacity of UK industry that to have endowed it with a level of equipment in the manufacturing sector alone commensurate with that enjoyed by overseas competitors would have required an investment of £100,000 million.

Pollard's comments on the effects of the stop-go cycle are not original but his work is unusually polemical and it commands attention as a sustained indictment of the course of post-war economic policy written by one of the UK's foremost economic historians.[29] It was the Treasury, obsessed by 'symbolic figures and quantities like prices, exchange rates and balances of payment', which neglected 'real quantities like goods produced and traded'. Thus, at the core of policy making there was a 'contempt for production' in the Treasury-dominated civil service élite and over the years this was reinforced by the predilection of academic economists for theoretical studies with limited application to the 'real economy'.[30]

In one major sense Pollard overstates his case since other OECD economies experiencing similar or greater fluctuations in output grew much faster than the UK. This suggests

> that the problem with the British economy was not so much any 'stop-go' pattern imposed by government policy, but

rather the slowness of the rise in the underlying trend in output. Possibly the 'stop-go' pattern appeared more marked in the UK than in most other industrial countries because in those countries output was still rising significantly when it was below trend, whereas in Britain there tended to be virtually no rise at all in the 'stop' phases.[31]

It certainly does not follow from this that 'stop-go' failed to discourage long-term investment programmes. It does, however, underline the point that there were other forces at work which have accounted for and reinforced the comparative sluggishness of Britain's rate of economic growth. In defence of the Treasury it can also be argued that its sensitivity to the needs of the external balance cannot be divorced from the role of sterling as an international reserve currency. In reality, this function was forced on the UK financial authorities, first by obligations incurred to the USA as part of the original Bretton Woods agreement of 1944, and second by the survival into the post-war period of the Sterling Area group of countries to whom the UK acted as international banker. In this context the question of whether or not the Treasury was obsessed by the priorities of short-term stabilisation is largely irrelevant: it is sufficient to note that its central role in policy formulation served to direct attention away from consideration of the long-term growth prospects of the 'real' economy.[32]

In a similar vein it can be argued that the post-war commitment to full employment – the most important legacy of the Keynesian Revolution – implicitly assumed that if only demand was right supply could look after itself. In the 1930s, in conditions of mass unemployment and with the UK enjoying some measure of protection from overseas competition, such a view was understandable, but in the post-war period the Keynesian consensus served to draw attention away from supply side issues to the detriment of the long-term growth potential of the industrial sector.[33] Again, in defence of policymakers, this factor was recognised by governments from time to time, such as in the early 1960s when Harold Macmillan's Conservative government created the National Economic Development Council (NEDC) in recognition of the adverse consequences of stop-go policies and the need to enhance industrial performance by means of indicative planning. In 1964 the incoming Labour government established the Department of Economic Affairs (DEA) which was specifically designed to act as a counterweight to the Treasury in the policymaking machine. The DEA's National Plan, however, combining targets for the growth of output, exports and incomes, was soon forgotten in the debacle surrounding the sterling crisis of 1966 – the prelude to devaluation in 1967.

The creation of the NEDC and the DEA was not, of course, the only governmental initiative on the side of supply. It is possible to point to other forms of intervention, such as the creation of the Monopolies Commission in 1948, the Restrictive Practices Act of 1956, and the Industrial Training Act of 1964, as evidence of an enduring concern with supply. But recurring balance of payments crises and the need to protect the exchange value of sterling inevitably directed attention away from long-term policy issues and enhanced the role of the Treasury whose function it was to maintain external equilibrium.

VI

The argument that industrial investment was constrained by macroeconomic prerogatives assumes in part, at least, that the UK industrial community – defined in the broadest sense to include businessmen and trade unionists – was only too anxious to innovate. In the case of the UK there is sufficient evidence to suggest that this is a facile judgement. As far as the trade union movement is concerned Britain is the prisoner of its past – the first industrial nation with the longest established tradition of trade union activity. The growth of union power at the end of the nineteenth century took place within a structure of labour processes dominated by customs and norms dictated by inherited craft traditions. This meant that in comparison with other countries where trade unions remained weak or had yet to achieve real bargaining power the collective bargaining structure which evolved in the UK was 'highly decentralised, uncoordinated and relatively unsuited to the later needs of mass production'.[34] Taking a long-term view, the craft system in UK industry perpetuated high manning levels and restrictive labour practices, thereby retarding technical innovation. It thus played its part in the process of industrial decline by inhibiting the growth of productivity.

It should also be noted that across a wide spectrum of UK industries the decentralisation of labour organisations was com-

plemented by fragmented industrial structures. In comparison
with their counterparts in other countries, notably the USA and
West Germany, UK businessmen lagged behind in the innovation of large-scale corporate enterprise characterised by 'industrial oligopoly, hierarchical managerial bureaucracy, vertical
integration of production and distribution, managerial control
over the labour process, and the integration of financial and
industrial capital'.[35] All of these factors facilitated the introduction of mass production techniques with relative ease, while UK
industrialists remained committed to disintegrated market structures − preferring the 'invisible hand' of competition to the
visible hand of the modern corporate economy. It was not until
the 1960s that advanced corporate forms of organisation based
on multidivisional enterprise began to make real headway in UK
industry, but even then it is difficult to prove that there was a
direct link between managerial reorganisation and improved
business performance. Again, it might be said that the post-war
programme of nationalisation in the UK went some way towards
reducing the problem of horizontal fragmentation. It did not,
however, address itself to the need for vertical integration, and in
its post-1970 form (the nationalisation of firms or industries in
imminent danger of financial collapse) it failed to provide
convincing evidence of its relevance in combating the cumulative
legacy of technological backwardness, weak management and
union job control at a time of intense international competition.
Thus, historical weaknesses in industrial organisation also contributed to Britain's economic decline, at least until the 1960s.

VII

In offering some concluding remarks on the longer term causes of
deindustrialisation it is worthwhile highlighting some of the more
ephemeral aspects of weak industrial performance in the UK.
Much attention has been focused recently on the inherited value
system of a society which, according to some observers, has never
come to terms with 'industrialism', despite a desire to enjoy the
fruits of economic growth. This view has been presented in an
extreme form by the American historian Martin Wiener who has
argued that the deeply ingrained cultural norms of British society
have retarded technological change and productivity growth.[36]
According to Wiener these norms were established in the latter

half of the nineteenth century when key elements in the middle and upper strata of British society reacted sharply to the growing political power of the newly emergent manufacturing class by creating a social and intellectual climate inimical to rapid industrial advance. By the end of the nineteenth century there was little evidence of the mid-century adulation of industrial pioneers such as I. K. Brunel and George and Robert Stephenson. On the contrary, industrialisation was perceived increasingly in subjective terms as being synonymous with 'dark satanic mills' and the despoliation of 'England's green and pleasant land'. Industrialists themselves reacted to the new social climate by accommodating themselves to it. Successful industrialists whose forebears had challenged the power of landed society now chose the path of assimilation: public school education followed by classical studies at the ancient universities were the chosen routes for their sons, while they themselves indulged in minor political activities, complemented, wherever possible, by the acquisition of a country estate.

The Wiener thesis seemed to strike a responsive chord for it was greeted with much critical acclaim when it was presented in the UK in 1981. It does, however, portray an extreme stereotype and unqualified image of the business community, grounded in selectivity and tending towards gross caricature. In the absence of a wider cross-section of individual business histories it is as easy to prove as it is to disprove.[37] Nevertheless, it cannot be denied that British society has for long accorded low social prestige to technical education and vocational studies to the detriment of industrial performance. This was already a notable phenomenon before 1900 at a time when Germany and the USA were beginning to make striking advances in such educational provision. Throughout the twentieth century, moreover, the more talented of the nation's youth have been attracted into the established professions, avoiding the world of industry which has presented an uncongenial image to school leavers. It is also possible to identify the long persistence of entrepreneurial perspectives rooted in nineteenth century experience. In terms of corporate structures, for example, the unitary or departmental form of company organisation, the internal recruitment of directors, and the retention of family owners in entrepreneurial positions survived long after 1945. Although family enterprise was by no means synonymous with failure there is growing evidence to suggest that even professional managers obeyed 'the

god of continuity' in the modern corporate era. In short, it was
the 'clubby, gentlemanly approach' of British managers, firmly
rooted in the existing 'culture of the firm' which precluded
radical institutional change in a wide spectrum of industries.[38]

A final observation is worth making in the longer term
perspective. In the generation before 1914 the growing import
penetration of the domestic market by German and American
enterprise resulted in a reappraisal of Britain's international
economic position which was ultimately reflected on the political
plane in the Conservative Party's espousal of tariff protection
and imperial trade preferences. Such a system was eventually
introduced in 1932 when it was a justifiable response to the
collapse of the international economy, and the UK certainly
reaped financial gains from its commanding hold over Empire
and Commonwealth markets in the decade after 1945. But the
price that was paid in catering for the needs of markets with a
relatively low preference for manufactured goods of high unit
value was the reinforcement of managerial and shopfloor complacency in UK industry. In buttressing existing institutional
rigidities the protectionist legacy served the country ill when an
outmoded industrial structure was exposed to the full force of
international competition which followed in the wake of the post-
war liberalisation of trade and payments during the 1950s and
1960s.[39]

It will be seen that the themes which are common to an
examination of Britain's economic performance in a long-term
perspective are both institutional and cultural. As Mancur Olson
has pointed out in his classic study of economic growth and
decline:

> With age British society has acquired so many strong organisa-
> tions and collusions that it suffers from an institutional scler-
> osis that slows its adaptation to changing circumstances and
> technologies.[40]

Such sclerotic tendencies invariably relate to the UK's early start
in the process of industrialisation, or the proclivity of successive
governments to sustain the country's international prestige
whether in the fields of finance or defence. The former gave rise
to the neoclassical economy of the nineteenth century which
institutionalised the small-scale firm and labour power over
work processes in the pre-mass-production era. The response of

industrialists to mounting foreign competition after 1880 was to
retreat into imperial and latterly Commonwealth markets – a
movement which obviated the necessity for radical institutional
change. All of these trends were compounded by cultural factors
– the general contempt for technical education, the growing
resistance to the values of 'industrialism' and the consequent low
status of industrial management as a profession. The illusion of
imperial grandeur and victory in two world wars may also have
served to prolong unrealistic attitudes to the inexorable rise of
foreign competition by perpetuating a xenophobic concern with
international prestige which manifested itself for much of the
post-war era in unprecedentedly high military expenditures in
peacetime and an obsessive concern with the exchange value of
sterling.

VIII

By the end of the 1970s two broad strategies were being
advocated for reversing Britain's economic and industrial decline.
For convenience they can be defined as the 'centrist' and 'anti-
centrist positions'.[41] In the former, great stress was placed upon
the need to emulate certain features of the Japanese, West
German and French economies. Thus, the advocacy of more
broadly-based R and D expenditures was a reflection of the belief
that West Germany and Japan had achieved important market
advantages as a result of their earlier concentration on consumer-
oriented manufacturing industries. Similarly, the advocacy of
institutional reforms, focusing upon the centralised direction of
investment, was inspired by French and Japanese practice where
the framing of industrial policy was alleged to have benefited
greatly from the interchange of personnel with shared backgrounds and experience between government and business, and
also by these countries' ability, through national agencies, to
back new strategic technologies according to broadly based and
informed assessments of long-term national priorities.[42]

    In the context of centrist opinion as a whole the above policies
are hardly controversial. There were, however, those economists
associated with the 'New Cambridge School' who argued that an
active industrial policy would need to be supplemented by some
form of protection. Devaluation to improve foreign competitiveness was ruled out since it would promote domestic inflation

(given the inelasticity of UK import demand) and in any event UK manufacturing industry generally was viewed as being incapable of responding vigorously to the advantages conferred by enhanced price competitiveness in overseas markets. British exporters were handicapped by non-price factors, such as delivery dates, quality of design, and reliability of performance, which were the principal causes of market failure.[43] These deficiencies could only be rectified by a sustained programme of state-sponsored investment under a protectionist regime. This would provide UK industry with a 'breathing space' during which the enhanced opportunities for expansion in a more self-sufficient home market would generate business confidence and so facilitate the introduction of successful investment programmes.

In contrast to the centrists were those who argued that effective industrial regeneration could only be accomplished by improving the functioning of the market economy. Monetarist doctrines were central to this view since the control of inflation was a necessary prerequisite for the lowering of industrial costs. A restrictive monetary policy would also provide the means to curtail the rate of growth of public expenditure. Other features of the market strategy included the privatisation of public sector assets, the reduction of the monopoly power exercised by the trade union movement, and finally a reduction in direct subsidisation of industry in both the public and private sectors.[44] Inspired in part by the Bacon and Eltis thesis the market strategy also derived much of its rationale from the writings of F. A. Hayek and Milton Friedman, the arch-liberal economists of the post-1945 era.[45] Higher levels of industrial productivity and profitability could be guaranteed only by the discipline of freely competitive markets, a discipline, moreover, which had been progressively weakened by the tendency for post-war British governments to protect the industrial sector from the consequences of market failure by means of subsidies or precipitate acts of nationalisation.

The fundamental rationale of the centrist position lay in its analysis of the current acute difficulties being experienced by much of the industrial sector, together with the chronic nature of the UK's economic decline in the light of the persistent inability of UK businessmen to respond effectively to market signals. In its 'New Cambridge' guise it was, in effect, an emergency programme for dealing with a deeply-rooted structural crisis which threatened the stability of the entire economy. It was flawed, however, in a number of respects. In the first instance the telling point could be made that despite the basic continuity of government industrial policies and their tendency to become increasingly interventionist over time, the secular rate of unemployment had continued to rise since the mid-1950s. Would 'more of the same' reverse this apparently inexorable trend? Secondly, the whole concept of a centralised 'industrial strategy' was attacked on the grounds that it neglected the principle of comparative advantage in international trade and ignored the problem of future uncertainty in a rapidly changing world. Thus, in view of the UK's peculiar factor endowment there might be positive advantages in belonging to the 'second division' of industrial countries, with less concentration on expensive and risky high-level technologies.[46] In a similar vein it can be argued that much of centrist opinion was characterised by a misplaced belief in the UK's 'manifest industrial destiny' – that it was right and proper that UK industry should be constantly striving towards a structure which reflected the current world technological frontier. As several commentators remarked: 'In so far as such attitudes prevail, a more assertive industrial strategy is likely to give rise to a succession of dubious or wasteful projects.'[47]

As for the 'New Cambridge' case for protection it is far more difficult to defend, if only because of the heroic assumptions on which it was based. The dangers of foreign retaliation were underplayed, as were the political ramifications of breaking international treaty obligations. This applies also to the assumption that protectionist measures would be consistent with the achievement of higher levels of industrial productivity. On the contrary, they could well perpetuate shop-floor opposition to technical change and in securing the home market in finished manufactures, resurrect the dangers of the kind of complacency which characterised the days of imperial commerce. Above all, the Cambridge policy totally neglected the fact that protection would be more than likely to damage UK exports directly: much of the advanced equipment, components, and semi-manufactures needed for industrial regeneration can only be obtained abroad, and unless UK exports were subsidised they would rise in price. Furthermore, although protection would increase domestic production for the home market, this would ultimately be a self-limiting exercise in that UK producers would be increasingly unable to exploit the economies of scale available to foreign producers catering for the needs of a world market. It is an irony for the UK that economies of scale can only be achieved by exporting, but extra investment in manufacturing capacity in response to protection is likely to produce those goods in which the UK is most disadvantaged in export markets.

In the event the election in 1979 of a Conservative government, inspired by the Hayekian belief in the liberal market order, ensured that anti-centrist policies were to be implemented in an attempt to rejuvenate the British economy. The broad policy implications were twofold – first to 'roll back the frontiers of the state' in economic affairs and secondly to enhance the role of market forces in order to encourage allocative efficiency. In practice this entailed the introduction of a medium-term financial strategy aimed at restraining the growth of public expenditure and reducing inflationary pressure via lower interest rates, thereby creating a macroeconomic environment conducive to the efficient functioning of the market economy. The subsidies payable to nationalised industries were reduced, as was the overall level of expenditure on industrial support programmes for the private sector. A new emphasis was placed upon revitalised competition policy, not least in the service sector, and the monopoly powers of specific public corporations were reduced. Similarly, the government sought to reduce trade union bargaining power: incomes policies were rejected in the belief that they introduced rigidities into the labour market and endowed trade union leaders with excessive political influence. Trade union legal privileges were also curtailed and an attempt made to enhance the quality of the labour force and to alleviate skill shortages by the introduction of new measures for industrial training. A new emphasis was placed on encouraging the formation of small businesses in the belief that they had a valuable role to play in stimulating structural diversity and in offsetting the risk averseness of large-scale firms by encouraging the development of a Victorian-style 'enterprise culture'. In this respect too, substantial reductions in direct taxation were clearly identified as a long-term objective consistent with the view that tax incentives were an essential component of a flourishing market economy. Finally, an increasingly ambitious programme of privatisation was implemented. This was motivated in part by budgetary considerations but it was also a product of the belief in the innate superiority of private enterprise over state-run bureaucracies. The common theme uniting these attitudes and policies was a profound scepticism concerning the legitimate role of the state in economic affairs, and the rejection of an approach to economic management which could be labelled 'strategic' or 'planned'.

Any judgement on the achievements of the Thatcher administration is clouded by the relatively short period in which the new policies have operated and also by the fact that the performance of the economy during the 1980s can be interpreted in two diametrically opposed ways. Thus, critics of the government would point out that taking the period from 1979 to the end of 1988 the trend rate of growth of GDP was distinctly lower than in the two previous decades, and that although it matched the performance of the French and West German economies it was below that achieved in Japan, the USA, and Italy.[48] More specifically, the growth rate of manufacturing production was also relatively low – less than 1 per cent per annum on average – about the same as in the 1970s and substantially below the level of the 1960s. As for the competitive performance of British industry, a notable feature of the 1980s was the progressive deterioration in the balance of trade in manufactures. Initially, this was masked by a significant improvement in the oil balance, but as this too began to fall away, at the same time as the balance of services began to deteriorate, the current account balance of payments moved into substantial deficit on a scale comparable to that experienced in the USA. The record on unemployment and inflation is, at best, ambiguous. By the end of the 1980s the former was higher in the UK than in Japan, the USA and West Germany, but below the level in France and Italy. The inflation rate, after falling consistently throughout the 1980s, began to accelerate after 1987, a record at the end of the decade worse than in all other advanced economies except Italy. Business investment (incorporating private investment in new housing and investment by all businesses classed as public corporations at the beginning of the period) also exhibits unclear trends. For the greater part of the 1980s it stagnated, and although it began to rise strongly after 1987 it seems that a high proportion of the increase was accounted for by the financial and commercial sector. In overall terms the level of gross investment was approximately 3 per cent lower in the period 1980–8 than in the previous nine-year period, reflecting the catastrophic fall during the first two years of the Conservative administration. Finally, it might be thought that one unequivocal achievement of the 1980s was the acceleration in the rate of growth of labour productivity in manufacturing industry from 2.5 per cent per annum in the 1970s to 4.3 per cent per annum in the period 1979–88. However, this improvement was certainly not reflected in enhanced competitiveness in the world or, indeed, in the domestic market.

A defence of the Conservative record in office would point out that the early fall in output notwithstanding, the whole of the period from 1981 to 1988 witnessed substantial and accelerating economic recovery which was eventually reflected in falling unemployment from 1987.[49] The improvement in manufacturing labour productivity has already been noted, and this was complemented by a steep rise in capital productivity in response to the more effective deployment of labour and capital in the face of diminishing trade union power and a reassertion of managerial preogatives in shopfloor organisation. Overall productivity growth, moreover, improved, although it remained below Japan, France and West Germany. It is hardly surprising, therefore, that the 1980s was marked by a major improvement in the rate of profit employed in manufacturing industry to the extent that it can be argued that there has been a fundamental change in the competitive ability of British industry. This, it can be claimed, augurs well for the future, all the more so since the improved performance appears to be spread fairly evenly across the manufacturing sector as a whole, with conspicuous improvements in metals, motor vehicles and electrical engineering. Supporters of the government would argue that the apparent enhancement of the supply-side responsiveness of the economy has been policy-induced. In this respect, the legislative curbs on trade union power and the facing down of key strikes in coal and printing are viewed as having had a crucial role to play. Even more importantly, it has been claimed that the government's consistent refusal to 'accommodate' rising costs and poor productivity by depreciating the exchange rate ensured that macroeconomic policy was effectively forcing the industrial sector to become more efficient and to improve product quality. Judged in this light the induced contraction of the economy in 1979–81, much deplored by the government's critics, was the price which had to be paid for moving the economy to a higher growth plane. It represented a long-overdue shake-out of redundant and inefficient capacity, and ensured the adoption of improved managerial and work practices among surviving businesses.[50]

It would be premature to claim that the 1980s have witnessed a 'supply-side miracle' leading to a permanent enhancement of

Britain's economic performance of sufficient magnitude to arrest the process of relative decline. The resurgence of inflationary pressure towards the end of the decade, together with the onset of large deficits on the current account balance of payments, are all reminiscent of the 'stop-go' era of the 1950s and 1960s, and they have serious implications for the future stability of the economy. The contraction of 1979–81 may have produced a leaner and fitter manufacturing sector, but experience after 1987 points to the persistence of serious supply constraints within the domestic economy. The expansion of consumer demand, after 1985 facilitated by government monetary and fiscal policy, has resulted in a resurgence in manufactured imports, reflecting a shortage of domestic manufacturing capacity. In view of current trends in the export of services and property income from abroad, the UK industrial sector remains too small to pay for import requirements at the full employment level. The deindustrialisation of the 1960s and 1970s, capped by the contraction of 1979–81, has not been reversed, and damping down the economy by monetary restriction in order to restrain inflation and rising labour costs could well have harmful effects both on the level of employment and on business confidence. If industrial investment falls in these circumstances, as seems likely, the economy would be dangerously near the point when a process of

> circular and cumulative causation will set in, with manufacturing decline affecting adversely exports and imports, while the deteriorating balance of payments itself, by imposing constraints on domestic demand, further worsens the prospects of manufacturing industry. The dependence of competitiveness on productivity growth, and productivity *growth* on output growth provide the linchpin of such a model of downward and cumulative causation.[51]

Even if it is accepted that the Conservative government has succeeded in laying the foundations for the creation of a highly competitive and dynamic free enterprise economy by virtue of its frontal assault on monopolies, state-run bureaucracies, the 'dependency culture' of the welfare state, and other growth-inhibiting institutions, the supposedly invigorating effects of these changes by their very nature can only bear fruit in the longer term. In the meantime we are left with a depressing scenario, well described by the House of Lords (Aldington) Committee on

Overseas Trade, whereby a series of massive balance of payments deficits leads to international indebtedness of such magnitude that the necessary corrective action, at the behest of creditors, carries with it baleful consequences for living standards, levels of unemployment, and Britain's place and standing in the world.[52]

3. Enterprise and the Welfare State: A Comparative Perspective

JOSE HARRIS

Do 'welfare states' enhance or subvert economic enterprise, civic virtue, private moral character, the integrity of social life? Though these questions have a piquantly contemporary ring in modern British politics, they are nevertheless old quandaries in the history of social policy. Since the seventeenth century, if not earlier, practitioners, theorists and critics of public welfare schemes have argued for and against such schemes in contradictory and adversarial terms; claiming on the one hand that social welfare schemes would supply a humanitarian corrective to the rigours of market economy; and on the other hand that they would support and streamline market forces by enhancing individual effort and collective efficiency. Similarly, for several hundred years models of civic morality which emphasise independence and self-sufficiency have jostled with alternative models which emphasise paternalism, altruism and organic solidarity.[1] Few phases of social policy in Britain and elsewhere have not contained elements of more than one approach. Even the New Poor Law, notorious for its subordination to market pressures, nevertheless harboured certain residual anti-market principles and often lapsed into practices that were suspiciously communitarian;[2] while Edwardian New Liberalism, famous for its philosophy of organic solidarity, in practice tempered social justice with the quest for 'national efficiency'.[3] These varying emphases have all been reflected in the fashions and phases of welfare state historiography; fashions and phases that appear to have been at least partly determined by the vagaries of prevailing political climate. Thus, in the aftermath of the Second World War historians tended to portray the history of social policy as a series of governmental battles against private vested interests;

battles in which the mantle of civic virtue was worn by an altruistic administrative élite, while civic vice was embodied in the motley crew of doctors, landlords, employers and insurance companies who viewed social welfare as a commodity in the market.[4] A slightly later generation of historians, influenced by 1960s-style Marxism and French structuralism, then shifted towards a different stance – emphasising not the conflict but the symbiosis between welfare and private enterprise. Social policy appeared increasingly not as the brake but as the tool of industrial capitalism, transmitting into the social democratic era the self-help maxims of the age of Cobden and Smiles; and social policymakers and public administrators were recast not as Davids of social reform but as Goliaths of the capitalist state.[5] Fashion is fickle, however, and the 1980s have brought to the fore a third vein in writing about the history of social welfare; a vein in which administrators and reformers once again appear as villains, but guilty now not of regulating the proletariat but of sapping and subverting that very same entrepreneurial capital-ism which only a few years ago they were reproached for supporting. This argument has lurked for several decades in the writings of the Institute of Economic Affairs,[6] and for long was treated somewhat disdainfully by the academic establishment; but it was brought to the forefront of historical debate by Corelli Barnett's *The Audit of War*, published in 1986, which portrayed the welfare state as one of the major links in the chain of Britain's post-Second World War national decline.[7]

Corelli Barnett's thesis seems to me an important one, less easily dismissible in many respects than some of its critics have supposed. And its message is doubly important in that, regard-less of the accuracy of its account of the more distant past, it has undoubtedly been helping to *make* history over the recent decade – in that no less a person than Mr Nigel Lawson cited 'Corelli's book' as a major source of authority for his fiscal and social policies as Chancellor of the Exchequer.[8] This paper will review the interpretation of the history of the welfare state set out by Corelli Barnett and assess its strengths and weaknesses. It will then discuss some of the questions which Barnett raises about the wider historical significance of welfare states and their influence upon social structure, economic behaviour and entrepreneurial skills.

What then is the connection between the rise of the welfare state and the secular decline of Britain as set out in Corelli

Barnett's *The Audit of War?* Barnett catalogues the substance of this decline in fairly familiar terms: loss of empire; loss of world power status; slippage from being the 'workshop of the world' to being fourteenth in the league table of world industrial nations, with a massive adverse trade balance, high unemployment, low domestic investment, weak entrepreneurship and low factor productivity, and a per capita output of little more than one-third of that of West Germany – once Britain's main industrial rival.[9] And what was the cause of this decline? Barnett's answer is a very simple one: Britain threw away the historic moment of reconstruction and recovery at the end of the Second World War, and instead of investing in the modernisation of industry and technology, frittered away her dwindling resources on building a comprehensive system of state welfare, which turned the mass of the British people into a 'segregated, subliterate, unskilled, unhealthy and institutionalised proletariat hanging on the nipple of state maternalism'.[10] And at the same time the Education Act of 1944, which purported to be bringing about secondary education for all, merely replicated the traditional faults of the British education system by ignoring science, technology and productive skills and by shoring up the cultural hegemony of an arts and classics trained gentlemanly élite.[11] And who or what brought about this state of affairs? Here Barnett's analysis is slightly more ambivalent. The main thrust of his attack is upon a wartime conspiracy of evangelical, nonconformist and humanitarian Christians – headed by William Beveridge, Clement Attlee, Hugh Dalton, Harold Laski, William Temple and many other leading members of the British Labour and Liberal parties – whom he portrays as corrupting the people with promises of a social New Jerusalem when they should have been facing up to the chill realities of economic bankruptcy and industrial reconstruction.[12] And behind this wartime conspiracy lay another more long-term and deep-seated factor. Ever since the early nineteenth century, a romantic-cum-Christian evangelical and 'Victorian' inheritance had weaned the British people away from productive and entrepreneurial values and substituted instead an ethic of humane learning, gentlemanly personal behaviour, pacific internationalism and disdain for materialism; an ethic mediated among the working classes by nonconformist chapels, and among the upper and middle classes by the public schools.[13] The all-pervasiveness of this ethic meant that over the previous 150 years Britain had *never* been well adapted to the highly competitive, disciplined and organised framework of advanced industrial capitalism. Even Britain's much vaunted technological miracles of the Second World War had been propped up by the American lend-lease programme; and British per capita wartime productivity had been considerably lower than, not merely that of German workers, but also that of 'the hundreds of thousands of foreign workers recruited onto German soil' (by whom Barnett presumably means workers conscripted by the SS into slave labour camps). This point introduces one of the main underlying subsidiary themes of Barnett's thesis; namely, the long-drawn out structural and cultural superiority of Germany at all stages of nineteenth and twentieth century British history. Even in the 1930s and early 1940s, Barnett argues, Germany had a basically strong and well-functioning social, political and economic system which had been temporarily hijacked by a handful of lunatic gangsters whom he sees as wholly extraneous to Germany's wider history. Nazism had only to be eradicated for healthy normality to be restored;[14] whereas Britain had a much more congenital and engrained problem of stagnation, sentimentalism, misplaced egalitarianism and deep-seated hostility to industrial and technological modes of life and thought.

This paper will leave on one side the wider issue of Britain's loss of world power status, and concentrate particularly on the equation between national economic decline and the setting up of a welfare state. It will also try to go beyond the rather generalised criticisms that have been put forward by many historians of the general plausibility of Correlli Barnett's thesis, and look instead at the factual and archival evidence with which he supports his case. In particular, it will focus upon the evidence for three cardinal points. Firstly, *was* the British economy burdened from the mid-1940s onwards by excessively high welfare state expenditure which sapped investment and enabled Britain to be rapidly outstripped by more realistic commercial rivals? Secondly, can the faults in Britain's welfare and education systems be ascribed to the extravagant idealism and disdain for enterprise of the Second World War reconstruction movement? And thirdly, what evidence is there to suggest that (in a ghostly echo of Gibbon's account of the Roman empire) it was the debilitating influence of Christianity that was the secret cause of Britain's decline and fall?

Firstly, then, the volume and impact of welfare state expenditure. As several of Barnett's critics have pointed out, Britain was by no means unique in introducing new and comprehensive social security plans in the late 1940s; and something which can loosely be described as a 'welfare state' emerged in nearly all western industrial countries in the decade after the Second World War. Is there nevertheless a case for saying that Britain, widely regarded at the time as the *locus classicus* of the 'welfare state', was crippling her economy with a disproportionately large amount of welfare expenditure that ate into the national dividend and national wealth creation in a way which did not happen elsewhere? What are the facts? Data relating to all European social welfare systems are readily available in many forms: in EEC and OECD reports on public expenditure, in the comparative studies of social policy carried out by Gaston Rimlinger, Peter Caim Kaudle and others; in the digests of European historical statistics published by Brian Mitchell; and most spectacularly in the massive volumes of data on European welfare states published since 1983 by an international team at the European University in Florence under the direction of Professor Peter Flora.[15] None of these very obvious sources was cited by Corelli Barnett, and indeed consideration of the welfare systems of any country other than Britain is conspicuous by its absence from his whole account. What support does such evidence lend to the view that Britain's poor economic performance since the Second World War has been peculiarly linked to the crippling fiscal and demoralising moral impact of the British welfare state system?

Some at least of the facts are as follows. Britain's new social security and national health legislation came into operation in 1948, and comparative data are available for social services expenditure in nearly all European countries from 1949 or 1950 onwards. Even in 1950, in a year when much of Western Europe had only recently been rescued from economic collapse by the first instalments of the Marshall Plan, Britain's spending on social security as a percentage of gross domestic product was lower than that of West Germany, Austria and Belgium. By 1952 her social security expenditure was also lower than that of France and Denmark, in 1954 it was outstripped by that of Italy, in 1955 by Sweden, in 1957 by the Netherlands, and in 1970 by Norway and Finland. From that time onwards until the early 1980s (the time for which full comparative data are available) Britain consistently devoted a lower proportion of national income to social security purposes than any other European country, with the sole exception of Switzerland.[16] But what about the national health service – that institution which in Correlli Barnett's eyes more clearly than any other symbolised the subordination of competitive economic values to social, egalitarian and solidaristic goals? Here again we have detailed and reliable sources of comparative data although they are not cited by Barnett. Studies of the 1950s and early 1960s showed that although the per capita health spending channelled through central government *was higher* in Great Britain than in other European countries, the aggregate volume of per capita health expenditure through central, local and private agencies was *lower* in Britain than anywhere else in Europe except Italy and Ireland. In other words the volume of investment being putatively siphoned away from wealth creation by expenditure on health care was considerably lower than elsewhere; and a committee appointed by a Conservative health minister in 1956 to investigate the problem of rising health costs concluded that, by comparison with possible alternatives, the National Health Service was both cheap and cost-effective.[17] Moreover, even if we confine our discussion solely to *public* sector health expenditure, Britain's lead under this head did not last very long. West Germany's combined public expenditure on social insurance and health care was already proportionately greater than that of the United Kingdom in 1949, and by the early 1950s Britain was overtaken in these spheres by Austria, Belgium, Denmark and Sweden. By the early 1970s Britain's expenditure on health care and health benefits was lower than that of all West European countries except Austria and Switzerland, and her joint expenditure on health care and pensions lower than that of any other European country with no exceptions.[18]

These findings are corroborated by many other studies. A comparative study of international patterns of public expenditure by Dr Jurgen Kohl found that throughout the period Britain devoted a lower proportion of its gross national product to social transfer incomes of all kinds (pensions, insurance, public assistance, benefits in kind) than all the large Western European countries and most of the smaller ones.[19] European Economic Community data show that throughout the 1970s Britain's social expenditure as a proportion both of national income and of gross domestic product was lower than that of any other community member except Ireland; and also that the rate of growth of its social expenditure was lower than that of any other EEC country.[20] Even more germane to the question of the impact of welfare on enterprise, data published by the OECD in 1985 showed that over the period 1960–81 Britain's annual growth in gross domestic product had been lower than that of all other OECD countries; and at the same time the rate of growth of Britain's expenditure on social services had *also* been consistently lower than that of the other eighteen OECD members.[21] As Harold Wilensky observed in an OECD conference paper of 1980 the 'big spenders' on social welfare such as Germany, the Netherlands, Norway and Belgium were all near the top of the international league table for economic growth rates; whereas what he called the 'lean-spending democracies' such as Britain, the USA, Canada, Australia and New Zealand were all somewhere near the bottom.[22]

The generalised case for the existence of a parasitic welfare state, which since the 1940s has crippled the economy of Britain but not that of its economic rivals, therefore looks weak. Like other forms of taxation, however, the fiscal burden of welfare spending can fall in many ways, and although Correlli Barnett is clearly *wrong* in suggesting that the global volume of British welfare state expenditure from the 1940s onwards was disproportionately high, nevertheless he *might* have a case if he argued that British welfare funding was either levied in such a way or spent in such a manner as to do more economic damage than similar funds levied elsewhere. Barnett at no point even considers any argument as relatively complex and historically specific as this, but in order to get at the historical truth of the matter, this possibility must be considered. Is there any evidence to suggest that Britain's relatively small welfare state was more economically burdensome than the relatively large welfare states of its continental neighbours?

One fact that very clearly emerges from the data compiled by the Peter Flora study is that far more of the cost of welfare expenditure in Britain fell upon the direct taxpayer and far less on employers and workers than in nearly all other European countries throughout the period 1948 down to 1982.[23] In other words it seems probable that the British social security system was at least marginally more redistributive than that of most other European countries. And another point that appears to emerge is that a comparatively *low* percentage of Britain's welfare budget was channelled through contributory social insurance; while a much higher proportion than in most European

countries was channelled through means-tested public assistance. This meant that a lower proportion of Britain's social
security expenditure was allocated to active workers temporarily
sick and unemployed (that is to say, to servicing the efficient
working of the productive sector of the economy) and a higher
proportion to support of those who were marginal to or wholly
outside the labour market. Moreover, this disparity grew over
time. Whilst in Britain the share of social security spending
absorbed by public assistance doubled between the late 1940s
and the mid-1970s, in Germany, Austria and Italy it fell dramatic-
ally over the same period.[24] In France centralised public assistance was wholly abolished in 1966, leaving the long-term poor to
a localised system of *aide sociale* far more marginal and limited in
scope than the British system of 'supplementary benefit'. In fact,
paradoxically, although Britain was believed to be the homeland
of the kind of 'universalist' social insurance system which was
identified with the 'Beveridge Plan', almost the opposite was
really the case. It was the European countries, most notably
France and Germany, which most wholeheartedly adopted a
comprehensive, contributory social insurance system (albeit differing from the Beveridge scheme in many important respects).
Whereas Britain, for all its much vaunted abolition of the Poor
Law, retained in addition to social insurance a substantial
means-tested, tax-financed welfare system, directly inherited
from the Poor Law, but shorn of much of the Poor Law's aura of
deterrence and stigma, and shorn also of its local democratic and
communitarian controls.[25] This latter system, in marked contrast to the contributory national insurance system, was primarily
concerned with relief of poverty and was almost entirely divorced
from market or actuarial constraints (except in so far as these
were mediated through political pressures). The same emphasis
on relief of poverty as the prime aim of social policy can perhaps
be seen in the policy of support for families. Whereas many other
European countries in the post-war era paid substantial child
allowances and other forms of family grant, Britain until the late
1970s paid very small 'universal' family allowances (excluding
first and only children) and channelled the bulk of its family
support services through means-tested public assistance.[26] In the
National Health Service priorities were different, in that the old
Poor Law principle of concentrating public services upon the
poor was abandoned in favour of equal access for all citizens. But
again the financial structure of Britain's health service was very

different from that of its continental neighbours, and Britain alone among the major European countries had a national health system offering total coverage and funded primarily by taxation rather than contractual social insurance.[27]

To this extent Correlli Barnett's critique of the welfare state as a hidden cause of Britain's poor economic performance may have some foundation. Though it is *not* true that Britain's global social security expenditure was larger than anyone else's, it appears to be the case that both the financial structure and the substantive priorities of Britain's welfare state *were* different. The non-economic goals of unconditional relief of poverty and, particularly in the case of the health service, of equality of access for all citizens, were more strongly built into the British welfare system than those of most other European countries, while the welfare systems of many European states and particularly of France and Germany were much more directly concerned with contractual entitlement and promotion of industrial efficiency. In other words, contrary to what most academic commentators and popular folklore have believed,[28] it was not contributory social insurance, but 'free' services financed out of direct taxation that most distinctively characterised Britain's welfare state system in the 30 years after the Second World War.

If one adjusts and amplifies Barnett's argument in this way, however, one automatically torpedoes the *second* major plank in his case against the British welfare state, which is that the sentimental, egalitarian rot set in with the wartime social reconstruction movement – because that reconstruction movement was overwhelmingly devoted to promoting a Beveridge-based contractual insurance system and to abolishing the centuries-old system of relief of need through the Poor Law. This brings us to the second major objection to Barnett's thesis, which is that he largely misrepresents the content of the wartime social reconstruction movement, and particularly that part of it mediated through the ideas of William Beveridge and the famous Beveridge Plan of 1942. Barnett portrays Beveridge throughout his book as the veritable incarnation of that 'Victorian', sentimental, Christian, pacifistic, classical, public school, Oxbridge culture, which he believes to have been the Achilles heel of British public life over the previous century. And he portrays Beveridge's plan of 1942 as the high peak of the hysterical surge of popular wartime feeling that demanded the instant sunshine of 'Brave New World' and ignored the cold reality of national bankruptcy.[29] The papers of Beveridge's social insurance committee reveal, so Barnett claimed in a resumé of his thesis published in the *Daily Telegraph* in 1987, that Beveridge deliberately set out to create 'the most lavish welfare state in the world', regardless of limited national resources and market criteria.[30] Beveridge's proposals were instantly taken up by that sentimental Christian pacifist sector of public opinion which thought that the Second World War needed some other purpose than mere military victory: the very *same* people, Barnett states, who only a few years earlier had been to the forefront of appeasement of dictators.[31] Beveridge's orchestration of public opinion ultimately forced a weak-kneed coalition government, deeply penetrated by sentimentalist Christian Labour elements, into acceptance of social welfare commitments which it knew to mean economic ruin.[32] Much the same forces were at work, Barnett suggests, in the planning of the 1944 Education Act, where scientific and technological imperatives were wholly ignored, and an Act passed whose main ingredients were the retention of compulsory religious education and the continued entrenchment of sectarian control within the nation's secondary schools.[33] This whole dismal story Barnett claims is enshrined in the public archives of the Second World War, sheltering behind all the deceptive rhetoric about patriotism and digging for victory.

It is impossible in a brief article to cite every instance in which the documentary evidence is open to a wholly or partially different interpretation from that which Corelli Barnett suggests, but we shall confine ourselves to a few key examples. First of all, the person of Sir William Beveridge. Contrary to the account given by Barnett, Beveridge was not at any time in his life a Christian, nor had he been brought up as a Christian, which was unusual for an upper-middle-class person born in the late nineteenth century. His only formal religious affiliation, abandoned after early childhood, was with the Unitarians, a sect notable in British welfare history for producing a long line of social theorists and reformers strongly committed to 'state sternness' in the treatment of the poor and to gearing social policy to the cause of industrial efficiency.[34] Beveridge was also never at any stage a pacifist, and throughout the 1930s he had been a powerful critic of appeasement. It is true that he had a first-class degree in classics (that alleged litmus test of incompetent idealism), but he also had a first in mathematics which Barnett does not mention; and throughout the eighteen years in which he had been director of the London School of Economics (1919–37) he had been a powerful advocate of the kind of business, vocational and practical studies that Barnett sees as having been at such a discount in British education.[35] Beveridge was of course a 'Victorian', in the sense that he was born during the reign of Queen Victoria; but since Victoria died only 38 years before the Second World War broke out this was necessarily true of all middle-aged leaders of public opinion during this period. More immediately relevant to this paper, Beveridge throughout his life had been a protagonist of the disciplined and highly organised 'Prussian' model of government which Barnett admires so much.[36] As a civil servant in the Board of Trade during the First World War period Beveridge had been one of the earliest (if not the earliest) advocates of the view that large-scale modern public administration needed not classicists and philosophers but technocrats and business managers.[37] Throughout his life he had been a strong defender of the maintenance of rational incentives and market criteria in state systems of social security.[38] Not perhaps unreasonably in the context of the Second World War, he had come to the conclusion in the early 1940s that at the level of macroeconomic management a pure free market had irretrievably broken down, and that both national and international economies in the future would need much more government direction.[39] But there is no suggestion in the Beveridge Report that market criteria were to be ignored at the level of paying benefits to the individual citizen. In fact quite the contrary is true. The definition of subsistence on which Beveridge's estimates of welfare benefits were based was deliberately kept to a very basic spartan minimum, partly to encourage private saving and partly to maintain the traditional Poor Law principle of a substantial incentive gap between wages and benefits – the so-called 'principle of less eligibility'.[40]

The same is true of Beveridge's whole construction of a total social security budget. The only glimmer of support for Barnett's (inherently unlikely) claim that Beveridge deliberately set out to devise the most expensive welfare system ever known, lay in the fact that early on in his enquiry he made a notional calculation of what a national social welfare system *would* cost, if all forms of want were to be universally covered by a subsistence minimum.[41] Having made this calculation he used it as a benchmark of what was socially desirable, but then proceeded with the help of advisers from the Treasury and the Economic Section of the

War Cabinet to prune it down to what was economically and fiscally viable.[42] Barnett portrays this process of amendment as mere reluctant cosmetic tinkering on Beveridge's part; a view scarcely borne out by the fact that it involved the jettisoning of such items as subsistence-level pensions, state insurance for industrial injuries, family allowances for first children, insurance for housewives, and benefits for persons unable to work because they were caring for sick or aged relatives. The result was that the 'social security budget' eventually included in the Beveridge Plan amounted to less than one-fifth of the initial 'utopian' calculation. Moreover, the vast bulk of the Beveridge committee papers which are held in the British Library of Political Science and the Public Record Office are devoted to discussions with the Treasury, the Government Actuary and the Whitehall social policy departments about methods of keeping costs down; and to statistical and nutritional inquiries about how to define the lowest possible level of provision for basic human need compatible with both healthy existence and budgetary reality.[43] A major consequence of this pruning process was that, in place of the originally hoped-for subsistence-level pensions, the Beveridge scheme recommended only a gradual increase in pension rates over a period of 20 years, to allow for the accumulation of the necessary insurance contributions; scarcely a proposal of wild imprudence or fiscal impetuosity.[44] Beveridge doubtless personally regretted the need for such economies. But regret is one thing, obtuse refusal to bow to facts quite another; and the final text of the Beveridge Plan firmly stressed the need to make the burden of social security 'as light as possible' in the aftermath of war, 'in accord with the probable economic and political requirements'.[45]

Moreover, central to Beveridge's whole philosophy of social welfare was the principle that the non-contributory Poor Law – with its means-tested benefits paid for out of general taxation and its consequent penalisation of effort and thrift – was servile and quasi-feudal and wholly unsuited to an advanced industrial economy. Instead, in Beveridge's view, people should pay for, and indeed wanted to pay for, their own welfare benefits. In the course of cross-examination of witnesses before the Social Insurance committee, he scathingly invoked the image of 'the Santa Claus state' as the epitome of the kind of welfare system that he was determined to avoid; an ironic commentary upon the 'Father Christmas system' foisted upon him by Correlli Barnett.[46]

'Benefits in return for contributions, rather than free allowances from the State is what the people of Britain desire', was perhaps the key sentiment in the whole of the Beveridge report and the one most often quoted by contemporary commentators.[47] 'Contract' not 'status' was the fundamental theoretical basis of Beveridge's conception of state social policy.[48] And, in addition, Beveridge envisaged that people who attempted to exploit the social security system were to be subject to a stringent labour test, 'conditions as to behaviour', and programmes of compulsory industrial retraining of the kind envisaged in an earlier generation by Sidney and Beatrice Webb.[49] ('No man should be subject to criminal penalties in peace for refusing work however unreasonably. But he should not be assisted to be unreasonable by provision of an insurance income.') The serious enforcement of such personal controls was never to be politically acceptable in post-war Britain, but Beveridge's advocacy of such controls could scarcely be more remote from the tender-hearted sentimentalism with which Barnett endows him. Moreover, though Barnett quotes extensively from Whitehall authorities who feared the costs of the Beveridge scheme, he makes no reference at all to the many expressions of the contrary view; to the economists and administrators in Whitehall and elsewhere who pointed out that the Beveridge subsistence-level benefits were actually in many cases lower than those currently payable under the Poor Law, who thought that the Beveridge system in sum would cost no more than all the fragmentary and overlapping services of the 1930s, and who believed that comprehensive insurance would help rather than hinder industrial recovery.[50] 'On balance the scheme should improve rather than worsen our economic conditions', wrote one such adviser to Lord Cherwell in 1943; 'the Beveridge scheme should not, therefore, be regarded as something desirable on altruistic grounds but perhaps too expensive in practice, for its cost, so far as one can see, will be less than nothing.'[51]

The historic cost of the welfare state is a subject that could be pursued in far greater detail than there is space for here. There is, however, very little evidence to suggest that welfare state spending in Britain got out of control before the mid-1960s; and, if it did so then, this was by no means a peculiarly British problem, but a European-wide and even global phenomenon. In many advanced countries between 1950 and 1970 social security payments soared ahead of economic growth and the margin between wages and benefits substantially narrowed.[52] But while it is not hard to imagine that this may have had an adverse effect on both savings and work incentives, it can scarcely be invoked as an explanation of the peculiar difficulties of Britain. In nearly every country, one of the most powerful pressures upon the upward spiral of welfare expenditure was demographic: the wholly unprecedented and at least partially unexpected burden of old age. But, in so far as social policies were influenced by cultural factors, it may be argued that the welfare state explosion stemmed, not from the utopian visions of the 1940s, but from precisely the opposite source. The stern, sober and somewhat spartan limits to state welfare imposed by planners in the 1940s began to be challenged in the 1960s by utopian thinking of an entirely different order: by academics and pressure groups and social policy lobbyists who wanted to make welfare rather than wages or investment a first charge upon national income and who looked with moral disdain upon the efforts of earlier reformers to harness social policy to economic and entrepreneurial goals. That epoch of the late 1960s fits the cap woven by Correlli Barnett far more closely than the austere and cautious 1940s. In other words, as T. H. Marshall argued long ago, the Beveridge-based welfare state was the 'child of austerity' and it broke down, not because of its extravagance, but because its spartan, minimalist, safety-net character increasingly clashed with the values and aspirations of a more affluent and millenarian age.[53]

This discussion of Barnett's ideas concludes by commenting briefly on the third aspect of his welfare state thesis; namely, his claim that it was the all-pervasive influence of Christianity that led to the setting-up of a comprehensive welfare system and to the consequent enervation of the British economy and corruption of the British state. That there is some kind of underlying connection between Christianity and welfare states is not quite so fanciful a thesis as many of Barnett's critics have supposed, since one of the major findings of the international survey carried out by Peter Flora and others was that throughout Europe confessional parties and particularly Catholic parties have been the most ambitious and open-handed social welfare spenders – far more markedly so than parties of the secularist left.[54] But Britain of course has no confessional parties and little tradition of social catholicism, and the interaction of its politics with religious opinion has always been more varying and nebulous than elsewhere. Nevertheless, is there any evidence to sustain the view that in Britain, as elsewhere, there has been some direct causal connection betweeen Christian conviction and the growth of a welfare state; and that, as Barnett claims, Christianity seduced the nation away from the struggle for economic survival? Whether he means all forms of Christianity or just some of them is not quite clear, as he frequently qualifies the noun Christian with pejorative adjectives; the terms 'Evangelical', 'nonconformist', 'Christian socialist', 'humanitarian' and 'godly notable' are used throughout his book apparently interchangeably. As exemplars of the Christian ethic he cites specifically Beveridge, Keynes, Hugh Dalton ('wearing his shovel hat as a Christian and a Socialist'), Clement Attlee and Archbishop William Temple, and at times suggests that the whole Liberal and Labour movements were embodiments of a particularly crass and worm-like Christianity; a Christianity that he also holds responsible for the 1930s policies of appeasement of dictators.[55] Just occasionally there is some slight suggestion that he is aware of something amiss with this thesis; as, for instance, when he aims a passing blow at Stanley Baldwin and Neville Chamberlain (both of whom he explains were 'liberals at heart' and had a 'family connection' with nonconformity).[56] But that there is something far *more* wrong with his thesis than that must be obvious to anyone who has the slightest familiarity with the *dramatis personae* of British history in this period; namely, that many of the people whom Barnett cites as leaders of the social reconstruction movement were not in fact Christians at all, let alone nonconformists, Christian Socialists or evangelicals. The nonchristianity of Beveridge has already been mentioned; but the same is true of nearly all the rest. Clement Attlee was an agnostic, J. M. Keynes a self-confessed 'immoralist', while Hugh Dalton's only adult connection with Christianity was the fact that his father had been an Anglican dean.[57] Barnett acknowledges Harold Laski to have been a Jew, but persists in treating him as a kind of honorary Christian gentleman. Of the major villains cited by Barnett the only one who was self-evidently a Christian was William Temple, and he could scarcely avoid being one as he was Archbishop of Canterbury; but the evidence of Temple's substantive influence on the planning of the British welfare state is minimal (other than the fact that he appears to have been responsible for popularising the term). Of the post-war Labour front bench the most prominent practising Christian was Sir Stafford Cripps: but Barnett explicitly exempts Cripps from his diatribe against the rest, on the grounds that Cripps was 'oddly realist'.[58]

That there *were* individual Christians and groups of Christians in the social reconstruction movement is undeniable (indeed it would be odd if there had not been in a country in which about one-tenth of the population were still active churchgoers and the vast majority still claimed to subscribe to the Christian ethic). And undoubtedly some Christians were tender-minded, leftist-inclined, enterprise-despising, libertarian utopians of the kind that Barnett finds most abhorrent. But the involvement of at least some of these reformist Christian groups was of a character quite opposite to that which Barnett suggests. One of the most vocal and organised Christian groups within the reconstruction movement was that which advised the Secretary of State for Education, R. A. Butler, on the reconstruction of the post-war secondary education system. Headed by the publisher and historian, Geoffrey Faber, this group included the high master of St Paul's School, Walter Oakeshott, and a number of prominent conservative business men and manufacturers. Whether by accident or design nearly all the members of this group were active Christians or Unitarians, and their reconstruction proposals were strongly imbued with the goal of rebuilding a post-war Christian commonwealth. The group drew much of its social theory and many of its practical ideas from the refugee Hungarian sociologist, Karl Mannheim. In particular, it was strongly influenced by Mannheim's view that the libertarian chaos of Britain's past history had got to be replaced by a morally integrated organic state, functionally adapted to the technological and organisational needs of modern industrial society.[59] This group set out a programme for the reform of the post-war education system, based on state takeover of the public schools, compulsory technical and vocational training for all 14–18 year olds, conscription of youth into organised youth movements, the replacement of classics by a national curriculum of science and technology, and the inculcation of public spirit through the teaching of Christian doctrine. Such a programme, it was argued, would equip Britain to meet the challenges of international competition and advanced modernity at the end of the war. With the sole exception of the emphasis on Christian doctrine, this programme was an almost exact replica of the kind of policies that Correlli Barnett appears to think *should* have been adopted by Britain's wartime planners. The programme was submitted to the Conservative Party's Central Council in September 1942, and rejected root and branch by the Conservative Party faithful as an obnoxious form of 'Christian Fascism', 'stark totalitarianism', Bismarck-inspired 'new liberalism' and the 'importation of the Hitler Youth'. It would mean a 'brass-bound sausage machine' designed to 'turn out thousands upon thousands of loathsome young prigs' and would deprive the nation's youth of their freeom, leisure and pleasure.[60] It was the total defeat of this scientific and technological programme by the rank and file of the Conservative Party that shifted R. A. Butler's educational thinking and planning towards the more bland compromise of the 1944 Education Act. This whole sequence of events within the wartime reconstruction movement is totally ignored by Barnett, and indeed like most abortive policy proposals has been largely ignored by historians in general. Yet it shows very clearly that cultural resistance to technological and organisational change had no necessary connection with support for Christianity, and that defence of traditional libertarian values was by no means confined to the nonconformist chapels.

What if anything is to be learned from this discussion about the modern history of the welfare state and its impact on national culture and economic decline? Although it has been critical of many specific points of Corelli Barnett's thesis, the overall significance of his study can be seen as being far from wholly negative. He is surely correct in suggesting that historians should investigate the welfare state, not simply as a series of episodes in high politics but as a complex of institutions and values that interact with the lives of citizens at many levels, on a par with churches or property-ownership in earlier epochs. If, for good or ill, particular welfare policies do encourage particular types of economic, moral or civic behaviour, then historians should not be too squeamish to acknowledge and inquire into this fact (a view that the Victorians whom Barnett so much despises would have fervently endorsed). Where Barnett goes astray, however, is in implying that all welfare policies have an identical and undifferentiated character, and in his curiously insular assumption that the welfare state stops at the English Channel. These perspectives underscore the need for historians who write about social welfare to define their terms and categories much more clearly. When we talk about the welfare state, do we mean by it a

Beveridge-based system of contractual social insurance? or do we mean the modern residue of a much older system rooted in economic status and citizen rights? or do we mean the whole complex of social and educational policies and institutions which in modern societies bear upon individual and collective socio-economic needs? Do we mean something peculiar to Britain, or do we see some form of welfare state system as well-nigh universal throughout the developed world? Although there is still a residual tendency among British writers to refer to the welfare state as quintessentially British, European and North American historians have long ago moved away from the view that the pure form of the welfare state, rather like constitutional monarchy, is only to be found in Britain. Indeed, it is ironic, in view of Barnett's sustained admiration for all things German, to recall that the term 'welfare state' was originally coined, not by English social reformers, but by the old Prussian right in the dying embers of Weimar Germany who (in terms very resonant of *The Audit of War*) blamed their country's moral and economic ills on *der Wohlfahrstaat*, and sought to cure them by a mixture of retrenchment, deflation and authoritarian rule.[61]

In the British context popular parlance often equates the welfare state with the proposals of Beveridge. Yet a comparative perspective suggests that in many respects this is a mistake, and that the peculiarity of the English in the context of state welfare lies not in Beveridge but in the Poor Law. It is the continuing institutional inheritance of an absolute statutory right to non-contributory public relief, rather than the national insurance system, that has most markedly distinguished Britain's welfare state from that of most other parts of Western Europe.[62] Progressive historians, following faithfully in the footsteps of the Webbs, have been inclined to treat the residue of the Poor Law as a mere pathological anachronism in twentieth century British social policy. I would like to suggest that this view needs reconsideration: that on the contrary the underlying continuity between the Poor Law and the British version of the welfare state is much more tenacious and much more functionally and ideologically complex than is often supposed. And conversely, if we are looking for a structural embodiment of Beveridgean principles, we may find at least some of those principles embodied in the schemes of continental reformers such as Pierre Laroque and Dr Erhard as strongly as in the welfare institutions of post-war

Britain. The whole question of the similarities and differences – economic, fiscal, political and philosophical – between the welfare policies of different countries seems to need more detailed and discriminating exploration than it has so far received. And only when this has been done will wider claims about the impact of such policies upon enterprise, incentives and economic efficiency be either sustained or refuted.[63]

A final point is that the intellectual, ethical and political roots of mid-twentieth century social policies need more rigorous scrutiny from historians than they have so far received, in order to liberate the subject from naïve assumptions about the goals and character of practitioners of 'social reform'. The archives of the Second World War and studies of wartime reconstruction thought make it abundantly clear that the welfare state was not the creature of any one particular group in British society, but something in which many diverse groups and ideological traditions had shaping hands; groups that included business men, accountants and enthusiasts for Prussian-style state corporatism, as well as the more obvious advocates of brotherly love, community, progressivism and democratic socialism. Social policies may be about helping people but they are also about power, and there is a case for arguing that social welfare in the twentieth century has joined the traditional spheres of defence, public order and protection of property as one of the quintessential and definitive purposes of the state. It has become one of the 'ends' which potentially reconcile citizens to the unpalatable fact of state dominion. If that is so, then historians must move beyond the kind of blanket perceptions of 'social welfare' that were noted in the introduction to this essay, as a guaranteed repository of either vice or virtue. As with foreign policy, the relevant question for historians to ask is not, did a particular state *have* social welfare policies? (One can be sure that it did in some form or another.) Nor should one ask, is the existence of such policies a good or a bad thing? (There is no sensible answer to that question.) Instead, the questions should be: what sort of policies were they, what was their specific rationale and purpose, how were they related to economic behaviour, political philosophy, culture and social structure? The answers to such questions will not be found in knee-jerk condemnation or exaltation of welfare states, but will vary according to content and context. Like the struggles over the emergence of the state itself in the sixteenth and seventeenth centuries, the welfare state should be analysed by historians, not as the marginal territory of a minority of high-minded do-gooders, but as part of the continuing contest over the structure, character and distribution of power and resources in the modern world.

4. Trade Unions, the Government and the Economy

CHRIS WRIGLEY

I

In the 1960s and 1970s industrial relations were often at the forefront of British politics. All manner of 'British diseases' were diagnosed at a time when the economies of the countries defeated in the Second World War – West Germany, Japan and Italy – were overtaking the British economy. Often prominent in such diagnoses were strikes and various other ills attributed by many to the actions of the trade unions.

Before the 1960s, although there was much criticism of the trade unions, there were relatively few major clashes between them and governments. In the decade after the end of the Second World War both Labour and Conservative governments were eager to win organised labour's cooperation in achieving economic growth. Clement Attlee's post-war Labour government (1945–51) needed trade union help to achieve wage restraint as Britain's economy, severely exhausted by the war, was rebuilt. In this ministers were helped by the warm support given to the government by the major trade union leaders, and the presence in it as Foreign Secretary, until March 1951, of Ernest Bevin, the most powerful trade union figure of his generation. With the return to power of Churchill in 1951 the Conservatives were restrained in their criticism of the trade unions. Walter Monckton, the Minister of Labour, later recalled, 'Winston's riding orders to me were that the Labour Party had foretold grave troubles if the Conservatives were elected, and he looked to me to do my best to preserve industrial peace'.[1] The 1950 Conservative general election manifesto had proclaimed that Conservatives 'from the days of Disraeli' had held 'that the trade union movement is essential to the proper working of our economy and of our industrial life', and had gone on to appeal to trade unionists

59

disillusioned with the Attlee government's wages policy with the promise that the unions would soon 'regain their function of obtaining for their members a full share of increasing productivity through free collective bargaining'.[2] In the early 1950s, with the emphasis in economic policy on growth, much of Conservative criticism of trade unions was centred on the need to remove restrictive practices in British industry.

However, by the mid-1950s there was growing concern among employers and in the government at the impact of inflation on British industry's competitiveness. Such concern was reinforced by sterling's difficulties in 1955, 1957 and 1961. The British Employers' Confederation pressed for wage restraint from the autumn of 1955, at a time when profits in most export trades were being squeezed. In 1957 the employers in shipbuilding and engineering rejected any general wage increase and faced major national strikes in an attempt to break the pattern of expected annual wage rises.[3] Although the government resolved these disputes by setting up Courts of Inquiry which resulted in a 6.5 per cent pay settlement, from roughly this time domestic price stability became a prime government economic objective. Through the 1960s and 1970s voluntary or statutory prices and incomes policies became major instruments of governments' economic policies. Alongside such anxiety about levels of pay settlements, there was growing concern about the impact of strikes on export industries during a period of recurrent balance of payment problems. In 1969, with the Conservatives promising tough trade union legislation, Harold Wilson and his Secretary of State for Employment, Barbara Castle, tried to pre-empt them with their own package of measures (entitled *In Place of Strife*) to deal with turmoil in British industrial relations. Though these proposals did not reach the statute book, they marked the beginning of a series of trade union enactments running through to 1990.

II

'British economic policy since 1945 has often resembled an inept juggler trying to keep three balls in the air, but with one or other frequently coming down and hitting him on the head. The three balls – or policy objectives – have been steady economic growth (of a magnitude comparable to other industrial nations), full employment and price stability. Where there has been failure, it has been marked by the economy being hit by high inflation, balance of payments and sterling crises, stop/go government economic policies and rising unemployment. Government involvement in industrial relations, and in collective bargaining in particular, has usually been a result of major problems in the economy. However, it also has been near to inevitable as a result both of the sheer size of the public sector and because of the demand management philosophy behind most governments' economic policies. The size of the public sector has made the government, directly or indirectly, a party to much collective bargaining and consequently many industrial disputes. Following the Second World War the growth of central and local government activities, the nationalisation of various industries and the reorganisation and expansion of health provision under the National Health Service were all major contributors to the increased size of the public sector. By 1961, 24 per cent of all employed persons were in the public sector, and by 1980 nearly 30 per cent were.[4] With both Labour and Conservative governments committed to managing the economy, it was not surprising that public sector pay-bargaining was used frequently by governments in an attempt to lower the level of expectations in all collective bargaining. Public sector pay has been the key issue both for incomes policies and for government control of public expenditure.

High wage settlements were seen as one of the major causes of inflation. During the 1950s inflation ran at 3 per cent. While this was low by later standards, by the middle of that decade it had become worrying for the government as by then it was clear that British manufactures generally were competing less successfully than their foreign rivals in the markets of the booming international economy. By the late 1960s it was felt that near full employment was creating very favourable conditions for trade unions to push up wages, which would add to manufacturers' costs and much of which then would be passed on in higher prices. Such concern had been given a theoretical underpinning by the economist Professor A. W. Phillips in 1958. He suggested a relationship between unemployment and wages, which implied that there was a link between wage changes and price changes. Drawing on data for the period 1861 to 1913 he suggested that there was an inverse relationship between the rate of change of money wages and the level of unemployment, which when depicted on a graph revealed a curve (hence the name for the relationship, the Phillips Curve).[5] Phillips' analysis of the impact of demand for labour on the level of inflation was especially influential during the 1960s, when the Phillips Curve could be shown to fit the period 1948 to 1966 with an impressive degree of accuracy (though thereafter it broke down as prices rose more rapidly and, later, as Britain experienced both economic stagnation and high unemployment).[6] The Phillips Curve could be used to reinforce the case for the control of incomes as a necessary concomitant of a policy of near full employment if the level of inflation was to be kept down.

III

The form of incomes policies changed between 1948 and 1979, reflecting the gaining of experience from previous difficulties.[7] However, generally they were marked by governments enforcing them with some degree of success in the public sector where there was often national-level collective bargaining, with low paid workers being among those most affected; while in the private sector, where there was much more plant level bargaining, there was widespread evasion.

In 1948 Attlee's government declared that there was 'no justification for any substantial increase of individual money incomes unless accompanied by a substantial increase in production'. This policy, which was not statutory, had considerable success until the cost of living index rose by 6 per cent in the year following the government's devaluation of the pound in September 1949. Such success was due to the General Council of the TUC supporting the government, even though there was extensive wages drift in the private sector, employers' organisations were less effective in keeping down levels of dividends and the government itself was removing price controls and ending rationing rather than making a major effort to restrain prices.

The moderate trade union leadership of the 1950s appears to have practised restraint in wage claims, but was unwilling to enter into negotiations with the Conservative governments of the mid-1950s for a voluntary incomes policy. After the settlement of the engineering and shipbuilding disputes of 1957, the government set up the Council on Productivity, Prices and Incomes. The TUC at first gave evidence to the Council but boycotted it after its first report. This was not surprising given that the report advocated a lower level of demand and higher unemployment as a remedy to high wage claims. With the TUC rejecting formal wage restraint, the government adopted a tough line on wage claims, one illustration of which was the government standing firm against a major strike by London bus workers in the summer of 1958.

From 1961 there were repeated attempts by both Conservative and Labour governments to introduce incomes policies, the most sophisticated being those from 1972. The early 1960s were marked by voluntary policies. In 1961 Selwyn Lloyd invited the private sector to follow the government's lead in imposing a 'pay pause' in the public sector. When this was evaded, the government in 1962 set a pay norm of 2.5 per cent, and referred for examination certain higher settlements to a new body, the National Incomes Commission. With the return of Labour in 1964 the National Incomes Commission was abolished and between December 1964 and April 1965, the government introduced in stages a voluntary prices and incomes policy in consultation with the TUC. This set a norm of 3.5 per cent, in line with the hoped for level of productivity set out in the government's *National Plan*. Although the TUC attempted to vet wage proposals centrally, local wage bargaining continued to push up actual take-home pay. Following a major sterling crisis in July 1966, Wilson announced a statutory prices and incomes policy involving a six-month standstill, followed by a further six months of severe restraint. Thereafter, between mid-1967 and mid-1968, the government maintained a zero norm, mindful not only of continuing economic problems but also that in earlier wage bargaining the 3.5 per cent norm had frequently been treated as a minimum. When the government did sanction pay rises again, the norm fixed for mid-1968 to mid-1969 was set at 3.5 per cent, with higher exceptions for genuine productivity agreements. As with the Attlee government, the impact on prices of devaluing the pound – this time in November 1967 – played a considerable part in undermining the policy.

With Edward Heath's Conservative government there was little prospect of trade union cooperation in formal or informal incomes policies. For one thing, trade union members had revolted at the Wilson government's prices and incomes policies. For another, the Conservatives' commitment to trade union legislation was anathema to the trade union leadership. So the trade unions embarked on 'gloves-off' free collective bargaining. From the autumn of 1971 the government followed an informal incomes policy based on the government setting an example by negotiating progressively lower settlements in the public sector. Faced with more rapid growth in real wages and rising unemployment Heath's government then brought in a statutory five-month freeze on wages, prices and dividends. Stage Two of this policy, in its attempt to be fairer to the low paid, recognised that pay norms expressed in percentages gave most to the better paid and provided good grounds for resentment among the low paid, who were worst hit by the higher cost of living. Hence wage increases for the year were limited to a flat rate of £1 plus 4 per cent of existing earnings with an upper limit of £250. There was a degree of flexibility within the policy as the total sum allowable under the formula for a particular group of workers could be distributed as felt best, subject to the £250 maximum. Stage Three offered a higher version of Stage Two. In order to cut out rises linked to guesses as to future inflation, the Heath government introduced 'threshold agreements' which provided for a further increase of up to 40 pence for every 1 per cent increase in the price level above 7 per cent. However, this proved to be disastrous when oil and other international commodity prices rose steeply following war in the Middle East in October 1973. It was finally wrecked by the NUM refusing to stay within the Stage Three formula, as the miners were angered that most of their 1972 gains in wages, as measured against comparable groups of workers, had been lost.[8] In February 1974 Heath lost a general election on the issue of whether the miners or the Conservatives should rule Britain.

Following the return of Labour to office, efforts were made to achieve a broad agreement with the unions of the kind which had been proposed by the TUC to Heath in the autumn of 1972 before his government introduced a statutory policy. The government offered as its part of a 'Social Contract' various measures including the repeal of Heath's trade union legislation, the introduction of new price control regulations, the freeze of rents for a year, increased old age pensions and tax changes. In return the General Council of the TUC agreed to cooperate with the remaining period of Heath's Stage Three policy (which ran out in July 1974) and urged that pay claims generally should be made only once a year, that negotiators should give productivity agreements priority and that otherwise trade unions should aim only to maintain the real incomes of their members. Denis

Healey, the Chancellor of the Exchequer, later observed that 'the value of services provided by the government, which we tried to get people to see as their "social wage", amounted to about £1000 a year for every member of the working population. But the unions defaulted on their part of the contract'.[9]

With inflation in the first half of 1975 reaching nearly 30 per cent, the 'Social Contract' was given teeth. Following suggestions from Jack Jones, General Secretary of the Transport and General Workers' Union, Healey secured TUC support for a single flat rate wage increase for the ensuing year as a measure which would protect the real value of most people's earnings and could benefit those on low wages. With the Second Phase, the government (now led by James Callaghan) went back to a percentage guideline in order to prevent further erosion of differential pay rates for more skilled workers.

By the summer of 1977 it was apparent that trade union leaders such as Jack Jones could no longer carry support for a third wage agreement. The government then unilaterally set a 10 per cent maximum for the next year, with the TUC only agreeing to support the view that pay rises should be negotiated once a year. In 1978 the government went a stage too far, or at least set the limit much too low, when it introduced a 5 per cent limit. The resulting revolt of trade unionists, especially among the low paid in the public sector, was a major contributor to Labour's defeat in the 1979 general election.

A major feature of the 'Social Contract' was Healey's use of the budget as a 'sweetener' for wage restraint. Tax levels have been seen by many economists as one trigger for union wage demands.[10] Healey in his 1976 and 1977 budgets explicitly recognised the link by making certain cuts in taxation conditional on there being lower wage settlements. In 1976, £900 of £1200 million and in 1977, £900 of £1300 million of tax relief was offered in this way, thereby proposing increases in average take-home pay of about 4.5 per cent without adding to British industry's costs.[11] This approach to the problem was not entirely new. While Healey made a very formal link between tax relief and wage restraint, Reginald Maudling, when Chancellor of the Exchequer in 1963, had earlier tried to secure lower wage demands by allowing £269 million to exempt 3.75 million people from income tax liability.[12] Another major feature of Healey's approach to wage restraint was to adopt the ideas of neoclassical economics as to the relationship between wage levels and jobs. After the October

1974 general election victory the government drastically reduced the rate of increase of the money supply, and in April 1975 Healey introduced a notably deflationary budget. If the offers of tax relief were carrots to encourage wage restraint, then these monetary and fiscal policies were a big stick with which to beat trade unionists into line or face substantial job losses.

IV

Assessing the effectiveness of prices and incomes policies is not easy, since comparisons need to be made not simply with before and after the application of the policies but with estimates of what would have happened had the policies not been applied. However, it does seem clear that in the period 1948 to 1979 those most successful in reducing the rate of change of wages were those applied at times of economic crisis when not only trade union leaders but the trade union membership and the general public appear to have supported them. This was the case in 1948 to 1950, when Britain was struggling for economic recovery from the Second World War, and in 1975 to 1978, when the government was successfully endeavouring to get inflation down from 24 per cent following both the rapid rise in world oil and other commodity prices in 1973 and also the inflationary fiscal policies and the threshold agreements of the Heath government.

Most economic studies of the 1948 to 1950 period have agreed that increases in money wages were lower that they would have been had not the government and the TUC acted to achieve a degree of wage restraint. Most have put this at 2 per cent lower for weekly wage rates. In 1975 to 1977 the incomes policy played a major part in achieving a deceleration of wage increases for two successive years and in getting the annual rate of increase to under 10 per cent for the first time since the late 1960s.[13] Between 1975 and 1977 the annual rate of increase in average weekly earnings declined from 27 per cent to 9 per cent, and the rate of inflation fell from 24 per cent in 1975 to 8 per cent in 1978. Although other factors also played a part − notably stable commodity prices, a rising exchange rate, monetary and fiscal policies and a rise in unemployment.

There is less agreement about the effect of the incomes policies of the 1960s and of the Heath government. Assessments of the 1961 and 1966 to 1967 incomes policies have varied between suggesting that they achieved between 0 and 1.15 per cent lower increases in weekly wage rates. However, the impact is clearer when the incomes policies are divided between 'harder' and 'softer' phases – in the former there were marked dips in the rate of increase of wage rates in 1961–2, 1966–7 and 1972–3. With Heath's incomes policy, earnings rose at a faster rate under Stage Two than in the previous two years; but then the impact of the incomes policy was affected by the rapidly expanding monetary supply and the escalating world commodity prices. One recent study has suggested that the econometric analyses have been too severe, and that Heath's policy may have lessened real wages by 3–4 per cent. This argument was supported by case studies of several industries. It is clear that there was a catching-up effect of wages after incomes policies, making their benefits temporary. The ending of incomes policies was marked by large pay claims, especially from public sector unions in 1969–70, 1974–5 and 1978–9. Even so, during the operation of the policies in the late 1960s and 1970s, there was the benefit that they did stop wage negotiations from becoming more frequent than once a year.[14]

Most of the incomes policies were seen as operating unfairly on public sector workers. In 1957 the Conservative government reduced Whitley Council recommendations for National Health Service and local government workers and held down wages for railway workers. In 1961 Selwyn Lloyd's pay freeze was applied to the public sector with employers in the private sector simply being urged to follow suit (an appeal which most ignored). Similarly under the 1964 to 1970 Wilson governments, public sector workers were most closely monitored, had less opportunities for productivity bargaining and consequently many found their real wages to be static or declining. Miners and NHS workers were especially hard hit.[15] In contrast, wages and salaries in the private sector were less rigorously controlled. The incomes policies reinforced the existing trend to plant bargaining and there was much scope for evasion either by such means as reclassification of work or productivity deals, real or imagined. In such circumstances public sector wage restraint could only be short term in the absence of any, or any effective, private sector wage restraint. There was also discontent during the earlier incomes policies aroused by the belief that profits and prices were either uncontrolled or inadequately controlled. Thus during the Second Stage of Heath's incomes policy company profits rose by 16 per cent and real dividends by 28 per cent. However, the impact of incomes policies on the share of profits in the national income was mixed. Recent analyses of that show that profits fell in 1961–2 and 1966–7 but rose not only in 1972–3 but also in 1976. But profits were squeezed very markedly in 1974–5 and 1979–80, after incomes policies had ended.[16]

In the mid-1970s Healey introduced cash limits on spending by government departments in order to pose more starkly the choice between gaining higher wages or maintaining levels of employment. But this policy was accompanied by an incomes policy within the 'Social Contract'. During 1976–9 it is probable that the working of the incomes policy helped to stabilise the level of unemployment, as was probably the case with the incomes policies in 1967–9 and 1972–4. After 1979 the Thatcher government combined cash limits in the public sector with restrictive monetarist policies, thereby pushing down inflation for several years without having recourse to an incomes policy. But the price was high unemployment. That had the cost to the economy of losing the benefit of the labour of large numbers of people as well as being expensive in terms of unemployment repayments. In turning its back on incomes policies the Thatcher government was following the demand-pull, or monetarist, school of economic thinking. This has argued that unions can increase wages at the expense of the overall level of employment, but that market forces, not unions, determine the rate of wage inflation. In this view, as one textbook puts it, 'incomes policies designed to reduce the rate of increase of wages by voluntary or statutory restraint on trade unions cannot be successful in curbing inflation. Since inflation is essentially a process determined by the forces of monetary demand, only monetary restraint can curb it.'[17]

However, such theories are hostile to trade union activities. The Thatcher government's attacks on trade unions were underpinned by faith in simple general equilibrium models of the working of the economy. In these, successful trade union bargaining, by gaining higher pay in the unionised sector of the economy, loses jobs and pushes up the natural level of unemployment in the whole economy, thereby making the working of the economy less efficient to the detriment of all. Indeed trade union strength in merely resisting wage cuts, according to some who hold such views, is culpable for being a restriction on what they deem to be an ideal free market where wages go down as unemployed people compete to do for lower wages the work currently being done by those still employed. Hence, in such views, trade unions are economic impediments and all diminution of trade union strength is a benefit to a free market economy. Such views, or milder versions of them, played their part in reinforcing what has been described as 'the anti-trade union, anti-corporate, anti-bureaucratic element' in the Conservative Party, and in ensuring under the Thatcher government an end to the 'creeping corporatism' epitomised by the negotiations between government, employers' organisations and TUC which took place during the various prices and incomes policies of 1948 to 1979.[18]

V

Strikes have been central to the diagnoses of 'the trade union problem' made by those who have seen trade unions as major contributors to Britain's economic difficulties. During periods of wage restraint, strikes frequently undermined government policy. In the 1987 general election Mrs Thatcher claimed that if the Labour Party won: 'The unions would be back in the driving seat. ... Under Labour production lines would grind to a halt, orders would be lost and investment plans cancelled. Foreigners would no longer be able to rely on the prompt delivery of British goods and the country would cease to pay its way in the world.'[19]

There was periodic government concern about the effect of strikes on the economy in the two decades after the end of the Second World War. This was especially notable during Attlee's post-war Labour government when the British economy was in a precarious state. Strikes were illegal until August 1951, when the wartime Conditions of Employment and National Arbitration Order No. 1305 was abolished. With the country anxious to achieve economic recovery and with the trade union leadership warmly supporting the first Labour government with a majority in the House of Commons, the level of days lost through strikes was low. In fact the number of days lost through strikes in 1945–51 amounted to only 6 per cent of those lost after the First World War in 1919–24, and compare reasonably well with the relatively quiet years of 1933–8 (being only 8 per cent higher). However, the government was very concerned about some major official strikes. In the case of a series of dock strikes, which affected exports, the Attlee government repeatedly resorted to the Emergency Powers Act and used troops.[20]

By the 1960s strikes were becoming a major political issue. This was partly to do with a wave of strikes between 1957 and 1962. These included several official major industry-wide disputes, often sparked off by the government's attempts to impose wage restraint. By this time the Conservatives and the trade union leadership had returned to a state of barely disguised hostility. Throughout the decade, there was growing concern at the number of unofficial strikes (often 90 per cent of all disputes in the 1950s and 1960s). The 1965–8 Royal Commission on Trade Unions and Employers' Associations (chaired by Lord Donovan) observed that 'the prevalence of unofficial strikes, and their tendency (outside coal-mining) to increase, have such serious economic implications that measures to deal with them are urgently necessary'. In addition the Wilson government felt that its economic policies were being thwarted by a seven-week-long merchant seamen strike which began on 16 May 1966. It was the one major official dispute of the 1960s, and it aroused in some ministers the paranoia of Communist subversives that had been displayed during some of the dock disputes faced by the Attlee government between 1945 and 1951.[21]

By the second half of the 1960s some form of trade union legislation was widely seen as a political necessity. Suggestions as to what the nature of the reforms should be came from three directions. The Donovan Commission reported in June 1968 in favour of the voluntary reform of collective bargaining. It specifically rejected various proposals to lessen the problem of strikes by statutory means such as requiring before strikes cooling-off periods (enforced delays to industrial action while attempts to settle the issues in dispute took place) and compulsory secret ballots, and the Commission deemed to be undesirable the making of collective agreements into legally enforceable contracts. In contrast to Donovan, in May 1968 the Conservative Party published, under the title *Fair Deal At Work*, proposals to set British industrial relations within a legal framework. These proposals included requiring trade unions to be registered and to be given corporate legal status, making collective agreements legally binding, and placing sympathetic strikes, inter-union disputes and strikes to support closed shops outside the legal protection afforded to trade disputes. In addition, the Conservatives proposed that the Minister of Labour should have the powers to refer a major dispute affecting the national interest to a National Industrial Court for arbitration, to apply to the Industrial Court for an injunction to secure a cooling-off period, and to order a secret ballot.

The third source of proposals for trade union legislation was the Labour government. Wilson felt that the voluntarist proposals of the Donovan Report, which were generally in line with TUC thinking, were not sufficient. The government's White Paper, *In Place of Strife* (published 17 January 1969), stated that its package of proposals tackled Britain's 'special problem' in industrial relations which stemmed 'from sudden industrial action taken before adequate negotiation or discussion of the problem'. These included giving the Secretary of State powers to order 28-day 'cooling-off' periods where strikes were imminent that breached collective agreements, to require a ballot before an official strike could take place which threatened the national interest, and to impose a settlement in an inter-union dispute. In arguing the case for these measures Wilson claimed that they were crucial to improve Britain's balance of payments and for economic recovery. There was also a political dimension. Richard Crossman, the Secretary of State for Social Services, noted in his diary that Wilson realised that his proposals 'would upset the trade unions and the Labour Party but felt that didn't really matter because this was going to be a great popular success'. Clearly the Prime Minister was much attracted to upstaging the Conservatives on one of their major election issues. However, the three proposals which abandoned voluntary principles and could result in fines led to a major clash between the Cabinet and the trade union movement, with much of the Parliamentary Labour Party in revolt. As a result Wilson, who had offered to drop the offending clauses if the TUC could come up with something 'equally urgent and equally effective', was forced to compromise and accept the TUC's 'solemn and binding' undertaking to try to resolve inter-union disputes and to discourage unofficial strikes.[22] Wilson's failure to press ahead with his original proposals was widely felt to be one of the major reasons for the government's defeat in the 1970 general election.

Following the return of the Conservatives to office, much of *Fair Deal At Work* was put into law in the Industrial Relations Act, 1971. Its operation became a major political issue, with the Labour movement doing all it could to undermine the Act and Heath being unwilling to lose face by amending those aspects of it which soon proved to work in a disastrous manner. The introduction of a special court, the National Industrial Relations

Court, into industrial relations proved to be an especially unhappy experiment. When, in March 1972, dockers committed what was deemed to be an unfair practice, boycotting containers that had been loaded by non-dock labour at road hauliers' depots, the Transport and General Workers' Union was fined £55,000 even though the men's action was unofficial and the union could show that it had tried to stop the boycott. In July 1972 the Court sent five dockers to Pentonville Prison for disregarding an injunction forbidding them to boycott such containers. In commenting on the judgment of his court, Sir John Donaldson observed: 'The purpose of this Court is to promote good industrial relations and none of us imagines for one moment that the making of committal orders will achieve this result. But the issue is whether these men will be allowed to opt out of the rule of the law.' Nevertheless, after a national strike of 170,000 dockers and the threat of a one-day general strike, the men were released, still unrepentant for being in contempt of the National Industrial Relations Court. The government was also embarrassed when the imposition of a 14-day cooling-off period and a secret ballot in a rail dispute in April 1972 strengthened the trade union leaders' hands since the result of the ballot showed that they had overwhelming rank and file support.

The effective life of the Industrial Relations Act 1971 came to an end in the summer of 1972. From that time the Heath government, which was anxious for trade union cooperation with its incomes policy, no longer operated it. Before then it already was apparent that many employers preferred not to worsen relations with their workforces by using the Act. Following the defeat of the Heath government in the February 1974 general election, the 1971 Act was repealed. Under the Labour governments and their Social Contract (1975–8) the level of days lost through strikes remained high compared to the 1950s and 1960s, but was at only half the level of the Heath years (1970–3) until 1979 (and then many of the days lost through strikes occurred under the Conservatives).

The major industrial unrest of early 1979 (the 'Winter of Discontent'), together with widespread public unease at the apparent strength of the trade unions in the state, played a major part in the defeat of Labour in the 1979 general election. The Conservative manifesto devoted much space to trade union reform, including promises to introduce legislation on picketing, the closed shop and to 'provide public funds for postal ballots for union elections and other important issues'. Between 1980 and 1990 there was a series of Acts which carried out this programme and went further in curtailing the activities of trade unions.[23]

While it has been repeatedly asserted since 1945 that strikes are very damaging to the British economy, it is difficult to come up with figures which show that they have had a major impact on the whole economy (as opposed to the particular industries affected). Obviously in most cases it would have been better for output if strikes had not occurred. (There may be a minority of cases where there was stockpiling, and a strike or lock-out simply avoided a later lay-off.) The same applies to the loss of working days through back complaints, colds and influenza, or simple absenteeism. But the reality is that there was 'a silent majority' not involved in industrial stoppages at all. A Department of Employment survey of the years 1971–3 found that in manu-facturing industry an average of 98 per cent of establishments were free of stoppages, and these establishments covered 81 per cent of workers in manufacturing. Moreover, even when there were strikes in large plants, many workers were not involved at all. Hence it is not surprising that such careful studies of strikes as that by Durcan *et al.* suggest that even in 1972, a year with one of the three highest strike levels of the post-1945 period, 'the impact of stoppages in the UK was to cause an output loss of not more than 0.25 per cent'. In contrast, these authors suggest that if unemployment had been reduced to a quarter of a million then that 'would have permitted additional output equivalent to 2.5 per cent of Gross Domestic Product'.[24]

This points to the impact strikes can have on particular industries. The Donovan Report argued that unofficial strikes damaged British industry by preventing firms meeting delivery dates and so risking the loss of future orders, that where strikes were against the introduction of new technology they could inhibit the modernisation of industry and the achievement of higher productivity and that such strikes, or the threat of them, often caused local wage drift (i.e. increases above national agreements). However, later studies of strikes have thrown doubts on strikes being sufficiently widespread, except in a few instances, for them to have such a major impact. The Depart-ment of Employment survey, which followed up the Donovan Commission, found in its analysis of industrial stoppages in manufacturing in 1971–3 that 'a mere 5 per cent of the small minority of plants that had stoppages . . . accounted for almost a quarter of recorded stoppages and for two-thirds of the working days lost'. Earlier Ministry of Labour figures for stoppages showed a problem of strike-proneness in a very small minority of establishments, usually large ones. In 1965 there were 31 and in 1966 27 establishments which had five or more stoppages in the year. The Department of the Employment survey concluded: 'It is abundantly clear that Britain does not have a widespread strike problem but rather a problem of stoppages concentrated in a small minority of manufacturing plants and in certain non-manufacturing sectors'.[25]

There have been several industries which have accounted for a high proportion of strikes at various times since 1945. Thus, for example, between 1946 and 1952 43 per cent of all working days lost due to industrial disputes were in coal mining. Excluding the coal industry, half of all major strikes in those years were in non-electrical engineering, shipbuilding, motor vehicles, the docks and road passenger transport. Similarly between 1970 and 1975 the industries in which most working days were lost were coal mining, the docks, motor vehicles, tractors and shipbuilding.[26] In some cases the main causes of the strikes were problems in adapting to change, such as an industry contracting, the introduction of new technology, or management enforcing new work practices in the face of foreign competition. In some cases, such as the contraction of the coal industry between 1957 and 1968, the changes took place with relatively few strikes. In others, such as the introduction of containerisation in the docks and the introduction of different work practices in the motor car industry, the changes were marked by major industrial unrest.[27] Whatever the cause, industrial stoppages in these more strike-prone industries were a considerable problem.

Yet strikes and other trade union action often provided an excuse for not tackling other, probably more important, causes of company or even national economic poor performance. Thus in 1985 the labour relations director of Ford was reported as saying, 'If the trade unions have been significantly weakened by economic pressures or by industrial legislation, it has whipped away the crutch which managers have been using for the past 30 years'.[28] Similarly, by the end of the 1980s, after a decade of trade union legislation and several years of relatively low levels of strikes, it was increasingly hard to ascribe Britain's economic ills to strikes. When Britain's strike record is compared with other western industrial nations it becomes clear that the British level

TABLE 4.1   Industrial disputes in the United Kingdom 1945–1988

Year	Number of stoppages beginning in the year	Aggregate duration in working days of stoppages in progress in year (000s)
1945	2,293	2,835
1946	2,205	2,158
1947	1,721	2,433
1948	1,759	1,944
1949	1,426	1,807
1950	1,339	1,389
1951	1,719	1,696
1952	1,714	1,792
1953	1,746	2,184
1954	1,989	2,457
1955	2,419	3,781
1956	2,648	2,083
1957	2,859	8,412
1958	2,629	3,461
1959	2,093	5,270
1960	2,832	3,024
1961	2,686	3,046
1962	2,449	5,798
1963	2,068	1,755
1964	2,524	2,277
1965	2,354	2,925
1966	1,937	2,398
1967	2,116	2,787
1968	2,378	4,690
1969	3,116	6,846
1970	3,906	10,980
1971	2,228	13,551
1972	2,497	23,909
1973	2,873	7,197
1974	2,922	14,750
1975	2,282	6,012
1976	2,016	3,284
1977	2,703	10,142
1978	2,471	9,405
1979	2,080	29,474
1980	1,330	11,964
1981	1,328	4,266
1982	1,528	5,313
1983	1,352	3,754
1984	1,206	27,135
1985	887	6,402
1986	1,053	1,920
1987	1,004	3,546
1988	770	3,702

SOURCES: H. Pelling, *A History of British Trade Unionism* (4th edn, 1987), pp. 299–300. *Department of Employment Gazette*, August 1989.

of strike activity is far from unique, and so should not be deemed to be an 'English disease'. Between 1975 and 1979 Britain still came behind the United States, Canada, Australia, Italy, Ireland and Spain in International Labour Organisation statistics on strikes. Yet the fact that major industrial competitors such as West Germany, France and Japan lost less time from strikes suggests, nevertheless, that high levels of strikes are probably both symptomatic of, and a contributory factor to, relatively poor performances in some industries.[29]

VI

The trade union movement's problems have not been confined to the actions of governments. The strength of trade unionism has been linked to long-term structural changes and to booms and slumps in the economy. Much of the growth of British trade unionism in the late nineteenth and early twentieth centuries was concentrated in a number of major industries. After the Second World War these industries were shedding labour. In the cases of cotton, coal mining and the railways, where trade union membership (or density) covered 85.5 per cent of the labour force, employment fell as a proportion of the total British labour force from 8.3 to 4.0 per cent between 1948 and 1968.[30] Hence for British trade unionism to maintain its strength, it needed to adapt to changes in employment.

In the late 1960s there was an upsurge in trade union membership marked by considerable growth in manual unionism and by a dramatic growth in white-collar unionism. The growth in the latter was important especially given the steady increase of this area as a proportion of the labour force. From 1951 to 1971 white-collar workers increased from 30.9 to 42.7 per cent of the British labour force. In these years the union density rose from 31.3 per cent to 34.3 per cent. Between 1951 and 1964 white-collar trade union membership grew swiftly but not as rapidly as the growth of employment, so union density dropped between 1951 and 1966.[31] Between 1964 and 1970 white-collar union membership grew by 33.8 per cent at a time when the white-collar labour force only increased by 4.1 per cent. This growth continued at a slower rate in the 1970s, with the union density continuing to rise. By 1979 about 44 per cent of all white-collar workers were in unions, and of all British trade unionists 40 per

cent were white-collar workers. In the case of the increase of
unionisation of manual workers from the late 1960s it resulted in
higher union densities among a smaller labour force. Between
1964 and 1979 the British manual labour force fell by about 2.2
million (15.5 per cent) but union membership within it went up
from about 53 to 63 per cent.[32]

Changes in the structure of the economy provide part (but
only part) of the explanation for the fall in trade union membership in the 1980s. The world recession hit the British manufacturing and construction industries hard, and the Thatcher
government's economic policies accentuated the world recession's
impact within Britain. Between 1979 and 1981 output fell by 14.1
and 14.9 per cent in manufacturing and construction respectively,
and in 1985, in the midst of what the government deemed to be a
'boom', output was still 5 and 5.4 per cent respectively below the
1979 level. Between March 1980 and March 1989 the numbers of
people employed in manufacturing dropped by 28 per cent, from
7,082,000 to 5,096,000.[33] United Kingdom trade union membership (Table 4.2) fell rapidly in the early 1980s, notably between
1979 and 1983 when it dropped by 15.5 per cent. This fall was
highest among unions in manufacturing industry. That the widespread closure of factories in the early 1980s was a major element
in the fall of trade union membership was confirmed also by the
1980 to 1984 Workplace Industrial Relation Surveys. The data of
these surveys point to the disproportionate closure of, or shedding of labour by, large, and so usually unionised, factories as
being the major reason for a very marked fall in the presence of
manual unions in their sample of private manufacturing companies.[34] The continuing redistribution of employment away
from the north to the south had a minor reinforcing role in this.
Various studies have shown that individuals in the north of
Britain were much more prone to join unions than people working in the south. Moreover most of the employment opportunities
in the south were in industries and small-scale workplaces which
were less likely to be unionised anywhere.[35]

However, for the unions the most worrying feature of membership losses in the 1980s was that numbers continued to fall, albeit
at a slower rate, when the economy picked up in the mid-1980s.
If the 1980s United Kingdom trade union loss of membership is
compared with the 1930s, the more recent loss appears very
serious. From a high point in 1929 trade union membership fell
by 9.6 per cent by 1933, but had risen 20.3 per cent above the

TABLE 4.2   Union membership 1945–1987

Year	Union membership (000s)
1945	7,875
1946	8,803
1947	9,145
1948	9,363
1949	9,318
1950	9,289
1951	9,530
1952	9,588
1953	9,527
1954	9,566
1955	9,741
1956	9,778
1957	9,829
1958	9,639
1959	9,623
1960	9,835
1961	9,916
1962	10,014
1963	10,067
1964	10,218
1965	10,325
1966	10,259
1967	10,194
1968	10,200
1969	10,479
1970	11,187
1971	11,135
1972	11,359
1973	11,456
1974	11,764
1975	12,026
1976	12,386
1977	12,846
1978	13,112
1979	13,289
1980	12,947
1981	12,106
1982	11,593
1983	11,236
1984	10,994
1985	10,821
1986	10,539
1987	10,475

Note that the 1986 and 1987 figures have not yet been adjusted by the Department of Employment.
SOURCES: G. S. Bain and R. Price, *Profiles of Union Growth* (Oxford, 1980), p. 38. *Department of Employment Gazette*, November 1977 to September 1989.

1929 level by 1937. In contrast trade union membership fell from a 1979 high point by 15.5 per cent in 1983, and by 1987 had dropped 21.2 per cent below the 1979 level. This scale of loss in a recession was not unique in the United Kingdom. The 1921 to 1922 economic recession was especially severe. Then trade union membership fell from a higher level than 1929. By 1923 numbers had declined by 35 per cent. A significant point in making comparisons between the impact of recessions on trade union membership is the strength of union membership at the outset. Both the 1921–2 and 1979–81 recessions followed ten-year booms in trade union membership. Overall trade union density fell from around 45 per cent in 1920, from about 55 per cent in 1979 and from only about 26 per cent in 1929. Recovery of trade union membership by 1937, or for that matter by 1939, had not reached the levels of 1918 to 1921.[36] Thus, like the economy as a whole, bigger falls in trade union membership have taken place from higher starting points (e.g. 1920 and 1979 rather than 1929).

In explaining why trade union membership moves up and down, most writers have offered explanations involving a mix of broad economic factors with more particular ones such as employers' policies, industrial structure and the actions of government. Various econometric studies of the relationship between the business cycle and the rate of change of trade union membership have argued that the main (economic) determinants have been the rates of change of retail prices and of wages and the level of unemployment. Both prices and earnings moved more rapidly between 1969 and 1979 than in the previous two decades. After 1979 earnings often barely kept up with prices, so for many workers real earnings were squeezed, and for some groups their real earnings fell at various times in the 1970s. This squeeze on real earnings was especially acute for white-collar workers. Hence Professor Bain and others have pointed to these movements of retail prices and earnings, which encouraged more workers to join trade unions in an attempt to protect their standards of living, as being a major explanation for trade union growth from 1969. However, while this explanatory model is satisfactory for the period from 1969, it is notable that earlier periods of inflation, such as 1950–2 and 1959–62, were not accompanied by such dramatic trade union growth. After 1979, in spite of retail prices and earnings moving up quickly at first, the scale of the increases in unemployment was the main economic reason for the sharp decline in trade union membership.[37]

VII

Another problem for trade unions has been to adapt to changes
in the way that work has been organised. This has always been a
necessity throughout the history of trade unionism. In the 1970s
and 1980s the changes were not only widespread and rapid but
also were of a kind that in the past had not favoured unionisation. These changes included the growth of capital-intensive
rather than labour-intensive, high-technology firms; a proliferation of small firms (the total number of manufacturing establishments rose from around 70,000 in 1968 to 102,000 in 1982);
increased subcontracting; more outwork; and a larger number of
temporary workers.

The combination of economic recession, high unemployment
and a government committed to pushing labour costs down produced an economic climate in the 1980s which was favourable for
employers who wished to casualise part of their workforces. In
this way some employers removed part of their labour force,
usually the less skilled part, from being near to a fixed cost and
instead obtained that labour by hiring the workers on short-term
contracts or subcontracting the tasks out altogether. In this way
flexible contracts of one kind or another shifted some economic
risk from the employer to the worker, though this was often at the
cost of a high labour turnover. In 1986 about one-third of those
employed could be deemed to be part of the flexible workforce.
The proportion of the flexible workforce varied across the economy, with the highest levels being in agriculture (60 per cent),
hotels and catering, distribution, construction, repairs and business and professional services.

As for which forms of flexibility were preferred, choices varied
across the economy. An Advisory, Conciliation and Arbitration
Service (ACAS) survey of 584 establishments, which was made
between April and June 1987, found that the employment of
part-time workers (30 hours or less a week) was much more
prevalent in service industries and the public sector than in
manufacturing industry – though in manufacturing nearly 90 per
cent of companies employing over 1500 workers did employ some
part-timers. The survey found that the employment of temporary
workers was less widespread, and was highest in chemicals and
in the extraction or manufacture of metals. The most widespread
way of securing flexibility in the size of the labour force was to
use outside contractors, as did 90 per cent of the manufacturing

firms in the survey. For the unions such developments often led to a loss of members, either through redundancies or because the newly created peripheral workforce was much harder to organise.[38]

As in the rest of Europe there was a considerable expansion in part-time employment from the 1950s, and this growth was associated with greater female participation in the workforce. Between June 1971 and March 1989 the number of part-time workers grew by a little over 50 per cent, to 5.2 million. Women

TABLE 4.3 Employees in the United Kingdom 1971–1989 (in thousands)

| | Full-time | | | Part-time | | |
	Male	Female	Total	Male	Female	Total
June 1971	13,124	5,619	18,743	602	2,793	3,395
June 1978	12,669	5,632	18,302	728	3,759	4,487
Sept 1981	11,768	5,433	17,222	738	3,856	4,594
Sept 1984	11,173	5,437	16,610	797	3,939	4,736
Sept 1987	10,919	5,741	16,660	908	4,211	5,119
March 1989	10,919	5,863	16,782	908	4,283	5,191

SOURCE: *Employment Gazette*, November 1989 (figures not seasonally adjusted).

made up 82.5 per cent of those workers. Part-time work was always most prevalent in the service sector. In the 1980s roughly 90 per cent of all part-time workers were employed there. In that sector there was ample demand for part-time workers to carry out work which was not just fractions of full-time jobs. Part-time workers can meet labour needs in periods of peak demand, such as late-night or Saturday shopping, rush hours or meal times in hotels. As well as hourly wage rates for such work being generally low, in the 1980s part-time labour was also cheap for employers as those working less than 18 hours per week were not covered (until after 5 years of continuous employment) by legislation relating to maternity pay, redundancy or unfair dismissal. Hence a study of 21 organisations between 1979 and 1982 found that in the service sector up to 70 per cent of those employed worked fewer than 16 hours per week. It also confirmed that part-time workers were usually in the lowest graded occupations, and that within the part-time labour force there was discrimination against women when workers were selected for dismissal on grounds of redundancy.[39]

Efforts to cut labour costs in the public sector were very

marked in the 1980s under the Thatcher government. Cuts in the
Rate Support Grant paid by central to local government and the
'rate capping' of many local authorities were intended, in part, to
force a shedding of labour and/or a cutting of real wages. The
1987 ACAS survey found that the number of part-time employees in public administration had increased in the previous
three years, and in some establishments part-timers amounted to
10 per cent of the workforce. Similarly the use of short-term fixed
contracts was most prevalent in the public sector, and the
practice had increased markedly in the previous three years.[40]
Privatisation of services was marked more notably by cutting the
wages bill (either by lower wages and/or less labour) than by
greater efficiency. Often low paid workers tendered for their
existing work at even lower pay. Where alternative outside
contractors came in, the greatest savings achieved frequently
were in the wages bill. In Lincolnshire, for example, an outside
cleaning contract in 1986 was operated with wages of £1.70p
replacing a previous wage rate of £2.41p an hour.[41] Such
developments in the public sector, which threatened to worsen
considerably the pay and other conditions of work, encouraged
workers to join or stay in unions such as the National Union of
Public Employees. Generally the levels of success of the unions in
recruiting part-time workers paralleled their levels with full-time
workers. Unionisation of part-time workers was weak in catering
and distribution but effective in the health service, education and
local government.[42]

     However, another area of recent growth, the area of self-
employment, has always been less fruitful for union membership.
After the numbers of self-employed had fluctuated for many
years around the 2 million mark, they rose rapidly during the
1980s. In June 1979 there were 1,906,000 self-employed in
Britain, out of a total workforce in employment of 23,365,000 (7.5
per cent of the total). By March 1989 the numbers had risen to
3,079,000 self-employed out of a total employed workforce of
26,272,000 (11.7 per cent of the total). A notable aspect of this
was the increasing number of self-employed women, from
357,000 (18.7 per cent) to 761,000 (24.7 per cent of the total self-
employed). Self-employment did provide many women with a
route into, or back into, the workforce. But, as Catherine
Hakim's study of the self-employed in the year between spring
1986 and spring 1987 showed, most of the new self-employed had
previously been employees. Many had become redundant, or

perhaps had gone from jobs before they were pushed out, and this encouraged them to try to make a success of some venture that they had long considered trying. However, the study also showed a remarkably high turnover of self-employed: with 440,000 entering self-employment and 250,000 leaving it.[43]

Some aspects of flexibility in working practices were less contentious than substituting part-time or self-employed workers for full-time workers. This was particularly so with changes in hours of work and payment systems which rewarded the acquisition of new skills. In the 1980s in white-collar work there was a marked growth in the operation of flexible working hours and some increase in the practice of job sharing, especially in the south-east of England. Such patterns of work, as with part-time work generally (with working hours ranging from the half day to 'twilight'), often suited female workers very well – which some unions were slow to grasp. However, the unions and the women workers were well aware that such practices were often marked by low pay status. Professor Hakim has suggested that in the late 1960s and early 1970s flexibility in work arrangements was promoted primarily for the benefit of the workers, whereas in the 1980s the focus of such schemes was adjusted to the benefit of the employers. In manufacturing industry in the 1980s, as the 1987 ACAS survey found, there was greater flexibility over demarcation lines in work. In the case of companies with much modern electronically or computer controlled plant there was a reduction in boundaries between clerical, technical and craft workers. Such changes were seen as essential to help raise productivity, and there was much evidence that, as the ACAS survey put it, 'the presence of trade unions has not appeared to inhibit the introduction of new working practices'.[44]

VIII

By 1990 the impact of the Thatcher government on trade unionism and on industrial relations generally appeared less innovatory or dramatic than many of its proponents or opponents claimed. Probably the biggest impact came from the government's economic policies, notably those which resulted in levels of unemployment soaring and in the devastation of British manufacturing industry, especially in 1979–81. At the level of national politics the government carefully marginalised the TUC by consulting it less and by ensuring that it was represented on fewer public bodies. It broke away from the tripartism of the 1960s and 1970s in which the TUC had been consulted frequently on some major aspects of economic policy. In the mid-1970s trade union figures such as Jack Jones and Hugh Scanlon had appeared to many people to be as powerful as Cabinet ministers. Indeed in one of the many alarmist writings of that period, Anthony Burgess' novella *1985* (1975), England was rechristened Tucland, with the trade unions in control and the closed shop being the only effective law of the land. However, even in the mid-1970s the trade union impact on economic policymaking often remained weak, with the TUC not being consulted on such key decisions as the application for a $3.9 million loan from the International Monetary Fund in the autumn of 1976,[45] although in the area of incomes policies, not surprisingly, both Labour and Conservative governments felt the need to seek the TUC's cooperation. The abandonment of full employment as a top priority of economic management, with North Sea oil funding unemployment benefits, carried with it less necessity for either an incomes policy or consultations with the TUC.

Whatever else may have followed from the Thatcher government's economic policies, a near strike-free era was not one of them. Much of the industrial unrest of the 1980s was in the public sector and stemmed from tight cash limits restricting wages and/or leading to substantial loss of jobs in the industries or services. The government's cash limits affected levels of real earnings and encouraged people to go from the public to the private sector. The government dealt with the many disputes with varying success. It lost public sympathy when dealing with such groups as nurses and ambulance personnel. It won some major setpiece industrial battles, notably the miners' strike of 1984–5. The miners not only were defeated in the strike, but thereafter saw (as the NUM leadership had predicted) wholesale pit closures and a massive reduction in employment. In the case of British Steel the workers in 1980 won a 16 per cent pay award after a lengthy strike, but afterwards experienced a two-thirds cut in the workforce. After ten years of Thatcherism Britain was far from being a strike-free zone. Indeed the wave of strikes in the summer of 1989 led the media to talk of 'a summer of discontent', making a damaging comparison with what they had dubbed 'a winter of discontent' under the Callaghan government.

The Thatcher government's policies were notable more for

encouraging the acceleration of some existing trends in the labour market, rather than introducing major changes. These trends included the use of more part-time workers, more sub-contracted labour and various flexible practices in the workplace. But the combination of heavy unemployment and government encouragements to 'enterprise initiatives' did take the numbers of self-employed people to a higher level than had been the norm in previous decades. The impact on industry of the government's industrial relations policies was less marked. Employers generally were reluctant to alienate their workforces by aggressive use of the various trade union legislation of the 1980s, with the exception of gaining injunctions against picketing on some occasions. The much vaunted strike-free agreements and single union deals of the early to mid-1980s covered some 10,000 workers and were not widely followed later in the decade.[46] According to the Confederation of British Industry (CBI) surveys of 1979 and 1986 the proportion of establishments which recognised trade unions remained much the same: 72 per cent in 1979 and 70 per cent in 1986.[47] The CBI surveys also suggested that in private industry there was a shift towards plant level bargaining, with more pay and other conditions arranged at the local level.[48]

The trade unions fared less badly under adverse circumstances than was suggested at the time by many commentators in the media. The economic situation of the 1980s favoured employers not unions in industrial relations. The effects of mass unemployment in weakening the unions' bargaining position were reinforced by trade union legislation, part of which placed considerable restrictions on industrial action. However, the level of unemployment, the changing structure of employment and the changing practices of work probably caused the unions more problems than the legislation. Unions such as the General Municipal, Boilermakers and Allied Trades Union (GMBATU) and the National Union of Public Employees (NUPE) were among those which responded with considerable success to the needs of part-time workers – and, in the case of the latter, to the problems arising from the putting out to tender of much public service work. However, generally, trade unions remained dominated by masculine presumptions and prejudices and often were not quick to respond to the needs of women workers.

The Thatcher government's trade union legislation was marked not simply by hostility to political opponents and – in the case of some ministers – by an economic creed that held that any trade union action was detrimental and a cause of unemployment. It also was influenced by a belief that many trade union leaders were out of touch with the views of their members. Unlike the 1971 Industrial Relations Act, the Conservative legislation put financial penalties on unions rather than individuals, thereby avoiding politically embarrassing martyrs, and combined restrictions on unions' actions with the giving of rights to individual members. The effect of some of the latter changes – such as regular secret ballots for top trade union posts – was to strengthen the trade union movement. In the case of the requirement in the 1984 Trade Union Act that unions hold periodic ballots to maintain political funds, ministers misread rank and file trade unionists' attitudes, and the resulting campaigns within unions for a 'yes' vote were a major boost for trade union morale – with 3 million trade unionists in 37 unions voting by large majorities to maintain their political funds and 4 million more voting to set up political funds for the first time. Moreover, the trade unions are likely to benefit from various EEC policies, such as the Fifth Draft Directive on Company Law, a series of directives on health and safety, and the Vredeling proposals from the Social Affairs Committee of the Commission. The Labour Party's leadership in December 1989 dropped support for the closed shop in order to be able to back the whole of the proposals in the European Community's Social Charter.[49]

The policy change which had the biggest impact on the unions was the Thatcher government's determination to confront inflation at the immediate expense of employment (though the Callaghan government had gone some way even in this). This undermined the earlier situation (especially of the 1950s and 1960s) when trade unions had been in a strong bargaining position in an economy with near to full employment and relatively high growth rates. In pushing up real wages they had played a part in generating the excess demand in the economy which had led to a wage-price spiral, and from 1968 added a wage-push element to the inflation of the early 1970s. However, in its approach to the problem of inflation, the Thatcher government accentuated the problem of unemployment, at a heavy human and economic cost.[50] Moreover, in spite of high levels of unemployment in the 1980s, employers in Britain continued to pay their employees considerable rises in real earnings. This appears to have been encouraged in part by the government's preferred mode of collective bargaining; that was at the local rather than at the national level, with employers paying for increased flexibility in workplace practices out of high profits. As one American commentator has observed, 'there is nothing to indicate that anything has been done to alter permanently the inherently inflationary character of Britain's decentralised wage-setting institutions'.[51]

Indeed, there was not much sign of the fundamental problems of British industry having been resolved during the 1980s. Thus, for example, in spite of North Sea oil, investment in British manufacturing dropped from 3.6 to 2.7 per cent of Gross Domestic Product between 1979 and 1989; the amount spent on research and development stagnated at a low level; and the lack of training in British industry was reaching a crisis point in some sectors by the late 1980s. If in its economic and industrial relations policies the Thatcher government was placing its faith in a return to a form of classical economics as well as a return to Victorian values, then it was attempting to go back to some of the conditions which, arguably, had led to the economic retardation of the British economy in the late Victorian period.

5. The Jerusalem that Failed? The Rebuilding of Post-War Britain

JOHN STEVENSON

FEW areas have reflected changing intellectual fashions and political ideologies more visibly and publicly since 1945 than the attitude towards housing and planning. Britain emerged from the Second World War with a strong tide of collectivist fervour running in favour of building, quite literally, a 'New Jerusalem' from the rubble and squalor of the past. Within a generation unease with what was being done in the name of progress had become evident and, from 1979, was to be reinforced by a reaction against planning and state control under the influence of the 'new liberalism' personified by the Conservative governments of Mrs Thatcher. Housing and planning were to become battlegrounds in a debate with wide intellectual and sociological repercussions, as well as a direct impact upon housing and planning policies. Long before 1945, social reformers had sought to achieve a reshaped physical environment which they believed would cure the ills of industrial society: crime, poverty and ill-health. 'Homes fit for Heroes' and the slum clearance campaigns between the wars began the process. By the end of the 1930s enthusiasm for 'planning' and the wholesale redevelopment of Britain's cities was growing apace. Financial stringency, however, prevented the implementation of any of the more visionary schemes to destroy the old and build the new. The Second World War broke this impasse. As part of the articulation of its war aims, the British government launched a propaganda campaign promising the creation of a better Britain in peacetime. At the same time, bombing was leaving millions homeless and destroying cities all over Britain. Plans shelved for lack of funds and visionary sympathy in the 1930s were dusted off in the 1940s and the building of the New Jerusalem began. Faith in modern planning as the panacea for all the ills of industrial society encouraged local authorities in the late 1950s to raze large tracts of town centres to build elaborate ring roads, shopping precincts and housing developments. But disillusion crept in; by the late 1960s it was apparent that the old social problems had persisted, and indeed, had been joined by a new set of social and political difficulties. By the 1980s 'planning' was almost considered as a bankrupt word and architects were widely blamed for a social disaster. The aim of this essay is to assess the origins and nature of the housing and town-planning movement in post-war Britain and the accuracy of the condemnation which has occurred in recent years. To what extent were the aspirations for this 'New Jerusalem' fulfilled and how far were its critics justified?

I

Almost no issue better encapsulated the collectivist enthusiasm of the post-war era than the idea of rebuilding a new society from the ruins of the war-ravaged and industrially-scarred Britain of the past. Already by the inter-war years rehousing the slum dweller ranked as one of the highest priorities for social advance. Lloyd George's 'Homes fit for Heroes' campaign at the end of the Great War was the first in which the government took a leading role in encouraging the housing of the people. Although the detailed history of the Lloyd George scheme is not one of the concerns of this essay, its importance was considerable.[1] The legislation to implement the house-building drive, in the two Addison Housing Acts of 1919 with their subsidies to local authority housing and their obligation upon the larger local authorities to survey their housing needs and to draw up plans for future housing development, set the tone for a whole era. Although the Addison Acts ultimately fell prey to the onset of the depression and the financial cutbacks of 1921–2 in the 'Geddes Axe', over 200,000 houses, both 'council' and 'private', were built under their provisions. The generous financial provisions of the Act allowed the building of houses which were to be a landmark in the design and quality of mass housing. The house designs were in a traditional vernacular style, spacious, light and well-ventilated, and built to very high standards. At an early stage some of the house designs were vetted by representatives of the Women's Cooperative Guild whose preferences for separate

parlours as against through-plan living rooms, for example, provided an early example of the potential for divergence between
the rational solutions of architects (who sought to maximise light
and ventilation) and the actual requirements of their potential
inhabitants. The aims of the Addison scheme proved an unful-
filled aspiration in the financial climate of the 1920s, but tackling
the housing problem remained a high priority of governments as
witnessed in the series of housing initiatives undertaken throughout the inter-war period. Almost 500,000 houses were built under
the more restrictive provisions of Chamberlain's Conservative
Housing Act of 1923 before it was withdrawn in 1929, while over
500,000 council houses were constructed under the Wheatley Act
of 1924 before its suspension in 1932. Most significant of all,
however, was the 'Greenwood' Act of 1930 which provided for
slum clearance by the local authorities with graduated subsidies
according to the total number of families rehoused and the cost of
clearance; in addition, local authorities were obliged to produce
five-year plans for slum clearance. When this was interrupted by
the financial crisis of 1931 a fresh Act in 1933 drew up new plans
for slum clearance with the same subsidies as under the original
Greenwood Act, aiming to clear 266,000 slum dwellings, build
285,000 houses, and rehouse some 1.25 million people.

Whatever the shortcomings of government policy in other
areas, the Acts of the inter-war years established housing as a
responsibility of national governments operating through the
agency of the local authorities and began to have significant
impact on the situation by the end of the 1930s. Although it was
the private house-building boom and the growth of semi-
detached suburbia which attracted attention during the era and
subsequently with over 2.5 million houses built for sale or rent
between the wars, the provision of council housing was by no
means negligible and was rapidly gathering pace in the period up
to the Second World War. Indeed, by any standards, the results
were impressive. More slum houses were cleared in the decade
before 1939 than in any other similar period. Between 1931 and
1939 local authorities cleared 250,000 slum properties and built
over 700,000 houses, rehousing four-fifths of existing slum dwellers. Already a pattern was developing of building traditional
style homes in a much diluted version of the 'garden suburb'
style as extensive estates on the fringes of main towns and cities,
or as 'satellite estates' on completely green field sites, such as
Norris Green and Speke, near Liverpool, Solihull and Longbridge

outside Birmingham, Wythenshawe to the south of Manchester
and a series of London County Council estates around the
capital. The best of these did offer a fair attempt at capturing
something of a pleasant, semi-rural character with tree-lined
avenues, spacious verges and open spaces, generous gardens and
traditional 'cottage' type housing. Some were undoubtedly the
product of deep commitment and considerable thought. The only
true 'satellite town' was Wythenshawe, built on land owned and
given to the City of Manchester by one of the foremost writers
and practical housing pioneers of the inter-war years, Sir Ernest
Simon. Planned for a total population of 100,000, 7000 houses
had been built by 1939. It formed part of a comprehensive plan
to redevelop the rundown, crowded slum districts of central
Manchester, rebuilding them at lesser density, and decanting the
surplus population to the new satellite towns.[2] But Wythenshawe
and the privately funded Welwyn Garden City were the only two
'new towns' built between the wars. Most suburban estates were
envisaged as an integral part of the existing urban communities
with public transport forming the crucial link with the major
employments and services to be found in the old town and city
centres.

It was here that the first flaws in the local authority rebuilding
and slum clearance programmes began to show up. Some of the
new estates provided little in the way of amenities, lacking com-
munal facilities such as pubs, shops and meeting places. In what
was to become a persistent refrain about suburban housing
developments, the dwellings were built and the people moved
before any community facilities were prepared. In many instances
it was a matter of poor coordination, but in certain cases it was
deliberate. Some of the early Liverpool council estates were built
without any licensed premises as an act of policy, depriving the
inhabitants of one of the natural points of focus in the old slum
communities. Family networks too were disrupted by the strand-
ing of young families miles from their relatives and the support
networks of kin which had been such an important feature of
economic and social survival in the slum districts. The close-knit
and highly textured life of the working-class districts conjured up
after the war in the writings of Robert Roberts and Richard
Hoggart, and given formal exposition in the work of urban
sociologists such as Wilmot and Young's post-war survey of East
London, was not yet fully perceived. The costs of the new
'council' houses also created problems for the tenants. Higher

rents, greater heating costs, and the need to find more furniture
and equipment for larger houses were already charged in one
influential pre-war study with depressing the living standards of
those who had been rehoused.[3]

Moreover, as the new estates grew in numbers, the overall
quality deteriorated and an almost inevitable complaint about
monotony, dullness and poor standards of construction began to
develop. But it was hardly surprising that, in contrasting them
with the appalling physical conditions of the old slums, many
commentators were blind to some of the new problems that had
arisen and concentrated on what they saw as their most important characteristic, the provision of basically sound houses,
free from the worst physical dilapidation of the slums. Optimism
about the new estates was assisted by their largely traditional
design, cottage or terrace-style houses, built of brick with pitched
roofs and gardens.[4] Although some of the younger architects had
begun to be attracted by the more 'modern' architecture of
central Europe and Scandinavia, particularly the large blocks of
workers' flats built in Vienna, and there was already a lively
discussion about the relative merits of flats versus traditional
houses, the debate was largely decided in terms of tried and
trusted designs. Only in inner-city areas where land was in short
supply was it considered necessary to build maisonettes and
these were usually restricted to 'walk-up' developments of no
more than four or five storeys. The giant Quarry Hill scheme at
Leeds, completed in the late 1930s, when 2000 slum houses were
demolished and replaced by a comprehensively designed block of
938 flat dwellings, drawing closely on continental models, was
the exception rather than the rule.

It was, however, a pointer to the future. Some of the more
ambitious architects and planners were increasingly attracted by
large-scale redevelopments in both housing and town planning.
'Planning' became something of a vogue word in the decade
before the war; architects and town planners were in the forefront
of those who saw a comprehensive and rational approach to
social and economic problems as the key to a better and more
progressive future. In architectural circles 'modernism' and the
so-called 'international style' were becoming fashionable. From
them flowed growing interest both in the visionary schemes of the
Swiss architect Le Corbusier for giant blocks of flats and for a
spare, rational architecture. It was increasingly fused with the
idea of comprehensive planning, stimulated by the largely

unplanned sprawl of private housing and industry between the wars and the mounting pressure of road traffic. It was also recognised that left unchecked and unregulated there was a tendency for new development to concentrate in the south-east and especially around London, offensive not only because of its contribution to the crowding of the south-east but also because other parts of the country were still suffering from industrial decay and unemployment. As a result, on the eve of the Second World War a number of tendencies were converging upon the idea of greater planning controls to force development away from the south-east to less favoured parts of the country, to rationalise the growth of London by encircling it with a 'Green Girdle' or 'Green Belt' as a barrier to urban development, (actually enacted in the Green Belt Act of 1938), to build 'New Towns' to take overspill populations from the large urban centres, and to adopt comprehensive 'plans' for the redesign and rebuilding of the older city centres. Many of these larger schemes provided the framework within which local authorities and housing officers were to operate after the Second World War.[5]

II

The Second World War had a decisive impact in a number of directions. Already by 1939 the threat of aerial bombardment had led to a policy of industrial relocation and controls over the siting of factories. The Barlow Commission of 1937, which reported in 1940, has been seen rightly as the 'planners' breakthrough', with its recommendations for greater government control of industrial and urban growth, especially in the south-east of England. The Scott Report of 1942 urged the setting up of a planning system to embrace the countryside as well as the town, mainly with a view to preserving the best agricultural land from urban development, but also recommending the setting up of National Parks. Moreover, the bombing of Britain's cities in the blitz provided a powerful impetus to plans for rebuilding Britain. Positive encouragement was given by the appointment in October 1940 of Sir John Reith as the head of the new Ministry of Works, not only to supervise the repair of bomb-damaged buildings but also to coordinate with other Departments and organisations in the post-war rebuilding of Britain's cities. One of Reith's first actions was to appoint a panel of consultants to advise him on post-war planning. A series of objectives was drawn up which followed closely the views of progressive planners. This included controlled development and utilisation of land, the limitation of urban expansion, redevelopment of congested areas, the correlation of transport and other amenities, improved architectural treatment, and the preservation of places of historic interest, national parks and coastal areas. One result was the appointment of Patrick Abercrombie and the LCC architect J. H. Forshaw to draw up a scheme for the rebuilding of London. The result was the *County of London Plan*, published in 1943, and a further report, tackling the whole of London's environs, the *Greater London Plan* of 1944. Schemes were also inaugurated for the reconstruction of some of the most badly bombed cities on a more comprehensive scale than ever before and to bring about a complete refurbishment of the urban landscape.[6] The example of Coventry illustrates to what extent pre-war efforts dovetailed with the effects of the blitz. It was one of the first cities to set up an Architects Department, and an exhibition in May–June 1939 *before* the war broke out illustrated plans for a redesigned civic centre. With the devastation of the city centre in November 1940, these plans were mobilised rapidly by the General Purposes Committee for a wholesale replanning and redevelopment of the city. Within six months of the raid on Coventry, an exhibition of sketches and plans outlined a redesigned city centre based on pedestrian shopping precincts, zoned development, and an inner city ring road.[7] Although Coventry was something of a showcase, many other towns and cities took the opportunity to articulate plans for rebuilding. Cities as diverse as Sheffield and Oxford were the subject of planning studies which attempted to translate into practice what had prior to the war remained largely visionary ideas. In that sense town planning became the symbolic standard-bearer for post-war reconstruction. The building of a better urban environment captured many of the highest hopes for the post-war world. In the 'Plan for Britain' issue of *Picture Post* in January 1941, the young architect Maxwell Fry summed it up with the phrase 'The New Britain Must Be Planned'; plans were required for every sphere of Britain's post-war future, in industry, housing, education, welfare and transport. But for Maxwell Fry the centrepiece was urban redevelopment, a large double-page spread contrasting the old, blighted townscape of polluted air and rivers, factories and housing jostling with each other, inadequate open

space and poor facilities for modern transport with the planned
townscape of residential blocks of flats, wide straight urban
highways, and zoned development for factories, shops and
housing.[8] Hundreds of town and city plans produced in the war
and the immediate post-war years were to echo these themes as
part of the conventional wisdom about what the rebuilt Britain
should become.

And these were not idle dreams. The Second World War gave
enhanced credibility to planning as well as a tremendous boost to
plans to build a better Britain. The elements became fused in
wartime propaganda which stressed that the British people were
fighting for a 'better tomorrow', a 'tomorrow' which was to be
shaped decisively by the progressive ideas of planners, architects
and experts of all kinds, and in which the same 'planning' which
had organised the war effort would be turned to meet the needs of
peace. The creation of the Ministry of Town and Country Planning in 1943, followed by the Town and Country Planning Act of
1944, provided both the machinery and the powers for comprehensive redevelopment on the lines envisaged by progressive
opinion. Subsequently, the 1947 Town and Country Planning
Act brought almost all development under control by making it
subject to planning permission; development schemes were to be
prepared for every part of the country, the powers being transferred away from the small district councils to the county and
borough councils, with coordination of local plans carried out by
the Ministry of Town and Country Planning.

The most thorough-going expression of the comprehensive
approach to solving the nation's housing problems lay in the
New Towns. Abercrombie's *Greater London Plan* had proposed
ten new towns beyond the Green Belt to relieve urban congestion
within the capital without adding further to the peripheral expansion of the metropolis. Others, in Durham, South Wales and
Scotland were planned to provide new facilities and amenities in
areas which needed substantial new housing, while Tyneside, the
Midlands and Merseyside also eventually were recognised as
areas where relief from urban overcrowding could be met by the
same means. The New Towns Act of 1946 represented the full
expression of the new machinery of planning; the Act provided
for the setting up of Development Corporations to plan and
create new towns where considered 'expedient in the national
interest'. The corporations were given wide powers of acquisition
and management of the requisite areas and generally 'to do

anything necessary or expedient for the purposes of the new town or for the purposes incidental thereunto'. Fourteen new towns were designated by 1950, eight in the 'London Ring' with a proposed population of over 600,000, with the other six taking the total almost to a million. Another seven were added by the mid-1960s, bringing the total of proposed new town dwellers to over 1.5 million people.[9]

If the New Towns were the most dramatic example of the reconstructionist mood and the faith in planning, the Labour government which came to power in 1945 faced a more mundane but pressing housing crisis. Pre-war local authority housing had been directed primarily at rehousing the inhabitants of the slums, and considerable progress had been made, but there remained the problem of a growing population, increased marriage rates, and a larger number of households. Although house completions were running at an average rate of 330,000 a year between 1935 and 1939 this was barely sufficient to keep pace with demand. Voluntary migrations of population to seek work had already created pockets of temporary housing ('shack development') in some areas and considerable pressure on rented accommodation, especially in parts of the south-east. The Second World War hugely exacerbated the problem. It brought both private and municipal building to what was a virtual standstill at less than 5000 houses per year. Meanwhile the backlog of houses due for demolition increased. In 1939 there were still 550,000 houses waiting to be demolished under the slum clearance acts and another 350,000 'marginal dwellings' on the brink of classification as slums. To this backlog had now to be added 475,000 houses destroyed or made permanently uninhabitable by enemy action and an even larger number damaged to a greater or lesser degree. Moreover the war had added a further twist to the upward spiral in the demand for houses; a rush of 2 million wartime marriages was followed quickly by a 'baby boom', an equally high divorce rate, large movements of population from one part of the country to another, and the need to accommodate thousands of foreign servicemen and ex-POWs who decided to stay in Britain.

The extent of the problem was well illustrated by the case of Liverpool, an authority with one of the worst housing problems prior to the war but one which in 1939 was making substantial inroads into slum clearance, building an average of 3500 houses a year. The war, however, saw almost 13,000 houses either destroyed or rendered uninhabitable, with another 19,000 seriously damaged. Moreover, the city had 'lost' the further 17,500 houses it would have completed at pre-war rates of building. The combined effect was an 'immediate' demand for 32,000 houses even before considering fresh clearance of insanitary and worn-out properties. When overcrowding and the rapid deterioration of the older housing stock were taken into account it was estimated that a further 40,000 houses were needed. The populations involved were large: with its often large working-class families, the city had more than 200,000 people which it needed to rehouse with some degree of urgency.[10]

But if the Labour government of 1945 was pitchforked into a first-class housing crisis it also had no doubt that housing was a major priority and in a mood of optimism not unlike that of 1919 set about a crash programme with a target of building 240,000 houses a year through generous subsidies for local authority rented housing. Immediate short-term problems were met, with some success, by such expedients as the estates of 'temporary' pre-fabs which soon became a permanent feature of many war-damaged cities, but the government's target proved hopelessly unrealisable amidst the competing claims of the export drive, the creation of the welfare state, and acute shortages of materials. In 1947 the housing programme was in serious difficulties with completions dropping to 12,000 houses. Although the Labour government eventually completed 900,000 houses by 1951, it had fallen disastrously behind its own target figure and was vulnerable to Conservative attacks on its failure. The Opposition's promise to build 300,000 houses a year was undoubtedly one of the major factors behind its electoral victory in 1951. The Conservatives' Housing Act of 1952 raised subsidies to local authorities to build houses but also increased the supply of licences to private builders. As a result the Conservatives redeemed their pledge with 319,000 houses built in 1953 and a record 348,000 in 1954. In fact the number of local authority completions fell as they were allowed to devote half of their allocation to private building and the Conservative government established the position that local authority housing was primarily to deal with particular problems, mainly the backlog of slum clearance. The 1953 White Paper, *Houses: The Next Step*, followed by the 1954 Housing Repairs and Rents Act reduced subsidies for 'general needs' housing while retaining them for slum clearance. In 1957 all subsidies for 'general needs' housing were

THE REBUILDING OF POST-WAR BRITAIN

removed apart from slum clearance and special needs such as one-bedroomed dwellings for the elderly. By the late 1950s housing policy was being directed primarily to private building and improvements to existing stock. The 1957 Rent Act decontrolled rents in the hope of reinvigorating a sector which was already dwindling rapidly in the face of the growth of owner occupation and a rising number of council tenants.

TABLE 5.1   Types of housing tenure in England and Wales: sample years

	Owner-occupiers (%)	Council tenants (%)	Private tenants (%)	Other (%)
1947	26.0	12.0	58.0	7.0
1958	39.0	20.0	37.0	3.0
1966	46.7	25.7	22.5	5.1
1977	54.0	32.0	9.0	5.0
1985	61.9	27.3	8.3	2.5

III

In all during the 1950s almost 2.5 million houses were built in England and Wales, two-thirds of them in the local authority sector; before the Conservative government fell in 1964 another 500,000 were added. Persistent problems remained, however, which ensured that housing retained a high profile in the political debates of the era. In spite of a respectable rate of house completions, governments were running hard to stand still amidst major demographic and social changes which were rapidly expanding the number of households. The figures spoke for themselves: the population of England and Wales grew from 38 million in 1921 to 48 million in 1966, but in the same period the number of private households almost doubled from 8.7 million to 15.7 million.[11] Changes in demand for type and quality of housing, in particular for young couples and single adults, both in the younger age groups and amongst a growing body of elderly people, were only the most obvious problem areas. The rapid shrinkage of the private rented sector, much of it demolished in slum clearance schemes, also created severe problems for many of those unable either to become owner-occupiers or to reach the top of council house waiting lists. In essentials, the two main thrusts of housing policy since 1945, to clear the slums and build houses for owner-occupation, had simply been insufficient to meet housing needs, particularly of those who were forced into the overcrowded and expensive rented sector of the major cities. By the early 1960s, problems such as the eviction of tenants from slum properties preparatory to refurbishment, associated with the case of the slum landlord, John Rachman (the so-called 'Rachmanism'), homelessness, and the plight of specific groups such as the elderly and immigrants were increasingly vocal concerns. One effect was to force the Conservatives to revive the 'general needs' subsidy graduated according to the needs of particular areas. A further Act in 1964 set up the Housing Corporation specifically to encourage the building of homes at low cost rents. The year the government fell from office a new record for house-building was reached with 374,000 completions, but even this figure was insufficient to match housing needs. The post-war era had seen the immediate problem of housing shortage arising from the war met in one form or another and some inroads into slum clearance, but the backlog of elderly and unfit dwellings was huge: in 1951 one-third of the housing stock was more than 80 years old; more than a third of houses had no bath; one in five had no sole use of a toilet or piped water supply and one in twenty lacked even the basic amenity of a kitchen sink. The number of unfit dwellings had actually risen from 472,000 on the outbreak of the war in 1939 to 847,000 in 1954. Eleven years later the figure was little changed, at 824,000.

The Labour government which came to power in 1964 had an ambitious housing target of 500,000 houses per year, divided equally between the private and public sectors. But as in the 1940s the economic crises of the mid-1960s slowed the programme significantly with the result that the five-year period 1965–9 produced only 1.8 million houses compared with the target of 2.5 million. Although comfortably beating the record of the Attlee administrations and matching the 300,000 plus of the Conservative governments before 1964, the rate was once again insufficient to meet demand. Although slum clearance was proceeding at the rate of 60–70,000 a year, more than double that of ten years earlier, it was not enough to prevent the backlog of unfit houses from growing. While 900,000 slum properties had been demolished since 1945, a new nationwide survey in 1967 by public health inspectors working to a uniform standard estimated that there were 1.8 million 'unfit' dwellings, a further 3.7 million needing repair, and 2.3 million lacking indoor sanitation.[12]

As well as a continued decline in the housing stock, there were clearly some errors in policy which sprang from good intentions but exacerbated an already serious situation. For example, the redevelopment of whole areas meant that many houses which might have been repaired were demolished. Wholesale clearance and the declaration of areas as due for clearance prevented the piecemeal refurbishment of a portion of the older stock which might have eased the overall shortage of accommodation. Equally serious, the Labour government's attempts to meet the widespread outcry over 'Rachmanism' produced the 'fair rents' legislation of 1965 which reintroduced rent control over the great majority of privately owned, unfurnished accommodation. However justified, one effect was to continue the reduction of rented accommodation available as landlords found letting an increasingly unviable proposition. Between 1966 and 1977 the proportion of housing tenure rented from private landlords was more than halved to under 10 per cent of the total in England and Wales. Homelessness, particularly in the larger cities, was intrinsically linked to the failure either to provide sufficient public housing to cater for low income groups or to encourage the provision of low cost rented accommodation which had met these needs in the past. The gradual drying up of what many saw as an essential lubricant to both the housing and labour markets was to make the problem of 'homelessness' a persistent refrain in the housing debate even as a reaction was beginning to set in against some of the new housing that had been built.

Between 1945 and 1968 something over 2.5 million people were relocated as a result of slum clearance. Whatever shortcomings there were when measured against total housing needs, the scale of the process was evident in the transformation of whole areas of both town and country by slum clearance and new building. In the latter half of the 1960s, in spite of the economic problems of the Labour government, more houses were built in England and Wales than in any previous five-year period since the First World War. But the character of the new developments was beginning to attract criticism. In spite of the high hopes with which they had been launched and the attention they received, the New Towns, including some freshly designated overspill towns in the late 1960s, contributed only a fraction of the new housing built in the post-war period. By 1972 their total

population was 611,000 and accounted for only just over 200,000 dwellings, in total less than one year's 'build' during most of the post-war period. On balance, they were usually well designed or, at least, attracted a higher degree of attention from architects and planners. This could, however, prove a mixed blessing. New Towns were a prey to whatever fashion seemed most in vogue at the time in the architectural profession. Some, such as the first wave of the 'London Ring' in places such as Harlow were built in the somewhat anonymous but inoffensive architecture first pioneered in Scandinavia and the Low Countries before the war.[13] The later wave, however, offered some bolder experiments. The first New Towns had assumed fairly low levels of car ownership, only 10 per cent of houses being allowed a garage, with the majority of the population moving by bicycle and public transport. By the 1960s it was recognised that the age of mass motoring had to be catered for. New Towns such as Milton Keynes were built around the premise of a majority of the inhabitants owning cars and were designed on the basis of a network of roads linking deliberately dispersed residential and working areas. The price paid was an inevitable anonymity, a town which seemed more like a series of linked roundabouts rather than a living community.[14] Similarly, experiments such as the Cumbernauld New Town, intended to service Glasgow overspill, and Runcorn in Cheshire, to house people from Merseyside, suffered from a failure of even the most well-meaning planners and architects to solve the riddle of creating viable living environments for their new populations. The problems varied: Cumbernauld suffered from its bleak, windy site and the malaise which affected it through the loss of employment caused by the contraction of Scottish manufacturing industry; Runcorn was to be beset by problems with some of its architecture and building methods, producing long-running battles between residents and the architects deemed responsible.[15]

But the problems of the New Towns paled into insignificance beside the evidence of discontent with some of the new estates. Although many of those rehoused were generally satisfied with the improved amenities of the new council houses, some became a by-word for bleakness and anonymity with an intensification of the problems already beginning to be evident on the pre-war estates. Kirkby, outside Liverpool, was to become a symbol of all that could go wrong. The opportunity existed for Liverpool to develop a 750-acre industrial estate and a 'complete community' four times larger than the largest pre-war satellite estate at Speke. By 1965, 50,000 people had been moved in and the relative prosperity of the 1960s ensured that reasonably full employment was available. By the early 1970s, however, the industrial estate was in trouble and as social problems of unemployment, rent arrears, crime and vandalism grew, Kirkby became a by-word for neglect and dereliction. Building on a larger scale had created more problems, not less. It was beginning to be recognised that slum clearance had destroyed not merely slums, but communities, communities which no amount of desktop and drawing board work by architects and planners seemed able to recreate to a reliable formula.

The formula for new housing was tested to destruction in the taste for giant schemes, similar to those pioneered at Quarry Hill. When, filled with enthusiasm for Le Corbusier's Marseilles block, opened in 1952, the Sheffield architects planned a huge development of the Hyde Park complex, towering above the city's main railway station, they scored both successes and failures. The idea of designing 'streets in the sky' to recreate on a vertical plane the old pattern of street life but now free from traffic and serving homes with modern amenities worked well enough in the first phase of development at Parkhill, where many residents expressed satisfaction with their new homes, although there were some complaints about noise and rowdyism. However, the next phase, the Hyde Park flats, crowning the site, proved a disaster. Its towering decks were soon found to be totally unsuitable for families with children, its exposed site was bleak and forbidding, and by 1976 it was decided to thin out the larger families and replace them with single people. Within ten years, demolition of what had been designed as a showcase was considered more than likely.[16] Up and down the country, the same problem with high-rise developments began to be apparent. To a considerable extent they were a product of the intense phase of development in the 1960s when the 'numbers game' was most in evidence. Local authorities were being urged by central government to build at ever greater rates and positive encouragement was given to high-rise developments using new and relatively untried methods. The system-built tower block seemed to offer the perfect solution to enable redevelopment at high densities, while still making sufficient land available for roads, schools and playing fields. Prior to 1955 several cities, for example, had followed the pattern of building only 'walk up' four or five storey maisonettes in the crowded central areas. Flats of this type were actually dearer to build than conventional 'cottage-type' houses and such survey evidence as existed showed them to be far less popular than houses with gardens. System-build, however, provided a much cheaper option and it was fondly believed that it was only a matter of time before people would get used to a new type of housing. Above all, however, they offered a speedy solution to what was recognised as the need to build more dwellings as quickly as possible. The example of Liverpool is again instructive. In spite of the wishes of the city architect from 1948, Ronald Bradbury, to experiment with high-rise blocks, shortages of steel for their construction and local opposition prevented their realisation and it was only in 1956 that the first ten-storey block was actually built. Tower blocks seemed to open the vista of a sudden break-through in a city which recognised that it was rapidly falling behind in the race to meet housing needs. As a result, the city turned to system-building with a vengeance. Following a visit by planners to Paris in 1962, the city ordered 22 Camus towers, 6 of twenty-two storeys. By 1965 Bradbury could report 110 tower blocks built or under construction. [17] Liverpool was not alone; flats and maisonettes accounted for 55 per cent of all tenders for local authority housing approved by 1964, although the proportion of tall blocks of over five storeys was lower, reaching a peak of 26 per cent in 1966. [18]

The tower block was to become the symbol of all that was wrong with local authority housing in the post-war era. Continental cities and even parts of Scotland with different civic cultures and traditions proved an unreliable guide for English conditions and social habits. It was quickly realised that high-rise was unsuitable for families with young children and that without constant maintenance and attention broken-down lifts and blocked rubbish chutes soon turned them into a nightmare for their inhabitants. 'Airy' streets in the sky took on a different complexion in a bitter English winter, while passage-ways, stairwells and ground-floor garage areas which could not be overlooked by the residents soon succumbed to graffiti, vandalism and litter. System-build soon revealed its own problems, whether the result of shoddy construction or intrinsic to the designs themselves; heating costs, damp and condensation soon proved some of the most persistent complaints of residents. Moreover, although some people undoubtedly found high-rise dwellings reasonably tolerable, there were thousands of others appalled at the scale and barrack-like construction of some of the new developments. Even where local authorities did not build particularly high, the giant 'deck access' complexes at places such as Hulme and Ardwick in Manchester were intimidating barracks, heartily detested almost as soon as they were completed.

IV

The collapse of part of the Ronan Point tower block in London in 1968 following a gas explosion was one of those chance occurrences which became symbolic of a whole sea-change in attitudes. Behind the subsequent narrow concern with the safety of using gas in tower blocks built with the new techniques, was a more generalised disquiet. There was a growing disillusionment and dissatisfaction with the 'New Jerusalem' which the architects and planners had built. The headlong rush to build a better world seemed to have run up against not just a minor technical hitch but a host of far more complex and deep-seated problems than originally envisaged. It was becoming apparent that more satisfactory lives could not be created in bricks and mortar alone, still less in system-built tower blocks and breeze-block modernism. The long-standing faith in 'experts' and a willingness to trust planners and architects was dwindling rapidly. On almost every side the planners and architects were under attack by the 1970s and many of the most visionary schemes were seen as a disaster. Birmingham, Britain's first city to grapple comprehensively with the problems of motorised access and through-routes for traffic, found its Bull Ring centre widely unpopular with anyone other than motorists. By the mid-1980s it was scheduled for a complete overhaul. Following American precedents, the first tower blocks were being demolished or sold off by councils who found the costs of repair too high to cope with and whose tenants refused to live in them. Moreover, the economic problems of the 1970s left whole areas cleared with no prospect of substantial or speedy rebuilding. Town and city plans lay abandoned and unfinished, along with ring roads which ended abruptly and urban motorways which led nowhere.

In part, at least, the disenchantment sprang from the articulate middle classes and growing concern at what redevelopment might mean to much loved existing townscapes. Warning notes had sounded early in the post-war era with outcries over the demolition of the Euston Arch in London in 1961, the ravaging of many of London's Georgian squares by redevelopment and the damage inflicted on some smaller towns like Worcester. Two famous victories over the planners at the end of the 1960s – the overturn of proposals for comprehensive redevelopment of Covent Garden in London and the final defeat of plans to drive a by-pass road through Oxford's Christ Church Meadow – symbolised that a more conservation-minded era had begun. Combined with that other social movement of the 1960s and 70s, the development of tenants' associations and local action groups, the bland optimism of the earlier period now seemed distant.

By the 1980s, the wheel apparently had turned full circle. At least three different strands of criticism were levelled at the post-war architects and planners. First, they were blamed for having destroyed more than they had created; that in the redevelopment of the cities and towns they had actually failed to provide something better than that they had set out to remedy. Undoubtedly in places this was true; the worst of the new estates, tower blocks, and redeveloped city centres seemed to lack any of the sense of community which was associated with the original rundown areas and the unimproved town and city centres and, at their worst, provided an almost intolerable environment for their inhabitants. It was difficult, however, to disassociate some of the criticisms from social changes for which it was not always clear that architects and planners were to blame. Growing affluence, the motor car, the greater mobility of the young, the unwilling-ness of young couples to share housing with their parents, and the greater longevity of the elderly were social phenomena which contributed to the break-up of the traditional communities and brought problems of loneliness and isolation, vandalism, crime and insecurity. The economic problems which created unem-ployment and political decisions which affected local authority finances clearly lay outside the scope of architects to deal with; similarly the cost restraints on many of the developments made compromises inevitable, so that a major argument of architects was that their schemes were rarely provided with the resources which might have made for better results.[19] Elsewhere, however, it was difficult for architects to escape blame for some of the cruder attempts to warehouse whole populations in what were even to a casual observer soulless and ugly environments. Architects who wanted the new public housing 'to reflect the grittiness of working-class life' through bare concrete and rough, harsh surfaces, and who could pronounce that 'tough working-class lifestyle demanded a tough architectural response' required few condemnations from others.[20]

Indeed, where the middle-class revolt against redevelopment and grassroots objectors to the new housing developments stood on common ground was in their objections to schemes and plans which bore little relation to the wishes of those who would have to live in them. The spirit behind 'community architecture' lay in the demand by local people to be consulted and involved in the processes of redevelopment. In some cases, that was in effect a rejection of wholesale clearance and a desire to refurbish and improve existing dwellings, a trend which began to receive increased encouragement in successive housing Acts from the late 1960s. In others, as in the well received Byker Wall scheme in Newcastle, it involved going ahead with large-scale redevelopment, but with deliberate attempts to involve the people concerned at every stage of the process.[21] In effect it meant an end to the wholesale, 'top-down' redesign of communities by architects, planners and local authorities without the consent and participation of those involved. The charge of arrogance, of imposing an alien and unwelcome environment upon a silent and suffering majority in the name of progress, was one which was not easily evaded, there was too much evidence on every side that this was exactly what had been done.

But lurking behind the debate about the damage done by architects and planners was the aesthetic critique of 'Modernism'. Many of the failings were put down to the uncritical adoption of the modernist style, irrespective of the preferences and tastes of the population at large. The crisis of confidence in the rebuilding of Britain was as much aesthetic as anything else. Popularised in a series of speeches by Prince Charles, the revolt against Modernism had earlier roots.[22] The rise of conservation movements, which by the late 1980s had 300,000 members, with some 600,000 protected historic buildings and 5000 conservation areas, dated from the 1950s with the enthusiasm for Victorian and Edwardian architecture popularised by people such as Sir John Betjeman. Galvanised by the worst excesses of redevelopment in the 1960s, groups such as the Victorian and Thirties societies provided a springboard for those who rejected the whole of the Modern Movement in architecture. There was plenty of ammunition, not only in some of the disasters of the new estates and tower blocks, but in prestige commissions carried out by some of the country's leading architects. The 'New Brutalism' did much to discredit the whole architectural profession; by the 1980s the Modern Movement was in headlong retreat in the face of a neoclassical revival and the bitter divisions about what was, in fact, an appropriate architecture for the last years of the twentieth century.

V

The much publicised stylistic debates in the 1980s and the serious questioning of the whole post-war record of rehousing and planning obscured important points. The first was that whatever the criticisms, a great deal of the legacy of post-war planning was still in place and proved remarkably durable. The planning machinery became an intrinsic part of local government and was widely used as a defence against unregulated development. Indeed, it was the planning machinery which was used to such effect by those who sought to slow down and halt some of the controversial developments so that the public enquiry became the typical battleground between planners, developers, pressure groups and the public. The Green Belts were widely regarded as a success and as something to be defended, as were the National Parks established after 1945. Although limited in their scope, the New Towns were largely successful and in spite of the many examples of poor, substandard local authority estates, there were many others which came close to providing their inhabitants with something of the improved environment which had been on the agenda since the Great War.

But in many respects the whole structure of the debate had begun to change. Growth in owner-occupation, a trend which had been rising steadily of its own accord, was reinforced by Conservative 'right to buy' legislation of 1980, so that consequently the local authority sector had declining importance. The balance of house-building which had swung decisively towards the private sector in the 1970s became overwhelming in the 1980s. In the period 1980–5, only just over 250,000 local authority dwellings were built, as opposed to three times that number in the private sector. By 1988 there were less than 25,000 local authority houses built, a reduction from what had still been over 100,000 a year in the late 1970s. Increasingly the emphasis was on owner-occupation and half-way stages to house purchase, such as housing association tenancies. By the end of 1985, 631,000 public tenants in Great Britain had bought their 'council' houses and by 1987 Housing Associations owned another 500,000 dwellings. The number of local authority and New Town houses in 1988 was only 86 per cent of the figure in 1981. With these changes, the era of mass clearance was virtually at an end. Conservation and renovation were the watchwords, except where 'new slum' blocks were being demolished and those areas such as the London Docklands where a fresh start was possible on derelict sites. A series of urban renewal programmes concentrated upon refurbishing rundown inner city areas, converting disused offices and warehouses into flats and encouraging private investment in housing and other amenities. Glasgow's Eastern Area Renewal Project and the Merseyside Docklands scheme were amongst 191 initiatives which received over £480 million between 1982 and 1987.

In crude terms, the shortage of dwellings which had bedevilled virtually the whole of the post-war era ought to have been ended. There was, by 1987, with over 22 million dwellings a crude surplus of homes over the estimated number of households, yet the problem of homelessness remained as acute and prominent as ever. The number of families accepted by local authorities as homeless had doubled in ten years, from 76,000 in 1979 to 146,000 in 1988, and the numbers of those sleeping rough in major cities had visibly increased.[23] In spite of a paper adequacy of dwellings, it was evidently the case that sufficient homes in the right place at accessible prices were still not available. Housing provision still did not match need. Even with attempts to re-invigorate the rented sector, the country lacked the right types of housing to meet the requirement of housing all its people. Critically, the drying-up of local authority housing and cheaper rented accommodation deprived the housing market of the ability to meet the needs of sectors of the population which could not afford or fell out of owner-occupation or could not afford high private rents. Moreover, even after nearly half a century of house-building since the war, the rate of construction had not kept pace with the erosion of the quality of the existing housing stock. Various estimates were made in the 1980s, but one assessed the backlog of improvement costs at almost £4 billion. Nothing of that order looked likely to be available.

Rebuilding Britain had absorbed vast energies and huge sums

of money since 1945. One of the flagships of post-war reconstruction, it had remained a part of the consensus right up to the late 1960s. But the heady ideals of the post-war era had been tempered by increasingly bitter experience that what was being done was both unpopular and inadequate to meet its objectives of giving people a better life. The criticisms levelled against architects, planners and local authorities from the late 1960s undoubtedly stopped further progress down the route of wholesale clearance and 'quick fix' architectural solutions, more or less discrediting some of the most unpopular forms of rebuilding, but the housing question seemed never to go away, only to reappear in new forms. With an estimated 700,000 'homeless', people sleeping in the streets of the capital, and an ever growing backlog of repairs required to maintain the standards of existing stock, the 'new Jerusalem' seemed as far away as ever.

6. The Rise (and Fall?) of State-Owned Enterprise

TERRY GOURVISH

I

ONE of the main barometers of British industrial policy since 1945 has involved those enterprises taken into public ownership after the war. The nationalisation of inland transport (chiefly the railways), coal, gas, electricity, airways and steel was undertaken by the Labour governments of 1945–51 in a spirit of economic and political idealism about the advantages of industrial management by the state, although the precise aims of the new enterprises were left rather vague, and the legacy of government-industry relations during the inter-war years played an important part in the process, as will be argued below. There then followed a long debate about the organisation and performance of the public sector model in a mixed economy. Criticisms of the alleged inefficiency of the nationalised industries gained ground in the 1960s and reached a crescendo in the more difficult economic conditions of the 1970s. The post-1979 Thatcher administrations pursued a consistent and determined policy of 'rolling back the public sector', such that 'privatisation' became the watchword of the 1980s quite as much as 'nationalisation' was in the late 1940s. In this chapter the main features of these developments are sketched out, and an attempt is made to provide a long-term perspective on state-owned enterprise in Britain.

First of all, we must define our terms. By 'state-owned enterprise' we mean any public corporation whose assets are publicly-owned, whose board is appointed by a Minister of State, whose employees are not civil servants, and whose revenues are derived primarily from a direct trading relationship with customers. Such a definition obviously embraces only part of what may be termed the 'public sector'. It excludes decentralised public services such as health, education, and the social services, enterprises which were directly run by the government, such as the Post Office and the ordnance factories, limited companies in which the government has held a stake, such as British Petroleum and Rolls Royce, and a miscellany of quasi-public bodies.[1] Nevertheless, it matches the working definition adopted by the Treasury, embraces elements conventionally regarded as defining such enterprises internationally, and isolates those industries which came to be organised according to the 'public corporation' model advocated by Herbert Morrison in the 1930s.[2] On this basis, the State-Owned Enterprise was very much a creation of the period 1945–51. The Labour Party had been committed by its election manifesto of 1945 to 'public ownership of the fuel and power industries . . . inland transport . . . and iron and steel',[3] and a healthy overall majority in the Commons of nearly 150 made action on this plank of policy inevitable. In the first three parliamentary sessions legislation established the following corporations: the National Coal Board (1947); the British Transport Commission (1948), charged with the ambitious task of integrating most of inland transport, including the railways, a sizeable chunk of road transport (both passenger and freight), London Transport, and the railways' docks, inland waterways and hotels; the British Electricity Authority (later renamed Central Electricity Authority) of 1948, responsible for power stations and the National Grid, and 14 Area Boards, concerned with distribution and sales; and the Gas Council (1949), which presided over 12 more independent Area Gas Boards. The nationalisation of Britain's iron and steel industry, which was neither a utility nor a victim of post-war difficulties, was more fiercely debated. The Iron and Steel Corporation was provided for under an Act of 1949 but was not formally established until February 1951, after the 1950 election, when Labour was returned to power with a very small overall majority. The airways were also nationalised. Anticipated by a Conservative measure of 1939, which established the British Overseas Airways Corporation (BOAC), Labour created two additional bodies in 1946: British South American Airways Corporation (merged with BOAC in 1949), and British European Airways. The Bank of England was also formally nationalised in the same year, together with Cable & Wireless.[4]

Thus, by 1951 a considerable part of British industry had been taken into the public sector. As Table 6.1 shows, six state industries produced a combined turnover in 1951 of £2235

TABLE 6.1   State-owned enterprise in 1951

Industry	Turnover (£m)	Employment (000s)
Inland Transport	616.5	888.1
[Railways]	[384.9]	[599.9]
Coal	541.1	780.0
Iron & Steel	502.4	292.0
Electricity	269.4	181.9
Gas	261.0	148.0
Airways	44.4	24.9
TOTAL	2234.8	2314.9

SOURCE: Nationalised Industries' Reports and Accounts, 1951 and 1951–2.

NOTES
1. Transport: British Transport Commission; turnover excludes minor miscellaneous income; calendar year 1951.
2. Railways: Railway Executive including collection/delivery but excluding shipping, catering, hotels; calendar year 1951.
3. Coal: National Coal Board; calendar year 1951; employment estimate based on colliery workers (698,600), non-industrial staff (40,400), plus October 1953 figure for other industrial workers (41,600, from NCB, *Report & Accounts, 1953*, p. 139).
4. Iron & Steel: Iron & Steel Corporation; turnover estimate based on sales 15 February–30 September 1951 (£314.0m, excluding sales to companies within the group); employment estimated.
5. Electricity: British Electricity Authority, Area Boards, year to 31 March 1952; North of Scotland Hydro-Electric Board, calendar year 1951 (turnover includes £0.92m sales to British Elec.Authority).
6. Gas: Gas Council and Area Boards; year to 31 March 1952.
7. Airways: British Overseas Airways Corporation, British European Airways; year to 31 March 1952.

million – equivalent to 17 per cent of Gross Domestic Product – and employed 2.3 million persons, nearly 10 per cent of the total employed workforce.[5] More significantly, the new enterprises were giants in the economy, consuming a considerable proportion of the nation's scarce post-war investment resources. The sheer scale of the new corporations hardly needs emphasis. The two biggest, the British Transport Commission and the National Coal Board, dwarfed the largest manufacturing companies in the private sector, such as Imperial Tobacco, Imperial Chemical Industries (ICI), and Unilever. Even gas and electricity, which were much smaller in terms of turnover and employment, were comparable with companies such as ICI, which in 1951 had a turnover of £263 million and a labour force in the UK of 131,000.[6] With investment, which was subject to strict government control during the austerity period (*c.* 1945–53), priority was given to fuel and power and to iron and steel. Consequently, public corporations were responsible for 19 per cent of total gross domestic fixed capital formation in 1951.[7]

II

How and why had these activities come to be taken into the public sector? First, it must be admitted that the story of Labour's post-war nationalisation programme has been told many times, for example by Rogow and Shore, Eldon Barry, and not least by Sir Norman Chester in his monumental study published in 1975.[8] Conventionally, Labour's strategy is seen as primarily political, rather than economic, one of drawing into public ownership the essential infrastructure elements of the economy on the assumption that 'socialist' management would be fairer and more efficient than that of the private sector. The policy was of long vintage, but its chief political origins lay in Clause IV of Labour's 1918 Constitution, which identified coal, transport and electricity as prime candidates for nationalisation, and in the Party's programmes of the 1930s, for example in 1937. It may be regarded as part of an intention to direct the economy, but this aim was only tentatively pursued, and was inadequately linked with planning or the pursuit of industrial efficiency. The programme was one of the more radical gestures of a reformist, moderate government.[9] At the same time, many commentators have pointed out the relevance of government industrial policy in the inter-war years, which involved the Conservatives quite as much as Labour. Right-wing support for 'rationalisation' usually focused upon the reconstruction of manufacturing industry via defensive merger, but it could also embrace a limited amount of nationalisation, as was demonstrated by the creation of public corporations such as the Central Electricity Board and the British Broadcasting Corporation (both in 1926), the London Passenger Transport Board (1933) and BOAC (1939).[10] Finally, there is the significance of the immediate post-war condition of industries such as coal and transport. Both were heavily used during the war but undermaintained and starved of investment. The resulting deterioration of these assets is regarded as making their nationalisation 'inevitable'.[11]

Recently published monographs on electricity, coal and the

railways certainly emphasise the importance of the legacy of past operation in the private sector, and the significance of pre-1945 relations with government. The railways, for example, invited government intervention from their inception, as they did in other countries. In Britain statutory control was tentative and piecemeal at first, but by 1900 the state had powers to intervene in most areas of business management. During the inter-war years the regulatory environment was made even more restrictive, the most important measure being the compulsory amalgamation of the railway companies into four giant oligopolistic concerns. Thus, although private ownership remained intact until 1948, state control was far-reaching. Nationalisation was in fact first proposed in legislation as early as 1844 and the issue was seriously debated in parliament in 1918–21. The railways were considered to be a potential monopoly (notwithstanding the rise of road transport and the strong hold on bulk freight of coastal shipping), one which demanded control in the public interest. The experience of the inter-war years did little to dispel the notion that private sector operation under government control was unlikely to resolve fundamental problems of overcapacity and underinvestment. The establishment of the four giant companies did not eliminate inter-railway competition, as had been envisaged, and profitability came under pressure in the wake of the depression of 1929–33. All this was reinforced by the war and its aftermath. The assets deteriorated markedly while financial viability was threatened by a government freeze on fares and charges. The industry's net earnings fell from an estimated £63 million in 1945 to *minus* £16 million two years later. The legacy of state control, both in the long and short run, served to make nationalisation almost a formality. It could justifiably be argued that the railways were in effect a state-run enterprise long before the formal transfer of ownership.[12]

The experience of coal was not a dissimilar one. The state's *direct* interest in the industry, though of more recent origin than that in the railways, also intensified during the inter-war period, exacerbated by a declining market for the product and a spectacular deterioration in industrial relations (notably in 1921 and 1926). Like the railways, coal was a prime candidate for possible nationalisation in 1919, and state intervention grew steadily after that. The Coal Mines Act of 1930 encouraged an element of cartelisation and at the same time (and not without contradiction) created the Coal Mines Reorganisation Commission with

authority to encourage mergers and formulate schemes of compulsory amalgamation. The latter policy was not successful, but the
former was strengthened in 1934 and 1936 with the result that a
centralised marketing organisation was established. Furthermore,
in 1938 coal royalties, i.e. mineral rights, were nationalised with
effect from 1942.[13] During the war the government's anxiety about
production levels, wages and control was not unlike that directed
at transport in general and the railways in particular. However,
the main difference lay in the fact that although the government
had already intervened to rationalise the structure of the railway
industry, it had patently failed to deal with the fragmentation and
diversity of coal. Here there was a very real problem. The scope
for economies of scale was more limited, given that the mine was
the basic unit of production, and none of the large coal companies was keen to incur costs in taking over inefficient pits
merely to close them down. Some concentration had taken place:
by 1945 the fourteen largest enterprises employed just under 25
per cent of the colliery workforce. But most of the 800 or so
mining companies were small, and there were still about 1470
collieries on the eve of nationalisation.[14] On the government side,
cartelisation, which helped to maintain employment, was preferred to rationalisation, which did not. At the same time, sharp
criticisms of private sector performance and of structural shortcomings, enshrined in the influential Reid Committee's report of
1945, were widespread, and were certainly not confined to the
political left. Thus, a combination of managerial weakness, union
demands for public ownership, and the industry's rundown
condition after the war proved to be a potent cocktail. As with
the railways, although with more justification, the private sector
was held to be incapable of making the necessary adjustments to
new market conditions without producing an upheaval which
would have been socially and politically unacceptable. Wartime
production crises only served to strengthen this view. The
nationalisation both of the railways and of coal may have been
part of an ideological stance, but it was also a logical reaction to
the difficulties experienced by these industries since 1914.[15]

The experience of electricity was different. Here the state's
concern was with a successful and potentially monopolistic
supplier of energy, an industry whose growth and profitability
had been considerable since 1900. It was an industry of the
Second, rather than the First, Industrial Revolution, one of the
'commanding heights' of the economy which the Labour Party

asserted should be harnessed to socialist principles of equity and public service. However, once again 'legacy' factors played their part in the nationalisation process. First of all, state involvement can be found at the birth of electricity in the 1880s, when Acts of 1882 and 1888 granted first 21-year, then 42-year franchises to private companies with the option on expiry of purchase by local authorities. Indeed, the latter were actively encouraged to participate in electricity supply, such that by 1910 they were responsible for about two-thirds of total sales.[16] The private sector remained more important in generation and bulk supply; indeed, as late as 1935 half of the electricity used in industry was privately generated. But here also the presence of the State was evident. In 1919 Electricity Commissioners were established to preside over the development of electricity, and in 1927 a Central Electricity Board was created to take over responsibility for the planning and construction of the major transmission network (and from 1933 the National Grid). The success of this 'business-led' public corporation served to demonstrate the advantages of larger administrative units and to indicate that there were economic arguments for public control, if not public ownership. The need for more concentration in electricity – there were still over 600 separate supply undertakings in the 1930s – was advocated by the Snell and McGowan Reports of 1931 and 1936, and accepted by both Conservative and Labour politicians and by engineers and other specialists inside and outside the industry. Their anxiety was heightened by the imminent expiry, in the late 1930s and early 1940s, of many of the 42-year franchises, where local authority purchase threatened to *reduce*, rather than increase, the level of concentration. The coming of war placed a moratorium on local authority acquisitions, but it also caused an investment backlog, inviting a more directed response in the future. In any case, by this time about two-thirds of electricity's capital investment was under public control. The war also saw a further move towards state ownership when a publicly-owned Board was set up in 1943 to supply hydro-electric power to the north of Scotland.[17] Public ownership therefore dominated electricity before the formal act of nationalisation, and the process was encouraged by the support of several senior managers, who shared a 'public service' culture reminiscent of that to be found in the railway industry.[18]

Thus, our case-studies underline the importance of the industrial inheritance of the inter-war years and the long-term relationship between government and the industries concerned in inviting a public sector solution to their post-war difficulties. The same could be said of gas, where about a third of the industry was owned by local authorities, where wide-ranging controls existed in the inter-war years, and the Heyworth Committee Report of 1945 was quite as influential as the Reid Committee Report for coal, in emphasising the value of centralised control and larger scale operating units.[19] Labour's programme, though pursued against a backcloth of post-war planning zeal and reconstruction aspirations for a rundown economy, focused upon industries which had been steadily moving towards state control and which had historically attracted arguments justifying nationalisation, including technological efficiency, the avoidance of wasteful competition, targeted capital investment, and the need to improve industrial relations.[20]

Iron and steel was a very different proposition, however. The industry had not been mentioned in Labour's 1935 election manifesto, and was a late inclusion in that of 1945. Here there was no legacy from the past and the decision, prompted by recognition of steel's strategic importance in manufacturing, provoked the most bitter political battles. Here, too, Labour moved more cautiously, and the establishment of the Iron and Steel Corporation in 1951 did not involve a loss of identity for the existing private companies. It was therefore no surprise when the Conservatives swiftly returned the industry to private hands in 1953, together with the long-distance road haulage interests of the British Transport Commission. Subsequently, steel became a political football, renationalised by Labour in 1967 and denationalised again in 1988.[21]

III

The way in which the industries were taken into the public sector, or more precisely, the type of organisation adopted, also deserves attention, particularly since many commentators have been influenced by Emanuel Shinwell's remark that on taking up his post as Minister of Fuel and Power in 1945 with the task of preparing legislation to nationalise coal, he found Whitehall's cupboards bare of blueprints: 'Nothing practical and tangible existed ... I had to start on a clear desk'.[22] In fact, this was something of an exaggeration, belittling the extent of pre-1945 discussion within Labour circles, for example by Hugh Dalton, Herbert Morrison and Evan Durbin,[23] broader discussions on reconstruction, including J. R. Bellaby's influential book,[24] and wider debate about how to tackle in operational terms those industries ripe for public intervention such as coal and the railways.[25] On the other hand, an examination of the public records indicates that *detailed* plans were rather scarce in 1945, but more importantly reveals that business advisers and leading civil servants played a decisive role in shaping the initial organisations of the nationalised industries. What Barry Supple has called 'the more covert but in the end more influential discussions among civil servants and technocrats' can be found, for example, in the work of Sir Ernest Gowers, Chairman of the Coal Commission, 1938–46, and Lord Hyndley, Controller-General in the newly-created Ministry of Fuel and Power, 1942–3, in the war-time deliberations on coal. Together with temporary civil servants such as Harold Wilson they formed a secret committee in 1942 which gave considerable impetus to the idea of a public corporation solution to the industry's problems.[26] At the same time Sir Cyril Hurcomb exerted considerable influence on both transport and electricity. As Director-General of the Ministry of War Transport from 1941 he did much to restrain the enthusiasm for a radical post-war solution for inland transport, as displayed by Sir Alfred Robinson, a Deputy-Secretary in the Ministry, and Dr W. H. Coates, seconded from Imperial Chemical Industries. Hurcomb also acted as Chairman of the Electricity Commissioners, 1938–47, taking part in the work of a special subcommittee set up in 1942 to examine the future organisation of electricity. Both Hyndley and Hurcomb, moreover, went on to chair two of the bodies which eventually materialised, respectively the National Coal Board and the British Transport Commission.[27]

Organisational planning by a few 'experts' and key civil servants had several weaknesses, however. There was little or no attempt to involve senior managers from the industries affected, and much of that planning was rather vague. This and the consequent haste with which legislation was subsequently drawn up in 1945–7 had a considerable impact on the way in which industries such as coal and inland transport were to function organisationally in the 1950s and beyond. With coal, the main challenge was to control a heterogeneous collection of businesses, but wartime discussions did not really address this problem, and the National Coal Board began in an overcentralised form. The lack of experience of the initial Board members, together with the unwillingness of several managing directors of the larger coal companies to join the nationalised industry, compounded this error, discouraging a thorough examination of organisational policy. Sir Charles Reid, former chairman of the committee of 1945, resigned from the Board in frustration in 1948, with the parting shot that 'most of those appointed had little or no experience of running any business at all, not to speak of a really large-scale enterprise'.[28] Defects were readily apparent in a management hierarchy headed by functionally responsible board members, but with a long and imprecise span of command embracing five or six tiers; a failure to improve either the quality of managerial staff or management techniques; and an inability to control senior managers at Area level, who were frustrated by their limited authority.[29] A similar tale could be told about inland transport, where not only the organisation but the strategy set by government was flawed. Wartime planning had rejected the idea of nationalising inland transport as a whole, and after 1947 a fair amount of road transport was left in the private sector to compete with the British Transport Commission. Yet the Commission was given a statutory duty to provide an 'efficient, adequate, economic and properly integrated system of public transport'. This would have been a tough assignment with a suitable organisation. However, with the structure established by the Transport Act of 1947 it resembled the Holy Grail. The Commission was intended to fulfil a planning and policy role, and below it five functional Executives were created, for Railways, Road Transport (from 1949 subdivided into Road Haulage and Road Passenger), London Transport, Docks and Inland Waterways, and Hotels. Contrary to Labour expectations, the Executives tended to act independently, and the Commission was too small to impose its authority upon them at a detailed level. The clash between the Commission and its Railway Executive, and between the Railway Executive and its regional managers, created all manner of problems before the Executives were wound up in 1953.[30]

IV

The first long period of Conservative government (1951–64) was characterised by the identification of organisational defects as the source of the nationalised industries' difficulties, thereby tending to mask more deep-seated problems, as for example, with coal and the railways, which were suffering from falling demand, underinvestment, and inadequate managerial attention to pricing and cost-control.[31] Decentralisation was the watchword, supported by contemporary critiques, such as the Acton Society Trust's reports of 1951 and Clegg and Chester's *The Future of Nationalisation* of 1953.[32] An impetus was given to railway decentralisation with the new (if unwieldy) organisation of the British Transport Commission of 1955. This attempted to fill the void left by the abolition of the Railway Executive by strengthening executive management at regional level and establishing an Area Board for each of the railway regions.[33] In the electricity industry responsibility for Scottish electricity was placed entirely in the hands of local bodies with the creation of the South of Scotland Electricity Board in 1955, and after the Report of the Herbert Committee in 1956 generation and transmission functions in England and Wales were separated, the Central Electricity Authority being replaced in 1958 by the Electricity Council (contrary to the Herbert Committee recommendations modelled on the Gas Council) and the Central Electricity Generating Board.[34] With coal the problem was rather different. Another committee of enquiry, the Fleck Committee of 1955, found that there had been unintentional decentralisation, encouraged by a weak Board at the top. The suggested solution was to reform the National Coal Board, strengthening its central authority by emphasising functional roles for its members, and to stimulate an improvement in the quality of middle management.[35]

These changes did help to improve the operations of the enterprises concerned, but the main thing to stress is how little was done by the Conservatives either to change existing structures or to clarify the relationship between the government and the state-owned corporations. What is striking is the absence of a clear remit from government for its nationalised industry managers, or, as in the case of inland transport, the existence of conflicting expectations, the Transport Act of 1947 requiring the British Transport Commission to 'provide ... an efficient, adequate, economical and properly integrated system' and at the same time to break even financially, 'taking one year with another'.[36] There is no doubt at all that a confusion of roles, and the acceptance by nationalised industry managers of a public service duty with only a vague idea of how that translated into economic performance as conventional businesses in the private sector would have understood it, was a marked feature of public sector weakness throughout the 1950s and, indeed, in the following two decades. Whenever serious problems surfaced, as for example, the mounting losses made by the railways, which persisted in spite of a major investment programme sanctioned in 1955 (the 'Modernisation Plan'), the government's response was primarily organisational. Thus, following the investigations of the Stedeford Advisory Group in 1960, the British Transport Commission was wound up by the Transport Act of 1962. London Transport, the docks and inland waterways, and the Commission's road haulage and bus interests were transferred to separate boards, and the British Railways Board was established with a prime duty to run the railways. It is true that with the appointment as British Rail chairman of Dr Richard Beeching from ICI, who had been a member of the Stedeford Group, business as well as organisational changes were anticipated. But all too often the government's response was to intervene without encouraging anyone, whether ministers, civil servants, or public sector managers, to get to grips with the more fundamental facts of business life, and, in particular, the profit and loss account.[37]

This situation did not persist, of course. The Select Committee on the Nationalised Industries, established in 1957, intensified its work in the 1960s, subjecting every activity to the closer scrutiny of parliament. Furthermore, new blood and new thinking in the Treasury after 1958 produced a growing emphasis on the need for state-owned enterprises to behave more commercially. Here, a government White Paper on *The Financial and Economic Obligations of the Nationalised Industries* of April 1961 was a notable landmark in beginning the search for more precise guidelines; it was followed in November 1967 by another White Paper, *A Review of Economic and Financial Obligations*. These encouraged nationalised industries to satisfy specific profit targets over a five-year period, to work to minimum rates of return on investment (8 per cent was recommended initially), and include discounted cash flow (dcf) techniques in their project appraisals. All this reflected the greater influence of economic as opposed to administrative prescriptions for the public sector in policy-making circles.[38] Under both the Labour governments of 1964–70 and 1974–9 and Edward Heath's Conservative administration of 1970–4, the emphasis on commercial performance was maintained. However, there was a distinct shift to interventionist solutions, including government subsidy, in industrial policy, and in some cases a preference for a more centralised organisation was expressed. Thus, steel was renationalised with the creation of the British Steel Corporation in 1967, and new bodies were created, notably the British Airports Authority (1966), British Airways (a merger of BEA and BOAC in 1972), and British Shipbuilders (1977). Businesses which had been directly run as government departments, such as the Post Office and the Royal Ordnance Factories, were converted into public corporations (in 1969 and 1974 respectively). The gas industry was encouraged to function in a more centralised manner after the Gas Act of 1965, in response to the discovery of natural supplies in the North Sea, and its Area Boards were abolished in 1972.[39] The recourse to state intervention was reinforced by the willingness of successive governments to provide financial support to private sector enterprises in difficulty (later dubbed 'lame ducks'). Casualties of British manufacturing's competitive weakness were sustained first by the Industrial Reorganisation Corporation of 1966–71, then by Heath's Industry Act of 1972, and finally, by the National Enterprise Board from 1976. Cash subsidies and other forms of financial support, usually accompanied by a measure of government control, were provided to bail out companies such as British Leyland (1975, 1977), Chrysler UK (1975), and Rolls Royce (1971, 1978). Poorly performing nationalised industries also received considerable assistance, with capital reconstructions being introduced to rescue coal (1965, 1973), the railways (1962, 1968, 1974), and steel (1969, 1972).[40]

At the same time, the performance of the nationalised industries was subjected to intensified government scrutiny. The investigations of the Select Committee on the Nationalised Industries were supplemented by the work of new institutions, notably the Prices and Incomes Board of 1965–71, and there were numerous *ad hoc* inquiries, particularly where enterprises were making losses. The railways, for example, continued to suffer serious financial deficits, despite the attentions of Beeching and his successors, and a special Joint Steering Group (British Railways Board/Ministry of Transport) was established in 1966. Its inquiries led to the Transport Act of 1968, which was welcomed in that it made the innovative distinction between 'commercial' and 'social' (i.e. subsidised) elements of the railway system. However, the way in which the subsidised part was identified, by fixing specific grants for each of a discrete number of passenger services, increased the involvement of Whitehall officials at a detailed management level.[41] When one realises that there were two other inquiries examining the railways in detail, one by the Prices and Incomes Board (1967–8), the other a pay/productivity exercise sponsored by the Minister of Labour, and that several consultants, including Cooper Brothers, Price Waterhouse, and McKinsey, had been appointed to probe into dark corners, it is no surprise to find a later British Rail chairman, Sir Peter Parker, declaring that his business was in a state of 'perpetual audit'.[42]

But for all this activity, it is by no means clear that the governments of 1964–79 fared much better than their predecessors in imposing an 'efficiency audit' on the state-owned enterprises. Some progress was undoubtedly made, since a closer monitoring was an inevitable consequence of the increase in nationalised industry borrowing, and the importance of that borrowing in the overall Public Sector Borrowing Requirement. Those industries which were expanding, such as electricity, gas and the airlines, were given specific profit targets over a five-year period (first to c. 1967/8, then to c. 1973/4), following the guidelines established by the 1961 and 1967 White Papers; their performance turned out to be fairly close to expectations. On the other hand, encouragement of both marginal cost pricing and the balancing of costs and revenues represented a clash between economic and financial criteria, while the vaguer instructions to the declining sectors – coal, steel and the railways – to 'break even' or 'reduce the deficit' were unsuccessful.[43] In large measure the government was its own worst enemy, since it reserved the right to interfere in ways which often challenged a commercial objective. Interventions in the pricing, wage-setting, strikes and major investment programmes of nationalised industries were all too frequent, coinciding as they did with times of economic crisis, such as 1967, and the early 1970s. Here, the public corporations were the victims of 'stop-go' expedients, used as instruments of macroeconomic management to serve the 'national interest'. Pricing controls, which as in 1972–4 were applied more rigorously in the public sector, could thus be said to be subsidising private sector customers. In such circumstances, it was difficult for nationalised industry managers to feel they could, or should, operate according to profit-maximising principles.[44]

V

How well, then, did the state-owned enterprises perform in the 30 or so years after their establishment in the late 1940s? To what extent were their managers responsible for their financial results? Was their performance inferior to that of the private sector? These key questions are not easy to answer, and we must tread a careful path through what is undoubtedly a quagmire of criticism, much of it affected by political intent. There is also a great deal of dubiety in interpretation, particularly on the part of less polemical critics, who recognise that the conditions under which state-owned enterprises recruited senior managers, raised money, invested, priced their products, and settled pay demands were very different from those which obtained in the private sector, and that competitive conditions were often very different.[45] The writings of the economist Richard Pryke are a good example of the way in which assessments of performance have fluctuated. In his seminal investigation of nationalised industry operations to 1968, published in 1971, he concluded that the enterprises concerned had performed creditably, particularly in the period 1958–68, in comparison with both British manufacturing generally and comparable enterprises in other countries. However, in 1981, when he came to assess the period 1968–78, he came to a quite different conclusion, and later on was even more trenchant in his criticisms. He has argued that the private sector was more efficient and profitable than the public in airlines, ferries, and gas appliances, and has condemned the National Coal Board for its cross-subsidisation policies, noting that the investment strategies of both coal and electricity had been 'marred by a series of major errors'.[46] To some extent such shifts in the verdict on nationalised industries are either a reflection of the performance indicators selected (productivity and profit measures often yield quite different results) or else a reflection of the economic climate generally (British industry *as a whole* found the 1970s a tougher proposition than the 1960s, for example).[47] On the other hand, while there have been some defenders of the public sector in the 1980s, such as Robert Millward, the majority of analysts now tend to regard state enterprise as comparatively inefficient, with its capacity for entrepreneurial response apparently fettered by government.[48]

Numerous calculations have been made of the weak financial performance of public corporations in the aggregate. In Table 6.2

TABLE 6.2 The financial performance of public corporations, 1961–81 (unweighted averages)

Period	Revenue net of estimated capital consumption minus labour costs and interest (£m)	Financial deficits plus subsidies/contribution to GDP (%)	Financial deficits/GDP (%)	Profit Public (%)	Profit Private (%)
1961–5	−202	–	2.2^a	–	–
1966–9	−264	–	2.3	–	–
1970–3	−900	23.0	2.1	5.0	17.7
1974–7	−2410	29.0	3.0	3.8	16.3
1978–81	–	17.2	1.8	3.9	16.9

SOURCES: Col. 1: W. Eltis, *Lloyds Bank Review* (Jan. 1979), cit. in Peter Curwen, *Public Enterprise. A Modern Approach* (Brighton, 1986), p. 73; col. 2: John Vickers and George Yarrow, *Privatization. An Economic Analysis* (Cambridge, Mass., 1988), p. 144; col. 3: I. C. R. Byatt, 'The Framework of Control', in John Grieve Smith (ed.), *Strategic Planning in Nationalised Industries* (1984), p. 75 (receipts of government transfers are excluded); cols 4 and 5: Vickers and Yarrow, *Privatization*, p. 143 (profit here defined as gross trading profit expressed as a percentage of net capital stock at replacement cost).

NOTE
^{a} 1962–5

a few of these have been combined to offer a rudimentary insight into the position in the 1960s and 1970s. The figures produced by Eltis, for example, show how the failure of the corporations' revenue to cover labour costs and interest was a persistent element in the 1960s and intensified thereafter (even allowing for inflation). It can also be seen that in relation to GDP the Corporations' deficits were a serious drain on resources in the 1970s, before the government imposed a tighter financial regime. With profits it is difficult to compare like with like, but even if we concede that considerable margins of error may exist, the contrast between private and public returns revealed by Vickers and Yarrow is still very striking (Table 6.2). On the other hand, estimates of labour productivity growth often provide more comfort for state-owned enterprises, particularly when they appear in disaggregated form (as in Table 6.3). The performance of coal and steel may have been disappointing, but electricity, gas and the airlines did rather well on this basis, and even British Rail achieved good results by cutting its labour force.[49] Even allowing for the fact that the public sector has been criticised for making low returns from its capital investment – the estimates of Total Factor Productivity growth in 1968–78 shown in Table 6.3 certainly suggest that this was the case – it would be more difficult to argue that overall productivity growth in the public sector since the war has been markedly inferior to that in British manufacturing as a whole.[50]

If the overall performance of the state-owned enterprises often appears to have been disappointing – important for a sector which consumed 19 per cent of fixed capital investment and employed 8 per cent of the labour force in the mid-1970s – then why has this been so? As we have emphasised, simple prescriptions must be treated with caution. Some commentators have clearly been tempted to explain poor financial performance as the product of poor management, but there is more to the argument than that. It is quite true that the quality and morale of senior managers were affected by the low ceilings placed on public corporation salaries from the late 1940s, and by the frustrations caused by an inability to respond quickly and decisively to market opportunities in 'politically sensitive' areas, such as the pricing of rail travel and the closure of loss-making coal mines and steel plants. Executives who joined the public sector from private industry frequently expressed surprise (and dismay) at the extent to which their freedom of action was

TABLE 6.3 Productivity measures for state-owned enterprises, 1948–78, with turnover and employment in 1979

Enterprise	Labour productivity growth (average per annum)				Total factor productivity growth (average per annum)	1979 or 1978/9:	
	1948–58 (%)	1958–68 (%)	1960–75[a] (%)	1968–78 (%)	1968–78 (%)	Turnover	Employment
Railways	0.3	4.3	5.8	0.8	n.a.	£2,295.6m	244,080
Coal	0.9	4.7	1.7	−0.7	−1.4	£2,989.4m	294,900
Steel	–	–	−1.4	−0.2	−2.5	£3,288.0m	186,000
Electricity	4.6	8.0	6.3	5.3	0.7	£6,081.2m	177,620
Gas	1.6	5.5	8.9	8.5	n.a.	£2,971.8m	102,870
Airways	14.0	8.9	7.1	6.4	5.5	£1,640.3m	57,740
UK manufacturing	1.9	3.7	3.4	2.7	1.7	–	–

SOURCES: cols 1 and 2: output per man-hour (railways per man-year), from Richard Pryke, *Public Enterprise in Practice* (1971), p. 20; col. 3: NEDO, *Study of the UK Nationalised Industries* (1976), cit. in Richard Molyneux and David Thompson, 'Nationalised Industry Performance: still third-rate?', *Fiscal Studies*, VIII No. 1 (1987), 57 (output per head); cols 4 and 5: Pryke, *Nationalised Industries* (1981), cit. in Molyneux and Thompson, 'Nationalised Industry Performance', 58 (output per head, TFP); cols 6 and 7: nationalised industry reports and accounts.

NOTE
[a] Dates vary. Railways: 1963–75; steel 1968–75; airways 1960–74.

constrained. The application of price and investment controls was a common complaint, particularly in the 1970s. Such interventions by government must be accepted as a major element in the performance of industries such as coal and steel, but they affected all activities. For example, the failure of British Transport Hotels, a subsidiary of the British Railways Board, to develop its considerable hotels estate in the 1960s and 1970s may have been a product of complacent management, but the managers themselves complained bitterly that they had been accorded a low internal priority by a Board which was suffering from tight investment allocations.[51] In other ways, too, condemnations of public sector managers may be challenged. Nationalised enterprises such as the railways proved to be just as responsive to developments in British corporate practices, including corporate planning and the application of more sophisticated investment appraisal techniques, as their private sector counterparts.[52]

At the same time, it must be recognised that for managers in the public sector the complex relationship with government could be a prop as well as a source of vexation. Managers could create delay, and obstruct or confuse the government when it suited them. There is also some truth in the suggestion that they were able to fall back on the government if serious mistakes were made, secure in the knowledge that 'bottom-line' responsibility was shared. The existence, whether notional or not, of a government 'lifeboat' served to support a less than dynamic approach to business problems. On the railways, for example, government support for the 'social' elements of the system became, under the 1974 Railways Act, a blanket annual subsidy to the whole of the passenger business. This payment, known as the PSO or Public Service Obligation, began in 1975. It may have been a step in the right direction in management accounting terms; it was certainly an improvement on the arrangements under the 1968 Act (see above). But for the rest of the decade it encouraged managers to regard the PSO not only as a legitimate payment for services provided but also as a sum which was largely irreducible – a situation which scarcely encouraged an aggressive attack by British Rail managers on their operating costs. The possibilities were later demonstrated when in October 1983 the government asked for a cut of 25 per cent in the real level of the PSO. This target was comfortably achieved by the Board in the stipulated three-year period.[53] Wherever the balance between the government and internal managers lies in responsibility for the running

of state-owned enterprises, it is generally agreed that the relationship between the two required clarification in the late
1970s. A confusion about goals and the absence of precise
objectives – a situation highlighted by the NEDO study of
nationalised industries in 1976 – combined with excessive
ministerial intervention at an operating level, the latter often at
odds with the limited targets which had been set. This can only
have produced suboptimal responses in management.

VI

As is of course well known, a new climate for Britain's public
sector was established by the Conservative administrations led
by Margaret Thatcher from 1979 to 1990. A prime objective was
the reduction of the PSBR or Public Sector Borrowing Requirement, which had increased by 130 per cent from 1977 to 1979;
there was also a determination to reduce the burden upon it of
the public corporations, whose share had risen from 24 per cent
in 1975 to 28 per cent in 1979.[54] Other considerations also
influenced the policy of 'rolling back the public sector': the wish
to remove the government from the pay bargaining process;
enthusiasm for wider share ownership and employee share
ownership; and a belief that private sector status was synonymous with efficiency and successful entrepreneurship. To some
extent, the change of attitude pre-dated the Thatcher years. For
example, an emphasis on financial targets as the main control
mechanism can be traced to 1976, when external financing limits
were introduced. Two years later, a White Paper on *The Nationalised Industries* brought more sophistication to the setting of target
rates of return, and required each nationalised industry to produce performance indicators, while the extension in 1980 of the
powers of the Monopolies and Mergers Commission to include
efficiency audits of public sector enterprises was the culmination
of much earlier policies.[55] But the Conservatives pushed much
harder, sustained by their deep-rooted conviction that nationalised industries were a drain on market enterprise, and that
ownership of the assets held the key to bottom-line responsibility.
Tougher, subsidy-reducing regimes were introduced, with the
prime aim of eventual disposal of the assets, or 'privatisation'.
Entrenched attitudes in the public sector were to be transformed.
As Sir Geoffrey Howe, the new Chancellor of the Exchequer, put

it in June 1979: 'Finance must determine expenditure, not expenditure finance'. Managers were to respond to the finance that was available, rather than working from existing levels of service and then looking for the necessary finance to support them. This was a fundamental change of emphasis.[56]

Privatisation proceeded fairly cautiously at first, with the main emphasis on enterprises which were trading in competitive markets. For some activities, a partnership with private sector capital was encouraged at first, although after 1981 'escape from the public sector' was interpreted to mean outright sale. And after the 1983 election the pace quickened, as the Conservatives turned their attention to the larger corporations which had a monopolistic or quasi-monopolistic status, such as British Telecom (the communications part of the old Post Office) British Gas, and British Steel. Sales of these three enterprises in 1984–8, together with subsequent stock transactions, raised over £13,500 million net for the government (Table 6.4). Altogether, the government raised £25,250 million over the nine years 1979/80–1988/9, the vast bulk – 90 per cent – being realised after 1983/4.[57]

TABLE 6.4   Major privatisations, 1982–8

Corporation	Date(s) of asset disposal	Proceeds (gross) (£m)	Under-valuation (£m)	Proceeds (net) (£m)
British Petroleum	1979/83/87	855[a]	11[a]	6090[b]
British Aerospace	1981/85	699	87	390
Cable & Wireless	1981/83/85	1101	40	1021
Britoil	1982/85	998	5	1053
British Telecom	1984	3916	1295	4701
British Gas	1986	5603	519	6533[b]
British Airways	1987	900	315	854
Rolls Royce	1987	1360	496	1031
British Airports	1987	919	174	1223
British Steel	1988	–	–	2418[b]

SOURCES: cols 2 and 3: Vickers and Yarrow, *Privatization*, p. 174; col. 4: Treasury, *Government Expenditure Plans 1990–91 to 1992–93*, 1990, Cm.1021, Table 21.5.13.

NOTES
[a] Excludes £7.2bn offer in October 1987.
[b] Includes estimated return for year 1989–90: BP £1370m; Gas £400m; Steel £1280m.

Cols 2 and 3 relate to the gross proceeds of the original offer or tender, under-valuation being the difference between the offer price and the price on the first day of trading. Col. 4 gives the net proceeds to government, but includes subsequent transactions.

The outcome was a fundamental assault on the PSBR, which became negative in 1987 and 1988, and on the element represented by the public corporations, which also became negative, in 1981 and 1985–8.[58]

It would be premature to try and offer a considered judgement on the experience of state-owned enterprise in the 1980s, or an assessment of the broader economic implications of privatisation policies. However, one or two observations may be made. The first concerns the price at which assets were sold. As Table 6.4 indicates, the major privatisations were carried out in a way which produced a substantial discount on the market price. The 'undervaluation' column in the table is based on the difference between the government's offer price and the price which obtained on the first day of Stock Exchange trading. The figures for the nine enterprises quoted add up to a substantial £2900 million, representing a discount to purchasers of 18 per cent on the gross proceeds. The sale of shares in British Telecom was particularly noteworthy in this regard. Here the government 'lost' the opportunity to secure an additional £1295 million, or 33 per cent of the gross proceeds. There is another side to this, of course. It must be admitted that the fixing of an offer price for 'unique' assets such as British Telecom was extremely difficult. Furthermore, the Stock Exchange 'crash' of October 1987, which wrecked the government's £7200 million sale of its remaining (32 per cent) stake in British Petroleum, had the effect of passing back some of the earlier 'losses' made on privatisation to the financial sector. Nevertheless, one is left with the distinct impression that considerable private profits have been made out of the process of asset disposal.[59]

On a more positive note there is the claim that the privatisation climate has freed managers from their public sector shackles and raised the performance of *all* state-owned enterprises, whether privatised or not. The data on productivity for 1978–85 certainly support this interpretation, since they provide growth rates which are higher than in 1968–78 for many of the major nationalised, or previously nationalised, businesses.[60] The balance sheets also contain evidence of substantial improvement, even in the formerly ailing businesses of steel, coal and the railways.[61] It would be wise to retain some scepticism about the situation, however. Undoubtedly, some of the improvement has resulted from the strong economic upturn which followed the recession of 1979–82. It is also a matter for argument whether similar results might not have been achieved by changes in the regulatory environment together with firmer financial targets, without a change in ownership.

Finally, we are left with the question whether state-owned enterprise, having risen in the late 1940s, has now experienced a fall. While privatisation has produced a substantial contraction in the public sector (a contraction which with the imminent privatisation of electricity is still proceeding), two of the giants of the late 1940s, railways and coal, remain in public hands. The latest listing of the top companies in the UK revealed British Coal as the 24th largest company on a turnover basis, and the British Railways Board, although shorn of its non-rail subsidiaries (hotels, shipping, engineering, property, etc.), was the 49th.[62] In addition the government has retained substantial holdings in some of the new companies, notably a 50 per cent stake in British Telecom, and has retained a 'Golden Share' in several companies, in order to ensure that takeovers and asset sales are subject to its approval.[63] Ownership may have been transferred in large measure, but the government retains a close, regulatory involvement in many industries. There still is a public sector, and a substantial degree of government control. How the new, efficiency-conscious managements will fare over the next decade or so is, however, a matter for forecasters and not for a historian.

7. The Defence of the Realm: Britain in the Nuclear Age

MICHAEL DOCKRILL

BEFORE the Second World War the tasks of the British armed services could be defined relatively easily – the British army was largely engaged overseas as an imperial police force, the Royal Navy was concerned with the protection of Britain's seaborne trade and the defence of British interests in the Mediterranean and the Far East while the Royal Air Force was intended as a deterrent against a German aerial assault on the homeland. Not until 1939 did the government accept unreservedly that in the event of a continental war a British Expeditionary Force should be sent to France.[1]

After 1945 this pre-war pattern was to a very large extent re-established. The army was spread across the globe, having recovered the territories lost to Japan in the Far East – Malaya, Burma and Hong Kong. The Royal Navy was still regarded as essential for the defence of Britain's commerce and overseas possessions while the Royal Air Force, confident that its bombing campaign against Germany had made a decisive contribution towards victory in Europe, saw a new role for itself as the main counter to any future Soviet aggression. Inevitably Britain's acute financial and economic difficulties, the result of its wartime sacrifices, demanded the rapid demobolisation of its swollen armed forces, but the government was not able to achieve the substantial savings it had hoped for as a result of this process. One reason for this was the very extent of the overseas territories for whose defence and internal policing Britain was now responsible. Indeed these were more extensive than before the war, since in addition to the British Empire, it now had to maintain occupation forces in zones in Germany and Austria, and in liberated Trieste and Libya.[2]

The granting of independence to India in 1947 did not lead to any substantial reduction of Britain's burdens. Indeed before independence Britain had been able to rely on the Indian army as an imperial reserve for use in operations in the Middle East, Burma and Malaya. However, India refused to cooperate militarily with Britain after 1947. As an alternative, the Labour government (elected in July 1945) sought a British sphere of influence in the Middle East by encouraging the Arab rulers to enter into defence pacts with Britain in return for British financial and military assistance. In August 1949 the Foreign Secretary, Ernest Bevin, informed the Cabinet that:

> in peace and war, the Middle East is an area of cardinal importance to the United Kingdom, second only to the United Kingdom itself. Strategically the Middle East is a focal point of communications, a source of oil, a shield to Africa and the Indian Ocean, and an irreplaceable defensive base.[3]

Thus British military, air and naval power would continue to defend the area from Britain's huge Suez Canal base. Eventually Britain was unable to sustain the ambitious role it had set itself – lacking the means to do much to assist the Arab countries economically while Egyptian nationalists called for the evacuation of the Suez garrison – and guerrilla attacks on Suez after 1948 rendered it untenable as a base.[4]

In April 1947 a severe financial crisis forced Britain to abandon Palestine, where its troops were tied down in a futile effort to prevent civil war breaking out between Jews and Arabs, and to hand over the financial responsibility for the Greek government's long post-1944 struggle against a communist insurgency to the United States. However Britain was, in the following year, faced with a Communist uprising which broke out in Malaya. Malaya was the chief supplier of Britain's rubber and other raw materials and its crucial importance to the British economy led to the commitment of 35,000 troops to an arduous campaign which did not come to an end until 1957.

The heavy demands which Britain's overseas commitments imposed on the British army compelled the Labour government to reintroduce conscription in 1946 (it had been abolished at the end of the war).[5] The government was determined that Britain should continue a global role, the basis of its claim to be a great power. It had emerged from the war as one of the three victorious powers and the economic difficulties which the costs of the war had imposed on the country would, the government believed, eventually be overcome. In March 1945 a Foreign Office paper concluded that:

> There are several reasons for hoping that financial difficulties will be a temporary phenomenon, for this country possesses all the skill and resources required to recover a dominating place in the economic world.[6]

With the rapid demobilisation of the American army after the defeat of Japan the British army was now the largest military force in the West, and Britain spent more of its Gross Domestic Product (GDP) on defence than any other country outside the Soviet Union: 6.6 per cent of GNP in 1950 whereas the United States devoted 5.1 per cent of its GDP to defence in the same year. France, the third largest western spender, allocated 5.5 per cent of its GDP to defence but a large proportion of this was spent on the conflict in Indochina.[7]

All this meant, however, that few resources could be spared for the defence of Europe. It soon became apparent to the British that the wartime alliance of Britain, the Soviet Union and the United States would not survive after 1945. The United States was not interested in continuing the post-1941 'special relationship' with Britain after the war. In August 1945 wartime lend lease assistance to Britain was abruptly terminated by President Truman. The Combined British and American Chiefs of Staff Committee in Washington was abolished and in 1946, under the Atomic Energy Act, Congress prohibited the sharing of nuclear information with other powers, despite wartime agreements between Roosevelt, Mackenzie King and Churchill that collaboration between the United States, Britain and Canada in atomic research would continue in peacetime. As a result in 1946 a secret Cabinet committee of senior ministers ordered the production of a British atomic bomb, despite the additional burdens the expensive manufacturing facilities would impose on the Exchequer. Britain's status as a great power appeared to depend on possession of this awesome weapon of mass destruction while, in the absence of any American help in the defence of Western Europe, a British bomb seemed to be the only means of deterring Soviet aggression in the future.[8]

Britain's other main wartime ally, the Soviet Union, was transforming the countries of Central and Eastern Europe it had occupied towards the end of the war into Soviet satellites and was showing increasing hostility towards British interests in Iran and the Mediterranean. While western estimates of the size of the Red Army stationed in Central Europe varied and often were exaggerated, it was still infinitely larger than any forces the western powers could field. In 1950 western intelligence estimated that the Soviet Union had 210 Red Army divisions stationed in Eastern Europe (including 22 in East Germany) while NATO could muster only 14 divisions in West Germany.[9] However, American intelligence did not consider that the Soviet Union, after its devastating losses during the Second World War, was in any condition to embark on another war for several years,[10] and in an attempt to restrain military expenditure, the government ruled that defence planning should be based on the assumption that there would be no major war for at least five years. In British eyes the presence of strong Communist parties in France and Italy was far more dangerous to western stability, with their potential for subversion and even the seizure of power in those countries.[11]

If, on the other hand, the Red Army should invade Western Europe Britain had no intention of sending an expeditionary force to the Continent. In this event the weak British and American occupation forces in Germany would be evacuated to the British Isles, and the Royal Air Force would bomb Soviet oil and industrial installations from Britain's Middle East bases.[12]

The United States finally committed itself to an anti-Soviet policy in April 1947, when it agreed to assume financial responsibility for the Greek and Turkish armies – the latter had been continuously mobilised since 1945 in the face of Soviet threats to Turkish security. With this decision the 'Cold War' really began. In the following year the United States went even further and began to encourage the emergence of a western bloc by providing the countries of Western Europe with Marshall Aid[13] to enable them to rebuild their wartorn economies and prevent them from succumbing to communism.[14]

Then, in April 1949, the United States, Canada, Iceland, Denmark, Norway, Britain, France and the Benelux countries signed a mutual assistance pact, the North Atlantic Treaty Organisation (NATO), directed against the Soviet Union. This was a major break with America's long tradition of not becoming involved in alliances with European countries. Britain and the United States hoped that their entry into NATO would encourage the Western Europeans to rebuild their armed forces and to this end the United States agreed to provide them with military aid and financial assistance. Neither power intended to send reinforcements to Europe in the event of war – the United States monopoly of the atomic bomb was regarded as a sufficient guarantee of European security. Not until March 1950 did the Cabinet's Defence Committee reverse its policy and authorise the despatch of two infantry divisions to reinforce the British Army of the Rhine (BAOR), thus making Europe, rather than the Middle East the first priority in British strategy.[15]

With the United States now committed to the defence of Europe, Britain succeeded in its aim of restoring the 'special relationship'. American financial and military aid helped Britain to recover from the effects of the Second World War and at the same time enabled it to uphold its great power status. Britain hoped that its atomic bomb would be successfully tested during the early 1950s, while the government had ordered the construction of a fleet of long-range jet bombers – the Valiant, Vulcan and Victor – which would provide the Royal Air Force with the capability to bomb European Russia in the mid-1950s. The Labour government calculated that, as a result, Britain would be regarded by Washington as a valuable ally, which would enable it to play a large part in influencing American policy in directions which suited British interests. Britain's progress in atomic development might also persuade the United States to resume the exchange of nuclear information which had been broken off in 1947.[16] However, British and American satisfaction with the course of events was rudely shattered when, in August 1949, the Soviet Union successfully tested an atomic bomb, three years ahead of Anglo-American expectations. The loss of the American nuclear monopoly created a deep sense of insecurity inside the United States which was enhanced by the Chinese Communist takeover of mainland China in October 1949. The Truman administration ordered the development of the hydrogen bomb, infinitely more destructive than its atomic predecessor, and embarked on a major rearmament programme after North Korea invaded South Korea on 25 June 1950.

The Korean War militarised the Cold War. Truman was convinced – wrongly – that the invasion was masterminded by the Soviet Union as part of a worldwide Communist thrust against western interests and that it would be followed by renewed Soviet pressure on Western Europe while the attention of the United States was distracted by events in the Far East.[17] He believed that if the United States displayed weakness in the face of North Korea's attempted takeover of the South, American credibility as leader of the western bloc would be undermined. He therefore despatched American naval, air and later ground forces to assist the beleaguered South Koreans, while United States resolutions passed the United Nations Security Council condemning North Korea for its aggression and calling on all members of the United Nations to assist South Korea. As a result Britain and the Commonwealth, France and other countries sent forces to South Korea, with Britain anticipating that its willingness to cooperate with the Americans would enable it to exert greater leverage over American policy in the Far East, thus further developing the 'special relationship'.[18]

In order to convince Moscow of United States determination to defend European security, despite its involvement in the Korean War, the Truman administration presented to NATO in September 1950 a 'package proposal' which offered to increase American forces in Germany from four to six divisions, to furnish the European NATO allies with additional military aid, and to appoint Dwight D. Eisenhower as Supreme Allied Commander in Europe (SACEUR). However, in return the United States demanded that the allies agree that Germany should contribute troops to NATO. While the allies welcomed the American offer of more troops and money, none of them, after their unhappy experiences during the Second World War, wanted to see the re-emergence of a rearmed West Germany. Although the Americans eventually secured the reluctant approval of most of the European allies to their 'package proposal', France adamantly refused to agree to it. The Americans argued in vain that given the reluctance of the West Europeans to provide sufficient troops to make the defence of Europe credible, a West German contribution was essential. Furthermore NATO in 1950 was also planning to move the western defence perimeter from its existing line along the Rhine to a new line along the frontier with East Germany near the Elbe. This would enable NATO to defend West Germany's resources, instead of allowing them to fall into Soviet hands in the event of a Russian invasion, but it also increased the pressure on the West to secure West German forces to contribute to the defence of this expanded area.[19]

In an attempt to resolve the ensuing deadlock, France put forward a counter-proposal for a federal European Defence Community (EDC), in which West German military effectively would be merged into a European army and thereby placed under tight European control. The Benelux countries and Italy agreed to join France in the Community, as did the Federal Republic of Germany. Britain, however, refused membership, on the grounds that it would undermine British military sovereignty, special relationship with the United States, and world power status. After considerable discussion the West European powers finally signed the EDC treaty on 25 May 1952, but in 1954 the French National Assembly refused to ratify the Treaty.

Britain feared that the collapse of the EDC would lead to the withdrawal of the United States, which had grown increasingly frustrated by the slow progress of the EDC negotiations, from the defence of Western Europe. As an alternative, Britain secured the agreement of its allies to the admission of both West Germany and Italy into NATO and the Brussels Pact in September 1954, with West Germany agreeing not to manufacture atomic or chemical weapons. France was persuaded to accept this solution by a British pledge that it would retain four British divisions and the Tactical Air Force in Germany for 40 years, thus calming French fears that they would be left unaided to deal with a future rearmed West Germany.[20]

Britain and France had followed the United States example by introducing major rearmament programmes of their own, in order to demonstrate their loyalty to the alliance and to head off accusations by neo-isolationists and 'Asia-Firsters' in the United States that Western Europe was leaving the United States to carry all the burdens of the Cold War. However, the cost of Britain's rearmament programme, which in January 1951 had been set at £3700 million over three years, was proving too much for the fragile British economy to bear and as a result inflation soared and Britain's balance of payments went into deficit. In 1950–1 defence expenditure as a percentage of GDP was 5.8 per cent while in 1951–2 this increased to 7.5 per cent and to 8.7 per cent in the following financial year. In 1950 the balance of payments showed a surplus of £307 million, but in 1951 this had turned into a deficit of £700 million.[21] In an effort to bring the economy under control, Winston Churchill's Conservative government, which defeated Labour in the October 1951 election, decided to stretch the three-year rearmament programme over a longer period. Churchill also ordered the Chiefs of Staff to review British strategy in order to suggest areas where economies in defence expenditure could be made.

As a result of these deliberations the chiefs produced a *Global Strategy Paper* in 1952 which was influenced strongly by the opinions of the Chief of the Air Staff, Marshal of the Royal Air Force Sir John Slessor, who was a firm believer in the war-winning capabilities of long-range bomber forces carrying the atomic bomb. The successful test explosion of Britain's atomic bomb in the Monte Bello islands in the Pacific in October lent weight to Slessor's arguments that aggression against Britain's interests worldwide would be deterred if an enemy was aware that Britain could inflict devastating damage on its cities and industries. If the Royal Air Force thus became the mainstay of Britain's defences, substantial reductions could be made in the army and navy. The army and navy chiefs rejected Slessor's proposal, which threatened their services with virtual extinction, and countered that a nuclear war would not be short and decisive, as Slessor claimed, but would be followed by months of 'broken backed' warfare in which the army and navy would be engaged in mopping up and destroying the enemy. In order to present a united front to the politicians, the chiefs incorporated both these concepts – deterrence and 'broken backed' warfare – into the *Global Strategy Paper*. As a result it contained no suggestions for any major cuts in defence expenditure. As Slessor commented subsequently: 'It was essential that we had all three Chiefs of Staff behind us and the broken-backed war thing I never believed in, and neither did Bill Slim [Sir William Slim, the Chief of the Imperial General Staff]. But we had to put it in for the sake of little Rhoddy Mcgrigor [Sir Rhoderick MacGrigor, the First Sea Lord] because otherwise if there was no broken-backed war there was no cause for keeping a large Navy.'[22]

Successive Ministers of Defence down to 1956 attempted to grapple with soaring defence estimates, but without much success. In January 1947, under the Ministry of Defence Act, the Attlee government had attempted to streamline the pre-war structure of defence administration by adopting Churchill's creation in 1940 of the post of Minister of Defence, which he (Churchill) had occupied, as a means of ensuring strong central control over the country's wartime strategy. The Act created a Ministry of Defence as a permanent government department. The Minister was a member of the Cabinet and vice chairman of a new Cabinet Defence Committee of key Cabinet ministers presided over by the Prime Minister. In practice the new arrangements made little difference to the existing situation: the minister had few powers and could only use persuasion to try to get the services to reduce their expenditures. The positions of the three service Secretaries of State were not affected by the changes and they continued to attend the Cabinet as of right. Thus the reforms neither imposed any effective restraints over the autonomy of the Chiefs of Staff nor did they result in many economies in defence expenditure.[23]

However, the humiliating circumstances in which Britain and France were compelled to withdraw from the Suez operation in December 1956 caused politicians to question the efficiency of Britain's conventional forces. It had taken nearly three months to organise the British expeditionary force, despite the relatively large sums of money that had been spent on defence since 1950. The invasion of Egypt by an Anglo-French expeditionary force, acting in concert with an Israeli advance across the Sinai desert, at the end of October, was almost universally condemned as an act of imperialist aggression but it was United States opposition to the venture which was decisive in forcing Britain and France to withdraw. The United States imposed financial sanctions on Britain which severely damaged its already ailing economy and, as a result, on 3 December Britain and France decided they had no alternative but to evacuate their forces from Egyptian soil.[24]

This blow to British prestige forced the resignation of the Prime Minister, Anthony Eden, the architect of the Suez operation, who had himself replaced Churchill in April 1955. Harold Macmillan, the new Prime Minister, was determined to mend broken fences with the United States and to restore the British economy to better health. The latter required cuts in public expenditure, especially in Britain's defence estimates, and Macmillan appointed Duncan Sandys as Minister of Defence with a mandate to secure substantial reductions in the size of Britain's armed forces. As Chancellor of the Exchequer in November 1955 Macmillan had insisted that in future 'we must rely on the power of the nuclear deterrent or we must throw up the sponge.'[25]

Tough and abrasive, Sandys forced through his April 1957 White Paper *Defence: Outline of Future Policy* in the teeth of bitter opposition from the service establishment.[26] He based British strategy for the future firmly on the Slessor concept of a British nuclear deterrent. The successful testing of a British air-dropped hydrogen bomb in that month, the development of which the Churchill government had authorised in 1954, together with the coming into service of the Vulcan bombers,

capable of hitting Moscow from United Kingdom bases with
hydrogen bombs after 1961, enabled Sandys to rely on the
nuclear deterrent with greater confidence than his predecessors.
When the Vulcan became vulnerable to improved Soviet anti-
aircraft defences after 1960, its life would be extended by Blue
Steel, a stand-off airborne missile which Britain was developing,
while the V-bombers would be replaced in the mid-1960s by a
British intermediate range surface-to-surface missile, Blue
Streak, production of which was being accelerated.

Future reliance on the nuclear weapon to deter potential
aggressors enabled Sandys to secure reductions in Britain's
conventional forces. He cancelled the production of a new
manned supersonic bomber and slightly reduced the size of the
navy. It was the army, however, which was affected most
seriously by the Sandys White Paper. Conscription was abolished and total armed services manpower was to be reduced from
690,000 to 375,000 by 1962. Defence expenditure was to be
reduced from the current level of 10 to 7 per cent of GNP by the
same year. The British Army of the Rhine was cut from 77,000
men to 64,000 – Sandys argued that the increased firepower
resulting from the introduction of battlefield or tactical nuclear
weapons justified this reduction – the number of divisions would
be kept at four. The Second Tactical Air Force was to lose 220
day fighters.

Sandys' famous reforms were hardly revolutionary. They were
the product of the long debate about nuclear deterrence which
had continued since the early 1950s. Suez had merely confirmed
the views of those who, like Sandys, believed that Britain should
rely for its defence on the nuclear option in future and that this
would result in considerable savings in conventional warfare
expenditure. The belief that nuclear weapons would be a
cheaper option in the long run was only true if the United States
was prepared to continue to supply them on favourable terms.[27]
While Sandys had substantially reduced the size of the British
army he had at the same time insisted that Britain would
maintain the bulk of its existing commitments. His White Paper
stated that 'outside the area covered by the North Atlantic
Alliance, Britain had military responsibilities in other parts of
the world, in particular the Middle East and South East Asia'.
Apart from minor reductions in some overseas garrisons, the
withdrawal of the small British contingent from South Korea and
of British troops from Jordan, there was little change else-

where.[28] Army chiefs estimated that to maintain these the regular army would require at least 240,000 men. In fact it was able to recruit an average of only 180,000 men after 1960. In 1958 the army numbered 340,000 men. By 1970 this was to fall to 176,740, admittedly after Britain had finally abandoned its East of Suez role.[29] This was during a period when Britain faced an increasing number of crises in its colonies which necessitated the despatch of troops to deal with them. When, in 1955, Britain decided to make Cyprus instead of Suez its Middle East base, this provoked a confrontation with the Greek Cypriot majority on the island, who sought union with Greece, an aspiration which clashed with Britain's determination to remain on the island. Escalating Greek Cypriot terrorist outrages against British military personnel and base facilities rendered Cyprus a diminishing asset as Britain was forced to send more troops to the island for internal security purposes until a temporary settlement was reached in 1960. Similarly an uprising against British rule in Kenya by Mau Mau tribesmen in 1952 required the efforts of 3500 British troops and local forces before it was finally put down in 1960.[30] In order to provide more troops for these extra-European commitments, the government reduced the size of the Rhine army to 55,000 in 1958 but when it sought a further reduction to 49,000 men in 1960 the storm of protest from its allies that Britain was reneging on Eden's pledge to NATO in 1954 forced the abandonment of further cuts. The Rhine army was to be kept in future at its 1958 level of 55,000.

Macmillan's skilful diplomacy led to the restoration of Britain's close ties with the United States. The Eisenhower administration was equally anxious to repair the breach between the two countries caused by the Suez debacle. Macmillan met Eisenhower at Bermuda in March 1957 and agreed to the stationing of 60 American Thor intermediate range ballistic missiles on British soil under a 'dual key' arrangement by which both powers would have to approve the firing of the missiles. At a further meeting in October 1957 in Washington, Eisenhower promised Macmillan that in view of Britain's progress with thermonuclear weapons he would persuade Congress to restore the exchanges of nuclear information between the two countries which had been terminated in 1946.[31] In 1958 the two countries signed an Agreement for Cooperation on the Uses of Atomic Energy for Mutual Defence Purposes, which, with a few exceptions, allowed for the resumption of the exchanges.[32]

When in April 1960 Britain was forced to cancel the production of Blue Streak, which was becoming increasingly vulnerable
to improved Soviet anti-ballistic missile defences and also extremely expensive – £60 million had already been spent on it and
it was likely to cost a further £500 million to put into production
– Macmillan secured Eisenhower's agreement to replace it by
American-built Skybolt air-to-ground missiles which could be
fired by the Vulcans at a distance from the target and would
enable the British V-bomber force to remain operational until
the late 1960s.

In 1961 John F. Kennedy became United States President. In
November of the following year, his Defense Secretary, Robert
McNamara, cancelled Skybolt production because of heavy cost
overruns and increasing vulnerability to Soviet counter-measures.
McNamara's action left Britain with the prospect that in the
future it would have no means of delivering nuclear weapons on
enemy targets. Macmillan flew to meet Kennedy at Nassau in
the Bahamas in late December 1961 to warn the President that
unless the United States provided Britain with a substitute for
Skybolt, Britain's continued adherence to NATO would be in
jeopardy. Before he left he cabled the British ambassador in
Washington, David Ormsby-Gore, that 'if we cannot reach an
agreement on a realistic means of maintaining the British
independent deterrent, all the other questions may only justify
perfunctory discussions, since an "agonizing reappraisal" of all
our foreign and defence [plans] will be required'.[33]

In the face of this threat, Kennedy agreed that Britain should
be provided with Polaris submarine-launched intermediate ballistic missiles for five British-built nuclear submarines. Britain
came out well from the agreement, having secured a virtually
undetectable deterrent at a much lower cost than would have
been the case if it had persisted with efforts to produce its own
missile system.[34]

However, as a result of these developments it was now
doubtful whether Britain's 'independent' deterrent was as independent as Britain's politicians liked to pretend. The advanced
technology and complex manufacturing facilities required made
it virtually impossible for Britain to afford its own missiles,
without making unacceptable sacrifices, and it was forced to rely
on United States expertise instead. This dependence meant that
it was unlikely that Britain could use its deterrent without prior
agreement with the United States. At Nassau, Kennedy insisted

that Polaris should be assigned to NATO, although Macmillan secured the right to use it unilaterally in cases 'where Her Majesty's Government may decide that supreme national interests are at stake',[35] but this was a somewhat empty gesture.

While Britain faced increasing problems with its nuclear deterrent, it was at the same time finding that its reduced conventional capabilities under the Sandys reforms could barely cope with all the demands made upon them. In 1958 British troops were airlifted to Jordan to prevent the pro-British king from being toppled by Egyptian-inspired unrest. In July 1961 a British taskforce was despatched to Kuwait (the source of half of Britain's oil supplies) to defend the country against a threatened Iraqi invasion. In 1964 British troops were flown to Kenya, Tanganiyka and Uganda to crush anti-government army mutinies, and in the same year nationalist disturbances broke out in Aden. And finally from 1963 to 1967 British ground, air and naval forces were engaged in a sustained campaign to thwart Indonesian guerrilla efforts to undermine the newly created Federation of Malaysia, for whose defence Britain had undertaken responsibility in 1957. The confrontation with Indonesia stretched British forces to breaking point.[36]

However, the Macmillan administration did allocate more funds to Britain's land and sea forces after 1960, while in 1963 and 1964 the Prime Minister and the Minister of Defence, Peter Thorneycroft, forced through changes in the defence structure which he (Macmillan) had decided against pursuing in 1957 in view of the bitter feelings the Sandys reforms had stirred up in the armed services. Macmillan commented at that time that 'the atmosphere in which our discussions were conducted had been at certain periods so disagreeable that I felt unwilling to reopen the question'.[37] In 1964 the Minister of Defence became Secretary of State in a centralised defence structure which involved the abolition of the three separate service secretaries and their replacement by three junior Ministers of State. The new Secretary of State became the sole representative for defence matters in the Cabinet and in the Defence and Overseas Policy Committee (which replaced the Defence Committee). He now presided over a defence establishment which was for most purposes entirely responsible to him. In 1968 the defence budget and the planning staffs were unified. As a result of these changes the autonomy of the Chiefs of Staff and the armed services was substantially reduced.[38]

These changes benefited Denis Healey, who became Defence Secretary in Harold Wilson's Labour government, which was elected in 1964. Healey remained in that office until Labour fell in 1970. The Labour Party's election campaign had called for 'the renegotiation of the Nassau agreement' and for major reductions in defence expenditure. However, both Wilson and Healey were convinced of the importance of maintaining Britain's nuclear deterrent. They merely cancelled one of the five nuclear submarines which the Conservatives had ordered. Both insisted upon the importance of Britain's 'East of Suez' role. Wilson informed the House of Commons in December 1964 that 'whatever we may do in the field of cost effectiveness, value for money and a stringent review of expenditure, we cannot afford to relinquish our world role'.[39] There were several motives behind Wilson's determination to hang on to Britain's extra-European responsibilities, despite the growing opposition of sections of his own party to Britain's overseas role. First the Labour leaders were as convinced as their predecessors had been that it was essential to Britain's continued status as a great power. Secondly they were equally determined to maintain the 'special relation-ship' with the United States – the murdered Kennedy's successor as President in 1963, Lyndon Johnson, claimed that Britain's overseas role was an essential contribution to global stability at a time when the United States was becoming increasingly dis-tracted by its growing involvement in the Vietnam War – when decolonisation, which had made rapid progress during the Con-servatives' final years in office, had produced a volatile situation. Thirdly they felt that Britain's role kept an increasingly disparate Commonwealth together, and fourthly that it was necessary as a means of protecting Britain's trade and investments overseas.[40] Perhaps an even more important factor, one not publicly articu-lated by a Labour government, was suggested by a leading economist of the period, in referring to Britain's economic difficulties in the 1950s:

> Perhaps the truth is that a military power on the wane tends to be more concerned than ever to show the flag at the various points around the globe where its sovereign authority can still be asserted. There is nothing essentially evil about this desire to show the flag. . . . But carried on in the unrestrained way in which it had been pursued since the [Second World] war, it can be abominably expensive.[41]

However, Labour was committed to cut defence expenditure, and Healey reduced it to a level of 6 per cent of GNP per annum from the 7 per cent annual level to which it had increased in the last years of the Conservative government. This meant that the armed forces came under considerable strain, as inflation reduced the total amount available for defence even further and the modernisation of army, navy and RAF equipment languished. In an effort to keep the defence budget within his 6 per cent maximum, Healey cancelled a number of expensive projects such as new fighters and transport aircraft, a new aircraft carrier and, in 1965, the TSR-2 strike and reconnaissance aircraft, which had been ordered by the Conservatives, which he replaced by purchasing 50 American FB-111 fighter bombers.[42]

This effort to maintain Britain's world role eventually proved to be more than the British economy could bear. In July 1967 the Wilson government, faced with a balance of payments crisis, finally admitted defeat and abandoned the East of Suez policy. Consequently Aden was to be evacuated immediately (in 1966 the government had decided to quit the colony when it became independent in 1968), while British forces in Malaysia were to be reduced by half by 1971 and withdrawn altogether in 1976. In November 1967 another financial crisis forced the devaluation of sterling and led to another round of public expenditure cuts, which in January 1968 resulted in the decision to withdraw from Malaysia in 1971, to scrap all Britain's aircraft carriers by the same date, and to cancel the order for the FB-111s.[43] Altogether these cuts were intended to produce savings of £110 million in 1969–70 and £260 million in 1972–3.[44]

The liquidation of the bulk of Britain's overseas military responsibilities – apart from small garrisons in Hong Kong, Gibraltar, Belize and the Falklands Islands – can be seen in retrospect as the belated and logical culmination of the retreat from empire which had begun with Indian independence in 1947 and had then been resumed, after a period when it was hoped that Britain could cling onto most of what remained, with renewed intensity in the late 1950s and early 1960s. It was not so much the vociferous opposition of many Labour MPs and their supporters in the mid-1960s to the continuation of Britain's overseas role that determined the outcome, but the impact of economic and financial pressures and the growing realisation amongst senior ministers and Whitehall civil servants that the effort had brought Britain no advantages internationally and had

saddled it with enormous costs. Britain's influence with the
United States declined rapidly after Kennedy's death – Wilson
and Johnson were never close – while Britain's presence overseas
had not given it any leverage over either side in the Arab-Israeli
war of 1967 or helped its abortive efforts at mediation between
the Americans and North Vietnamese. By 1966 Whitehall was
questioning whether it was worthwhile maintaining overseas
garrisons and naval forces to protect Britain's trade and invest-
mènts when other nations such as Japan, which had no significant naval or military forces, were expanding their overseas
commerce. Furthermore the Commonwealth was now regarded
as of declining importance both politically and economically.

Britain now began to look to Europe both for economic
salvation and as the focus of future British defence efforts. The
six continental powers had formed the European Coal and Steel
Community (ECSC) in 1951, designed to pool and regulate the
production of coal and steel throughout the community, and
based on the supranational principle. As a result of the success of
the ECSC, in 1955 the six set up the more ambitious European
Economic Community (EEC), which was to be bound by a common tariff and placed under the control of federal institutions.
Britain, then wedded to free trade, to the 'special relationship'
with the United States, to the Commonwealth and to its world
role, feared that all of these would be prejudiced by membership
of the EEC and had spurned admission. However, when Harold
Wilson decided to apply for membership of the Community in
1967, this was vetoed by France (an earlier British application by
the Macmillan government had been similarly rejected by
France in January 1962) on the grounds that British policy was
too closely tied to that of the United States and that Britain could
not therefore be 'truly' European. Nevertheless Britain did begin
to demonstrate a new found commitment to Europe, at least in
the defence field, during the late 1960s, when Healey began to
play a more active role in NATO, allocating more money for
Rhine army equipment and promoting the formation of a ten-
nation Eurogroup within the organisation as a means of press-
urising the United States into supplying more information to its
allies about the post-1969 strategic arms limitation negotiations
with the Soviet Union.[45]

Edward Heath, who defeated Labour in the 1970 general
election, was a far more committed Europeanist than any of his
predecessors at No. 10 Downing Street. Heath secured Britain's

admission to the European Economic Community in 1972 while his government agreed to spend £400 million between 1970 and 1974 on updating BAOR's equipment. Although the Conservatives had promised that if re-elected a Conservative government would restore some of the East of Suez cuts which Wilson had made, in practice such changes as Heath made were purely cosmetic: a commitment to send a British military contingent to Singapore as part of a joint British, Australian and New Zealand defence force; the construction of an Anglo-American naval base at Diego Garcia; and the reactivation of an agreement with South Africa, which Labour had abandoned, and which allowed the Royal Navy to use the facilities of South Africa's Simonstown naval base. The aircraft carrier *Ark Royal* was also to be kept in commission. On the other hand Britain withdrew its remaining naval forces from the Persian Gulf in 1971.

In a surprise election early in February 1974 Labour were returned to power. While there had been a slight increase in defence expenditure under Heath, the economic situation remained weak, and the country was now experiencing a new economic crisis as a result of the quadrupling of the price of oil after the Middle East war of October 1973. A miners' strike early in 1974 occasioned Heath's fall. Wilson's government wished to devote more resources to Britain's social, health and education services. This entailed further reductions in defence expenditure, the value of which was in any case being eroded by heavy increases in the cost of new weapons and equipment. A Defence Review in 1974 required expenditure to be reduced from 5.5 per cent of GNP in 1975 to 4.4 per cent by 1985. Heath's defence commitment to Singapore was abandoned and the Simonstown agreement terminated, service manpower levels were reduced, amphibious and airborne forces cut back and the navy lost one-seventh of its surface fleet. The government also announced that the Polaris force would not be replaced when it became obsolescent in the 1980s. In future Britain's 'strategic priority areas' would be the NATO Central Front, the defence of the Eastern Atlantic and English Channel, the defence of the United Kingdom and the maintenance of Britain's existing strategic nuclear deterrent. However, senior ministers did agree secretly to fund Project 'Chevaline', the modernisation of Polaris by providing it with multiple warheads, which would enable it to be deployed into the 1980s.[46]

By 1976, when Wilson resigned, Britain's defences were suffer-

ing from serious neglect. BAOR needed new tanks and other
equipment and the Royal Air Force now was virtually confined
to a tactical role in Europe but needed new fighters for the task.
The navy, having lost most of its aircraft carriers, now relied on
'through deck' or anti-submarine warface cruisers, mini-aircraft
carriers which had been ordered by the Heath government in
1973. These could carry a complement of helicopters and Sea
Harrier vertical-take-off jet fighters. James Callaghan, who replaced Wilson as Prime Minister in 1976, was anxious to arrest
the decline in Britain's defences at a time when tensions between
the West and the Soviet Union were increasing. In 1979 Britain
joined the other European NATO allies in agreeing to increase
defence expenditures for NATO purposes by an extra 3 per cent
per annum over the next five years. A new battle tank and
artillery were ordered for the Rhine army while Callaghan
promised that there would be no further reductions in army
manpower.

The May 1979 general election returned the Conservatives, led
by Margaret Thatcher, to power. In their election campaign the
Conservatives called for greater defence expenditure, and one of
the first decisions of the government was to award an immediate
pay settlement to the armed services of 33 per cent, designed to
arrest the decline in morale and the shortfall in skilled manpower
recruitment which had taken place during the late 1970s – a
result of a freeze on service pay and of the effects of inflation. The
government also agreed to continue Labour's policy of devoting
an extra 3 per cent to NATO until 1986. It scorned a vociferous
campaign by nuclear disarmers against the basing of 96 American cruise missiles in Britain, which had been agreed to by its
predecessor.

The new government was also pledged to effect reductions in
Britain's public expenditure and inevitably the increasing costs
of defence could not hope to escape coming under close scrutiny.
These costs were likely to rise even more alarmingly as a result of
a decision in 1980 by the Thatcher government to purchase from
the United States a replacement for Polaris – the Trident
submarine-launched ballistic missile. Moreover the need to maintain British troops in strife-torn Northern Ireland, where the gulf
between the Catholic and Protestant communities, which had
widened since 1969, provided fertile soil for terrorist outrages by the
Irish Republican Army and by Protestant para-military groups,
was also imposing additional burdens on the Exchequer.

When John Nott became Defence Secretary in 1981, he commissioned a new Defence Review, *The United Kingdom Defence Programme: the Way Forward*, which was intended to be a radical reappraisal of Britain's defence commitments and resources. The Labour government's decision in the late 1960s to withdraw from Britain's East of Suez role had not led to any significant long-run savings in defence expenditure. Any savings on that account had soon been swallowed up by the increasing cost of new weapons and equipment – estimated at 6 per cent above the current level of inflation. In an effort to stabilise the cost of research and development Britain had entered into a number of collaborative weapons ventures with its European partners – such as the Anglo-German-Italian Tornado multirole combat aircraft. Some of these, such as the Anglo-French variable geometry plane, had foundered, and in any case the different specialised roles which each of the participating countries required often loaded the weapons with intricate navigational and other equipment which made the ultimate costs very high.

In an effort to rationalise defence expenditure Nott focused on two of Labour's four priority strategic areas where reductions would yield substantial savings. These were the BAOR and the navy's surface fleet. Since any reductions in BAOR would anger Britain's European partners at a time when the government was seeking a reduction in Britain's financial contribution to the EEC, and might encourage those in the US Senate who were calling for American troop withdrawals from Europe, Nott decided that the only alternative was to reduce drastically the size of the fleet.[47] The number of frigates and destroyers was to be cut from 59 to 42, two remaining aircraft carriers were to be sold off or scrapped, and the navy's amphibious warfare capability was to be abandoned. Altogether 25 per cent of the surface fleet was to go. Neither Nott nor the Prime Minister were deflected from their course by the storm of protest with which these proposals were greeted in naval circles, or by the resignation of the junior Navy Minister. The government would now concentrate resources on the deterrent and on a land-based strategy in Europe, while in future the navy's role would be restricted to anti-submarine warfare and its nuclear submarines.

However, Nott's plans were upset not by internal dissent but by the intervention of an external threat to one of Britain's few remaining dependencies, the Falkland Islands.[48] Britain had long dithered about the fate of the Falklands, torn as she was between the insistence of the islanders, who had powerful contacts in the British Parliament, that they remain under the British flag, and the desire to be rid of an unwanted colony which Argentina had long claimed as rightfully belonging to it. Britain's inability to make up its mind about the future of the islands, the presence of only a handful of marines to defend them, the withdrawal under the Nott cuts of the only remaining naval vessel in the South Atlantic – the ice patrol vessel *HMS Endurance* – and the British government's sweeping cuts in the surface fleet, convinced the Argentinean military junta that Britain would not resist an Argentinean take over of the islands.

Poor intelligence and British complacency about the defence of the islands were responsible for the anguish with which Britain greeted Argentina's sudden invasion and occupation of the Falkland Islands on 2 April 1982. The Thatcher government, under intense attack from the opposition and from within its own ranks for its negligence, ordered the preparation of a naval taskforce at Portsmouth – fortunately the two aircraft carriers, which formed the core of the force, had not as yet been scrapped – which sailed for the Falklands on 5 April. When Argentina refused to evacuate the islands, British forces, after bitter naval and air battles, landed on the islands on 21 May and forced the Argentinean forces to surrender on 8 June. Although this conflict was a minor affair (except to those on both sides involved in the fighting) in comparison with the wars which have been waged in the Middle East and in Vietnam since 1945, Mrs Thatcher exalted at a Conservative rally on 3 July 1982 that 'the lesson of the Falklands is that Britain has not changed and that this nation still has those sterling qualities which shine through our history'.[49]

As a result of the Falklands crisis the government abandoned the bulk of Nott's naval cuts. The navy would now keep 50 destroyers and frigates, its aircraft carriers and its amphibious landing capability. In addition the Falklands now had to be expensively reinforced by the army. Consequently defence expenditure increased by 21 per cent in real terms between 1979 and 1985 – the only saving was the coming to an end of the extra 3 per cent per annum expenditure on NATO forces in 1986. From 1981 to 1986 defence expenditure averaged 5.2 per cent of GNP.[50] The Thatcher government refused to contemplate another major Defence Review after the fate of the 1981 Review in the wake of the Falklands War. Britain is still faced therefore with the continuing problem of matching defence expenditure to its overall resources, a problem which has bedevilled British defence planning since 1934. The problem is likely to become acute in the wake of renewed inflation and balance of payments deficits during and after 1989.

It has been the axiom of all governments since the end of the Second World War that Britain's prestige abroad and the success of its defence and foreign policies depend on a healthy economy. In practice this ideal has been difficult to achieve while Britain's dilemma in the future is likely to be increased by new scientific innovations – the American Strategic Defence Initiative (SDI or Star Wars) which was announced by President Reagan in March 1982 and which is designed to harness complex anti-ballistic missile systems to destroy incoming enemy ballistic missiles. If the Soviet Union succeeds in perfecting its own Star Wars defences in the 1990s or improving its anti-submarine war capability, Britain's Trident missile system will become vulnerable to interdiction. Furthermore so-called 'emerging technology' (ET), which will provide armies and air forces with greater firepower at greater levels of accuracy, might save army manpower in Europe but it will prove to be incredibly expensive for a faltering economy like that of the United Kingdom.

These are not the only imponderables. The advent of Mikhael Gorbachev as Soviet leader, and the new 'openness' both internally and in Russia's relations with the rest of the world, have resulted in a Soviet-American agreement to remove intermediate range missiles from Europe and a major relaxation of East-West tension. These and the recent traumatic events in Eastern Europe, which has seen the Communist Party lose its stranglehold on power there almost entirely will lead to further strategic arms limitation agreements and reductions in conventional forces on both sides of the former Iron Curtain. In October 1990 both East and West Germany were reunited and eventually the Red Army in East Germany will be evacuated to its homeland. The uncertainty that such developments have created is beginning to call into question the consensus about the need for NATO to continue as a defensive alliance. Will the British army continue to have a role in the defence of Europe if these changes continue? Many naval experts have suggested that the time has come for a reappraisal of the need for a continental commitment in the light of these prospects in favour of a maritime strategy, in which Britain possesses all the advantages of long experience and a distinguished tradition.[51] The August 1990 Iraqi seizure of

Kuwait and the subsequent despatch of American, British and other foreign forces to Saudi Arabia will no doubt strengthen the hands of those who argue that the world is too volatile to allow a too drastic reduction in Britain's defence posture. Other strategic commentators wonder whether the expenditure on the independent deterrent is justified in an era when new defensive techniques might render it obsolescent, and indeed the Labour Party has proposed that it should be bargained away in return for Soviet reductions in conventional forces in Central Europe. There is no sign that the British government has yet begun seriously to address these issues. So far all that has happened in the defence field has been piecemeal reductions across the board – for instance in navy personnel – which if continued to a logical conclusion will amount to what Lawrence Freedman has described as 'a defence review by stealth'.[52]

Whatever the future may hold, one can say that Britain has managed the transition from a post-1945 defence posture which relied heavily on a large conscripted army deploying relatively unsophisticated Second World War equipment to one which during and after the 1960s came to depend on highly sophisticated weapons systems deployed by relatively small forces in which there is a relatively large proportion of highly skilled personnel. David Greenwood has argued that the reduction in Britain's overseas commitments and the commensurate drastic cuts in the size of its armed force do not represent in any sense a 'decline' but a rational and relatively orderly adjustment to new conditions which have resulted in the three services possessing more firepower and greater capability in the 1980s than ever before.[53] On the other hand, many historians have tended to see this process as one of 'decline', which is reflected in Britain's reduced status in the world: from a great world power in 1945 to a middle ranking Eurocentric one in 1989.[54]

While Britain's defence planning has often been characterised by confusion and muddle, the changes that have taken place can be seen in hindsight as sensible adjustments to changing circumstances. Most of the crucial decisions which were taken were not sudden improvisations but were the product of much heart searching and careful consideration of the alternatives. Clearly, once the decision was made to grant independence to Britain's remaining colonial empire after 1958 and to downgrade Britain's role in the Middle East and the Gulf by 1966, the maintenance of large garrison and intervention forces was no longer sensible.

During the years of the Reagan presidency Britain managed to maintain relatively close links with the United States, especially in the field of intelligence gathering, albeit on a reduced level to that which existed during the early 1950s. However, critics allege that this has been at the price of British subservience to the United States in foreign and defence policies – Denis Healey told the House of Commons on 27 October 1987 that Britain faced 'a prolonged and humiliating dependence on the US which will cover the whole of our foreign and defence policy ... the 'rent-a-rocket' Trident programme ... made Britain totally dependent on the Americans and totally incapable of standing up to them'.[55]

Britain plays an important part in the defence of Western Europe. If the arguments over whether it should concentrate its scarce resources on a continental commitment or should return to a maritime strategy are to be revived, this is merely a further episode in a century old naval-military controversy and not the beginning of a new chapter in British history.

TABLE 7.1   British defence spending as a percentage of Gross National Product 1948–1978

1948	1949	1950	1951	1952	1953	1954	1955	1956	1957
7.1	6.5	6.6	7.9	9.8	9.7	9.2	7.9	7.8	6.9
1958	1959	1960	1961	1962	1963	1964	1965	1966	1967
6.7	6.4	6.3	6.3	6.4	6.2	5.9	5.9	5.8	5.9
1968	1969	1970	1971	1972	1973	1974	1975	1976	1977
5.6	4.9	4.8	4.8	4.8	4.7	4.9	4.9	4.9	4.8
1978									
4.6									

SOURCE: Keith Hartley, 'Defence with less Money? The British Experience', in Gwyn Harries-Jenkins (ed.), *Armed Forces and the Welfare Societies: Challenges in the 1980s* (1982), p. 11. Reproduced with kind permission of Dr Hartley.

8. Social Equity and Industrial Need: A Dilemma of English Education since 1945

MICHAEL SANDERSON

In 1933 a senior civil servant of the Board of Education after an acrimonious discussion with two Chief Education Officers wrote an aide memoire. He reflected and deplored that 'what was quite clear was that they regard the matter almost entirely from the point of view of the right of the individual boy or girl to rise and very little, if at all, from the point of view of the organisation and needs of industry'.[1] The civil servant in recording this high-lighted an essential dilemma of attitudes to the educational system which underlies contemporary English development, particularly since 1945. This was the dilemma of the 'right to rise' versus the 'needs of industry' as the 1930s official put it. It is not inevitable that there should be a conflict between the social justice and industrial efficiency motives in education. For the Edwardians it was not so. Indeed the advocates of education as the 'ladder of opportunity' through which able children of modest background could rise were also propagandists for the 'national efficiency' movement of the pre-1914 years. For Sydney Webb, Sir Robert Morant, Viscount Bryce, Lord Haldane and the rest the one set of attitudes was an essential part of the other since rising talent of whatever social origins would renourish all elites including those of science and industry.[2] Nor would this dilemma have been inevitable in the 1930s and after 1945 had the proposals of a prominent educationalist, Lord Eustace Percy (President of the Board of Education 1925–9), been adopted. Percy envisaged a system by which young people could pass from junior technical schools through to technical colleges which would become a part of higher education.[3] This in his view should become the technical counterpart to the secondary school–university sequence. In post-war terminology, he was advocating a parallel track consisting of secondary technical school leading to polytechnic or technological university. This would match the more traditional liberal education or pure science sequence of grammar school and university. Expanding opportunities for social mobility up this technical track would be directly of service to industry.

At the end of the Second World War these two considerations were strongly co-existent. There was a firm belief in the capacity of education to bring about 'equality of opportunity', which became a catchphrase of the 1940s.[4] It was a tradition from R. H. Tawney in the 1920s, through Archbishop William Temple and the genesis of the Welfare State. The expansion of opportunities for the working class to attend the grammar schools in the inter-war years was brought about by Morant's 1902 Act and the reforms which followed Sir Henry Hadow's report in 1926. The 1944 Act was borne along by these rising expectations. By abolishing fee paying in state grammar schools it hoped to increase working-class chances yet further and open up a highway through secondary education to the university. Expanding educational opportunities would bring about greater social justice in keeping with the 'People's War' idealism of the time.

The period at the end of the war no less emphasised the importance of education in science and technology for industry. The war itself had enhanced the prestige and glamour of the 'boffin' war scientist. Butler had stressed 'the need for industrial and technical training'[5] and two major reports on Higher Technological Education (1945) by Lord Eustace Percy[6] and on Scientific Education (1946) by Sir Alan Barlow[7] called for a considerable expansion of technical and scientific education and personnel to put industry on its feet in the post-war years.

Yet co-existent as these two preoccupations were, if rivalry should beset their relationship then social rather than economic factors would take preferment. In particular we would argue that since the Second World War there have been crucial areas where a concern about education for social justice or equality or expanding opportunities has been at odds with the need for education for industrial efficiency. The former has too often been allowed an unfortunate precedence. This has been notably the case in the failure of school technical education, the policies of polytechnics and the initial expansion of higher education in the

1960s. Percy saw education as being 'at the crossroads'. Taking the wrong direction of choice in such areas has contributed to the failure of the education system to support the economy and played its part in the relative economic decline of Britain in the post-war years.

I

The first and perhaps most important area where industrial needs were sacrificed to considerations of social capillarity was the fate of the secondary technical schools. The secondary technical schools had their origins in the junior technical schools of the 1900s. They provided technical and trade education for children from the age of 13 and were especially valuable in the engineering and construction industries and in preparing for some specialised trades such as tailoring, silversmithing and photography. The Spens Report of 1938 was intended to give them a powerful boost. Sir Will Spens saw these schools as the future main area of development and even suggested that there were too many grammar schools and that several should be converted to technical schools.[8] The war overtook Spens before anything could be done but it was an important set of ideas incorporated into the thinking behind the 1944 Education Act. Spens and Butler were old friends, respectively Master and Fellow of Corpus Christi College, Cambridge. Another intellectual influence behind the 1944 Act was Sir Cyril Norwood's report of 1943 which also gave an implied boost to the technical school idea.[9] This posited three psychological types: the academic, the mechanical and the concrete. The mechanical mind had 'an uncanny insight into the intricacies of mechanism' and clearly justified the existence of separate technical schools just as the grammar school was justified as the appropriate locus of the abstract thinker. The secondary modern schools were to receive those who 'deal with concrete things rather than ideas'.

The 1944 Act required LEAs to provide education for children according to their 'age aptitude and ability' without being specific about the types of schools which should make this provision. The lack of specificity in the Act left an element of discretion to the LEAs who might want to experiment with multilateral or bilateral systems. Yet the assumptions of the official Ministry of Education pamphlets were firmly tripartite in describing the three types of schools – grammar, modern and secondary technical. The last was the new name given to the old junior technical schools. They were now undoubtedly part of the secondary education system. The age of entry was reduced from 13 to 11 so that pupils entered the technical school after the 11+ examination on a par with the other two main forms of secondary schooling. The first official Ministry of Education explanation of the post-1944 structure praised the secondary technical schools and envisaged their thriving expansion as Spens had desired.[10] The 1947 rewriting of the Ministry statement was equally enthusiastic and – optimistically and prematurely – suggested that the new secondary technical schools were 'an important factor in the development plans of the local education authorities'.[11]

Yet these schools did not grow to produce the technicians needed by British industry. On the contrary, they declined in number from 321 in 1947 to 225 in 1962. The proportion of secondary school pupils they educated remained constant at a tiny 1.2 per cent between 1947 and 1962.[12] Sir Peter Venables pointed out that in 1952–3 there were seven times as many pupils in grammar schools as in secondary technical schools and nearly 17 times more in secondary modern schools. This curious ratio 1:7:17 was hardly a true tripartite system and 'the ratio provokes grave doubts as to whether this is a proportion appropriate to the needs of a commercial and industrial nation'.[13]

Various factors lay behind this. There was limited enthusiasm for secondary technical schools at the top. Ellen Wilkinson, who became Labour's first Minister of Education (July 1945), came to office with few ideas about education. She accepted the tripartite system yet was sceptical of secondary technical schools as a separate stream: 'the idea of boys building pig styes or making beehives and wheelbarrows and of girls doing laundry work or catering infuriated her'.[14] She increasingly thought of bilateral arrangements of technical streams in grammar schools to ensure flexibility and generosity of secondary education. Her successor George Tomlinson evinced no special interest in secondary technical schools and shared the same reservations about vocational education in schools. He specifically disapproved of using the extra year resulting from the raising of the school leaving age from 14 to 15 'to provide vocational courses of a narrow kind'.[15] He himself had left school at 12 or 13 to work in a cotton mill and knew the effect of the premature encroachment of employment on the young developing mind.[16] As Minister of

Education he obliged local authorities to keep the proportion of pupils attending technical schools deliberately low. For example Middlesborough planned for 28 per cent of its secondary school children to be in technical schools. Tomlinson, on the contrary, suggested that 'it is not to be expected that so high a proportion of the children as 28 per cent would find what they need in this kind and standard of provision'. [17] Tomlinson obliged the authority to restrict their technical scholars to 10 per cent and he seems to have been suggesting something like this figure for other authorities at the same time. [18]

One may appreciate the restrictive attitudes of Labour ministers to the secondary technical schools. For them the grammar school and the expansion of grammar school places were the golden gateway to opportunity for the working class. There was a long tradition of Left-wing suspicion of technical school education. It was seen as pre-empting the careers of working-class children, looping them prematurely back into working-class jobs and denying them the rounded general education that the middle classes claimed for themselves. Moreover, this was linked with a trade union suspicion that technical schools would lead to an overproduction of the skilled technician class, driving down their wage levels. The technical school was a relative dead end, the grammar school was the 'ladder of opportunity'. Hence the new Labour ministers considered that they best served the interests of the working classes who supported their party by accepting the tripartite assumptions of the 1944 Act but emphasising the grammar school and downplaying the technical school.

Whether secondary technical schools were to flourish or not depended not only on attitudes in Whitehall but also on those of the LEAs. Here many local authorities were less concerned to develop secondary techs as a part of the tripartite system than to absorb existing or provide new ones as streams in other kinds of schools. For example in London the post-war educational reconstruction plan had been approved in July 1944 and its principles were firmly multilateral – the future replacing of grammar, central and technical schools eventually with large comprehensive high schools. Immediately after the end of the war was too soon for costly rebuilding on these lines but in the 1950s the long-term plans were put into effect. For example the Borough Road Polytechnic junior technical school, one of the first, was transferred to a secondary modern school. Two secondary technical schools were absorbed into the new comprehensive school in Kidbrooke Grove. By 1961 London had 59 comprehensive and 21 grammar schools, but only 5 secondary technical schools remained of that proud London tradition of junior techs and trade schools.[19] A commentator who deplored the absorption of the secondary schools in London observed presciently, 'they will of course lose their identity as schools and this will be the ultimate fate of all the secondary technical schools'.[20]

In Rene Saran's study of a local authority in the south-east of England (which he calls 'Townley') he shows that it began the post-war years with tripartite assumptions.[21] But by 1949 the authority prepared schemes of modern-technical and grammar-technical schools on the grounds that the 11+ could distinguish grammar and modern pupils 'but was no indicator of suitability for a technical course'. If the grammar and modern scholar types could be distinguished then allowing them into technical courses would be more flexible than a tripartite structure. It was the policy of the Chief Education Officer and became 'Townley's' Conservative policy for the 1950s. The blunt politics of the situation was that the Conservatives were concerned to defend the grammar school and to resist the comprehensive at almost any cost. Their defence of the grammar school did not extend to all parts of the tripartite structure. 'Townley' was an authority very amply supplied with grammar schools with about 30 per cent of children attending them. In this situation there were few with appropriate aptitudes left over for secondary technical schools and no motive to create them to reduce the numbers going to grammar schools. Labour likewise had no wish to defend the tripartite system. They wanted comprehensives. With neither Left nor Right deeply committed to tripartism the loser was the separate technical school.

A root of the problem was the urgent desire of parents and local authorities for grammar schools. Spens thought that grammar schools had overexpanded in the first third of the century. Parents preferred grammar schools because they led to professional, clerical and white-collar occupations and not to labouring work. Behind this was the belief in the superiority of office work, the 'preference for the black coat of the office over the boiler suit of the workshop'. Behind that in turn was not merely snobbery but the experience of the 1930s that industrial employment was associated with insecurity: 'in bad times the man at the bench is stood off more quickly than the man at the desk'.[22] If the Ministry and the LEAs were ambivalent about genuine tripartitism so too were parents. The Ministry in 1951 observed that 'the implications of the 1944 Act are lost upon many parents. Authorities are subject to strong pressure to admit children who are unsuited to a grammar school course to what may appear to parents in some cases to be the only true secondary school available.'[23] These pressures, it was asserted, led to too many pupils being admitted to grammar schools for which they were academically unsuited and from which they failed to derive full benefit.[24] Many of these grammar school dropouts might have been better placed in secondary technical schools.

What is even more clear is that the expansion of other parts of the tripartite system and the growth of forms of multilateralism had a profound effect on secondary technical provision. Firstly there was an increasing absorption of technical studies into other kinds of school, either taking over existing secondary technical schools or failing to establish a technical school and starting technical streams in grammar, modern or comprehensive schools.

The decline in the number of secondary technical schools contrasts strikingly with the growth of bilateral technical-modern and technical-grammar schools in the 1950s and the soaring expansion of comprehensive schools with technical streams. Moreover even where secondary technical schools survived they were almost encouraged to become surrogate grammar schools. For example it is surprising that consistently through the 1950s

TABLE 8.1 Secondary technical and other schools 1950–1962

	Bilateral			Multilateral	
	Secondary technical schools	Modern-technical	Grammar-technical	Multilateral	Comprehensive
1950	306	4	8	4	10
1953	297	15	10	3	11
1956	303	16	20	2	31
				bi and multilateral	
1959	269	no longer classified separately see column 4		58	111
1962	225			63	152

SOURCE: *Reports of the Ministry of Education*: 1950, PP 1950–1 X Cmd 8244; 1953, PP 1953–4 XI Cmnd 9155; 1956 PP 1956–7 X Cmnd 223; 1959 PP 1959–60 XII Cmnd 1088; 1962 PP 1962–3 XI Cmnd 1990.

1.2 to 1.9 per cent of the staff of secondary technical schools were teaching classics. It is not many, but it is amazing that they were there at all. More strikingly, 11 to 14 per cent of secondary technical staffs in the 1950s were teaching modern languages. Foreign languages were undoubtedly suitable for higher and export management but hardly for the technicians these schools were intended to produce. For that reason foreign language study had been specifically excluded from the curriculum of the junior technical schools before 1944. Also from 1951 there were consistently more teachers of English in these schools than of mathematics and science – in contrast to the 1940s. This was especially odd in schools which were supposed to be oriented to science and technology but which in the 1950s were beginning to take on more of the liberal characteristics of the grammar school. Too much so. This was increasingly evident in the after careers of secondary technical students. Between 1950 and 1959 both relatively and absolutely there was a decline of those going directly into jobs (from 15,948 to 12,120) and a sharp rise of those proceeding to higher education (from 19 to 229).

A curious paradox began to emerge from the mid-1950s under David Eccles and Lord Hailsham. Great emphasis was placed on higher technical education. The Colleges of Advanced Technology were created and it was planned to spend £70 million on a great expansion of technical education in the period 1956–61. Yet the secondary technical school was to be kept constrained. 'The general principle was followed that the proportion of 13 year olds in grammar and technical schools, taking existing and projected schools together should be between 15 and 25 per cent.'[25] From this point (i.e. 1955–6) an increasing enthusiasm for higher technological education was counter-matched by a diminished willingness to accord any important role to the secondary technical school.

It is now clear that the crucial internal debate about the secondary technical school took place in 1955 under Sir David Eccles as Minister of Education. He broached the question at the end of 1954, remarking 'I do not have a clear idea of the importance of these schools'.[26] He was puzzled at their tiny role in the overall structure, wondered at the justification of their separate existence and called for a thorough departmental discussion in the New Year. Eccles was still fairly open-minded, he did not know whether grammar schools should develop technical sides.[27] But he thought bilateral grammar-technical schools acceptable.

As the memoranda from civil servants were drafted, this proved to be the basic division of viewpoint. Sir Toby Weaver, the Assistant Secretary, feared that the separate education of young people as craftsmen would be too costly a development 'if it is bought at the price of the loss of the values summed up in the phrase "the humanities" '. Weaver queried 'cannot the answer be found in the liberalised and technological grammar school?'[28] A. R. Maxwell Hyslop held the same view. He was impressed that there was no reliable way of discerning technical aptitude for selection at 11 or 13 and favoured bilateral grammar-technical schools.[29] The strongest anti-technical school arguments came from his fellow civil servant D. H. Morrell. He argued that schools should be divided by *ability* levels and not by *aptitude* types and claimed that 'the secondary technical school, as at present conceived by its supporters is essentially an "aptitude" school. This seems to me fundamentally unsound.'[30] He then embarked on a logical path which seems to have impressed Eccles. If technical schools were supposed to attract ability with particular aptitudes then this is what the grammar schools already did. If the grammar school was not providing for technology then the remedy was to encourage it to do so, not to locate the technology elsewhere. The prestige of the grammar school and pure science would always attract the best but if the technical school did attract people of ability then it was undesirable to educate them 'divorced from the liberal tradition of the grammar school course'. He finished bluntly. The technical school was a 'side turning'; the main road was developing a wider range of courses in grammar schools.

The defence of the secondary technical was upheld by Sir Anthony Part, the Under Secretary, and HMI Bray. Part's argument was that combining technical studies in grammar schools was not likely to be successful since 'many of them are not very good at these things because though they do produce recruits for industry, their tradition is mainly in the field of arts studies and black coated jobs'.[31] He preferred 'more variety among selective schools'. Mr Bray was even more direct. The old junior technical schools had made boys 'industry minded', all their output had gone into industry, if they had gone to grammar schools they would have been diverted to other occupations.[32]

The minister held his meeting on 23 February 1955[33] and the foregoing arguments were rehearsed verbally by their proponents. Part spoke persuasively and secured agreement that existing secondary technical schools should be removed from technical colleges, have selective 11+ entry and develop sixth forms. But there was clearly no commitment that separate secondary technical schools should be expanded. The minister had come to a view inimical to this specialised form as he soon made clear in his crucial speech to the National Union of Teachers in the following April. 'There will be *rare* [my italics] cases where the local need is so strong as to call for a new technical school, but I hope the general policy will be to distribute technical courses over as many schools as possible.'[34]

In the early 1960s with Sir Edward Boyle as Minister for Education the secondary technical schools seemed to have vanished from government thinking and even from roles which were intended to be specifically theirs. In Boyle's view 'the schools are not sub-assembly lines processing material for industry' and 'the schools do not need to ape the technical colleges'.[35] It was notable that while 120 Technical Colleges were praised for running pre-apprenticeship colleges there was no suggestion that this was exactly what secondary technical schools should have been doing or that they had a role to play in the whole apprentice and pre-apprentice training issue which was an object of attention at that time.[36] So diminished had the technical schools become that when an American scholar inquired about them he received the following admission of brutal frankness from the Ministry: 'it is therefore now pretty clear that not only do technical schools not yet enter into the picture in most cases but that they never will'.[37]

The pity was that the secondary technical schools had a special ethos disposed towards industry which the grammar school did not have. Indeed there was the fear that technically minded boys in grammar schools would be diverted into pure science and the professions whereas 'in the technical schools the boys are directed towards industry'.[38] Moreover secondary technical schools were linked with technical colleges which in turn had the direct links with local industry and firms which grammar schools did not. Merely debasing secondary technical schools to technical streams in grammar schools 'is likely to result in such technical streams being technical only in name' for 'the two atmospheres cannot properly be developed side by side in the same institution'. It became evident, almost too late, that secondary technical school pupils did indeed have an ethos different from grammar schools and in some ways more oriented to work and industry. For example, Thelma Veness found that when boys from different schools wrote imaginary future life stories, three-quarters of technical school boys wrote accounts in which work was the dominant theme, compared with 41 per cent of secondary modern and 44 per cent of grammar school boys. Secondary technical boys were more work-minded, regarded themselves as already starting their careers, nearly two-thirds regarded ambition as a good thing, thought work was the way to get on and looked forward to National Service as a rewarding experience. Here was a reservoir of keenness, positive attitudes oriented towards industry which the nation, to its cost, under-valued in the 1950s and 1960s and allowed to be dissipated.

The secondary technical schools were ultimately vanquished by being absorbed into the comprehensive schools of the 1960s. The motives behind comprehensivisation were predominantly those of social justice. There was the concern that the operation of the 1944 Educational Act and the supposed opening up of the grammar school by the abolition of fees had not greatly raised the chances of working-class children going there.[39] It was shown how far success in passing the 11+ examination to the grammar school was due not to innate intelligence but to family and parental support and background.[40] There was also a good deal of concern over the fairness of the 11+ examination as a mode of selection with its English component which favoured the lan-guage fluency of the middle classes against the 'restricted codes' of working-class speech. It also aroused suspicions that grammar school provision varied very widely throughout the country (from 18 per cent in the south to 35 per cent in Wales). Yet in each area and town exactly the right percentage of children in every place in every year happened to 'pass' the 11+ at the right level to fill the available grammar school places however few or many![41] Finally the ultimate justification of the comprehensive schools was that they rather than nationalisation or taxation were the gateway to social equality and socialism.[42] The pro-pounder of this view of the future of socialism, Anthony Cros-land, became the Minister of State for Education who set national comprehensivisation in train in 1965. Junior and secon-dary technical schools whose origins and existence had been justified on industrial grounds were to be swallowed up by grammar and comprehensive schools justified on grounds of social justice, equality and expanding opportunities.

The failure of the secondary technical school has had serious knock-on effects in the neglect of training for non-academic late teenagers. This is now increasingly recognised as one of the most serious deficiencies of the English system and a major cause of the skill shortage which weakens British industry even in times of unemployment. Several surveys in recent years indicate this. For example in 1976 Britain had only 5.7 per cent of 18 year olds in non-higher technical and vocational training compared with 51.8 per cent in Germany, 48.9 per cent in Switzerland, 30.3 per cent in Denmark, and 6.7 per cent in France at various dates in the late 1970s.[43] In the early 1980s Britain had 65 per cent of 16–18 year olds in some form of education and training compared with 85 per cent in Germany, 73 per cent in Japan and 66 per cent in France.[44] Finally John MacGregor, when Secretary of State for Education recently pointed out (1990) that in Britain 90 per cent of 16 year olds are involved in education and training which compares well with a comparable figure for Germany of 96 per cent. Yet the British figures decline sharply to 68 per cent of 17 year olds and 35 per cent of 18 year olds. By contrast the comparable German figures are sustained – 92 per cent of 17 year olds and 80 per cent of 18 year olds.[45] The secondary modern and comprehensive schools did not produce generations of post-school leaving age pupils eager for and capable of further training and education. The secondary technical schools already orienting their pupils to vocational training would certainly have done better. There is now much awareness of this issue,[46] but for most of the post-war years this has been a major area where education for industrial need has been neglected. In consequence the British workforce, in the harsh judgement of Sir Bryan Nicholson of the Manpower Services Commission, has become 'a bunch of thickies'.[47]

II

The expansion of the new universities in the 1960s was another area where interests of social justice predominated over the needs of industry. The social justice reasons were plain enough. There was the trend to staying on in the sixth forms, whose pupils rose from 32,000 to 53,000 between 1947 and 1958.[48] This 'trend' was achieved by a generation whose birth rate was falling in the 1930s. But behind them and exacerbating the problem rolled the birth bulge cohorts born in the aftermath of war.[49] Accordingly the number of 18 year olds rose swiftly from 533,000 in 1959 to a peak of 812,000 in 1965. As the effects of the bulge were added to the trend in the 1960s so in 1961 only 4 per cent of the university entrance group were admitted, although 6.9 per cent obtained entrance qualifications. If nothing were done then, Lord Robbins considered, by 1967 some 25,000 youngsters would be annually denied a university education which they merited and from which they could benefit.[50]

Problems of equity were also evident in the disparities between the social class chances of getting to university. One study suggested that 14 per cent of children born to professional and managerial families in the late 1930s got to university but only 0.5 per cent of children born to fathers in semi- and unskilled occupations.[51] Robbins found that a third of children born to professional and managerial fathers in 1940 were admitted to university but only 1 per cent of semi- and unskilled workers.[52] The working classes had increased markedly their proportion of going to grammar schools in the twentieth century (from 1–4 per cent pre-1914 to 12–15 per cent by the 1950s). It seemed inequitable that this improvement in access to the grammar school had not been followed by a commensurate increase in chances of university entrance. Robbins hoped to close this gap.

The equity motives for the expansion of higher education were plain and statistically incontrovertible. So too were the industrial and economic motives. The 1960s was a period of concern over Britain's slow comparative growth since the war. Its 2.5 per cent per annum growth of GDP was the lowest in Europe and its 2.4 per cent per annum growth of productivity the second lowest.[53] Low economic growth was seen as related to low levels of educational provision with England's 2 per cent GNP growth relating to its 20 university students per 1000 primary school students at the bottom of a league table led by Germany and Japan.[54] Robbins hoped that industrial growth could be served by raising student intake levels from around 4 to around 7 per cent[55] (French levels) and by increasing the output of technology as opposed to science degrees. Industry, through the Federation (now Confederation) of British Industry, supported Robbins enthusiastically on industrial grounds.[56]

If the equitable and economic motives were closely interwoven in the expansion of higher education yet its implementation reflected more of the former than the latter. Six new English universities were created: Sussex, Kent, East Anglia, Warwick,

York and Lancaster. Stirling and Ulster completed the picture. Most were in cathedral cities, on greenfield sites outside the cities and distant from centres of industry. The striking exception was Warwick, sited near Coventry and closely involved with industry.[57] This has proved to be arguably the most successful of the new universities, with six centres of international excellence including several of direct relevance to industry – mathematics, computing, engineering and business management.[58] Yet most new universities, especially in the early days, built heavily on the humanities and social studies. The same would be true of the Open University (1969) an imaginative and successful enterprise in teaching by radio, television and summer schools.[59] A commentator of the time noted that 'it is a paradox that whereas the talk of politicians was need for technologists and applied scientists the new universities devoted so much of their resources to the arts and social sciences'.[60] Nearly a third (29 per cent) of science departments of the new universities had no contact with industry by 1970 and only 20 per cent of their research students wished to take PhDs in conjunction with industry.[61]

Interlocking reasons lay behind the discrepancy between the rhetoric about education for industry and the neglect of science and technology. It was the national duty of the new universities to expand rapidly to absorb this potential shortfall to which Robbins had drawn attention. Moreover they wanted to continue to grow quickly to maintain the momentum of public attention as they competed among themselves for a high profile image. Yet it was evident that expansion on this scale (113,143 students in 1961 to 200,121 by 1967) could only be achieved without astronomic cost if the cheaper arts and social studies were encouraged rather than science and technology. For example in 1969 total educational expenditure, recurrent and capital per undergraduate, varied widely over subject areas from £1976 for social studies and £2339 for arts to £3350 for science and £4240 for engineering.[62] To maximise the number of students at minimal cost entailed expanding the cheaper subjects irrespective of the ultimate best interests of the economy. In addition this tactical decision was further dictated by student demand. In the 1950s there had been a swing towards science in the subject preferences of sixth formers.[63] However, in the 1960s the swing moved away from the sciences to social studies. This may reflect the decline in quality of science teaching in the schools as teachers' salaries were kept uncompetitive with those in industry whose demand for science graduates was strong from the 1950s. Accordingly the new universities had to seek their intakes from a generation of students with markedly different academic intentions from their predecessors. In these circumstances the new universities understandably trawled the rich shoals of arts and social studies sixth formers, especially since they knew that incomes could be expanded or contracted according to their capacity to attract students.

The Vice Chancellor of a technological university who had suffered cuts by trying to recruit scientists and engineers rightly deplored the situation.

> To allow the mutable preferences of sixth formers to determine the areas of higher education in which the nation will invest its resources is an abrogation of responsibility which will only encourage a greater swing away from science and technology than the present one.[64]

There was a clash here between higher education for technology and industry and expansion as an act of social justice in which the latter predominated.

It might be argued that the paths taken by the new universities were not damaging because alongside them were the so-called 'technological universities'. The technological universities (Aston, Bath, Bradford, Brunel, City, Loughborough, Salford, Surrey, Strathclyde and Heriot Watt) were created in 1966 and 1967 from Colleges of Advanced Technology which in turn had been formed in 1956 from select leading technical colleges. Many had roots in Victorian technical institutions and mechanics' institutes and were heirs to a noble tradition. But their dilemma was how far to cleave to this tradition and how far to relinquish it and become more like other universities with a wide humanities spread. In practice the technological universities drifted away from their prime commitment to industry and technology.

Various factors lay behind this. The technological universities were in the position of wanting to expand to serve industry but being committed to areas where there was insufficient student demand. For example in 1969 more than 1500 university places remained unfilled but these were chiefly in science and engineering.[65] Even the prestigious UMIST had 20 per cent of places unfilled in 1964, filled only a quarter of their course on machine tool engineering in 1965 and still had empty places in 1967, the peak of the bulge.[66] Such were the pressures and disappoint-

TABLE 8.2   Proposed and actual subject spread of technological
            universities, 1963, 1974

	Recommended by principals of CATS to Robbins	Actual spread 1974
Technology	65	43
Science	15	24.6
Social Science	10	19.6
Arts	10	12.8

SOURCE: Sir Peter Venables, *Higher Education Developments: the Technological Universities* (London, 1978) p. 295.

ments inducing technological institutions to fill their places in less industrially relevant subject areas. The technological universities, no less than others, experienced a sharp increase in applications for places in the social studies and a decline in the natural sciences and technology.[67] University Grants Committee grants forced the technological universities to go for growth irrespective of subject. A distinguished technological university Vice Chancellor, Sir Peter Venables of Aston, deplored that:

this inevitably reinforced the persistent swing away from science and technology which was a very disturbing, not to say threatening, factor in the developing programme of the Technological Universities: and this just at a time when national needs required a positive campaign to increase substantially the quantity and quality of students taking up science and technology.[68]

As more social and arts students were admitted so were more lecturers in the same subjects, which had further knock-on effects. Whereas a half of lecturers appointed before August 1956 had had industrial experience this fell to only 35 per cent appointed after August 1966. The newer non-science lecturers were less keen on maintaining a distinctively technological identity for their universities and were intent on throwing off their CAT origins and becoming more like orthodox universities with their high arts and pure science components. Symbolically, Bath dropped the designation 'University of Technology' from its title in 1971.

The technological universities have been diverted from their true purpose. Accordingly (in 1989) we have eight supposedly technological universities that in the latest Universities Funding Council survey of research performance can apparently muster only one excellent department between them (Pharmacy at Aston) but with 14 poorly rated departments. Of most concern is the fact that of the poorly rated departments in technological universities two each are in civil engineering, chemical engineering, electrical engineering and chemistry, and one each in physics and computing – the very subjects in which technological universities should be claiming and achieving excellence.[69] If more attention and resources had been devoted to their traditional technical college subjects and less to the arts and social studies then their overall performance in their distinctive sphere would have been better. As it is their achievement is considerably inferior to that of the new universities (with twelve excellent and only four poorly rated departments), let alone the civics.

III

The polytechnics were another area where the pursuit of growth and diversity led to a diversification of purpose away from their prime concerns of science and industry. The polytechnics were technical colleges of the level below those designated as CATs and Technological Universities. It was made clear by Anthony Crosland in his speeches at Woolwich in 1965 and Lancaster in 1967 that this next tranche of colleges would not be elevated to university status but would remain a local authority controlled part of a binary system of higher education. Their distinctive role was to be technology in the service of industry. Yet the polytechnics began a 'policy drift' away from their technical and scientific purposes, expanding by seeking more students in the arts and social studies. An early influential enthusiast for polytechnics noted as early as 1968 that there had been a 'phenomenal growth' of courses in the arts and social studies. Five years before (1963) 'the volume of degree work in these fields was negligible. Several colleges now have over 500 degree students in these subjects whereas they had few or none at all five years ago.' He added artlessly that all this 'has not been the result of any deliberate policy decision taken anywhere'.[70]

The drift over the 1960s and 70s was evident as Table 8.3 demonstrates. The relative commitment of polytechnics to their traditional science and technology diminished and that to social

TABLE 8.3   Subject spread of students in polytechnics 1965/6–1978/9

	Engineering & technology (%)	Science (%)	Social admin. & business (%)	Language & literature (%)	Arts (%)
1965–6	43.9	14	26	0.6	1.6
1968–9	32.8	13.2	34.2	0.9	1.5
1974	20.4	17.4	36.9	15.0	
1978–9		33.9	30.4	20.0	

SOURCE: For 1965–6, 1968–9, J. Pratt and T. Burgess, *Polytechnics, a Report* (London, 1977) p. 77. For 1974 Sir Peter Venables, *Higher Education Developments: the Technological Universities* (London, 1978) p. 231. For 1978–9 Alan Matterson, *Polytechnics and Colleges* (London, 1981) p. 67.

and arts studies increased. A. H. Halsey has recently observed that while pure science dominates university studies 'the comparable giant of the polytechnics is social science, including administration and business studies (31 per cent)' because 'the social sciences offered the cheapest form of growth'.[71]

The reasons for this shift were various. In 1965 the Council for National Academic Awards (CNAA) established its Arts and Social Science Committee to validate polytechnic degrees in these subjects. CNAA-validated students (almost all of whom were in polytechnics) soared with the same relative decline of science and rise of arts. Also there was a strong demand for places in sociology which far exceeded those supplied in universities in the 1960s. Polytechnics found that in this subject they could obtain passable results with students whose GCE grades were 'below normal' with 'inexperienced staff' in 'inadequate facilities'.[72] It was also easier to attract students with respectable A levels in social and arts subjects than in engineering, technology and science. Nearly half of engineering and science students had very low scores (0–3) and nearly half of social and arts

TABLE 8.4   CNAA-validated students 1965/6, 1973/4

	Science & technology	Arts & social studies	Total
1965–6	3,944 (97%)	129 (3%)	4,073
1973–4	23,843 (58%)	16,166 (40%)	40,162

SOURCE: Julia Whitburn, Maurice Mealing and Caroline Cox, *People in Polytechnics* (SRHE, Guildford, 1976) p. 149.

students had high scores (7–9+).[73] The polytechnics well understood that they could not secure large expansion by relying on school leavers with good science A levels. The decline of science teaching in state schools was hardly providing sufficient science undergraduates for universities, let alone polytechnics. There was also an element of power-seeking empire building in this quest for expansion. Polytechnic directors and staff could hope that a large fast-growing poly with an arts spread might even be designated as a university with all the expectations of enhanced salary scales, 'professorial' titles and so forth. As the Vice Chancellor of a technological university noted candidly of the polytechnics: 'given a choice between status, especially social status and relevance, for example industrial and economic relevance, status wins every time'.[74] This revealingly suggests the low status of technology which underlies the dilemma of choice just referred to and is a deep seated cultural factor in the whole theme of this chapter. Local authorities who controlled the polytechnics also welcomed expansion. A technical college merely teaching local youths brought no additional revenue to the town. But a large polytechnic with non-locals living in residences and spending in the shops not only brought prestige but swelled the trade of the city. Finally the government accepted this development because it enabled them to point to the general expansion of 'higher education' to mask the cuts imposed on the universities in the 1980s. Government could also hold up the polytechnics as an example to the universities of how to produce arts graduates cheaply. All these interlocking interests – school leavers with low A levels seeking degrees, CNAA seeking more degrees to validate, polytechnics hoping to enhance size and status, local authorities seeking revenue and central government welcoming a cheap demonstration effect – played their part in the drift of the polytechnics from science to the arts. The expansionist interests of many groups were served rather than the industrial needs of the nation. Even worse, there is evidence that in some institutions – the Polytechnic of North London and the Hornsey School of Art (part of Middlesex Polytechnic) – the increasing involvement with social or general studies was an element in profound disruptions and unrest around 1970.[75]

The general trend of movement to the arts and social studies can be exemplified in the cases of specific institutions. Enfield College in 1962/3 had 340 students, all of whom were studying technology. It then embarked on a decade of 'restless, determined, insatiable growth' which took the form of a rapid expansion of social studies and arts courses. By 1970 it had 952 of these non-scientists and still only 380 in technology.[76] Enfield is now part of Middlesex Polytechnic, 80 per cent of whose students are on arts rather than science based courses. Oxford Polytechnic shows a similar transition.[77] When it was a College of Technology in 1954 it provided a good range of vocational technology courses. It was designated a polytechnic in 1970 and student numbers nearly tripled over the decade from 1387 to 3573. Yet the Faculty of Technology fell from 26 to 20 per cent of the total. A 'modular course', 'designed to accommodate other fields of study and not to be limited to the sciences', took half the students and in 1977 a department of humanities was created, taking pride in work on Milton's sonnets and old Japanese history! Yet again massive expansion was achieved by a relative decline in the role of technology and a shift into areas unrelated to industry.

The latest official survey of polytechnics puts their position succinctly. In the eight years 1981–9 the students at polytechnics have increased by 74 per cent. Yet this expansion has only been achieved by a fall in costs per student (from £3800 to £3150 in real terms). This has resulted in a serious lack of equipment – 'the lack of up to date equipment which reflects modern industrial practice is impairing the students' experience ... much of that which is in use is obsolete' – and half the polytechnics have poor computing provision.[78] Large expansion and increased opportunities of access have been bought by overcrowding, reduced unit costs and an accepted deterioration of those very facilities of most relevance in preparing students for industry. Moreover the polytechnics' drift into the non-vocational arts has not met with market credibility. Unemployment rates for polytechnic graduates in such subjects are twice those of university graduates.[79]

While criticisms may be levelled at some of the policies of the technological universities and polytechnics yet certain factors mitigate these. Firstly we have stressed already that all institutions of higher education have been impeded in their development of science and technology by the restricted provision of such students by secondary schools. This reflected difficulties of science teaching and teachers' poor salaries in schools. Secondly the polytechnics (and the Open University especially) have performed valuable service in catering for women and mature students who found personal satisfaction in education which did not include aspirations to a career in industry. Thirdly it could be argued that the 1960s intentions that technological universities and polytechnics should concentrate on science and technology for industry were wrong-footed by the reversal in industry's fortunes in the 1970s and especially the early 1980s. The industrial unemployment of those years may have swayed the institutions and their students away from studies designed to cater for this shrinking market. Fourthly these institutions may also have been confused by the lack of clear demand from industry for graduates with specifically scientific or technological qualifications. Industry required lawyers, economists, accountants, and linguists as well as scientists and the universities and polytechnics provided these with obvious justification. Yet it seems more difficult to justify these industrially oriented institutions producing philosophers, historians, political scientists and literary critics. One possible justification has been the fact that British industry has traditionally liked the 'educated amateur'. This is in contrast to our American, German, French and Japanese competitors who prefer trained managers with professional qualifications and degrees closely relevant to their industrial careers. The poor performance of British industry in comparison with these competitors suggests, as does Shirley Keeble, that this recruitment policy was wrong.[80] The polytechnics' and technological universities' involvement in liberal arts education might have been exonerated if they had been meeting what industry required and if industry had flourished accordingly. British industry's present poor competitive position suggests otherwise.

The polytechnics faced their own dilemma within the broad one. They could seek parity with the universities in either of two ways. They could move into the territory of the universities, duplicating their activities in the humanities but as cheaper substitutes.[81] Or they could try to create a smaller but distinctly technological sector more like the German Technical High Schools,[82] building on their technical college foundations without spreading sideways into the liberal education humanities. It was the former strategy of spread which was chosen for it seemed as if polytechnics did not really believe it possible to create a credible, prestigious sector of higher education in England based on technology alone. To an extent the problems were interlocking. Lord Percy in the 1930s had hoped to see the development of technical schools for children leading to higher technological education on a par with universities. The failure to develop the school stratum contributed to the lack of flow of students with technical aptitudes into technological universities and polytechnics. It reinforced their drift into the humanities in the search for growth. Both were victims of the excessive English reverence for a humanities based liberal education and a reciprocal disparagement for the technical and vocational.[83]

They may also have been reflecting a change in the very meaning of 'technical education' in this time. From Victorian times through to the 1930s technical education was seen rather specifically as the education appropriate for artisans and directly relevant for industrial occupations. Yet since 1945 and especially in the 1950s something broader or more liberal was favoured as a more general education for those in industrial and commercial occupations or even as an education for all in a technological age.[84] For example, the Ministry of Education in 1959 observed officially that 'the new concept is that the technical colleges are first and foremost centres of continued education, not of narrow vocational education'.[85] This explains something of the cool view of secondary technical schools held by David Eccles and Edward Boyle and which set the tone for policy drift in the CATs and future polytechnics. But the rather denigrating undervaluing of vocational education was dangerous for industry and articulated a value system Britain is now urgently trying to reverse.

There is an increasing recognition of the dichotomy which we posed at the outset. Already in the late 1950s Lord Percy was deploring that the demand for 'equality of opportunity' in education had become in 'many minds ... a very crude form of idolatry' while over-reliance on the Welfare State had a 'dangerous tendency ... to breed a rather sickly distaste for "vocational" education'.[86] Eric Robinson, writing in the 1960s, admitted that 'our priorities in its [education's] development are argued in terms of social justice rather than economic return'.[87] Retrospectively Lady Warnock has noted that by the 1960s arguments about education 'were almost entirely concerned with the structure of the system' while teachers 'rejected absolutely the idea that education should be directed towards any service or economic end'.[88] Likewise Jean Floud, one of the most influential educational sociologists of the post-war years, considers that in the 1950s and 1960s they were more interested in the structure of the education system than in the content of its parts.[89]

In the 1980s there was a shift in recent policies over to

favouring the 'industrial need' side of the dilemma. The Education for Capability Committee,[90] the influential (if academically controversial) writings of Martin Wiener and Corelli Barnett and the Finniston Report have all emphasised the need for a greater concern for education for industry as an urgent necessity. Recent reforms seek to address the problem. The national curriculum will enforce the study of science and technology with benchmark standards. Differential salaries will provide the opportunity for higher pay for science and technology teachers at the expense of their arts colleagues. The City Technology Colleges, it is hoped, will revive in a modern form the abandoned tradition of the junior and secondary technical schools. The independent, non-LEA, status of the CTCs expresses implied displeasure with the LEAs which had failed to develop the technical school side of the Butler tripartite triangle and allowed the polytechnics to drift away from technology.

The preference for considerations of social equity over the needs of industry has contributed to Britain's present predicament. Our underemphasis on genuine technical training (as opposed to arts, pure science or social and 'business studies') underlies Britain's chronic and acute shortage of skilled labour even in times of high unemployment. The lack of skill handicaps industry's capacity to deliver goods the British consumer wishes to buy and contributes to an influx of foreign imports and to our massive balance of payments deficits (1989, 1990). This leads to pressure on the pound and consequent inflationary pressures, as do the high wage settlements necessary as firms poach (rather than train) the short supply of skilled labour. The curbing of this inflation is a prime priority and the restriction of public expenditure a key mechanism. The consequent inability to invest sufficiently in education and training and the strict incomes policy on teachers' pay have lead to actual shortages of teachers in the state sector, especially in technical areas. The inadequacy of technical education and the skill shortage continue and no market mechanism operates to break this vicious circle.

What is argued here is that that stream of education of technical school leading to genuine technological university which Eustace Percy had advocated in the 1930s did not develop in England after 1945. There have of course been notable achievements in English education in this period – the ladder of opportunity provided by the grammar schools for the meritocrat, the eradication of the unfairness in this by the comprehensives, the colossal efforts of the new universities in absorbing the Robbins shortfall in the 1960s, the expansion of the independent schools catering for new cohorts of the enriched middle classes. Yet the achievements have been chiefly in the fields of expanding and equalising opportunities rather than in the generation of productive knowledge and specialised skills for industry. Professor Aldcroft reminds us that the total resources devoted to education are not out of line with other industrial countries[91] but it is rather the direction in which the resources have been put. The over-concern with expanding numbers and opportunities has forced us into the cheaper alternatives of the humanities and away from more expensive but industrially relevant technological education. There have been too many Jim Dixons, Howard Kirks and Robyn Penroses, and too few Vic Wilcoxes, both in fact and in fiction.[92]

9. Towards Equal Opportunities? Women in Britain since 1945

PAT THANE

In the period between the end of the Second World War and the implementation of equal pay and equal opportunities legislation in the 1980s, the issue of equal pay for women with men and the, associated, wider questions of equal opportunities never wholly disappeared from public discussion, although they were certainly more prominent at certain times than at others. Discussion of these issues unavoidably touched upon, and for the historian provided evidence about, some of the main themes in women's lives. First of all, there was the relationship between domestic life and work in the paid labour market, experiences at home and in the paid workplace, and the processes of socialisation which shaped them. Second, there were the attitudes of women towards these experiences, attitudes which have varied over time, and which have sometimes been expressed in terms of a conscious feminism. Finally, there were the attitudes of men towards women, which were particularly important when the men concerned exercised influence over women, for example as husbands or employers. Hence the issue of equal pay provides a framework within which important themes in the changing and varied histories of British women over almost half a century can be discussed with some attempt at coherence.

I

In March 1944 the House of Commons voted narrowly for an amendment to the great Education Bill, to grant equal pay to schoolteachers. It was initiated by the Tory Reform Group and introduced by the Conservative MP Thelma Cazalet Keir. It followed pressure from the beginning of the century for equal pay in the public sector, which had taken on new vigour during the war. Cazalet Keir was supported by men of all parties and no member opposed the principle of equal pay. The amendment passed by 117 to 116 votes. On the following day the Prime Minister insisted that the House must delete the amendment. He demanded that this should be treated as a vote of confidence in the government and he threatened to call an election if it were lost. To the plea of Labour MP Emanuel Shinwell that equal pay for teachers posed little obvious threat to the war effort and that the House, which manifestly wholly supported the war, had amended other government measures without giving evident comfort to the enemy, Churchill responded:

> It is really impossible to distinguish between votes on domestic policy and votes on the general policy of the war, in this country [HON. MEMBERS: 'Nonsense']

After vigorous protests about the principle involved the House deleted the amendment.

Why the Prime Minister was prepared to interrupt his preparations for D-day and, in the midst of London's heaviest bombing of the war, trouble to prevent teachers receiving equal pay remains a mystery. The incident suggests the degree of feeling on both sides of the issue, and also the ambiguity of attitudes towards women at the end of the war: the strong inclinations both for and against change.[1] Indeed support for equal pay was so strong that Churchill was shortly forced to establish a Royal Commission on Equal Pay. Its main outcome was to illustrate these ambiguities more exhaustively.

II

Though the equal pay issue had simmered, gently, since the later nineteenth century it took on new urgency during the war. Craft unions in occupations which women entered in large numbers – notably engineering where 1 in 3 workers were female by 1943 – came to support equal pay, though for less than feminist reasons. They regarded women as guardians of the jobs of skilled men absent in the services. They feared – with reason – that employers would repeat their efforts of the previous war to modify and redesignate as less skilled jobs assigned to women in order to attach to them permanently lower pay-rates. The unions' defence against such moves was to limit the employer's room for manoeuvre by demanding, not always successfully, equal pay for men and women.

Women often shared the view that they were temporary workers. This did not necessarily mean that they willingly put up with lower pay and poor conditions. Not surprisingly many of them took seriously union assertions that they deserved equal pay. There were persistent strikes among women in engineering during the war. Surveys by the research agency Mass Observation uncovered evidence of discontent about low wages. In 1943 H. A. Emmerson, Bevin's right-hand man at the Ministry of Labour, reported that disputes relating to women's wages were 'proportionately more prone to result in strike action than where men are concerned'.[2] Male workers might support such strikes but they received at best reluctant support from the craft unions. After longer and stronger campaigns from the beginning of the century, women in white-collar public sector occupations had won support from their unions. Hence the 1944 amendment occurred against a background of active, if not overwhelming, discontent about women's conditions of work. There were indications that equal pay was an important issue for many women and had popular support. A British Institute of Public Opinion survey of 1940 claimed that 68 per cent of the population favoured 'equal pay for the same work'.[3] The reversal of the Commons vote led to protests from women which forced the government to establish the Royal Commission. However, unusually for such a body, it was not empowered to make recommendations; its role was just to investigate and to report on its findings.

The Report was issued in 1946. It provided a comprehensive description of the grossly unequal position of women in the labour market and of the attitudes of the major interest groups involved. It acknowledged the problem of defining 'equal pay'. 'Equal pay for equal work' evaded the problem that most of the labour market was strictly divided by gender. There was a general tendency for male jobs to be more highly paid than female and it was difficult to ascertain whether these pay differentials were due to the genuinely higher skill or responsibility content of male tasks or to discrimination leading to unequal pay for men and women doing work which in fact required comparable levels of skill or responsibility. One thing that stood out from the study was a clear difference between the position in the white-blouse public sector – chiefly the civil service, local government and teaching – and that in most other forms of employment. In the former occupations women were active advocates of equal pay, they were strongly unionised and their unions were mostly supportive of equal pay even when, as in the case of the civil service unions, they had majority male membership. In these occupations men and women most evidently did identical work for different rates of pay. Pay rates were clearly established on incremental and promotional scales so that differentials were quite clear. Also women formed large groupings in all of them, many of them evidently talented and working below their capacity due to limited alternative opportunities.

The Commission found that the precise relationship between male and female pay varied from occupation to occupation and from place to place according to no discernible rationale. In the civil service at the lowest levels men and women normally entered on the same minimum rates, but diverged during their twenties. Generally in the public sector differentials averaged 50 per cent at the bottom levels, 10 per cent for the few women at the top. For the problem was not simply one of pay, but of unequal recruitment and promotion. This inequality had been reinforced by the operation of the 'marriage bar', which obliged most women to leave these occupations on marriage. This had been removed in teaching, where it had been long resisted and often disregarded, by the 1944 Act and was ended in other public sector occupations at the end of the war. In a number of professional occupations, such as university teaching, the BBC, architecture, medicine and as Members of Parliament women formally had equal pay. However, in 1946 just 7198 medical practitioners out of 44,341 were female; 325 out of 9375 architects; and about 164 out of 17,102 solicitors.[4] Only 24 of 640 MPs elected in 1945 were female.

Representatives of management in local government and education expressed themselves strongly in favour of equal pay for equivalent work, generally with the proviso that it should be accompanied by an adequate scheme of family allowances. This was widely seen as the answer to the most frequent defence of unequal pay, that many more men than women supported dependants. Broadly, this was true. But it was also the case that many male workers had no dependants, while a significant number of women did, and also that male pay was not normally adjusted to take account of family size. Family allowances of 5s (25p) per week for the second and subsequent children were introduced while the Royal Commission was sitting. Welcome though they were to very many families as being better than nothing, their low level was widely criticized.[5] The representatives of the Treasury, on the other hand, insisted that the economy could not bear a costly pay increase for female civil servants and they held out no hope that an adequate system of family allowances could be paid in conjunction with equal pay. The Council of Women Civil Servants, representing women in the top grades of the service, wondered why the Treasury's concern for economy and for rational behaviour did not lead them to employ women exclusively.

Most women in paid work, however, were in the private sector, divided in roughly equal proportions among, first white-collar secretarial and clerical work, secondly retailing and similar services, and thirdly manufacturing. The stricter gender division of labour, the smaller scale of many operations, and the complex and often individual forms of pay negotiations, systems of payment and gradings (especially in industry) made the situation in the private sector hard to understand. They also made solutions to the clear gender division in pay and promotion less clear cut, while in many sectors, women were less disposed or less able to organise. According to the Ministry of Labour in January 1945 the average earnings of women in industry were 53 per cent of those of men. The Royal Commission's careful enquiry found that such averages were influenced by the much lower average age of female workers and disguised a great variety of earnings of women even when they were working at similar tasks within the same industry. One reason was that married women in particular had a tendency 'to come a bit late and go a bit early'[6] due to family responsibilities, which reduced their piece rate earnings; but local variations in earnings were harder to explain. The Commission concluded that in engineering and clothing (two major employers of female labour, employing about 1 million and 309,000 respectively in the UK in 1945), men and women were receiving, on piece rates, 'widely unequal sums for doing equal amounts of work so closely similar that it would commonly be described as identical'.[7]

The Commission's task was not assisted by contradictory assertions from employers and unions. The British Employers

Confederation (BEC) and other representatives of private sector employers almost unanimously stated that they were wholly in favour of equal pay – in those circumstances in which males and females did precisely equal work. But, they pointed out, unfortunately this was rarely the case. There were, they believed, excellent reasons for the gender division of labour which placed women generally in the lower status, less skilled, lesser paid occupations: men were more efficient, more flexible, more ambitious, took less time off, were physically stronger, less tolerant of monotous work, had a longer time commitment to a career and hence were worth the investment of training (which women, in any case, were said to be reluctant to undergo), needed higher pay in order to support their dependants and were better able to manage other men. The employers' representatives proved unable to provide evidence to support these assertions. They evaded suggestions from the Commission that women in wartime had been as productive as men and that heavy work could be adapted to women's capacities. They blamed the unions for restricting female access to higher pay and promotion. Furthermore, they argued that to raise women's wages would harm exports by leading to higher prices. They explicitly opposed the concept of equal pay for equivalent work, and showed no spontaneous awareness of the possible long-term consequences for the economy of the poor training and incentives available to most women.

The TUC based its statements to the Commission on responses to a questionnaire sent to all affiliated organisations. It too asserted support for equal pay, but only for 'equivalent' work, insisting that its restriction to 'equal' work would seriously limit the area of potential equalisation. It and representatives of the Amalgamated Engineering Union also asserted the need to improve women's limited access to training. They insisted that there was greater similarity in the work performed in private industry by males and females than employers were prepared to admit. This was because employers had long sought to create dissimilarity and to exaggerate its significance in order to maximise the use of cheap female (or when it was available cheaper less skilled male) labour and to reduce wage rates overall. They had not always been free, and they had not always desired, to do so. However, circumstances such as those in light engineering in the 1930s had been especially favourable because a number of sectors had undergone ɪapid change while being weakly unionised.[8] The two wars also had provided favourable environments for such attempts.

The union representatives did not deny that unions had in the past acted in a number of ways to preserve gender differentials. However, they no longer defended male demands for a 'family wage' now that wages had risen well above basic subsistence; and indeed they denied that it had ever played a major part in wage negotiation, as distinct from *post hoc* justification of differentials. They claimed that unions were now demanding the 'rate for the job', irrespective of gender. They recognised that even with equal rates of pay for equivalent work women would very often take home less pay than men, even when engaged in the same work, due predominantly to their disinclination or inability to work overtime and their tendency to work shorter hours. But women would at least acquire some choice in such matters. They implicitly recognised that this choice would be limited since they assumed that married women would continue to take primary responsibility for domestic matters. They stressed the need also to improve conditions of work in the home, recommending better housing conditions and social service support, to match improvement in one half of woman's double burden with the other. But however well intentioned the leaders of the trade union movement were on this issue they could not necessarily influence local bargaining. Whether all union leaders, or union members at other levels, shared these views is much more doubtful. The unions opposed legislation for equal pay, partly due to hostility to government intervention in any facet of wage bargaining. They argued that equal pay in the private sector should be achieved through greater unionisation of women, collective bargaining and a gradual process of evaluation to establish equivalence between male and female jobs.

The Commission also heard evidence from a range of women's organisations. These were strong in all public sector salaried occupations. Such surviving successors to the pre-1918 suffrage societies and inter-war feminist organisations as the London and National Society for Women's Service, the National Council of Women and the British Federation of Business and Professional Women, with the Fabian Women's Group, also gave evidence. The numbers of such organisations and their unequivocal statements of the inequalities experienced by women in all classes suggests the survival through the war, among some women at least, of a quest for a sexually just society. They were not wholly unanimous as to their goals or always willing to acknowledge the label of feminism, but there were large areas of agreement among them, as on the principle of equal pay for comparable work.

The Commission asked the advice of an array of medical specialists and psychologists and received a perfect spectrum of expressions of prejudice along with some useful information. Dr Sybil Horner, after 26 years as a Medical Inspector of Factories, argued that women needed higher pay in order to improve their poorer standards of health. Even more they needed rest: 'equal play with equal work'. From her experience and her official statistics she refuted some of the commoner complaints of employers about women workers: relatively few women were responsible for a very high proportion of 'absenteeism'; it was not the general female characteristic often assumed; indeed it was remarkably uncommon given the very long working day imposed by women's double load. Contrary to another popular assertion, menstruation, menopause and gynaecological disorders had very little effect upon the work of the great majority of women.[9] Dr Lane of Manchester University explained, however, that women's smaller skeleton rendered them incapable of heavy labour or 'sustained effort'. Menstruation and, still worse, the menopause, lowered efficiency. Men, he believed, suffered from less sickness because they were 'apt to regard their work in a more serious light'.[10] Ten economists gave a similar mass of contradictory advice.

In its final Report the Commission provided a comprehensive survey of most that could be discovered about the almost universally deplorable pay position of women. The commissioners concluded that in most cases the differentials between male and female rates of pay could not be explained in rational economic terms, i.e. as a reliable measure of higher male productivity. Rather they were products of a combination of the influence of 'assumptions drawn from the sociological background' with the effects of oversupply of female labour in the restricted range of occupations open to them. It was also important that the relative youth of most female workers brought down the average earnings of occupations in which they were employed in large numbers; also that most women did not remain in employment for long enough to acquire high levels of experience and promotion. The commissioners recognised that these factors were also products of social and cultural processes. They concluded that 'family wage' arguments had long ceased to play more than a small role in wage determination even if they had been important in the past. Decisions by employers influenced by pressures of supply and demand had a greater impact on wage rates than had trade union bargaining, although the latter, and the attitudes of the workforce, could constrain employer decision making. Once they had been established, social convention kept differentials in place.[11] They concluded that women's lesser physical strength currently debarred them from relatively few occupations, and many of the remainder could be so reorganised as to match their capacities.

The Commission put forward a strong argument in principle for equal pay for work of 'equal value', but they concluded that implementation in the near future would be harmful to the economy. Three of the four female members signed a minority report dissenting from the unwillingness of the Commission to make more positive recommendations. The Commission thus documented very fully the extent of gender inequality in the paid labour market and the reasons for it. The commissioners found 'No doubt in our minds about the extent and intensity of the present discontent' among women on the question, though it was stronger 'among women who look on their jobs as careers'. Nor did the evidence suggest to them that most men would resent equal pay.

III

Hence in 1946 there was a broad consensus that equal pay was desirable, but a range of definitions of its meaning. No one in a position of power was in any hurry to do anything about it. This included the Labour government, despite the fact that it was, reluctantly, committed by a vote of the annual party conference in 1944 to a policy of equal pay for equivalent work and that at the general election of 1945 a clear majority of women voters voted Labour.[12] At the same time Labour was anxious to keep women in the workforce. From 1943 the government had been aware of the likelihood of a post-war labour shortage and had started to plan to keep in the labour force as many as possible of the women who had entered it during the war. But as the war ended more women returned to the home than had been hoped. The 7.75 million women in paid work in June 1943 fell to 6 million in June 1947. From 1947 to 1949 the Ministry of Labour campaigned to persuade women to return to the labour market.[13]

Rather than being pushed from the post-war labour market, women left voluntarily. They did so overwhelmingly to start families, having delayed marriage or childbirth due to the war. The UK birth rate, having started to rise in 1942 from the historically low levels of the 1930s, was 16.1 per 1000 of the population in 1945, 19.1 in 1946, 20.7 in 1947. The closure of wartime day nurseries (which had always been intended to be temporary) despite the protests of many women, left most of them with little option but to give up work.[14] Many women indicated their intention to return to the workforce when their children were older.[15] Older women with completed families stayed in the workforce in significant numbers, whilst others re-entered it who had spent the war at home caring for small children.

Another theme of the post-war years was the fear that the birth rate would return to the low levels of the pre-war years, when anxiety about a dwindling and ageing population had been acute.[16] It soon became clear that the birth rate was maintaining higher levels after the war and, on the whole, the 1949 Report of the Royal Commission on Population – established in 1940 in response to the population panic – was reassuring. However, another relic of pre-war concerns, less easily dispelled, was concern about low levels of physical fitness in the population; to this was added a rising level of concern with psychological fitness. The psychoanalytic theories of Melanie Klein were popularised by D. W. Winnicott in radio broadcasts and publications (including a bestselling babycare handbook[17]) during and after the war, and by John Bowlby's widely disseminated studies of the psychological ill-effects of maternal deprivation in early childhood.[18] Although their prescriptions were derived from studies of the unusual condition of total maternal deprivation (e.g. of orphans living in institutions) and offered no clue as to how much or how little maternal care, of what kind, had measurably good or bad effects in more normal circumstances, they generated a remarkably pervasive climate of belief that well-adjusted people required to spend the bulk of their first five years in the company of their natural mothers.[19] Such intensive mothering was said to be the key to physical and mental fitness. In consequence health visitors, welfare clinics and baby manuals demanded exacting standards of mothers.

Hence mothers of pre-school children encountered both emotional and practical barriers to their combining motherhood with paid work. Also the government made it clear that it believed that they should remain in the home.[20] Rather the Ministry of Labour targeted its propaganda at women over 35. Wartime surveys had suggested the willingness of many women to return to work, at least part-time, as their children grew older.[21] Post-war inflation provided some incentive, though queues induced by shortages and the scarcity of such services as laundries to some degree pulled in the opposite direction. Nevertheless 1947 saw a net rise in the female workforce of 24,000 full-timers and 100,000 part-timers. The total numbers of working women in Great Britain grew by 300,000 in each of the following three years. By 1961 the total was 8.4 million, in 1981 8.7 million. The numbers recorded as working part-time are given in Table 9.1. They show a rise from 779,000 in 1951 to nearly 3.8 million by 1981. Recorded numbers continued to rise throughout the 1980s.[22]

TABLE 9.1   Female part-time workers, 1951–81

1951	779,000
1961	1,851,000
1971	2,757,000
1981	3,781,000

SOURCE: V. Beechey and Tessa Perkins, *A Matter of Hours. Women, Part-time Work and the Labour Market* (University of Minnesota Press, 1987), p. 24. (Derived from House of Lords Session 1981–2. 19th Report, table 1, p. ix, and *Employment Gazette*, December 1983, Census of Employment 1981.)

These numbers are, however, approximate. Following the 1981 census, official statisticians were convinced that the census under-recorded women's work, and especially part-time work, as it had long done. A comparison (in Table 9.2) of the census with other measures of employment suggests that this had been the case throughout the post-war period, and that, since each census collated slightly different information, the undercount was not consistent over time. More accurate figures derived from national insurance statistics still undercount women in casual jobs, such as domestic cleaning, who may evade national insurance contributions; in addition, there are members of the 'hidden workforce', who are employed in various forms of heavily exploited

TABLE 9.2   Census and departmental estimates of the working population, Great Britain 1951–1981 (millions)

	1951	1961	1966	1971	1981
	Employees in employment				
Females					
Census of Population	6.5	7.4	8.3	8.3	8.7
National Insurance					
(25% sample)	7.0	8.0	8.6	8.5	
Census of Employment[a]				8.2	9.1
Difference a	−0.5	−0.6	−0.3	−0.2	
b				0.1	−0.4
Males					
Census of Population	13.4	13.9	14.4	13.3	12.0
National Insurance					
(25% sample)	13.5	14.3	14.7	13.6	
Census of Employment				13.4	12.6
Difference a	−0.1	−0.4	−0.3	−0.3	
b				−0.1	−0.6
	Out of work				
Females					
Census of Population	.14	.19	.27	.44	.64
Register					
Wholly unemployed	.07	.08	.06	.08	
Claimants unemployed		.05	.04	.05	.62
Difference a	.07	.11	.21	.36	
b		.14	.20	.39	.02
Males					
Census of Population	.34	.49	.43	.85	1.57
Register					
Wholly unemployed	.15	.21	.22	.59	
Claimants unemployed		.16	.17	.48	1.59
Difference a	.19	.28	.21	.26	
b		.33	.26	.37	−.01

Census of Population adjusted for sampling bias, 1961 and 1966. 1981 employees include Armed Forces, all previous years Civilian only National Insurance, Employees and Registered Unemployment are averages for March and June. Differences calculated before rounding.

SOURCE: H. Joshi and S. Owen, *How Long is a Piece of Elastic? The Measurement of Female Activity Rates in British Censuses 1951–1981* (London: Centre for Economic Policy Research. Discussion Paper No. 31, 1984) p. 25.

NOTE
[a] Derived from interviews.

'outwork' for manufacturers in their own homes or by kin in small family businesses such as shops. Since the 1950s many female members of the growing ethnic minority populations have joined these latter categories.

Since pre-war statistics were at least as inadequate, it is unwise to argue, as is sometimes done, that more women became active in the paid labour market in the post-war period than earlier in the century. However, what was established after the war was a new life-cycle pattern for women, which has remained into the 1990s. In the inter-war years middle-class women had entered the labour market for the years between education and marriage and then overwhelmingly left it for good. Working-class women tended to take paid work after marriage whenever the household required it, which was most often when children were very young, and to withdraw when children became old enough to contribute to the household income. In the 1930s fewer such women were in paid work due to the combined effects of un-employment in the depressed areas and increased affluence elsewhere. In the 1930s compared with the 1920s more young women, mainly middle class, were in paid employment, compared with fewer women in age groups over 34.[23] From the late 1940s the numbers in the latter age group returning to paid work after a period of childrearing climbed, while most mothers took some years out of the paid labour market to care for children. A two-phase work pattern was established as the norm for most women.

In continuation of pre-war trends the overwhelming majority of women married; first marriages occurred at younger ages (between 20 and 24 for women) and at more uniform ages than had historically been normal; women had first babies at earlier ages and concentrated childbirth into a shorter time period. Family size remained small and the birth rate began to fall again in the middle 1960s. It fell from 18.8 births per 1000 of the UK population in 1964 to 16.2 in 1971. Thereafter to the mid-1980s it averaged 12.8. The fall coincided with the introduction and spread of the birth pill. This was a dramatic breakthrough in birth control technique, but it cannot unambiguously explain the decline since the birth rate had fallen to lower levels in the 1930s without such assistance. Its influence was almost certainly greater upon sexual attitudes and practices among at least a minority of the population – until the health hazards of long-term use became clearer in the 1970s and AIDS emerged in the later 1980s.

More people also divorced (in 1968 3.7 per 1000 of the UK married population, in 1970, 4.7, and in 1971 6.0. The divorce rate peaked in 1985 following a change in the law in 1984 which allowed divorce after one year of marriage instead of after three) and remarried, recreating in modern form the life-cycle and complex family patterns of past centuries. The proportion of families headed by a lone woman was as high in 1971 as in 1871; the cause then was death, now it is divorce, separation or non-marriage.[24] In the 1980s co-habitation seemed to be replacing marriage for some, with rising numbers of children born outside formal wedlock; but it is not necessarily the case that the relationships concerned are less, or more, stable than those sanctioned by marriage.

IV

The government in the late 1940s was more anxious to entice older women into the workforce than to extend their opportunities. It made clear that they were wanted for the jobs 'which it has always been usual for women to do'.[25] Women did not always accept this willingly. In May 1945, 400 women made 'strong protests' when they were ordered to leave a Ferranti electrical engineering factory in the north-west and go into the textile mills where wages and conditions were inferior.[26] And it indeed proved difficult to coax women back into this most traditional of female industrial occupations. Most, however, remained concentrated in lower status, poorly paid white-collar, service and industrial occupations. The pattern of women's work was also regionally uneven. The proportions in paid work were highest in the affluent south and east, low in Wales. The numbers in professional jobs rose only slowly. By 1961 there were still only 8340 female medical practitioners (15.9 per cent of the profession) and 1030 women in the whole legal profession (3.5 per cent); 1580 were surveyors and architects (2.3 per cent), and there were 25 MPs. Women made up 47.5 per cent of 'social welfare and related workers'.[27]

Government social surveys in 1943 and 1947 indeed indicated that 58 per cent of women believed that married women (with or without children) should not 'go out to work' (73 per cent of women surveyed in the US in 1943 thought this[28]). But this sentiment was weaker among younger women and surveys through to the 1970s showed its continuous decline. A high proportion of the women who left the labour force after the war to have families told interviewers that they intended to return to the labour market when their children had grown. Later surveys detected their doing so. The 1947 Government Social Survey showed that marriage was considerably more important than childbirth in determining withdrawal from the labour market. This was to change strikingly over the following decade.

The Labour government resisted repeated requests from MPs of all parties to act on the Report of the Royal Commission on Equal Pay. Repeatedly until their defeat in 1951 spokesmen stated that much as they supported the principle of equal pay, until the economy was strengthened to implement the report would destroy their economic strategy. The Conservatives included a vaguely worded commitment to equal pay in their manifestos for the 1950 and 1951 general elections. When they entered government they adopted exactly the stance of their predecessors. Meanwhile the campaign for equal pay did not die away. Women and trade unions in the white-collar public sector continued to demand it and to move a little way towards it by negotiation with management. But until the early 1950s their demands and those of women in industry were fairly muted, due probably to a real desire to support the Labour government's attempt to construct a full employment welfare state. From this women (2 in 3 of whom were not, after all, in paid work) certainly benefited, notably from the introduction of the National Health Service. Most women had not been covered by pre-war National Insurance arrangements and pre-war surveys demonstrated appalling levels of ill health among working-class women.[29]

Women gained also from the construction of more and better housing and from increased access to domestic technology as more equipment became available and more could afford it. The use of electric irons, vacuum cleaners, washing machines, refrigerators, more convenient kitchens, and more easily cared for furnishings spread gradually and unevenly but has contributed to a major change in the lives of women since 1945. Studies have consistently shown that the outcome has been rising standards of household care rather than reduced hours of housework, and that rising standards have created another source of conflict and guilt for women, but these responses have not been universal. Women who previously would have had no servants acquired choice about the time spent on housework. More universally they escaped the debilitating, physically heavy, drudgery that housework for centuries meant for women.

Nevertheless in the 1950s media reports of isolated housewives in new towns and housing estates conflicted with their other prevailing image of contented domesticity. And women in paid work were also grumbling. Women in the public sector put pressure on the government through trade unions and MPs, male and female, of all parties. When the Labour MP Charles Pannell raised the question of equal pay in the public services in the Commons in May 1952 he was supported by large demonstrations. Women protested and petitioned until at the beginning of 1955 the government gave in and announced that equal pay would be introduced into the civil service, local government and teaching, gradually over six years. There are also indications, though no systematic research, that women in industry protested about pay. In November 1955 the women at the Hillington engineering works near Glasgow struck. A strike in 1943 had gained them near equality with male pay rates, but the women protested that these had been eroded to 76 per cent. However, the success of the campaign among public employees did not lead to sustained pressure for equal pay in the private sector.

V

In 1956 Alva Myrdal and Viola Klein's *Women's Two Roles. Home and Work* sought ways to enable women to combine the 'two roles'. They argued for extended maternity leave of 1–2 years; work training for older women; better planned housing; and more services, including day nurseries and a shorter working day for men and women. There should be a 'fairer distribution of work and leisure between the sexes'. Employers should adjust work conditions to women's needs. Equally vitally, society should value both roles:

> all their productive efforts whether paid or unpaid, whether inside or outside their homes, should be taken into account; whether they educate children or spin cotton is of minor concern in this connection.

Currently, they argued, society was creating new dilemmas for women and indeed driving a wedge more firmly between the two roles, above all by imposing 'new and exacting standards of motherhood'. In particular they attacked the influence of theories of maternal deprivation, 'a new and subtle form of anti-feminism'. They accepted the need of the young child for security, but questioned whether this necessitated full-time care by the natural mother.[30]

Many of these ideas were less novel than Myrdal and Klein appeared to think. They had been alive in the 1920s,[31] and many were to be revived and extended in the 1960s and beyond. The volume appeared in an influential sociology series and remained in print until its second edition in 1968. It was one conduit channelling the feminism of the early part of the century to the later through a period in which it was by no means as dead as is often assumed, though it was not vibrant or visibly attracting more than a handful of younger women. Simone de Beauvoir's *The Second Sex* was translated into English in 1953 and had an immense impact upon individual women; as had the feminism of Doris Lessing's *Golden Notebooks* (1962).

Similarly small but persistent numbers of women in Parliament, in all parties, in academic and literary life, in trade unions and in the surviving women's organisations kept alive a certain discontent about gender inequalities. The issue of equal pay and opportunities continued to provide a focus for their efforts. Nevertheless, evidence collected in the 1950s and early 1960s suggested that such inequalities were changing at best very slowly; though the fact that evidence was collected at all suggests a continuing strand of awareness of the problems. Viola Klein, in a survey of *Britain's Married Women Workers*,[32] tried in 1957 to discover 'how ordinary men and women feel' on the question. By this time the birth of the first child had become the normal time to give up work. Greater affluence and the accessibility of rising living standards meant that couples opted for a period of accumulation before the birth of children. When women returned to work in later life the reason they most frequently gave was raising the family standard of living; less often than in the past to avoid starvation, rather to buy more comfort, although it should be remembered that pockets of periodic unemployment and severe poverty remained, most acutely on Merseyside and Clydeside. Klein concluded:

The outstanding impression gained from this survey is that women's lives, today as much as ever, are dominated by their

> role – actual or expected – as wives and mothers. . . . there is
> no trace of feminist egalitarianism . . . nor even is it implicitly
> assumed that women have the 'right to work' . . . the isolated
> references to the 'equality of the sexes' were made by men. . . .
> Men appear on the whole to be less conservative in their out-
> look in these matters than they are usually assumed to be . . .
> the majority of women seem to get moral support from their
> husband in their decision to take a job . . . the idea of marriage
> as a partnership is widely accepted today.

About a third of the men interviewed, however, did disapprove of
married women working outside the home and most disapproved
of mothers of young children taking paid work. Nor did it seem
that moral support extended to such active support as significant
assistance with housework. Klein also questioned employers and
discovered an extreme unwillingness to adapt to the needs of
married women.

Confirmation that employer attitudes had changed very little
came from a survey carried out for the Ministry of Labour in
1959 of 50 per cent of all women who had graduated in science
and engineering in Britain in 1954 and 1956 (only 708 in all) and
of a sample of larger employers in relevant industries. Of the
graduates covered 74 per cent were employed in teaching, at
various levels, or in other public services such as the health
service. The minority working in industry were concentrated in
research posts; they felt that they had inferior prospects of
promotion compared with males and many felt undervalued.
The employers' responses confirmed that their feelings had
substance. Though many considered women scientists 'particularly good at detailed work', 60 per cent paid higher rates to men.
They justified this with the arguments that men had a longer
term career commitment (not borne out by the interviews with
the women) and had dependants to support. For similar reasons
24 per cent allowed women no opportunities for promotion and
others limited the level to which they could rise in view of the
difficulties presumed to arise when women held authority over
men. Only 28 per cent of managers were wholly in favour of
employing women.[33]

A follow-up study three years later by Nancy Seear and
colleagues at the London School of Economics (LSE) was
undertaken at the request of a small group of industrialists who
feared that women's scientific and technical training was being

underused in industry. The report pointed out that the 1961 census showed 249,000 economically active people with qualifications in science and technology, 18,300 of them female. The recent Zuckerman report on Scientific and Technological Manpower had anticipated a shortage of 28,000 suitably trained people by 1965, rendering more urgent the greater use of womanpower. The LSE team surveyed older girls in 17 schools and found that a substantial minority were interested in training. But these girls encountered great difficulty in finding information about occupations not traditionally defined as female and serious discouragement in all quarters from entering them. They were well aware of the barriers women encountered and understandably:

> competing mainly with men was not a prospect which attracted many of them. They were chary of entering into a situation in which they would have to push in order to win promotion. . . . Not one girl expressed enthusiasm for breaking down prejudice simply because it was there.

Many of them opted for a teaching career because it was socially acceptable and could be combined with domestic roles.

Employers and teachers expressed the conviction that women could not perform well in the sciences. The research also uncovered a fine array of prejudices about women as managers ('Women have emotional crises and can't take being kicked' was an especially emotional reaction), and the distaste most girls felt for working in 'industry', of which they had a wholly negative image, especially if they came from working-class families. Interviews with women employed in industry showed that many of them were planning their careers on a lifetime basis, usually with a break for childrearing, but felt that they would find it difficult to obtain retraining on returning, and that in general their talents and skills were underused. Seear concluded:

> Prejudice runs like a scarlet thread all through the pattern of this study . . . so far we have not gained so much as a toe-hold . . . in the industrial world. The question is not whether women should be allowed better opportunities, but rather whether as a community we can afford to continue to waste their trained powers . . . of course there are difficulties (such as women's family responsibilities) . . . but these are not the fundamental difficulties. From this survey the basic problem seems to be prejudice.[34]

A much larger survey carried out in 1965 for the Ministry of Labour confirmed the findings of Klein and of Seear.[35]

Not that life was so wonderful for the majority of women who worked in the home. Suggestions about the isolation and discontent of housewives were given substance by Hannah Gavron's study of North London housewives in the early 1960s. Gavron found that the isolation of young mothers had been increased by the disappearance of their older neighbours and relatives back to the workforce; 35 per cent of the working class wives and 21 per cent of the middle class felt strongly that they had married too young. They said that they had done it primarily to break free of their families and, in the case of working-class girls, from monotonous low paid work 'and were now full of regrets for the things they had not done', primarily in respect of training and work.[36]

Most felt that their marriages were more egalitarian than those of their parents, though 62 per cent of working-class wives (only one middle-class wife) did not know their husbands' earnings. Of the middle-class wives 90 per cent had received training above school level and 77 per cent of them intended to return to work. Only 29 per cent of the working-class women had acquired some skill although 87 per cent intended to return to the labour market.

Gavron was struck by the similarity of attitudes and experiences between the classes and by the fact that few of the women 'saw their lives dominated by the role of wife and mother'. They were all aware of conflict between their roles as mother and worker, though no longer between those of wife and worker. She concluded that the worlds of education and work were too exclusively geared to the male life-cycle. School should prepare women for the life pattern that was becoming normal for most of them; and they should have access to training and further education in later life. The inadequacies of female education and training were a strikingly prominent theme of post-war surveys. The Report in 1968 of the (Donovan) Royal Commission on Trade Unions and Employers' Associations provided one of the bluntest confirmations that attitudes towards the training and employment of women was one of the enduring weaknesses of post-war British management: 'the facts are so disturbing and the implications – both social and economic – so important that they must be singled out for discussion'. Female access to apprenticeships was 'extraordinarily limited'. Though girls per-

formed as well as boys in O-level examinations, only 7 per cent
entered apprenticeships (mainly in hairdressing) compared with
43 per cent of boys. While 49 per cent of male workers in industry
were classified as skilled, this applied to only 29 per cent of
women. In 1966, 538,000 men were granted day release for
further training but only 87,000 women. On the basis of their
interviews with managers and trade unionists, and evidence from
another survey undertaken by Nancy Seear, the Commission
concluded that although family commitments did provide
obstacles to women's work and training, this was much less the
case for older women returners:

> Lack of skilled labour has constantly applied a brake to our
> economic expansion since the war and yet the capacity of
> women to do skilled work has been neglected ... forecasts of
> the size of the working population indicate that there will be a
> very limited increase between now and 1981. Women provide
> the only substantial new source from which extra labour and
> especially skilled labour can be drawn during this period. . . .
> Many of the attitudes which support the present system of
> craft training and discrimination against women are common
> to both employers and trade unionists and deeply engrained in
> the life of the country. Prejudice against women is manifest at
> all levels of management as well as on the shop floor. Among
> the professions there are to be found demarcation rules and
> rules for qualifying to practice which are no less strict and no
> less open to question than those practised in many crafts. [37]

Seear's survey for the Commission, conducted in 1966, found no
evidence of change since 1962. She commented that: 'Even the
most ardent feminist will agree that there is no great upsurge of
protest by women against the existing situation.' However, this
did not necessarily mean that they approved of it: 'Human
beings are remarkably adaptable and most people once they have
recognized a brick wall for what it is decide not to bang their
heads against it.' The biggest obstacle was that:

> in subtle and not so subtle ways an atmosphere is created and
> sustained which still makes it appear peculiar or comical for
> women to be both feminine and using their capacities to the
> full. This attitude thrives while a book reviewer even in a
> serious journal thinks it relevant to refer to an authoress as

'handsome', while BBC commentators make facetious asides about women in science and managerial jobs, while the public and press chatter nervously about the way to address a lady judge, while a girl in a mixed comprehensive school can be told that 'technical drawing is only for boys'.[38]

VI

There has been little sign in the past 25 years that the comments of Seear and the Donovan Commission fell on any but deaf ears. They were, however, in tune with a visible upsurge of organisation among women at the time. In the early 1960s a number of the organisations which were heiresses of the suffrage movement remained in being. None was large but from 1966 two of them, the Six Point Group and the Fawcett Society, initiated alliances among these women's rights groups and others such as the National Council of Married Women, the National Council for Civil Liberties and women's professional and employment associations. They aimed to coordinate constitutional pressure for equal opportunities, equal pay, equal taxation and better treatment for unmarried mothers. They encouraged women to join trade unions and supported the flurry of strikes for equal pay in the mid and later 1960s, most famously that of women machinists at Ford's at Dagenham. Simultaneously women within mixed sex organisations, in particular the TUC and the Labour Party, were increasingly active on questions of gender inequality, also building on a tradition which had never quite died away.[39] Labour won a firm majority in 1966, supported by a higher proportion of eligible female voters than they had obtained in any post-war election (in 1964 they had won their lowest post-war proportion of female votes). In 1967 the Labour Party set up a committee to investigate discrimination against women, which reported in 1969 and 1972.

Somewhat later, from 1968, a more radical strand of feminism emerged out of the Campaign for Nuclear Disarmament, the Vietnam Solidarity Campaign and various socialist organisations, often in reaction to the sexism of males in such groups. By 1969 there were 70 local women's liberation groups in London. The first national Women's Liberation Workshop, held in Oxford in 1970, drew 600 delegates. Its supporters became active in a variety of fields: welfare rights, organisation of low paid women (notably night-time office cleaners), wages for housework. They were more self-consciously radical, less hierarchical in their forms of organisation than the older groups and concentrated more on issues of sexuality, control over reproduction, gay rights, violence against women, and less on matters of work and training. They tended to be critical of orthodox political groupings, anti-institutional, and sceptical of the possibilities of legislation as a vehicle of change. The 1970 Women's Liberation Workshop voted only very narrowly to support demands for legislative changes.

Though there was cooperation between the two wings of feminism, there was also tension between them, similar to that between militant and moderate suffrage campaigners before 1914; and as with their predecessors, commentators have tended to credit the more public and militant strand with both such change and such regression as occurred. In both periods, however, it is probably more accurate to see the two strands as complementary and the tension between them as more creative than they perhaps realised. Between them they raised a wide range of issues, most of which have not since vanished from the public arena, and a more widespread awareness of gender inequalities, which also did not disappear, even though visible feminist activism, especially of the more radical kind, declined in the 1980s. *Both* public anger and quieter lobbying may be necessary to give a high profile to issues which have long been simmering, and to bring about and shape action. It is also clear that the radical movement, rather than being the sole or chief originator of the most recent wave of feminism, as it is sometimes seen, was itself a product and part of a wider movement detectable from the mid-1960s and with longer, if slender, roots in the movements of the earlier part of the century.[40]

The later 1960s, in fact, saw legislative changes which developed alongside rather than clearly grew out of the revival of the women's movement, since they pre-date its most active phase, notably the Abortion Reform Act, 1967 (introduced by Liberal MP David Steel). Also in 1967, Labour set up negotiations between the Confederation of British Industries and the TUC to try to negotiate a way forward on the equal pay issue. This only revealed that nothing had changed since 1946. The employers refused to go beyond commitment to 'equal pay for equal work' and regarded the TUC preference for 'equal pay for work of the same value' as far too open-ended and indefinite. That equal pay legislation followed in 1970 was partly a consequence of the breakdown of these talks (which convinced the TUC of the need for legislation) and of pressure from the broad range of women's groups. It was also important that a male Minister of Labour of no known feminist inclination, Ray Gunter, was replaced in 1968 by Barbara Castle. Her skill and determination played an essential part in pushing the bill through a cabinet which was not wholly enthusiastic and in rushing it through the House of Commons before the general election of 1970, which Labour lost. She admitted that the speed with which it was constructed and passed accounted for many of its deficiencies. The Act established equal rates of pay for the same or similar work, or work that had been rated as equivalent under a job evaluation scheme. Compliance was to be voluntary until 1975. Barbara Castle was well aware of the inadequacies and potential for evasion in the bill but argued that 'legislation cannot cover every possible development' and that it was essential for government to give a moral lead on this as on other issues.[41]

Its effects are hard to estimate. The legislation was designed to remove only that element in pay differentials due to direct gender discrimination, i.e. not those due to the younger age, lesser training or experience of females, though these may indirectly derive from discrimination. The acute problems of defining and measuring discrimination have led econometricians to widely varying conclusions.[42] The likely conclusion is that the Act had some effect, but it was small.

The Equal Pay Act left untouched the processes that excluded women from higher earning occupations. During the period of Conservative government, 1970–4, a succession of anti-discrimination bills were brought in by Members of Parliament. One drafted by Nancy Seear (by now a baroness and prominent Liberal) gave rise to a House of Lords Select Committee in 1972. Evidence to this committee provides a snapshot of attitudes comparable with that provided by the Report of the 1946 Royal Commission.

The Confederation of British Industries and the Engineering Employers Federation demonstrated that all too many employers still had learned nothing and forgotten nothing. Their explanations of the inferiority of female to male labour were unchanged. They still believed that to train most women was not worthwhile due to their short stay in the labour market; that the 'real problems' were far removed from discrimination and prejudice, to which they were opposed, although they insisted that it hardly existed in industry. The, largely male, Institute of Personnel Management provided clear evidence of discrimination in industry, in particular that it accounted for the tiny number of women in top positions, including in personnel management. They were supported by a memorandum from the Department of Employment on 'Sex discrimination in employment and training'. This provided statistics demonstrating yet again the concentration of female workers in low paid, low skilled sectors.

Lady Summerskill (formerly a Labour MP and long a campaigner for women's rights) asked the representatives of the TUC why they had done so little in the matter. They confessed the difficulty of even well intentioned union leaders in influencing their branches. Mrs Marie Patterson described the slow process currently under way to persuade bus driver branches of the Transport and General Workers Union to accept female drivers. Political and Economic Planning drew upon research it had sponsored in 1966–71 on women in top jobs[43] to provide evidence of discrimination in appointments and promotions to top professional posts, such as university chairs. Such discrimination was extraordinarily hard to prove, yet the statistical disparity between the numbers of women at the lower levels of most professions and at the top, left discrimination, often unconscious, as the only explanation. The Sex Discrimination Act of 1975 attempted to deal with this difficult area and established the Equal Opportunities Commission. Action against discrimination in Britain was taken further in the 1980s with support from the European Commission and the European Court of Justice.

The economic problems of Britain in the 1980s complicated the always difficult task of assessing change in the relative experiences of men and women; the more so because, as in any period 'women', like 'men', have had far from uniform experiences. Unemployment has risen less fast among women, but this is partly because government policies have tended to encourage the low paid, low skilled jobs which lie at the root of the difficulties of many women.[44] There are indications that significantly more women have entered the business world and professions such as the law and medicine. In 1988 50 per cent of entrants to the law were women. Females made up 21 per cent of solicitors and barristers, and 22 per cent of GPs. Yet only 3.2 per cent of surgeons and 0.5 per cent of engineers were women. A change from the 1950s was that more middle-class families came to expect their daughters as well as their sons to enter the professions. We have yet to see how far they will rise.

On the other hand more women than in the 1950s were single heads of families on low incomes. Legislation of the 1980s has complicated access to maternity pay and allowances and weakened employment protection for pregnant women. The rights of part-time workers were much reduced. The likelihood is that for women as for men the 1980s saw a polarisation between those who gained and those who lost a great deal.

10. Immigration

COLIN HOLMES

IT has been suggested recently that 'The one issue of which academic historians have still, so far, fought shy', is 'the diverse ethnic composition of these islands'.[1] This observation stands in need of qualification but it contains a substantial grain of truth. In particular, historians have seriously neglected the immigration which has occurred since the Second World War. This neglect is not mirrored among sociologists, urban geographers and political scientists. On the contrary, their footprints lie heavy on these years.[2] In the course of their work these social scientists have produced a mass of challenging concepts from which historians can benefit. Nevertheless, the marked reluctance of the majority of these writers to inject a substantial historical dimension into their work reduces its overall effectiveness.

This last emphasis needs to be substantiated. One way forward is to take the theme of continuity and change and consider it in relation to a number of selected areas in the recent history of immigration. But how recent is recent? In the case of sociologists and urban geographers their historical interest might stretch backwards from the present day to 1945, but for many of them the first two decades after the Second World War still remain 'a dark age'[3] and are therefore ignored. The historian, however, can spot dangers in any exclusive concentration on the post-war years or a fraction of this period: any such exclusivity opens up the prospect of unintended distortion. Against the background of such general cautionary and critical comment it is possible to become more specific.

There is no doubt that the years between 1945 and the early 1970s, on which attention is initially concentrated, constitute an important period in immigration into Britain as well as other European countries. However, in the case of British society, the full scope of developments is seldom revealed. The work under-taken by the vast majority of social scientists concentrates upon the arrival of blacks, in other words those of Afro-Caribbean origin, and Asians from the Indian subcontinent. This emphasis is important if only because the size of these groups increased significantly in absolute terms. However, such work often runs in parallel with the neglect of the earlier history of these groups in Britain.[4] Furthermore, it is often associated with a failure to recognise that the process of post-war immigration embraces more than blacks and Asians from the Indian subcontinent.

Up to 1971 the Southern Irish remained the largest single immigrant minority in Britain. In the census of that year the Irish-born population was counted at 957,830 with at least 615,820 from the Republic. Those born in the Republic, the majority of whom were Irish citizens, amounted in 1971 to 1.1 per cent of the total British population.[5] The reconstruction of British cities after the war and the development of the country's infrastructure resulted in absolute levels of Irish immigration which had not been witnessed since the late nineteenth century.

The concentration on blacks and Asians has also taken place at the expense of those groups who came to Britain from con-tinental Europe. Important in this regard are the Poles, wartime allies against Germany, who did not relish the prospect of return to a Poland dominated by the Soviet Union. Census statistics relating to the Polish community are notoriously difficult to analyse, owing to national boundary changes, but the 1951 figure of a Polish-born population of 162,376 marked a substantial increase over that recorded in the 1931 return. However, from the 1950s no significant increase occurred and, without a re-generating stream, by 1971 the size of the Polish-born minority had been reduced to 110,925.[6] Other continental European refugees included the so-called European Volunteer Workers or EVWs, consisting of Estonians, Latvians, Lithuanians and Ukrainians and other groups, who were brought to Britain from DP camps in Europe in order to fill specific gaps in the labour market. Similar schemes also led to the arrival of Belgians, German scientists and Italians. As a result of such official recruitment, and a process of independent migration, by the 1960s Italians had become the fifth largest immigrant minority in the labour force in Britain.[7]

In short, since 1945 immigration into Britain has developed a diversity which, to repeat, the overwhelming emphasis on blacks and Asians has tended to mask. This recent diversity can be further underlined by reference to a sample selection of other groups including the Hong Kong Chinese, and the Cypriots, as well as refugees from Czechoslovakia, Hungary, Chile, Vietnam and Sri Lanka.

Any exclusive concentration on the years since 1945, even if it recognises the variety of the immigration process, still runs the risk of obscuring an awareness of immigration into Britain as a continual process.[8] An appreciation of this important historical trend can be gleaned from a brief consideration of developments from the late nineteenth century up to 1945.

During these years a wide range of immigrant newcomers arrived. As a result of economic, social or cultural pressures, or a mixture of such influences, these groups took a decision to leave their native countries with the intention of staying temporarily or permanently in Britain. During the same period they were joined by refugees searching for a permament or temporary home in which to escape from a well-founded fear of political, religious or racial persecution, or a combination of these pressures.

From the late nineteenth century these immigrant and refugee groups included Germans, Russian Poles, Italians, Communard exiles from France, as well as Belgian refugees, over 200,000 of whom arrived during the First World War. The assorted refugees who sought exile from Fascism in the inter-war years, a continuing number of blacks, whose size increased from a low base during and after the First World War, as well as groups of Asians from the Indian subcontinent and a small Chinese minority, also deserve attention. Furthermore, at all times, we encounter the presence of the Irish who, down to 1945, remained the largest single immigrant minority. The historical tradition of immigration which all these various groups symbolised had a related consequence, summed up in the observation: 'The British are clearly among the most ethnically composite of the Europeans'.[9]

In entering this plea for a recognition of immigration as a continuing process, it has to be admitted that the absolute and relative size of such groups remained small. In the 1971 Census, for example, the total population born outside Great Britain, not all of whom incidentally would qualify as immigrants or refugees, amounted to no more than 6.6 per cent of the overall population.[10] Another important caveat needs to be entered. During the last 100 years Britain has functioned generally as a net exporter of population. At specific points in time, such as during the world economic crisis in the 1930s and also in the period immediately preceding the imposition of controls over Commonwealth immigration in the shape of the 1962 Commonwealth Immigrants Act, a net inward movement occurred. However, these periods are exceptions to the general flow.[11] Nevertheless, none of these statistical details reduces the importance of immigration as a feature of recent British history. To make one claim only, it acts as a social barometer of the fears, anxieties and tensions which are present in society.

This discussion of continuities in the process of immigration paves the way for a survey of continuities in responses in the course of which the frequently painted image of Britain as a tolerant country requires consideration. Those who paint this picture are able to draw sustenance from comments uttered by immigrants and refugees. The tribute paid by Martha Lang, a refugee from inter-war Austria who escaped the Nazi terror to find 'freedom and new happiness'[12] in her adopted country, reflects a gratitude shared by many other exiles. Such experiences which span more than one country serve as a reminder that the concept of toleration possesses a relative as well as an absolute dimension. However, at present little can be said regarding the relative strength of toleration in Britain. In part this difficulty persists because several acres of the history of immigrants and refugees in Britain still remain unrecovered. A more serious restriction is that little work, however tentative, which compares aspects of immigrant and refugee history in Britain with that of other countries, has yet been attempted. As a result, comparative assessments are premature at present: emotional, moralistic and essentially narcissistic claims about Britain's history or toleration in relation to other countries can be discounted. Even so, it is necessary to remind ourselves that, absolutely, Britain has often fallen short of its celebrated toleration of immigrants and refugees.

In support of this claim it is possible to draw evidence initially from the years between 1945 and the late 1970s. During this period opposition towards immigrants and refugees emerged in various forms. It appeared in public speeches. The opposition to Poles which surfaced at the TUC Annual Congress in 1946 and the vocal antipathy present within the National Front at the time when Ugandan Asians arrived in 1972, provide selected evidence from both ends of the chronological spectrum. It appeared also in published form. That section of the press associated with Oswald Mosley's post-war Union Movement was quick off the mark to attack Eastern and Central European refugees. Moreover, by the 1970s opposition towards black and Asian immigrants as well as other groups such as the Irish, had appeared in an extensive cross-section of the British press. This last emphasis is important. Spoken and written opposition did not pullulate exclusively on the fringes of British society: it had a much more extensive currency.

Speeches and written comment do not necessarily become translated into action. There is no automatic link between prejudice and discrimination. Since 1945, however, hostility has sometimes resulted in discrimination. To cite some of the most reliable data only, abundant survey evidence collected by Political and Economic Planning from the late 1960s to the mid-1970s leaves no doubt that blacks and Asians had to contend with differential treatment, even after allowing for the fact that discrimination on grounds of race is a slippery issue which is often difficult to prove conclusively.

Since 1945 some opposition has also been expressed through collective violence. Any reference to this form of antipathy creates a special discordance among all those who believe that Britain is a tolerant country.[13] Nevertheless, historical evidence cannot be washed away or, to borrow the imagery of Hannah Arendt, we are unable to cover over the dirt from our own history. Attacks on Jews in the north-west of England in 1947 at the time of tension in Palestine, violence against blacks in Liverpool in 1948 when fears surfaced over the prospect of unemployment, as well as the incidents in 1958 in Nottingham and Notting Hill when economic, social and cultural problems associated particularly with immigration from the Caribbean had assumed a sharper dimension, provide part of the post-war picture of collective violence. Even so, the catalogue does not end there. The late 1950s witnessed attacks on Cypriot café owners in London. A variety of evidence also reveals the persistence of violence into the 1970s.

These various developments are important strands in the tapestry of opposition towards immigrants and refugees, which is widely and often indiscriminately categorised as racism. In order to complete the picture, however, another prominent feature needs to be worked into it. Since 1968, in the wake of the state's increasing involvement in immigration control, a growing emphasis has been placed upon the significance of institutional racism. This term is not without its difficulties, but in drawing attention to the structural rather than individual dimension of the hostility which immigrants and their British-born descendants have had to endure, it serves an important function. Apart from the involvement of the state in immigration control, the action of local authorities reflected, for example, in housing allocation policies, provides an additional dimension to the institutional opposition which blacks and Asians have faced. This awareness of institutional discrimination is further heightened by recalling the earlier agreements as a result of which, in the terms of their employment, EVWs were placed at a disadvantage in relation to British workers.[14]

In discussing hostility it should not be assumed that such developments remain the exclusive preserve of the post-1945 world. In retreating once more and again briefly into the earlier history of immigrants and refugees, covering the period from the late nineteenth century to 1945, important patterns of continuity can be discerned.

Before 1945 both spoken and written hostility surfaced towards immigrants. Trade union voices rose against Chinese seamen in the years before the First World War; in the inter-war period the Seamen's Union pursued other seafaring minorities with similar zeal. As regards published antipathy, some of the fiercest anti-semitism ever produced in Britain leaps from the pages of Joseph Banister's *England under the Jews* which appeared in 1901. The rejection of Lewis Namier from a Fellowship at All Souls on the ground that he was a Polish Jew, and the treatment of Learie Constantine at the Imperial Hotel in London in 1943 provide classic cases of discrimination. Violence, too, featured in the history of immigrants and refugees before 1945 as it did after the Second World War. Indeed, the years between 1911 and 1919 constitute a major period in the history of collective violence against racial and ethnic minorities. Finally, it is worth recalling that institutional oppression is not a feature confined exclusively to the post-war years. The impositions of controls over alien immigration in 1905, 1914 and 1919 are important legislative landmarks: between 1826 and 1905 no such restrictions existed. At a local level, it is important to record the interpretation by the Cardiff police of the 1925 Aliens Order which led the force to deprive black British subjects and other imperial minorities of their British citizenship. This action, which had adverse implications for the employment prospects of these groups, provides one of the major cases of institutional oppression in the twentieth century.[15]

At this juncture we can reverse direction, leave the developing emphasis on continuity, and bring aspects of change into focus. After 1945 the size of the black population in Britain and that of Asians from the subcontinent grew absolutely on a scale which outstripped their increase in any earlier epoch. In 1945 these black and Asian groups were statistically insignificant and their representatives were widely regarded as anthropological curiosities even though, owing to deficiencies in official statistics, it is impossible to provide precise figures on population size. It can be estimated from the 1951 Census, however, that such immigrants numbered no more than 138,072. By the 1971 Census they had increased to a figure not greater than 707,110.[16] These post-war years also witnessed a significant increase in the number of Chinese in Britain even though census figures on this group are especially tricky to decipher. The majority of these newcomers arrived from Hong Kong and contiguous territories in South East Asia such as Malaysia and Singapore, rather than from the People's Republic.[17] Nevertheless, a degree of perspective is required. Notwithstanding the major increase in size of those groups who arrived from 'beyond the oceans',[18] the majority of the immigrants who came to Britain after 1945 were white. Such evidence, which amid a degree of change further underlines the process of continuity in immigration patterns, flies in the face of popular perceptions and gives no change to those who hypothesise on a future Britain dominated by blacks and Asians.

Since 1945 important developments have occurred in the occupational structure of black and Asian immigrant groups notwithstanding their continued and pronounced working-class character. In 1945 they were concentrated particularly in the merchant shipping industry. By the 1970s, however, a broadening of their occupational structure can be detected. In the north of England Pakistanis could be found in the remaining textile mills of Yorkshire and Lancashire. Some Pakistanis, modelling themselves on earlier Jewish entrepreneurs, had also become well-established in the Manchester rag trade. Asian groups in the Midlands had found work in the engineering trades and the foundry industry. Black workers, for their part, had assumed an important role in the public sector. Women from the Caribbean served as nurses in the National Health Service and their male contemporaries featured prominently alongside Asians in public transport.

Another significant occupational shift can be noticed in the case of the Chinese. This group, which in the years before the First World War had been concentrated in the merchant shipping industry, developed a growing presence in laundries in the course of the twentieth century. After the Second World War, however, their economic activity underwent another decisive shift as they developed their involvement in restaurants. This part of the service sector became the major source of employment for the Chinese, and Gerrard Street in London's West End emerged as the national focal point of this activity.

The occupational structure of the Irish also displayed a greater diversity than it had in earlier years. As a result, if their continuing involvement in heavy labouring work can still be traced, they were no longer as tightly concentrated in such activity after 1945 as they had been in earlier years.

This emphasis on change can be further substantiated with reference to some of the continental European groups who arrived after the Second World War. Various schemes took the Italians into the brickworks of Bedfordshire and the steelworks of South Wales. Their recruitment into this type of employment marked a departure from their earlier concentration in the service sector. However, there is not always a permanent fracture between continuity and change and, once their contracts had expired, some Italians redirected themselves away from heavy industry towards their traditional locus of service sector employment.

One clear element of change after 1945 relates to the spatial concentration of immigrants and refugees. A survey carried out at the end of the Second World War would have revealed the concentration of these groups in a limited number of locations. London had traditionally acted as a magnet for them. Indeed, the visible symbols of immigrants and refugees in London are legion.[19] The histories of a number of other cities such as Liverpool and Manchester also reflect long-standing cosmopolitan influences. The same applies to Cardiff and Glasgow. The fact remains, however, that by 1945 vast areas of Britain had never engaged in any direct contact with immigrants and refugees. This situation changed within a short space of time. The Chinese, who in 1945 had been concentrated almost entirely in a limited number of ports, soon became more widely dispersed. By the 1970s scarcely a town in Britain could be found which lacked a Chinese take-away. Whereas in 1945 blacks and Asians had been located in London, a number of ports, and as students in several university centres, by the 1970s these groups could be found in all the major conurbations in Britain. Within London new settlements had developed in areas such as Brixton and Brent. The post-war settlement of Poles and European Volunteer Workers took these Europeans into new parts of Britain.

Related to this change, there was an extension of the cultural influences associated with immigration. In London, a Greek Cypriot presence in Camden Town, evident in the 1950s, had become extended by the 1970s into other parts of the capital, particularly the Green Lanes area of Haringey. Southall, in the nineteenth century a market garden centre supplying London, was transformed by the arrival of immigrants from the Indian subcontinent into a little Punjab. Parts of Glasgow also witnessed the implanting of cultural influences from the subcontinent as a result of which the area around Nicholson Street became known locally as Burma Road. The post-war years also brought the first major influx from the subcontinent into Bradford. Not that these groups can be counted as the first post-war newcomers to arrive in that northern city. They were preceded by East Europeans, the Poles and EVWs, who settled initially in the Manningham Lane area, a part of the city which later became a centre of Muslim settlement; the Urdu sign 'Halal Fish and Chips' and the proliferation of mosques on the city's skyline graphically illustrate this latest transformation.

A final element of change deserves to be recorded. This relates to the role of the state. Whereas before 1945 the state had been reluctant to encourage immigration, except to a limited extent during wartime, it has been noticed already that the labour shortages after the Second World War led to the official recruitment of workers from the DP camps which proliferated in Europe at the end of the war. What did this entail? Keen to overcome labour supply problems and relatively relaxed about the recruitment of white Europeans to fill such gaps, the Labour government initiated schemes such as the Balt Cygnet programme and the Westward Ho! venture which brought various European groups to Britain. This kind of activity and the other schemes involving Belgians, German scientists and Italians, had no earlier peacetime parallel in the nineteenth and twentieth centuries.[20]

At the side of such initiatives, however, the post-war years witnessed unparalleled intervention to control immigration. There was nothing new about the state restricting the entry of aliens. The legislation in 1905, 1914, 1919 and the associated Orders in Council which threw a tight system of control over their entry, movement and deportation have already been emphasised. In the operation of such legislation no distinction can be made between Conservative or Labour administrations: both applied it with great rigour. The significant new development after 1945 involved the control of Commonwealth immigration. In 1948 the British Nationality Act had guaranteed freedom of entry into Britain for citizens of independent Commonwealth countries and also for the remainder of the Commonwealth's subjects, known technically as Citizens of the UK and Colonies. In asserting the principle of free entry at a time when restrictions were being imposed by some Commonwealth countries such as Canada, the British government reaffirmed a long legal tradition of access into the UK for Commonwealth citizens, all of whom were regarded as possessing British citizenship. A few years later this principle was thrown overboard.

In 1962 the Conservative administration of Harold Macmillan placed the first restrictions to be operated by the British government upon entry from the Commonwealth when it passed the Commonwealth Immigrants Act. This measure aimed to restrict the entry of unskilled blacks and Asians. Once that step had been taken, the prospect of further controls loomed large. In 1965 a White Paper issued by the Labour government tightened restrictions even more. Then, in 1968, in the form of another Commonwealth Immigrants Act, the Wilson administration, under strong pressure from public opinion, imposed voucher restrictions upon those Citizens of the UK and Colonies who had secured their British passports at British High Commission offices overseas. The 1968 Act was designed to control the entry of Kenyan Asian refugees at that time fleeing from the Africanisation policies of the Kenyan government.

The 1971 Immigration Act pulled together these measures of the 1960s. In that sense the 1971 Act can be regarded as a tidying operation but, for example, by increasing the state's powers over the deportation of illegal immigrants, it tightened control over immigration. The upshot of the new legislation was that after 1973, the date when the 1971 Act came into force, unrestricted primary immigration into the UK from the Commonwealth became dependent upon the possession of patrial status. In other words, all such intending applicants had to furnish proof of a close connection with the UK either through birth, descent, or settlement or because they had acquired their citizenship in the UK. Commonwealth citizens unable to satisfy one of these requirements were treated essentially as if they were aliens. Indeed, the 1971 Act replaced all previous immigration legislation, including those measures relating to aliens, although sections of the 1919 Aliens Act remained in force. In the 1971 Act citizens of the Irish Republic were treated as a special case; although they did not possess patrial status, the Act ensured that they were free from entry controls even if they remained liable to deportation. The cumulative changes relating to immigration, symbolised by developments in 1961, 1965, 1968 and drawn together in 1971, are some of the most significant initiatives in post-war British history. In the same year that the 1971 Act came into force the United Kingdom joined the EEC. In doing so it accepted the principle of free movement within the Community for the nationals of member states. However, this development, and its implications for immigration, generated no debate comparable to that which had taken place over Commonwealth immigration.[21]

Indeed, the debate over immigration from the Commonwealth extended into the heart of British politics. In 1962 the Labour Party took an initial principled stand against the imposition of controls over the entry of Commonwealth citizens. In the course of the 1960s, however, politicians of all persuasions played 'the immigration card' to gain favour with the electorate. In particular, the shock defeat of Patrick Gordon-Walker at Smethwick in the 1964 general election, after a campaign in which some supporters of Peter Griffiths, the Conservative candidate, had exploited the slogan, 'If you want a nigger neighbour vote Labour', brought home the strength of feeling on the immigration issue. 'Ever since the Smethwick election it has been quite clear that immigration can be the greatest political vote loser for the Labour Party if one seems to be permitting a flood of immigrants to come in and blight the central area of our cities', Richard Crossman confided in his *Diaries*, and on the same day he described immigration as 'the hottest potato in politics'.[22] By the late 1960s politicians had become a prey not only to pressures from within areas of settlement but also from wider strands of public opinion, some of which were gathered up after 1967 by the

National Front, an organisation whose immigration policy the major parties conveniently condemned in order, to some extent, to divert attention from their own policies and actions.

In this ambience a number of additional unprecedented official initiatives can be traced: these can be viewed as the British equivalent to the civil rights legislation which emerged in the same decade in the United States. In 1965, following its White Paper on entry control, the Labour government passed the first Race Relations Act. This legislation 'was an attempt to influence behaviour and attitudes by [laws] which declared that everyone in Britain will henceforth to be treated on the basis of individual merit, regardless of colour or race'.[23] The 1965 Act set up the Race Relations Board to deal with complaints of discrimination. The Act made it unlawful to discriminate on grounds of race, colour, ethnic or national origin in public places or on public transport. However, important areas where discrimination occurred, such as employment and housing, did not fall within its scope. In an attempt to rectify this situation, a new measure was introduced in 1968 in order, as cynics have observed, to mollify the impact of the 1968 Commonwealth Immigrants Act. This second Race Relations Act brought the key areas of employment and housing within the scope of legislation. It also provided the Race Relations Board with the power to investigate complaints and initiate proceedings. In addition, it established the Community Relations Commission and endowed it with the responsibility for promoting harmonious race relations and advising the Home Office on such matters.

In practice neither the 1965 nor the 1968 measures achieved the results for which social engineers had hoped. Since both appeared on the Statute Book in the shadow of restrictive entry legislation, the Acts did not secure the confidence of Britain's immigrant groups. Secondly, successive governments showed relatively little interest in making such legislation work or, to put it another way, they took a greater interest in curbing the immigration of blacks and Asians and, in the course of this activity, labelling such groups as social problems.

The final step in the race relations programme came in 1976 when the Labour government passed a third Race Relations Act. It abolished the Race Relations Board and the Community Relations Commission and replaced them with the Commission for Racial Equality. The CRE's role was to assist individuals who believed they had encountered racial discrimination; it was also charged with combating the general problem of such discrimination and, in this regard, its brief ranged over all the key areas of social life, including employment and housing. The 1976 Act also went further than the 1965 Act in regard to incitement. The later measure amended the 1936 Public Order Act in such a way that it was no longer necessary to prove that the accused intended to encourage such sentiments. The decision whether or not to initiate any action on this matter still lay with the Attorney General.

This legislation on race relations came under attack from whites who resented what they regarded as the intrusions of the 'race relations industry' and from many blacks and Asians who viewed it as tokenism, designed at best to draw the sting of oppression without eradicating it. Nevertheless, these measures did mark a new historical beginning. Earlier immigrants and refugees had been denied any similar protection. After failing to secure a full conviction in the case of *Rex* v. *Leese* in 1936, for example, the crown remained reluctant to intervene in order to protect the Jewish minority against seditious libel.[24] In the immediate post-war years legal opinion continued to advise the government that the specific protection of ethnic and racial groups lay beyond the scope of the law. At this time the advice of the lawyers reflected a wider sweep of public opinion. The legislative developments between 1965 and 1976, whatever their deficiencies, amounted to a significant historical reversal of that previous strongly held position.

III

So far our discussion has not ventured into the years of the Thatcher governments. That omission can now be remedied. Before doing so, however, a brief recapitulation might be undertaken. In discussing the period from 1945 into the 1970s an emphasis has been placed on a number of important points. A cautionary note has been sounded regarding the distortions which can arise from any exclusive concentration on immigration as a post-Second World War phenomenon. It has also been pointed out that Britain has generally functioned as a net exporter rather than a net importer of population. The powerful celebratory myth that Britain is a tolerant country has also been queried: the accumulated evidence on various forms of hostility

call this image into question and qualification. In discussing such
themes great emphasis has been laid on historical continuity. At
the same time, it has been recognised that after the Second
World War the history of immigrants and refugees did reveal
evidence of change. The absolute size of such groups who came
to Britain from beyond Europe increased significantly, even if the
majority of newcomers who arrived after 1945 were white. Other
evidence of change can be gleaned from a consideration of the
occupational patterns, geographical distribution and cultural
impact of immigrants and refugees, as well as certain developments associated with the state. In turning our gaze to the years
since 1979 a number of equally important emphases have a claim
on our attention. It can be argued with some cogency that
hostility relating to and resulting from the process of immigration
continued as a prominent feature of British society in the 1980s
and attention can now be focused upon this theme.

Following the tight system of control which by 1973 had been
placed over primary immigration from the Commonwealth, and
particularly over the entry of blacks and Asians, it might be
thought that any further restrictions would assume a low priority.
In fact, the 1980s witnessed a tightening of controls. A new bill,
introduced in November 1987, became law in August 1988. It
required Commonwealth citizen men to show proof that they
could maintain and accommodate their families without recourse
to public funds. The act also forbade the entry of second wives
of polygamous marriages. Furthermore, overstaying became a
criminal offence. Finally, the Act limited the right of appeal of
those immigrants who had lived in Britain for less than seven
years and faced deportation for overstaying or for a breach of the
conditions attaching to their residence. In conjunction with other
steps, including the Immigration (Carriers' Liability) Act of
May 1987, which laid down that airline and shipping companies
bringing people into the UK who had no right of entry faced fines
of up to £1000 for each offence, the later 1980s witnessed an
increasingly pronounced fortress policy on immigration.[25]

Such Little Englandism also came on display in the dying days
of 1989 when the government refused to grant a general right of
abode in the UK to the Hong Kong Chinese. These people, along
with other groups unable to claim patrial status, had been excluded from full British citizenship by the 1981 British Nationality Act. With the recent events in Tiananmen Square deeply
etched in their minds Hong Kong's ethnic Chinese become

fearful of what might happen on the island after its handover in 1997 to the People's Republic of China. Even the limited proposal made by the government to grant the right of abode to selected Hong Kong Chinese ran into opposition from a section of the Tory Party spearheaded by Norman Tebbit.[26]

These developments, taken in conjunction with the treatment of refugees such as the Vietnamese, some 20,000 of whom were grudgingly admitted under international pressure, and the fate of individuals, including the well-publicised case of Stancu Papusoiu, who tried unsuccessfully to enter Britain from Romania in 1983, further underline the tough stance on immigration which has been pursued since 1979. So does the hard line taken on Tamil refugees from Sri Lanka. A similar brand of political machismo came on display later in 1989 with the forced repatriation of Vietnamese refugees from the squalor of camps in Hong Kong to Vietnam, an action which the authorities pursued in the face of international criticism.[27]

During the period of Conservative government since 1979 we have been exposed to a flood of rhetoric which dwells upon the restoration of Britain's place in the world and the reassertion of Victorian values and virtues. Nothing in the government's immigration policy squares with this image. Its contours bear no relation to the liberal open door policy on entry which characterised the Victorian years. This is not to suggest that decisions such as those relating to the entry of Hong Kong Chinese are easily made. Important matters of political expediency and policy are at stake. Hard choices are inevitable. The fact remains, however, that the general failure of vision which had become particularly clear in the politics of immigration by the 1960s, still remains strikingly evident.[28]

The history of those groups who did manage to enter Britain is also revealing. Attempts are made to dwell upon success stories. However, there are limits to the extent to which such claims can be taken on board. In part, these accounts represent a continued attempt to present an image of Britain as a country of liberal openness in which immigrants and refugees can flourish and develop their potential. As such, the claims are celebratory. It is a celebration in which, as in the years before 1945, the newcomers have also joined. The reasons for their involvement in building this image are complex. In part, the retailing of success can be regarded as an attempt to justify their presence in Britain. In part, too, success stories can provide a degree of compensation

for present disadvantages. Irish workers have been noticed
dwelling on the important role of the Irish in the building trade,
hoping 'perhaps one of these days they themselves will take the
first plunge into sub-contracting after which there will no be
looking back, but only forward to Jaguar cars ... and the big
house in London's Highgate'.[29]

In attempts to project this image of success in the 1980s many
sermons have been delivered extolling the commercial enterprise
of the Ugandan Asians. This group, in particular, is widely portrayed as possessing all the Smilesean virtues which the Thatcher-
ite 'revolution' has attempted to promote. Not that it is the only
immigrant minority to receive attention. The least sign of any
form of conventional success among the Vietnamese, an acutely
disadvantaged group, is also avidly seized upon.

Such warm images provide only a partial picture of the history
of immigrants in Britain in the 1980s. It is possible to lay
alongside them the continuing evidence on hostility which these
groups have had to endure. Material relating to the problems
experienced by black and Asian groups, on whom an initial
interest can be focused, lies particularly heavy on the ground.
Visitors to areas of settlement soon encounter strands of hostile
sentiment. A writer sojourning in Bradford found herself treated
to the following emotive outburst against newcomers to the city.
'Contaminating the country that's what they're doing – contaminating us all! We all think they're horrible – no one likes 'em.
Live on filth they do – take my advice and keep well away –
catch anything off them you could.'[30] Newspapers such as the
Sun[31] presented this type of popular sentiment vividly and
persistently to a wider audience. However, in considering hostile
sentiment it is too restrictive to concentrate exclusively upon
working-class expressions and the tabloids. A more considered
message of opposition appeared recently in the Sunday Telegraph.
In this piece, written in the shadow of pressure from the Hong Kong
Chinese to secure a right of abode in the UK, the earlier
immigration of blacks and Asians from the subcontinent became
linked with the morbid possession of the white English by a cultural
death wish which had led to the destruction of the nation and the
race. 'The long unquestioned dominance of multi-culturalism has
sent England into hiding and forced English people to disinvent and
un-English themselves. By slow, shameful stages our country has
been taken away from us.' The article resulted in 241 readers'
letters, of which 189 were in agreement with its sentiments.[32]

Similar comment appeared in Parliament and among parlia-
mentarians. In 1988 one well-known Tory MP expressed his
concern about the unwelcome importation of 'tribes and cultures'
into Britain:[33] the language might have been different from
working-class Bradford but the message remained the same. At a
later date the responses of Muslim demonstrators to Salman
Rushdie's *The Satanic Verses* and the continued uncertainty over
the possible entry of some Hong Kong Chinese generated similar
opposition. 'England must be recaptured for the English', John
Townsend, the Tory MP for Bridlington, proclaimed in August
1989. Those immigrant minorities already living in England had
to recognise these priorities and there should be no weakening on
the question of entry.[34]

This necessarily limited spread of evidence on antipathy is
part of a wider opposition. In an investigation carried out in
1984, 90 per cent of the survey sample believed that blacks and
Asians in Britain encountered hostility.[35]

If the expression of such hostile sentiment provides a strong
link of continuity with earlier years, so does the practice of
discrimination. When, between February 1984 and March 1985
the Policy Studies Institute conducted tests in three major cities
to measure the extent of racial discrimination, it discovered that
one employer in three discriminated against black and Asian
applicants. Some of these applicants were immigrants but others
had been born in Britain – not that those who practised hostility
worried over this distinction since all members of minority
groups tend to be lumped together by those who oppose them.
Similar findings on discrimination emerge from other surveys. A
more recent report by the Law Society, based on an ethnic
monitoring survey and data compiled by the Society's race
relations committee, revealed the extent of discrimination in the
legal profession. The consequences of this action showed up in
the numbers of qualified legal personnel. Out of 48,494 solicitors
in England and Wales in 1986–7 only 618 came from ethnic
minority, i.e. non-white, backgrounds.[36] An official recognition
of such problems appeared in the government's 1989 White
Paper on employment for the 1990s. This publication depicted
racial discrimination as a barrier which blocked the country's
most effective deployment of its human capital.

These sentiments in the White Paper would doubtless be
echoed by those invisible and silent members of black and Asian
groups who in the 1980s featured disproportionately in the

anonymous statistics on unemployment. A 1981 report by the Home Affairs Committee of the House of Commons on Racial Disadvantage observed; 'At most times when it has been measured over the past ten years the rate of unemployment has been higher among ethnic minorities than among the rest of the population.'[37] The report particularly emphasised the vulnerability of young blacks and acknowledged that some of this disadvantage related to discrimination. Later sources, including the 1985 Labour Force Survey and the 1987 annual report of the Commission for Racial Equality, continued to draw attention to the relatively high levels of unemployment among blacks and Asians. The persistence of 'widespread and deeply entrenched' discrimination, which the Chief Executive of the CRE believed could be demonstrated beyond 'any reasonable doubt' as a major force behind such unemployment, led him in 1989 to enter a powerful plea for effective contract compliance.[38]

Apart from discrimination relating to employment, blacks and Asians continued, as in earlier years, to face difficulties in the housing market. In July 1987 the press obtained details of an investigation by the CRE into the housing allocation policies of Tower Hamlets council. The enquiry, published in the following year, concluded that the council had engaged in discriminatory practices to the particular disadvantage of Bangladeshi immigrants. Similar evidence appeared elsewhere in the 1980s. A 1989 CRE report on Liverpool, a follow-up to a survey which the Commission had produced in 1984, revealed that in its housing allocation policy the City Council continued to discriminate unlawfully on racial grounds. As a result, the local authority stood in contravention of the 1976 Race Relations Act.

A continuation of collective violence directed against blacks and Asians can also be traced. Data in *Searchlight* and the *Runnymede Trust Bulletin* provide ample confirming evidence. For those who prefer other sources it is possible to turn to the admission by Douglas Hurd, then Home Secretary, who in a 1989 speech to the Tory Reform Group admitted that the scale of racial attacks and harassment remained 'worryingly large'.[39] Many attacks occurred in inner city areas but by the late 1980s racial violence had also become a feature of prison life. It had also spread beyond these confines. The involvement of racial nationalist groups with the supporters of Leeds United and Chelsea football clubs is well known and at times this association brought racial violence in its wake.

If, at this point, attention is switched to central government policy, we can recognise a significant imprint left by the state on the pattern of developments in the 1980s. The tightening of entry controls has already been noticed. It is important now to set this development in a wider context. Since 1979 the Conservative governments have often adopted a populist stance which, when occasion required it, has translated easily into an emphasis on 'White British first'. In addition, some blacks and Asians already living in Britain were adversely affected in the early 1980s by the adoption of monetarism as official economic policy. Economic policy compounded the problem of racial discrimination and its impact on employment patterns. Aware of the consequent prospect of social unrest in the inner city areas, one other strand of government activity, related to its wider policy commitment to law and order, involved the heavy policing of the inner cities. In turn, however, this development became viewed in such areas as a form of institutional oppression. The police, visible local agents of law and order, became the first in the firing line of local resentment.

This cumulative policy background helps to explain the participation of some blacks and Asians, immigrants and British-born, in the inner city violence which proliferated in the 1980s. Events in St Paul's, Bristol, in 1980, in Brixton, Southall, Toxteth, Moss Side and Handsworth in 1981, and the Broadwater Farm Estate in Tottenham in 1985, are sombre landmarks reflecting various tensions between the state, at national and local level, and the black and Asian communities.[40] The involvement of black and Asian groups in this urban violence generated increasing hostility among those whites opposed to immigration. In particular, young blacks became portrayed as a subversive element, a culturally alien group without any future in Britain. Rastas often became symbols in this regard. On a more detached perspective, these urban developments provide the other dark side of the coin to the celebratory accounts of success stories and link the longer term consequences of post-war immigration with major social policy problems which will stretch into the 1990s.

At this point it might be asked: is such evidence exceptional? Can it be claimed that the Afro-Caribbean minority and the Asian groups from the subcontinent stand alone among the post-war immigrants and refugees in having to face antipathy in the 1980s? It would be difficult to defend any such claim. A random survey of developments reveals opposition towards other groups. Three emphases serve to make this point.

Firstly, the government's firm immigration policy was further revealed in the introduction, with effect from 23 June 1989, of new visa requirements for Turkish nationals, with the aim of restricting the inflow of Kurdish refugees.[41] This step was consistent with the growing involvement of the government in attempts to differentiate between 'real' and 'bogus' refugees, a distinction which, it might be remarked, is ultimately difficult to establish. Secondly, among those immigrant groups already living in Britain, the Chinese faced less hostility than they did in the years before 1914. Even so, they were not completely shielded from antipathy. A recent report on Sheffield claimed that owners of take-aways were particularly exposed to white boorishness and hostility.[42] Finally, studies of the largest single imigrant minority, the Irish, have tended to be especially celebratory, emphasising their tolerated position in Britain. However, this claim, always a simplification, has become increasingly threadbare in the course of the 1970s and 80s. The troubles in Northern Ireland have fashioned strong shafts of anti-Irish sentiment, particularly in popular newspapers, in the form of vicious articles and cartoons. This popular antipathy has also been reflected in the graffiti scrawled outside Everton's football ground. In 1982 similar sentiment led to the suggestion that citizens of the Republic should be denied their long-held capacity to vote in Britain.[43] No wonder that some spokesmen in the Irish community urged the need for a low profile, not that this strategy would necessarily provide protection against hostility.

These last observations suggest two related emphases. First, confident claims regarding the treatment of immigrants and refugees always deserve close scrutiny. Second, it is necessary to be aware that circumstances affecting the perception and treatment of such groups can change; events in Northern Ireland and their impact on the Irish minority are a case in point. In glancing further ahead, albeit tentatively, we might wonder how the possible trials of alleged war criminals currently growing old in Britain would influence responses towards exiled groups such as the Ukrainians.[44] Furthermore, we might also ponder the impact which the arrival in Britain of any Triad gangs from Holland following the relaxation of EC frontiers in 1992 might have on the responses encountered by the Chinese. This issue is already starting to attract attention and is ripe for exploitation.[45]

In pulling back from this passing speculative venture into the future and returning to the recent past, and also bearing in mind the significance of changing circumstances, there is room for one final observation. In considering the history of post-war immigration and its consequences, it is difficult to detect any automatic, inexorable cycle of development as a result of which immigrants and refugees have moved from an initial encounter with hostility, through a later stage of toleration, towards the nirvana of acceptance. Hostility sleeps lightly. It is soon awakened. Moreover, with John Bull's hazy notions of abroad, reflected in the popular view from Bradford that all East Europeans were 'bloody Poles',[46] hostility can scoop up unsuspecting individuals and groups with sudden speed into its confining net. Members of immigrant and refugee groups are well advised, consequently, to retain their frequently expressed sense of everlasting uncertainty. They, above all, can appreciate the sentiments of the Dutch-descended poet: 'O happy, happy Browns and Robinsons!'[47]

IV

In considering the post-war history of immigration some positive changes can be detected.[48] However, there is no shortage of evidence to indicate that since 1945 immigrants and refugees in Britain have encountered persistent antipathy and relative disadvantage.

Even so, these groups have not met with ceaseless hostility in all situations. Responses have often revealed a degree of complexity which cannot be ignored. The comments of a Liverpool taxi driver are revealing in this regard: 'I can take them or leave them the same as anybody else you know. I don't mind having a drink with a coloured chap. I've met some very nice coloured people but with regard to intermarriage I think I'd draw the line there.'[49] Such ambivalence has been emphasised in relation to other groups such as the Irish.[50]

After 1945 some variability in responses can be noticed between different areas. Following the Second World War Poles came to regard Bradford as a good town in which their settlement created relatively few problems. In more sombre vein it has been suggested that in the 1980s the environment for blacks is harsher in Liverpool than it is in London. In the former a razor-sharp divide excludes blacks from the city's economic and social life.[51] Judgements of this kind, however, require careful scrutiny and qualification. After all, in East London 'a locally based and socially transmitted vigilantist culture'[52] dating back to the anti-semitic campaigns against Russian Poles in the late nineteenth century, has continued to create problems for immigrant minority groups in the East End, particularly for Bangladeshis. In some cases these conflicts have left bloodstains on the streets.[53]

A number of political developments can also be deployed to qualify the heavy and frequently reiterated emphasis on bleakness. The installation in 1985 of Mohammed Ajeeb as Bradford's first Asian Lord Mayor and the return to Parliament of newcomers in the persons of Paul Boateng, Bernie Grant, and Keith Vaz, as well as Diane Abbott, a British-born black, in the 1985 general election are important positive political developments. A degree of business and professional success among groups such as the Chinese, the Greek Cypriots and the Ugandan Asians is also deserving of notice.

However, we need to return to fundamentals. It is a distortion to concentrate attention on success stories alone; the larger jigsaw of immigration since 1945 and its consequences cannot be composed chiefly out of such vibrant pieces. A number of Poles and European Volunteer Workers never overcame the initial obstacles they had to face: the same observation can be passed on a wide range of other groups. Furthermore, when it did occur, conventional forms of success, particularly in areas of self-employment, sometimes reflected the difficulties which immigrants faced in the labour market. Hence a black QC on the list of silks announced by the Lord Chancellor's Department in 1988 stated that this uncertain leap into legal independence was 'the only option' he could contemplate.[54] A reliance for cases on his white contemporaries at this stage of his career carried a higher risk. Such remarks are a reminder of the strongly held historical preference for self-employment among other groups, such as the Jews, for essentially similar reasons.

If all these pieces of evidence are taken on board, this survey of a selected number of themes relating to immigrants and refugees since 1945 reveals evidence of continuity and change. However, it discounts any major transformation as yet in the *general* condition of these groups in the years since 1979. With these brief observations the survey comes full circle in the sense that some of these assessments can be made only from a position of historical awareness and perspective, a plea for which was entered when this discussion began. Issues relating to immigration are too easily distorted if left entirely in the hands of sociologists, urban geographers and political scientists whose primary orientation is towards the present day. These issues are also far too sensitive to be placed wholly in the guiding hands of polemicists who, by virtue of their role, lack any noticeable sensitivity to the complexities of the world.

11. The Conservative Party since 1945

ANTHONY SELDON

No history of post-war Britain can be complete without a study of the country's most enduringly successful political organisation – the Conservative Party. Yet despite the party's record, it has been much less studied by historians and political analysts than its less successful rival, the Labour Party.[1] Readers of this chapter should, therefore, appreciate that many areas of major interest to an understanding of the Conservative Party either have not been investigated, or remain under-researched.[2] The chapter is divided into a number of thematic sections. It opens with a discussion of the party's electoral record, the dominant fact about the Conservative Party post-war, and there follow shorter sections dealing with the phases of the party's policies, ideologies and factions, organisation, social base and finance, concluding with an assessment of the party's six leaders and seven governments from 1945.

I

The Conservative Party has proved astonishingly successful at winning elections and gaining power with significant majorities. It has won seven of the thirteen elections since 1945. More significant, all seven victories saw it achieve majorities large enough to carry through whatever legislation it wanted in Parliament, whereas only two of Labour's victories, in 1945 and 1966, saw it achieve large 'working' majorities. Its remaining four successes saw either majorities of less than ten (1950, 1964, October 1974), which left it with constant fears of parliamentary defeats, or with no clear majority at all (February 1974).

Taking the last 40 years, from 1951–91, the Conservative record looks even more impressive. With seven of eleven general

233

elections won, it has held power for 29 years, nearly 75 per cent of the time. Labour in contrast only had a majority in the Commons of over ten for four years, 1966–70, i.e. only 10 per cent of the period. Conservative domination over Labour has indeed been impressive.

The first post-war general election (occurring in fact before the end of the war against Japan) came in May 1945. Because of the war, no general election had been held since 1935, and most expected the Conservative dominance over inter-war Britain to be reaffirmed. They were in the event greatly surprised by the result, which saw Labour winning 48.3 per cent of the vote to the Conservatives' 39.8 per cent. At the dissolution of Parliament, the Conservatives had held 398 seats to Labour's 166. After the election, Labour had won 393 seats to the Conservatives' 213, a remarkable turnaround. Many factors explained the 13.9 per cent loss of Conservative vote since 1935. Although fighting on a register which favoured the Conservatives, the electorate was disillusioned with the party for its inter-war record, especially for its association with appeasement and unemployment. The party was ill-organised at both the central and constituency level to fight a general election, and the leaders appeared stale. Churchill during the campaign squandered some of the fund of sympathy for him personally by making exaggerated remarks about the dangers of voting Labour.

Labour in contrast had arguably the better organisation, while the intellectual as well as popular mood of the country since the 1930s, bolstered by the wartime experience, had moved in the direction of socialism. During the war its principal leaders, Clement Attlee, Ernest Bevin, Stafford Cripps, Hugh Dalton and Herbert Morrison, had all gained experience in high office, and had amply displayed their patriotic credentials, regarded as especially important by the large numbers of middle classes who abandoned the Conservatives for Labour in the election.

The Conservatives learnt a hard lesson in the 1945 election, and a series of measures, described in more detail below, were put into effect which made the party far better prepared for the 1950 election (which came in February). Although the Conservatives failed to win, they reduced Labour's majority from 146 to just 5, winning 298 seats to Labour's 315, an achievement all the more notable as the Attlee government of 1945–50 had been highly active and generally popular. The Conservative manifesto, *This Is The Road*, was a big improvement on policy statements in

1945, and the party displayed a new-found confidence.[3] Labour lost some seats (25–30) because of the rearranging of constituency boundaries, and the new postal vote scheme may have gained the Conservatives an extra 10 seats. More significant, however, was the benefit the Conservatives derived from the reaction of the middle classes away from the post-war austerity and planning with which Labour were intimately connected. The Conservatives also benefited from their new moderate policies and from a sensible and well planned campaign.[4]

The party had to wait only another eighteen months before Labour were defeated. In the October 1951 general election, Labour won only 295 seats to the Conservatives' 321. With an overall majority of just 17 (and in fact 200,000 less votes) the Conservatives had their lowest majority of their seven post-war victories. Yet the small size of the majority did not prove a deterrent, except perhaps for a few months in 1952, and the party was able to press on with its favoured policies without serious risk of parliamentary defeat.[5] The rundown of Labour rather than any dramatic new initiatives from the Conservatives had resulted in their victory. Key Labour ministers (Bevin, Cripps) lost through ill-health, internal party divisions (culminating in Bevan's resignation in April 1951) and a series of economic and foreign policy woes all played their part. The collapse of the Liberal vote (to 2.5 per cent, their lowest post-war poll) though due, in part, to their fielding fewer candidates, nevertheless was to the benefit of the Conservatives.[6]

The popular mood in the country continued to flow in favour of the Conservatives in the May 1955 general election, which saw their majority rise to 58, and with 49.7 per cent of the popular vote proved to be their best post-war result. The Conservatives were able to boast a capable track-record since 1951, but as Labour's 1945–50 experience showed, election results are determined by far more than a government's record in office. The economic outlook in 1955, bolstered by an electioneering budget that April, appeared promising, as did the prospects of international peace, with the anticipation of further improvements to come. Labour in contrast did not offer an inviting prospect. Led by the ageing Attlee, the party had had a listless record in opposition since 1951, and was still rent by internal divisions.[7] Prospects for a Labour victory at the next election rose when the Conservative government under Eden failed to satisfy its supporters, culminating in what remains Britain's most humiliating and traumatic post-war episode, the Suez crisis of 1956. But with a new Prime Minister, Harold Macmillan, from January 1957, the fortunes of the party began slowly to improve. The Conservatives' popularity in the opinion polls recovered, and took the party to a sensational victory and a majority of 100 in the October 1959 general election. Conservative seats rose to 365, and Labour's fell to 258, with the Liberals remaining a politically insignificant force with just 6 MPs. The result in October 1959 was the first time since the Great Reform Bill of 1832 that a party had won three parliamentary terms in a row (an achievement subsequently repeated by the Conservatives in 1987, although, unlike in 1959, they benefited then from a divided opposition vote). Even more so than 1955, this was an election won by the Conservatives rather than one lost by Labour. Strongly led by Macmillan, on the solid bedrock of rising material prosperity, the party also pulled off a well organised campaign, fighting on the slogan 'Life's better with the Conservatives. Don't let Labour ruin it'. Analysis of the vote reveals that Labour suffered from abstentions: in those constituencies where turnout increased most, the Conservative vote tended to be smallest. The tendency towards the north–south divide in voting was given added impetus by most of the Conservative gains of 40 seats coming in the south-east and Midlands.[8] The largest gap in the post-war period between general elections followed, with the first occasion since 1722 that a Parliament ran its full statutory term. In the event, leaving the election till the last possible moment, October 1964, did not secure the Conservatives victory, although they did much better than polls indicated they might have done if the election had taken place six months earlier.[9]

The period 1959–64 has been much studied recently by analysts for the light it might throw on the problems of third-term Conservative administrations, with particular reference to Margaret Thatcher's post-1987 government. Although the electorate by the 1980s had become far more volatile, there are nevertheless striking parallels, above all the recovery of Labour two years after the election defeat. From 1962 Labour was steadily ahead in opinion polls, and was determinedly led first by Hugh Gaitskell and then, from 1963, by Harold Wilson. Conservative misfortunes, sometimes own goals, constitute the other main point of comparison. A number of events followed in swift succession: the checking of the steady economic advance since the 1950s; the recovery of the Liberals, notably at Orpington in

March 1962; Macmillan's ill-considered dismissal of seven Cabinet ministers in July; rejection by de Gaulle of Britain's attempt to join the EEC in January 1963; the Profumo sex scandal of that June; and finally the unseemly leadership battle under the glare of the nation's television cameras at the October annual party conference. Macmillan's successor, Alec Douglas-Home, did much better than many gave him credit for, but the task proved too much for him, especially when matched against such a wily debater and party tactician as Harold Wilson.[10]

The biggest puzzle about 1964 is why Labour did not do even better: they won 317 seats to the Conservatives' 304, and had an overall majority of only 4. Had a few voters in critical seats either abstained or voted for other parties, the result might have gone to the Conservatives. Yet Labour, for the first time since 1945–50, appeared the party most in tune with the national mood. The party also looked much more impressive and united under Wilson than it had done under Gaitskell, and its leitmotif during the campaign of modernisation and 'wasted opportunities' under the Conservatives struck home. Indeed it was now the Conservatives who appeared disunited, with two key ministers, Enoch Powell and Iain Macleod, refusing to serve under Douglas-Home. The principal feature of the 1964 election was the collapse of the Conservative vote. It declined by 6 per cent on the 1959 figure, a loss of nearly 2 million votes, the biggest post-war drop for any party. The main beneficiaries were not, however, Labour, but the Liberals, whose share of the vote rose by 5.3 per cent, yet only giving them 9 seats in Parliament. The results are also remarkable for the lack of a nationwide swing: considerable regional variation was in evidence. A factor accounting for the differential swing in certain areas was immigration, which had leapt up as a national issue since the 1959 general election. It has been calculated that three Conservative gains in the West Midlands may have been because traditional working-class Labour voters deserted the party for the Conservatives, deemed tougher on immigration.[11]

The period following the 1964 general election saw Conservatives engaged in an extensive rethinking exercise. With such a slender majority, the party expected Labour to call another general election as soon as its showing in the polls materially improved. They lost little time in replacing Douglas-Home by the younger Edward Heath, in 1965. In the event there was only an eighteen-month wait before Wilson called an election for

March 1966. Even in so brief a period, the Conservative reformulation had had time to bear fruit in the manifesto for the 1966
election, *Action Not Words*, which placed greater stress on
competition, incentives and efficiency, rather than on planning.
The popular perception of the Conservatives, their leader notwithstanding, remained that of Macmillan's and Home's party,
old-fashioned, upper class and out-of-touch.[12] The election result
revealed a major increase in support for Labour, which achieved
its biggest majority (96) since 1945. The Conservatives lost
600,000 votes from their 1964 total, and this was their worst
result since, unsurprisingly, 1945. The party's divisions over the
Rhodesia crisis did not help it but overall the election again was
won by the government rather than lost by the opposition.
Wilson, leading brilliantly, had succeeded in establishing Labour
as the more credible party, and the economy appeared, if only in
the short term, to be under control, with unemployment low, and
standards of living rising. The result worried many leading Conservatives: Wilson appeared to be well on his way to establishing
Labour as the natural party of government. Few foresaw that in
1970, within just four years of their landslide victory, the Conservatives would have succeeded in driving Labour from office.

The Conservatives returned to their policy rethink with renewed fervour after their 1966 defeat. It has indeed been called
the party's most thorough policy re-examination ever in
opposition.[13] Their party organisation was also modernised, and
the party had the opportunity to plant a new image in the minds
of the electorate, free from the associations of the 1950s and early
1960s. Under Heath's leadership, a younger generation of Conservatives had risen to the top echelons. The party was also able
to exploit the internal divisions within the Labour Party where
the leadership had become divided over the unsuccessful
attempts by Barbara Castle (Employment Secretary) to introduce trade union reforms. Discontent had also swelled over the
conduct of economic policy, and support for the United States in
Vietnam, and many Labour Party activists, becoming disillusioned, had left to join radical or revolutionary groups.[14] In
the end, however, Heath's new ideas set out in the manifesto *A
Better Tomorrow*, and Labour's divisions, mattered for much less
than a last minute and unforeseen swing against Labour, precipi-
tated by the publication of adverse balance of payments figures
two days before polling day. The 1970 election saw a 4.3 per cent
swing to the Conservatives from their 1966 result, and with 330

MPs to Labour's 287, a clear majority of 30. Neither of the two major parties proved popular with the electorate over the next three and half years. The general election of February 1974 saw a 5.9 per cent swing away from Labour, their lowest percentage of the vote since 1935, but a 6.6 per cent swing away from the Conservatives, an even worse result than in 1945. The break-up of the alliance with the Ulster Unionists further damaged the Conservatives. With 301 MPs to the Conservatives' 297, Labour were able to form a government, albeit a minority one, with an overall shortfall of 34 below what was required to establish a majority. What had gone wrong for the Tories?

The government's Industrial Relations Act of 1971 had introduced various laws applying to trade unions – succeeding in legislating where Labour had failed two years earlier. But the law, perceived to be much more hostile than Labour's abortive plans, sparked off major industrial unrest culminating in the miners' strikes of 1972 and 1973–4. The new legislation quickly acquired the reputation of being unworkable. Iain MacLeod had been Heath's first Chancellor of the Exchequer, but he died after a month in office, and his successor, Anthony Barber, lacked his skills. Heath became the dominant force shaping economic strategy, and unemployment and inflation mounted, exacerbated by the price rises following the oil crisis after the Yom Kippur War in the Middle East in autumn 1973. Heath had wanted to avoid an early election, but political friends persuaded him to call one. His efforts to reach an accord with the striking miners failed, and on 7 February Heath announced that a general election would be held at the end of the month. It took place during a period of three-day working weeks (in effect since early January) and in an atmosphere of industrial and political crisis. Heath himself stated the government's case as seeking a strong mandate to pursue a counter-inflation and incomes policy. The three-week campaign, the shortest post-war, did not go the Conservatives' way: Harold Wilson announced during it that Labour had secured a 'social contract' with the unions, i.e. that a future Labour government would work in close alliance with the unions; a pay commission (under Sir Frank Figgures) then reported that the miners were under rather than overpaid. Finally, three days before the election, Enoch Powell advised those Conservatives who were opposed to British entry into the EEC the previous year to vote Labour, which may have proved decisive in the election result.

Labour formed their seventh government which, like that of 1929–31, was a minority one. The next election could not be long away. The Conservatives were in disarray after their defeat. Home and Barber both retired, indicating a lack of confidence in the prospects of another Conservative government in the near future. Pressure mounted for Heath to retire. The split between middle-of-the-road or progressive Conservatives and those of the 'new right' who favoured a more free market approach came to the fore. Two prominent members of this faction, Sir Keith Joseph and Margaret Thatcher, formed a think tank, the Centre for Policy Studies, to advance their cause. Heath, as during 1965–70, often failed to get the better of Wilson in Parliament, and with Labour repealing the Industrial Relations Act and introducing two quick budgets, the initiative was soon firmly in their hands. By the late summer of 1974, Wilson felt strong enough to call an election for October. The Conservative manifesto, *Putting Britain First*, failed to excite the electorate, while Labour successfully exploited the internal divisions of the Conservatives. With a 2.1 per cent swing in their favour, and the same margin moving against the Conservatives, Labour achieved an overall majority of three. Despite this small size, Labour was able to sustain itself in office for over four years, bolstered by an unsatisfactory pact with the Liberals from March 1977 to mid-1978.

The period up to the 1979 election proved happier for the Conservatives than for Labour. Under a new leader, Mrs Thatcher, from 1975, the party gradually acquired fresh confidence and sense of purpose. A broad rethink on policy occurred, similar to those during 1945–51 and 1964–70. The manifesto produced for the election (*The Conservative Manifesto, 1979*) was similar in tone to that of 1970, and focused on the trade union 'problem', especially the issues of secondary picketing and the closed shop. The 'winter of discontent' of 1978–9 aided Tory plans by reducing union popularity. Party organisation, under the capable chairmanship of Lord Thorneycroft, was again in good heart. In April 1978 the party contracted with Saatchi and Saatchi to provide advertising, and the firm's hard-hitting and innovative campaign boosted Conservative appeal. Labour, with a tired and demoralised front bench, and fatally handicapped by the breakdown of their relationship with trade unions in the 'winter of discontent', came over as much the less convincing party. The Conservatives went into the campaign clear favourites (10 per cent ahead in the polls) and there were no mishaps during it to upset their lead. The election saw a massive 8.1 per cent swing back to the Conservatives from the October 1974 result, which gave them 62 seats more and an overall majority of 43. Labour dropped 50 seats and the Liberals, with a 4.3 per cent drop in voting support, won only 11 seats.[15]

The popularity of the Thatcher government slumped shortly after it came to power. As with the earlier government of Heath in 1970–4, economic troubles bit home, exacerbated by the 'second' oil shock of 1978–9 which further boosted domestic inflation. The nadir came in 1981, with unemployment soaring over 2 million, and inflation still on 13 per cent in February. Many in the Cabinet argued for a budget which was expansionist rather than deflationary. Mrs Thatcher, and her Chancellor Geoffrey Howe, refused to listen, and produced a tight budget in March to the anger of many on the left and centre of the party. The party's ratings in the polls, however, began to pick up from late 1981 with the popularity of the newly created Social Democratic Party (1981) beginning to moderate. There is a keen debate among political scientists on the extent to which the boost in popularity for the government during 1982 was due to the successful conclusion of the Falklands War in mid-1982, and hence the effect of the war on the 1983 general election result. David Sanders *et al.* argue that the war itself had little impact, pointing rather to improved prosperity, while Lawrence Freedman argues that the war did have an important effect on the 1983 election.[16] What is beyond doubt, however, is that Mrs Thatcher and the Conservatives went into the 1983 election in much better heart than they had been in 1980 and 1981. *The Conservative Manifesto 1983* boasted the government's achievements, and boldly announced further privatisations (British Telecom, British Steel, etc.) and the abolition of the Greater London Council. The result saw a 1.5 per cent swing away from the Conservatives' 1979 result, the party winning 42.4 per cent of the vote and 397 seats. The split opposition vote (Labour 27.6 per cent, SDP-Liberal Alliance 25.4 per cent) was greatly to the Conservatives' advantage, giving them an overall majority of 144 in the Commons.

The second Thatcher term (1983–7) had some severe traumas, notably the Westland Crisis (1986), but by the election the PM could boast of falling inflation, decreasing unemployment, and a solid record of achievement. Anxious to maintain the image of a party with work still to be done, the Conservatives echoed their

1964 manifesto slogan *The Next Moves Forward*. Despite a more popular Labour leader in Neil Kinnock (in place of Michael Foot who had led the party in 1983) and their much improved campaign, the Conservatives held on to their vote (42.2 as opposed to 42.4 per cent), sufficient for an overall majority of 102. Mrs Thatcher had indeed achieved a remarkable third election result and, for the next few months at least, her standing had never been higher.

What conclusions can be drawn from the party's post-war electoral record? The six losses all saw different factors at play, albeit with some uniting themes. When the party was divided, as it was in 1964 and 1974, then it lost support. Staleness, and over-exposure, were working against the Conservatives in 1945 and 1964. Economic difficulties, rightly or wrongly blamed on the government, played their part in 1964 and February 1974. All three factors, namely internal division, boredom and economic problems could work against the Conservatives to their detriment at the next general election. Success resulted from the image of a divided Labour Party, a factor present, to some extent, in all seven Conservative victories. Successful track records, and an avoidance of unpopular policies, played a part in 1955, 1959, 1983 and 1987. Superior party organisation and mastery of the electoral arts were particularly significant in 1951, 1959, 1979 and 1983. Divided opposition parties (splitting the non-Conservative vote into two camps) were a critical factor in the 1983 and 1987 election results.

The factors listed above pertained in different measures at various times. Another broad explanation of the conspicuous Conservative electoral success since 1945 has been that there have simply been more loyal Conservative voters in Britain. The steady haemorrhaging of the Labour vote from 1951–83 (with the exception of the 1966 'blip') lends credence to this view. Again there is a major academic debate about the correlation between class and party loyalty, and the extent that the contraction in size of the working class is damaging Labour. Suffice it to say that the jury, on this issue at least, is still out.[17]

II

Many ways can be devised of subdividing the post-war history of the Conservative Party. This author sees four main periods.

1. 1945–51: period of transition. The 1945 defeat had been a severe blow to the party, which had dominated politics ever since 1918. It embarked on a rigorous overhauling of party organisation and policy. The Conservative Research Department (CRD) under its chairman R. A. Butler became the focal point for the policy reformulation. Many younger men were involved in this work, notably Iain Macleod, Reginald Maudling and Enoch Powell, who were all to play prominent roles in the party in the post-war period. The *Industrial Charter* of 1947 was one of the more significant of the documents produced during the period up to 1951. In fact, the *Industrial Charter* and the other policy statements said little that had not been articulated at the 1945 general election, but they were significant as a further restatement of the party's new-found commitment to interventionism, welfare reforms, full employment and the mixed economy, in marked contrast to the laissez-faire approach of the inter-war years. In 1945 the electorate, and even many in the party, had tended not to believe that the Conservatives had changed their policies from pre-war: the policy review and the work of the CRD convinced them that there was no going back.[18]

2. 1951–65: acceptance of consensus. The rethink played a significant if unknowable part in persuading the electorate to vote Conservative in the October 1951 general election: it was even more significant in convincing the party itself that it had to adapt itself to what has subsequently been termed the 'post-war consensus'. Cemented by the Attlee Labour government of 1945–51, it owed its origins to the work of the Wartime Coalition (1940–5) and often to earlier precedents. The two principal intellectual influences on it were William Beveridge and J. M. Keynes. It consisted of five main aspects or 'planks': a commitment to full employment; an acceptance of the right of trade unions to consultation by government: the mixed economy; the welfare state; and a commitment to equality, in an attempt to mitigate the worst aspects of inegality.[19] Although the whole notion of consensus is open to criticism,[20] it is nevertheless a useful descriptive tool for comprehending the direction of post-war history. The party after 1951 embraced all five planks. The Churchill government of 1951–5 set the tone for the period in office to 1964. The party accepted its obligation to full employment, Churchill offering the Chancellorship of the Exchequer in 1951 to the moderate Butler in preference to the more hardline

Oliver Lyttelton. By pursuing a mix of fiscal and monetary policies, aided by a generally favourable international trading position, Conservative governments to 1964 ensured that the aggregate level of unemployment seldom rose above 2–3 per cent.

Trade unions had been intimately connected with the Labour Party since its foundation in 1900: partly for this reason the Conservatives had treated them with suspicion. During the inter-war period antipathy had reached a high point during the General Strike of 1926 when Churchill as Chancellor of the Exchequer played a key role in its defeat. During the Second World War, however (as to a lesser extent during the First) trade unions had been involved in the processes of government, and after 1945 the post-war Labour government maintained those close links. The expectation was that a future Conservative government might sever them, but in 1951 Churchill returned to power, determined to conciliate the unions. He appointed the moderate Walter Monckton Minister of Labour (now called 'Employment Secretary') with a brief to avoid industrial unrest. Monckton performed this task with such zeal that he annoyed industrialists, who felt he was giving away inflationary wage claims, and earned himself the nickname 'the oilcan' in the process. From 1961, with the adoption of income policies and the establishment of the National Economic Development Council (NEDC), on which sat representatives of government, industry and the unions, ties became even closer.

Third came the mixed economy, entailing a large role for government in the running of the economy, and hence the limitation of unbridled capitalism or the free market. This plank refers principally to the ownership of industry, instigated by the Attlee government's major programme of nationalisation, including the Bank of England, Cable and Wireless, civil aviation, coal, electricity, and road and rail transport, all during 1945–7, gas in 1948 and iron and steel in 1949. In total, 20 per cent of the economy was taken into public hands. However, as K. O. Morgan has argued, the nationalisations, with the exception of iron and steel, aroused little controversy, and the organisational structure adopted was also in a moderate form.[21] It was theoretically open to a future Conservative government to indulge in wholesale de-nationalisation, yet Conservative governments throughout 1951–64 chose to keep the majority of these industries nationalised: only road haulage, and iron and steel were privatised, both in 1953, and by creating the Atomic Energy Authority in 1954, the government even extended the principle of state ownership of industry. The state's role in housing was also boosted: in the 1950s over 2 million new houses were built, half of them through the public sector.

The 'welfare state' constituted the fourth plank. It has been argued convincingly that any government coming to office in 1945 would have established welfare reforms in some form; indeed, a limited welfare state was already in existence, when the war broke out in 1939.[22] What the Labour government of 1945–51 did was to establish, in a series of measures, including the NHS Act of 1946, a comprehensive system of free welfare benefits covering children, sickness, old age, unemployment and loss of the breadwinner. The services were provided by the state and were paid for by taxation or insurance. Many had expected the next Conservative government to trim back on benefits, introduce more charging for services or extend the role of private provision. In fact the Conservatives in 1951–64 left the welfare state largely intact. Initial plans to introduce more charges for the NHS were dropped, and in 1952 Churchill appointed another moderate, Macleod, as Minister of Health. Expenditure on the welfare state as a percentage of gross domestic product rose throughout their period in office.

Equality is the final aspect of the post-war consensus, entailing the use of economic, regional and social policy. Conservative governments in the period 1951–64 did not pursue this end with Labour's ardour; for example they reduced income tax and allowed regional unemployment to rise markedly when compared to the south-east. Nevertheless, in broad terms, the principle of striving for a sense of equality for all within the United Kingdom was followed.

The period of attachment to the post-war consensus lasted approximately until the election of Heath as party leader in 1965 in succession to Home. The period can thus be said to have ended the year after the party's defeat in the general election of October 1964.

3. 1965–75: period of transition. Heath came to lead the party with a policy statement *Putting Britain Right Ahead* which marked a clear breach with post-war Conservatism up to that point. Above all, it committed the country unequivocally to the European Community to an extent that the Macmillan government (1957–63) had never felt able to do.[23] The policy review which Heath initiated produced other important departures, notably the principle that agreement was not required from all sides before taking tough action. A future Conservative government was to be more decisive. The unions in particular were to be brought into line by trade union reform, a far cry from the conciliatory approach of Walter Monckton. In the event the Heath government was unable to carry out effectively many of its tougher and non-consensual policies. Opposition from the unions and mounting economic problems led to the abandonment of many of the policies – the 1972 'U-turn'. Following it, government became much more interventionist in the economy, and controls were introduced on prices and incomes. Of the five planks of the post-war consensus, all except perhaps one, the welfare state, came under threat during 1970–2, and then from 1972 until his defeat in February 1974, Heath returned to those same consensus policies. Heath himself argued that the retreat was merely tactical and would be temporary: in the event the loss of the election rendered him unable to prove whether he was right.[24]

4. 1975 onwards: Thatcherism. The second defeat in October 1974, and the failure to have executed a consistent policy when in office, were the catalysts for Heath's leadership to be challenged in 1975, with Mrs Thatcher emerging as victor. With her close political ally, Sir Keith Joseph, she had set up a free market think tank, the Centre for Policy Studies, the previous year. Together they started to champion non-consensus conservatism. With views similar in tone and substance to many of the policies attempted by Heath up to 1972, they gave the impression that this time they would not be deflected back to middle-of-the-road Conservatism when the going got tough.

And so it proved. In office from 1979, Mrs Thatcher systematically began to dismantle many aspects of the post-war consensus. Unemployment drifted to over 3 million, way beyond levels that would have been regarded as politically acceptable in the first 30 years after the war. The conquering of inflation was put above full employment as the primary objective of government economic policy, and so it remained throughout the 1980s and into the 1990s. The critical point came in 1981 when unemployment, which had stood at 1.3 million when the Conservatives came to office, threatened to escalate to unprecedently high levels following the 1980–1 recession. The pressure on Mrs

Thatcher to introduce expansionary policies, which would have boosted the economy and reduced unemployment, was immense. She refused, announcing that, unlike 1972, there would be no U-turn. Keynesian 'demand management' economic policies, which had dominated government approach since 1945, were jettisoned in favour of monetarist policies as advocated by the American economist Milton Friedman. Suddenly Keynes and Keynesianism had become dirty words.

'Conciliation' of trade unions was the second consensus plank to be abandoned. Much of the ire of the Centre for Policy Studies, influenced by the other main intellectual influence on Thatcherism, F. A. Hayek, was directed against trade unions. The subject dominated the Conservative manifesto in 1979. In the February 1974 election both the Labour and Conservative parties had been offering a 'corporatist' vision for running Britain, i.e. government working in close league with union and business leaders. Yet after 1979 first the informal and then the formal contacts with unions were unceremoniously ended. Mrs Thatcher deliberately set out also to win battles against unions, as Martin Holmes has argued, mostly notably in the miners' strike of 1984–5, and hence to reduce their power.[25] Legislation in 1980, 1982, 1984 and 1988, coupled with high unemployment and social and employment shifts, combined to make her task easier. By 1990 unions in Britain, as in many other industrial nations, had become far weaker than they had been ten years earlier.

Public ownership was another *bête noir* of Mrs Thatcher and Keith Joseph. Distaste for the public sector and trade unions went hand-in-glove with admiration for individualism and private enterprise. The extensive privatisation programme and the sale of council houses succeeded in tipping the balance of the mixed economy back in favour of private enterprise (if not as far as many Conservative supporters claimed or would have liked).

Only the welfare state survived largely intact into Mrs Thatcher's third term in office. But after 1987 even this last bastion of consensus came under attack, with the government's introduction of reforms in health and education which extended free market principles and reduced the role of the state as the main provider.[26] These reforms, especially in health, proved highly unpopular, and suggest the reason why the welfare state, alone of the five consensus planks, endured so long. Attachment to the equality principle came under attack early on in the Thatcher regime. Income tax rates have been reduced for the better off, and increasing reliance has been made on flat rate taxes such as VAT. The community charge, also being levied equally on the population, is likewise unequal in outcome as it hits the less well off the hardest. Regional policy also has been steadily reduced, with less cash available for the poorer areas of the UK. In consequence, the south of the country has become more prosperous under Thatcherism, and the north relatively less well off.[27] Britain under Margaret Thatcher thus became a more unequal society with the government standing by and in some cases even encouraging increasing divergence in income and regional wealth.

The fourth phase of post-war conservatism saw the successful implementation (unlike Heath's third phase) of a new style of conservatism, one drawing its inspiration from Friedman and Hayek rather than Beveridge and Keynes. It is an open question whether the phase will survive long into the 1990s. The likelihood is that the Conservatives under John Major from November 1990 will move into another transition period, and return eventually to a set of policies more in line with the post-war consensus, as Labour has returned to in its 1989 Policy Review, if for no other reason than this is what the electorate seems to want.

III

Considerable debate surrounds the Conservative Party and ideology. The interest concerns both whether there is an ideology of the Conservative Party, and if so, what it involves.[28] Supporters of a Conservative ideology refer to three influences in particular: Edmund Burke, with his belief in gradual progress and in change which is in harmony with the individuals in society and their traditions; Sir Robert Peel, who in his *Tamworth Manifesto* argued the need for the party to adapt to change, hence keeping it in line with changing society; and finally another Conservative PM, Benjamin Disraeli, who in a famous speech at Crystal Palace in 1872 set three great objectives for the party – maintenance of national institutions, the upholding of the empire, and 'the elevation of the condition of the people'.[29] The third of Disraeli's objectives, the belief that the party should represent 'one nation' rather than just advancing the interests of one section or class, has found repeated echoes since, notably in Harold Macmillan's important book, *The Middle Way* (1938).[30]

A further key thinker, whom supporters of a Conservative ideology look to, is Quintin Hogg (now Lord Hailsham). In *The Case for Conservatism* (1947) Hogg reiterated the need for gradual adaptation, and stated that patriotism lies at the heart of Conservatism: 'The nation, not the so-called class struggle is therefore at the base of Conservative political thinking'.[31]

Many authorities, however, deny that the Conservative Party is ideological.[32] Notable among them is Ian Gilmour, the journalist and former Cabinet Minister under Mrs Thatcher who was sacked in 1981. Gilmour writes that Conservatism 'cannot be formulated in a series of propositions which can be aggregated into a creed. It is not an ideology or a creed.'[33] The author of this present chapter confesses to scepticism about a consistent Conservative Party ideology, still more so to its indispensability to an understanding of the history of the Conservative Party in the post-war period. Rather he sees a series of influences operating on different people and groups at different times, ideological considerations playing second fiddle to a desire to gain and retain power. Thus the party could jettison Disraeli's second principle, attachment to empire, when in the 1950s and 1960s it no longer appeared practicable to retain Britain's colonies. In the later 1970s and the 1980s the party leadership was influenced by the ideas of Hayek and Friedman, which had far more in common with liberalism than Conservative theory. These ideas were mediated by the little-known international group, the Mont Pelerin Society, set up in 1946, and also by the Institute of Economic Affairs, established in 1957. After Mrs Thatcher new doctrinal influences are already coming into play. Indeed, a considerable debate has sprung up over whether Mrs Thatcher, the longest continously serving PM since Lord Liverpool (1812–27), was indeed 'a Conservative'.[34] This surely supports the case for not dwelling too long on the question of Conservative ideology.

More illuminating is an examination of the factions, or tendencies, within the Conservative Party. Such an exercise indeed illuminates the multiplicity of ideological influences on different sections within the party at different times. Richard Rose has written that the Conservatives are 'pre-eminently a party of tendencies'. Others have preferred to call these subgroupings 'factions', indicating a more coherent and better organised existence.[35] Although 'tendency' is the more accurate term for most of the period, both terms will be used below. Table 11.1

TABLE 11.1 Conservative factions

	Progressives	New right	Nationalists/neo-imperialists
Intellectual gurus	Ian Gilmour Iain Macleod Harold Macmillan	Milton Friedman F. A. Hayek Keith Joseph	Leo Amery Enoch Powell Roger Scruton
Contemporary advocates	Edward Heath (post-1972) Jim Prior Peter Walker	Margaret Thatcher Keith Joseph Norman Tebbit	Enoch Powell Julian Amery Teddy Taylor
Previous advocates	Rab Butler Walter Monckton Harold Macmillan Edward Boyle Lord Hailsham Robert Carr	Angus Maude Lord Coleraine Oliver Lyttelton Enoch Powell	Leo Amery John Biggs-Davison Lord Salisbury Lord Brookeborough
Causes	One Nation Toryism, limited Constitutional and social reforms. European integration	Free market economics, popular capitalism & privatisation, deregulation, anti-local government, Anglo-Americanism, British sovereignty in Europe	*Formerly* Imperial union, anti-decolonisation, especially for Rhodesia, anti-GATT, anti-EEC, pro-Suez and East of Suez *Currently* Anti-immigration, pro-South Africa, UK sovereignty in NATO & Europe. Ulster & Scottish Unionism, free market economics

Organisations	(1940s/1950s) Tory Reform Committee. One Nation Group (1960s/1975) Pressure for Social & Economic Toryism (1975–current) Tory Reform Group (Current) Charter Group	Institute for Economic Affairs Selsdon Group Centre for Policy Studies Adam Smith Institute Libertarian Alliance (ultra) (All current) Bow Group (1951–current)	East of Suez Group (1960s) Ulster Unionists/Orange Order (1882–1973) Anglo-Rhodesian & South African Friendship Societies Anti-Common Market League (1960s/1970s) Tory Action (ultra) Monday Club (1961 to current) Freedom Association
Spheres of Influence	'Wets'-Euro-integrationists: Conservative social reformers	Party mainstream: Parliamentary Tory majority, Central Office, Young Conservatives	'Old Guard', Ulster & Scottish Unionists, anti-Soviet & pro-South African lobbyists
Publications	H. Macmillan, *The Middle Way* (Macmillan, 1938) I. Macleod & J. E. Powell, *The Social Services: Needs & Means* (CPC, 115 1952 & 1954) Lord Hailsham, *The Case for Conservatism* (Penguin, 1949) I. Gilmour, *Inside Right* (Hutchinson, 1977)	A. Maude, *The Common Problem* (Constable, 1969) K. Joseph, *Reversing the Trend* (Barry Rose, 1975) M. Friedman, *Free to Choose* (Penguin, 1980) Rhodes Boyson (ed.) *1985: An Escape From Orwell's 1984* (Churchill Press, 1975)	J. Amery, *The British Commonwealth & Western Europe* (Longmans, 1952) L. Amery, *Thoughts on the Constitution* (OUP, 1953) E. Powell, *The Common Market: The Case Against* (Elliott Rightway, 1971) *Wrestling with the Angel* (Sheldon, 1977)
Journals	(*Cambridge Reformer*) *Tory Reform*	*Crossbow* *Daily Telegraph*	*Tory Challenge* *Salisbury Review* (*Monday World*)

delineates three clear factions in the party: the progressives or moderates, the new right, and the nationalists or 'neo-imperialists' (sometimes called 'old right'). Each has dominated at different times. Such is the hierarchical nature of the party that the leader can entirely imbue it with his own outlook: Churchill (party leader, 1940–55) was initially a nationalist/neo-imperialist, who turned progressive after the war; Macmillan (1957–63) a whole-hearted progressive; and Mrs Thatcher an apostle of the new right.[36] The dominant faction at any one particular time has tended to obscure the fact that the others have continued to have powerful advocates in the party, whose views often only find voice at times of party crisis. The three broad factions are not exclusive; many key Conservatives have moved from one to another, and some belonged to more than one at the same time, for example Enoch Powell, a member initially of the progressives, who went on to combine the beliefs of both the new right and the nationalist tendencies. The groups themselves moreover are not homogeneous, and each has considerable differences of opinion within it: they are indeed best understood, not as mutually exclusive, but as overlapping, circles. The nationalists/neo-imperialist tendency has been the dominant force in the inter-war party, and some key supporters lingered on into the Cabinets of the 1950s, notably Harry Crookshank, Oliver Lyttelton, Lord Salisbury and Lord Swinton. The late 1940s saw a younger brand of progressive Conservative, conspicuously Butler and Macmillan, move into top positions, and when Churchill set up his government in 1951 he gave many of them the key portfolios, including the Treasury (Butler), Housing (Macmillan) and Labour (Monckton). These progressive Conservatives looked back to the party's inter-war leaders, Stanley Baldwin (1923–37) and Neville Chamberlain (1937–40) and argued that their reformist zeal, especially Chamberlain's, had been overtaken by other priorities. They determined that this would not happen again, and together they helped convert and then attach the party to the post-war consensus policies, the visible form of the progressive tendency's views.

Progressive Conservatism was also the creed that found favour with the large numbers of younger Conservative MPs, many of whom entered Parliament in 1950. Together they formed the One Nation Group in 1950, the title harking back to Disraeli's call for Conservatism to appeal to the whole nation, not just one section of it. The new right looks to Peter Thorneycroft's brief period as Chancellor of the Exchequer (1957–8) as an early advocate of their views, but Macmillan soon reasserted his own brand of progressive Conservatism. Not until the 1960s did the new right begin to capture supporters in any number among Conservative MPs as they fell under the influence of the free market ideas articulated by the IEA (founded in 1957). Key advocates of new right thinking at this time in the parliamentary party were John Biffen and Enoch Powell, and to a lesser extent Geoffrey Howe. Powell ruled himself out of any future influence on the party leadership after his anti-immigration speech and subsequent dismissal from the shadow cabinet in 1968, but it was new right thinking which trickled into some of the policy statements, especially on industry and union matters, and subsequently influenced the policy of Heath's government from 1970 until the U-turn in 1972. The 'Selsdon Group' was formed at this time by young new right enthusiasts in an unsuccessful attempt to persuade the government not to return to progressive/ consensus policies. Not until after 1974 and the failure of the Heath government did the new right begin to win supporters on a large scale. There were several reasons for this upsurge. Progressive policies, it was alleged, did not work: they had burdened the country with unacceptably high levels of tax and government expenditure, had elevated unions to an overpowerful position and had encouraged a dependency culture where citizens looked to the state as a cure-all for their ills rather than to themselves and their families. Rising unemployment and inflation, and repeated economic crises, were cited as evidence of the failure.[37] As one leading figure on the new right told Dennis Kavanagh: 'By the mid-1970s [collectivists] had been [dominant] for thirty years and could no longer ask for more time.'[38] To the new right, post-war Conservative governments had been as culpable as those of Labour in their adherence to collectivist policies.

The old right by the mid-1970s was no longer a credible force to take over the party. They had fought one lost cause after another since the war: decolonisation; the decision in 1954 to withdraw from the Suez base; immigration; accession to Europe in 1972; sanctions against the white regime in Rhodesia; more overt support for the Protestant Unionists in Northern Ireland. Their main organisation, the Monday Club, had been formed in the wake of Macmillan's 1961 'Winds of Change' speech in South Africa which suggested that the days of white minority rule in

Africa were numbered. But only a small minority of MPs were involved in the Monday Club. Resistance to further moves to European integration, and to immigration from Hong Kong, proved that this wing of the party still had its supporters in the early 1990s, but its strength was at best static, and was probably waning. The old right, therefore, lacked the power base in the party, and a coherent policy prescription, to take over after the Heath failure. The new right, however, had both a clear policy, and growing support. In February 1975 Mrs Thatcher, a surprise candidate, ousted Heath as party leader. Her election should be seen as a reaction against Heath, whom many in the party wanted out at all costs, rather than as a victory for the new right, who were at this point in a minority in the party. Nevertheless, using her powers of patronage, Mrs Thatcher steadily promoted those of a new right disposition at the expense of progressives. This policy continued after she achieved power in 1979, and was seen most notably in 1981 when she sacked three leading progressives (by now dubbed 'wets', as opposed to new right 'dries'): Ian Gilmour, Christopher Soames and Norman St John Stevas.

Two Conservatives have had an 'ism' attached to their name – Enoch Powell and Margaret Thatcher. Powellism, combining an obsession with national identity with laissez-faire economics, was taken very seriously in the late 1960s and early 1970s, and became the subject of several books and doctoral theses.[39] But Powell's own difficult temperament, his lack of tact and unfortunate timing meant that Powellism withered on the vine before it had even flowered; many sympathisers in the party, but few supporters, mourned its passing. Had Powell planned his attack on Heath's leadership after it had been shown to have failed, rather than before he came to power in 1970, then history might have been very different.

Mrs Thatcher's timing, however, was perfect. (Ironically, it was Powell who said that Mrs Thatcher just happened to be in the right place when the roulette wheel stopped in front of her.) Apparently loyal to Heath from 1970–4, she (and Joseph) came out into the open with their attack just after the election defeat in February 1974. But what exactly was Thatcherism? The political historian John Campbell has written illuminatingly on the subject. He first comments on how rare it was for a single politician to be afforded an 'ism' (only Bevan apart from Powell in postwar Britain). It has to be conceded, even by her worst enemies, that in this respect Mrs Thatcher was exceptional. Indeed, it was her enemies as much as her supporters who gave the concept of Thatcherism its currency.[40] Campbell saw four ingredients to Thatcherism. The political *philosophy* denoted a concern with personal freedom under the law, with private property as against collectivism, and with capitalism as against socialism – in other words, the particular emphasis in Conservative thinking of the new right. Next came what Campbell called the intellectual *doctrine* of monetarism and the free market, with its strong preference for private rather than state provision of goods and services. Incomes policies, regional subsidies, support for national-ised industries and other key features of Keynesian economies were all downgraded or eliminated altogether. Third was the practical *agenda* of Thatcherism, i.e. the record of policies pursued by the government since May 1979, involving all those areas from local government via council houses and trade union powers to the universities, where her government made a decisive impact.[41] Finally, there were the underlying *instincts* of Thatcherism, her deep-rooted social values often derived from her early life experi-ences as the daughter of Alderman Roberts in small-town Grantham.[42] This last aspect of Thatcherism, an insistence on order and authority, clashed with the laissez-faire approach in economics, intent on rolling back the frontiers of the state. Andrew Gamble has written persuasively of this inconsistency, most recently in his *The Strong State Free Economy*. In it he shows how central government in Britain after 1979 has acquired extraordinary new powers – over local government, trade unions, the Civil Service, education, etc. – while at the same time extolling the need for personal responsibility and decentralised decision-taking, within the discipline of the market. A Thatcher-ite defence of this dichotomy was to say that government involvement over many aspects of individuals' and corporate life had proceeded so far this century, and especially since 1945, that a strong dose of authoritarianism was needed to redress the balance and set the country back on the right path.[43]

Not all commentators agree that Thatcherism was an impor-tant phenomenon. Prime among the sceptics is Ben Pimlott, who argues that it was 'mainly composed of developments that would have happened anyway, albeit with a different rhetoric, under Labour, and with probably much the same kind of rhetoric under Heath'.[44] To Pimlott the claimed successes of Thatcherism, the 'economic miracle', the taming of the unions, transformation of values and recovery of international reputation, have been exaggerated in importance, and many of the innovations, from monetarism to council house sales, either pre-dated 1979, or would have been undertaken by a Labour government. Indeed, the 1989 Labour Policy Review accepts many parts of the Thatcher reforms since 1979, further evidence that Labour might well have enacted them if faced with the same facts.[45] Pimlott also points to the evidence worldwide in the 1980s and early 1990s, from Lange's New Zealand to Gorbachev's Soviet Union, to indicate that to pin too much on Mrs Thatcher herself is misleading. He further highlights the role of luck in accounting for Mrs Thatcher, above all the divided opposition in the 1983 and 1987 elections, which allowed her to win landslides on small majorities (42 per cent of the total vote) and the unexpected windfall of a victory in a war (the Falklands, 1982).[46]

One can never know what might have happened had Mrs Thatcher not become party leader in 1975. Nevertheless it seems unlikely that another leader would have seen quite the same urgency for taking Britain in a similar direction. Mrs Thatcher's sheer stamina, persistence and belief in her own rightness did indeed make her a most unusual, perhaps unique, Prime Minister. William Whitelaw, Geoffrey Howe, Edward Du Cann and Jim Prior were all possible leaders after Heath: it is most unlikely that they would have changed the direction of the Conservative Party, and hence Britain, as much as Margaret Thatcher did in her eleven-and-a-half-year premiership.

IV

The Conservative Party has always been more hierarchical than Labour, and the authority of the leader and the parliamentary party has been more secure. This traditional view was given fresh voice when Bob McKenzie wrote his classic textbook on British political parties in 1955.[47] McKenzie argued that the Conservative Party was an 'overt oligarchy' for five reasons: the origins of the party were parliamentary, with the organisation in the country coming only in the later nineteenth century after the 1867 Reform Act, which extended the franchise; in consequence, the National Union of Conservative and Union Associations, the party's voluntary wing outside Parliament, had no role in policy-making; third, even the full-time party headquarters organisation, Conservative Central Office, was similarly subordinate to the parliamentary party, with the party chairman at its head appointed (and dismissed) by the party leader; next came the attitude of the Conservative rank-and-file, which was to defer to leaders and support them, often uncritically; finally was the party's non-ideological approach, which meant that policy could be flexible and turned to the electorate's changing preferences, with the party as a whole trusting their leaders to determine what the appropriate policy should be.[48]

Does McKenzie's hierarchical thesis (subsequently revised) still hold true today? The evidence conflicts. Most important, the leader's power has not been nearly as absolute as McKenzie imagined. To begin, in the year that McKenzie's volume was published, Churchill was all but bustled out of the party leadership (and No. 10) by discontented party colleagues.[49] In January 1957 Anthony Eden had to retire following the disaster of the Suez crisis of 1956, having lost the support of his Cabinet colleagues. Harold Macmillan retired reluctantly in October 1963 due to ill health, again having lost the confidence of key Cabinet colleagues. Alec Douglas-Home became subject to bitter attacks ('Sack Alec') following the October 1964 election defeat, and the pressure led to him retiring in 1965. His successor, Edward Heath, came under fire following the February 1974 defeat, and criticism crescendoed after the second election in October, until he was successfully challenged by Mrs Thatcher the following year. Even Mrs Thatcher was not unassailable. Criticism was always close to the surface. Even before the successful challenge to her leadership in November 1990, opposition had come out into the open in 1989, with Sir Anthony Meyer's formal leadership challenge in the autumn. On the other hand one could stress the reverse side. Churchill survived years of plotting against him (from at least 1947), Macmillan rode out crises in 1962 and early 1963, Heath lost three elections out of four and was not ousted until 1975, and Thatcher's durability was arguably more impressive than the attempts to unseat her. Further evidence also suggests that McKenzie's hierarchical model is in need of revision. New research by Richard Kelly finds that Conservative Party conferences, dismissed by McKenzie as of no policy significance, have become increasingly assertive. Reforms to married women's taxation in the 1980s, for example, have occurred in response to pressure from Conservative conferences. Within Parliament, as Philip Norton has shown, party leadership since 1970 has become subject to increasing backbench revolt and assertiveness.[50] Norton points to a wide range of issues, from the defeat of the Shops Bill in 1986 to student grants, nurses' pay and concessions in housing benefit where Mrs Thatcher was forced to moderate policy in the light of pressure from her backbenchers.

Evidence can also be advanced, however, to support the hierarchy thesis. Despite pressure from pro-democracy groups within the party (most notably from the 'Charter Group') the party outside Parliament remains with no formal policy role. The Conservatives are the sole major party where only MPs are able to vote for the leader. Party manifestos remain firmly the prerogative of the leader to decide, in marked contrast to the Labour Party, where the National Executive Committee has real policy power. Conservative Central Office remains tightly under the control of the party leader, and when Norman Tebbit as Party Chairman annoyed Mrs Thatcher he was calmly dismissed. The 1922 Committee, to which all Tory backbenchers belong, has probably less power while the subject committees (Defence, Northern Ireland, etc.) have more than in the 1940s. Mrs Thatcher, meanwhile, was often able to ride roughshod over her Cabinet during the 1980s, earning her the title of the most dictatorial Prime Minister since the war. The extent to which she was authoritarian, especially *vis-à-vis* her Cabinet is, predictably, the subject of another academic debate. Peter Hennessy has argued that she weakened Cabinet, George Jones that her alleged power as PM was much exaggerated.[51]

The period since 1945 has also seen some notable changes in policy machinery. Lord Woolton became Party Chairman in 1946 and set himself the task of building up Central Office and local organisation in the country. By 1951, party members had reached 3 million, which proved to be the post-war highpoint, with the newly-founded Young Conservatives being one of the areas of fastest growth.[52] The Conservative Research Department, which became fully operational again in 1947 after the hiatus of war, and the Conservative Political Centre, the party's revived education and propaganda arm, further served to give the image of dynamism at the centre of the party's organisation. In the years that followed the authority of Central Office fluctuated, in large part due to the personality of the incumbent Party Chairman, and the party leader's willingness to take his advice. Apart from Woolton, Butler (1959–61), Thorneycroft (1975–81) and Parkinson (1981–3) were notably influential.

If the power of Central Office fluctuated, that of the Research Department waned after 1970 until in 1978 it was relocated within Central Office. Increasingly in the 1970s and 1980s the party leadership turned for policy suggestions to bodies outside the formal party, notably the Institute of Economic Affairs, the Centre for Policy Studies and the Adam Smith Institute. These three bodies, indicatively, were all advancing new right rather than progressive Conservatism. The 1980s and early 1990s can be seen also as a time of growing professionalism within the party, often following the lead of the Republican Party in the United States, for example in the use of computers and direct mail.[53] The use of outside advertising agencies was first seen in the 1959 election, but reached new heights after 1979, as did reliance on media consultants and other public relations specialists. Resentment at this media management reached a highpoint at the 1988 annual party conference, when the leadership kept Northern Ireland off the agenda for fear that a heated debate could compromise the image of a unified party.[54]

The party's recruitment and the social background of its volunteers and professionals are under-researched areas. The little work that has been done indicates a small degree of broadening of the party's social base. Traditionally the Conservative Party had been the party of the upper or upper middle classes: by 1990 it was still more socially exclusive than any other party, but had become more middle class. Ramsden has reached several broad conclusions, as seen in Table 11.2.[55]

TABLE 11.2   Social background of Conservatives

	1951	1959	1970	1983
	The background of Conservative MPs (% of total)			
Occupation				
Professional	41	46	45	45
Business	37	30	30	36
Misc. white-collar	22	23	24	19
Manual	0	1	1	1
Education				
Public school	75	72	74	70
of which				
Eton/Harrow/Winchester	33	29	25	16

First, he shows that whereas the proportion of MPs from public schools has remained broadly the same, those from the elite three (Eton, Harrow, Winchester) have halved. Remarkable stability in occupational background is clearly indicated in the table. He further finds that the social structure remains a pyramid: Conservative voters are more middle class than Labour voters; party members are more middle class than voters, and so on, becoming ever more socially exclusive, via constituency activists and local councillors up to MPs and party leaders. Only gradual change has occurred in the party's finance structure. Throughout the post-war period the Conservatives have been better off than Labour, but their advantage has been declining. The routine (i.e. non-election) budget of Conservative Central Office was nearly three times the size of Labour's until the 1960s; by the mid-1980s it was only 20 per cent larger.[56] The sources of the party's funds have remained unchanged: corporated donations have contributed about 50–60 per cent of the party's central income, individual donations and bequests accounting for about 20 per cent, and the remainder has come from constituency association activities.

Whether the Conservatives have been more pro-business than they might have been without the cash is uncertain. Keith Ewing said that it 'would be wrong to say that the Conservatives are pro-business simply because they are financed by business'.[57] Michael Pinto-Duschinsky, however, thinks differently, arguing that corporate funding has been a 'significant influence' on the development of party policy.[58]

V

So where does this survey of the Conservative Party post-war leave us? Conservative dominance, it was suggested at the outset, has been the pre-eminent fact in post-war political history.[59] All seven governments have had achievements; in the absence of clear yardsticks for assessing governmental performance, the following judgements will be made.[60] The most successful administrations, in terms of policies and promises met, were those of 1951–5, 1979–83 and 1983–7. Two governments which started well but then became unstuck were those of 1959–64 and 1970–4. The improvement prize to the government which picked up most after an inauspicious start must go to that of 1955–9, while the poorest government of the seven is clearly that since 1987. All six party leaders had strengths and weaknesses. Churchill was past his best by the time he came to No. 10 in 1951, as was Eden in 1955. Two, Macmillan and Mrs Thatcher, began very promisingly but then lost their touch. Heath, in contrast, never fully had the feel of the parliamentary party, and when his policies came unstuck from 1972 few were prepared to stand by him. As popular with the party as any leader was the one who spent least time at No. 10, Alec Douglas-Home, who has consistently been the most under-rated post-war leader of the Conservative Party.

12. Labour as a Governing Party: Balancing Right and Left

MARTIN CEADEL

IT is a truism that British government 'is pre-eminently party government'.[1] The lack of an institutional separation or territorial division of powers, or of a bill of rights, means that whoever controls the House of Commons has almost unfettered constitutional authority. And a combination of a simple-majority, single-ballot electoral system and a political culture with only one major cleavage – that based on a largely dichotomised view of social class – ensures that it is what Harold Macmillan has called the 'essentially English' two-party system[2] which controls the House of Commons.

For the Labour Party, which became a full member in 1945 on winning its first parliamentary majority, this two-party system has proved a source both of opportunity and of difficulty. By offering the chance of single-party government, it has given Labour the opportunity from time to time – so far in 1945–51, 1964–70, and 1974–9 – to implement its programme as fully as it wished. But by marginalising parties of both the centre (such as the Liberals) and the far left (such as the Communists or ILP), it has forced Labour to accommodate within its own ranks almost the full spectrum of left-of-centre thought. The two-party system has, in other words, required Labour to live with both a right and a left which in other political systems might have split off into viable separate parties. However much the party has sought to play this fact down, the most troublesome aspect of its political life has been the division between those primarily concerned to offer an electable reforming alternative to Conservatism (which is how 'the right' will be defined in this essay) and those preferring to hold out for more fundamental social and economic change (which is how 'the left' will here be defined). And, however much

263

the issues which reveal this division have varied over the years, the question of how far the economy should be 'nationalised' has been the most important.

The state of relations between, and the relative strengths of, Labour's right and left have been among the key variables of post-war British politics. In view of the vast literature on the Labour Party – far bigger than that on the Conservatives – it is surprising that the shifting balance between right and left has not more often been addressed directly. This essay will attempt to do so, even at the price of neglecting other aspects of Labour's development since 1945 – such as its changing electoral basis – which have received exhaustive treatment elsewhere. It will therefore chronicle Labour's history as a full member of the two-party system in terms of six phases in which different balances of power between right and left can be identified.

I

The first phase requires the most attention since it has proved to be unique in Labour's history as a governing party: both left and right were united in their satisfaction with the policies on which the Attlee government had been elected. The right be- lieved that the manifesto embodied its own strategy. In the mid-1930s it had led Labour away both from the mixture of vague utopianism, syndicalist temptation and Gladstonian orthodoxy which had characterised party policy in the 1920s, and from the ultra-radicalism to which the party had succumbed in the immediate aftermath of the 1931 crisis. In their place Labour had formulated a specific and practical programme which satisfied the moderate majority in both the party and the trade unions.[3] When the Beveridge Report appeared in 1942, the right also welcomed its ideas: 'a free national health service, policies of full employment, a comprehensive system of social insurance, family allowances for second and further children, and abolition of poverty by a comprehensive system of social insurance, with benefits paid at subsistence level and as a statutory right.'[4] These were all policies that were sufficiently progressive for socialists to support while also being workable and popular.

The left liked the 1945 manifesto too. As Jonathan Schneer has put it: 'In 1945, for once, the party leadership said more than enough to satisfy the Labour Left.'[5] In the 1930s the left's grievances had been mainly tactical, such as the leadership's refusal to join a united or popular front against the National Government. On policy issues it had been able to draw comfort from Labour's continued commitment to public ownership. The proposals in the 1935 manifesto – banking, coal and its products, transport, electricity, iron and steel, and cotton – constituted (to quote David Howell) 'a list unrivalled in its specificity and length'.[6] Admittedly in March 1937 the right had succeeded in omitting banking, iron and steel, and cotton from the list included in 'Labour's Immediate Programme'; but the left had made little protest, claiming that this was merely a brief statement of short-term priorities which did not diminish the party programme as a whole. It is also true that during the war Herbert Morrison had attempted to ensure for a future Labour government as much flexibility as possible regarding both the industries to be tackled and the form of control to be imposed; but at the December 1944 conference a resolution, moved by Ian Mikardo and carried without a card vote over the executive's protests, had demanded the inclusion in the manifesto of commitments for the full public ownership of land, large-scale building, heavy industry, and all forms of banking, transport and fuel and power. Partly as a result of the Mikardo resolution, the election manifesto which was agreed in April 1945 included specific commitments to nationalise coal, gas, electricity and transport, the Bank of England, and iron and steel. Despite the fact that these pledges fell short of its maximum demands, the left preferred to hail them as a victory. The Beveridge commitments were also welcomed by the left. Although their intellectual pedigree was largely Liberal, they had to some extent been anticipated by Labour: a centrally funded national health service had been in the party programme since 1934; and several months before the Beveridge Report's publication the 1942 Labour conference had endorsed comprehensive social insurance and family allowances.[7] Another reason why the left warmed to the Beveridge proposals was that they had stimulated the one major rebellion by the Parliamentary Labour Party (PLP) against the wartime coalition: in February 1943, 97 Labour backbenchers had voted against the government's view that the Beveridge Report might be too costly to implement.

With right and left both enthusiastic about it, Labour's 1945 manifesto provided the basis not merely of a united and successful election campaign but also of a remarkable legislative programme. The nationalisations of the Bank of England, coal mines, civil aviation, Cable and Wireless, railways, road haulage, and electricity were all enacted by the end of the 1946–7 parliamentary session, as were the national insurance and national health service bills; and gas nationalisation and national assistance were legislated for in 1947–8. The government hesitated only over one major item, iron and steel nationalisation. In 1946 it merely set up a Steel Control Board as an interim arrangement while it considered the matter further; and in April of the following year John Wilmot, the Minister of Supply, backed by Morrison, a long-standing opponent of the nationalisation of an efficient, profitable industry with good industrial relations, persuaded the Cabinet to approve a form of nationalisation that would leave the structure of existing private companies intact although the government would compulsorily purchase their shares. In the summer of 1947, however, this decision was successfully challenged by the left, led by Aneurin Bevan. Wilmot was sacked; and the Cabinet agreed that iron and steel would be fully nationalised, albeit not until the 1948–9 session. The legislation was duly passed then, but vesting was delayed until after the 1950 election as part of a deal with the opposition over the 1949 Parliament Act, which reduced the Lords' delaying power to one year.[8]

The Cabinet row over iron and steel nationalisation was the first sign of the left-right dispute which was to become public as soon as the party, having enacted its manifesto, took stock of its achievements. Why had this dispute not broken out sooner? The delay cannot wholly be explained either by electoral euphoria or by ambiguity as to whether the 1945 manifesto was a first instalment in a plan of reform, as the left later claimed, rather than all that was achievable for the immediate future, as the right was to imply. A more important reason is that the left had exaggerated the effects of the reforms they had advocated. Nationalisation is a case in point – and not merely because Morrison's public-corporation model was used, generous compensation paid, and workers' control omitted. Because of the industries chosen, nationalisation failed to give the government control of the commanding heights of the economy. The failure to choose, say, the chemical industry cannot be blamed entirely on the caution of the right. The left itself seems not to have realised the extent to which Labour had become committed to nationalise

certain industries and not others because of pressure by trade
unions worried about industrial relations in their sector and not
about the strategic control of the economy. It was largely because
it had equated socialism with the implementation of an arbitrarily
accumulated agenda of nationalisation demands that the left
became discontented after the manifesto was fulfilled.

More surprising than the left's illusions about the effect of
nationalisation, however, was its failure to plan the remaining 80
per cent of the economy for such time as it was to remain in
private hands. Although interest in planning had become widespread even in non-socialist circles in the 1930s, had been
boosted after 1941 by sympathy and admiration for the Soviet
Union, and had been demanded by the 1944 conference, it was
absent from the 1945 manifesto. Once in power, moreover, and
despite inheriting an armoury of physical controls from wartime,
Labour made minimal efforts at planning (and this was true even
in regard to the public sector). It failed to continue with a
Ministry of Production or create one for planning, making do
instead with the Lord President's Committee until the 1947
economic crisis led to the creation in the Cabinet Office of an
Economic Planning Board under an industrialist, Edwin Plowden. The creation in September 1947 of a Ministry of Economic
Affairs was an expedient to head off a rebellion by Sir Stafford
Cripps and lasted only until the resignation six weeks later of
Hugh Dalton, following a convenient though technical and
harmless budget leak, which enabled Attlee to make Cripps
Chancellor. Although Plowden moved with him to the Treasury,
he was preoccupied with short-term crises; and Cripps abolished
the National Investment Council, a Labour innovation of which
little use had been made. Meanwhile Cripps's successor as
President of the Board of Trade, Harold Wilson, was beginning
to make a 'bonfire' of the controls inherited from wartime.

Historians have of course acknowledged that the Attlee
government's attempt to plan private industry was from the start
'half-hearted, indirect, and in many ways unsuccessful', and that
in the *Economic Survey for 1947*, for example, 'there was
remarkably little planning indeed'.[9] And they have been aware
that the left – for example the 'Keep Left' group of MPs –
complained more loudly about the absence of a socialist foreign
policy[10] than about the absence of planning. But they have not
come up with a persuasive explanation as to why this was.
Morrison's limitations as Lord President, though much com-

mented on, are not the whole answer, since there was little improvement once his power was reduced. Nor are economic constraints such as the dollar gap, severe though these were: compared with other Labour administrations, the Attlee government was reluctant to use the economic environment as an excuse, perhaps because it did not appreciate its true seriousness. Indeed Sir Edwin Plowden has recently written: 'I do not believe that, at that time, any minister, shadow minister, official, journalist, commentator or the general public truly grasped the real extent of our economic difficulties and our economic weakness.'[11]

Why, then, did the party not demand planning? One explanation is that it believed that Keynesian demand management, which had been accepted by the Treasury during the war, was achieving what planning was intended to do, notably the reduction of unemployment. Those, such as Arthur Deakin and the young James Callaghan, who had called for planning at the 1944 conference had given as their reason the need to prevent a repeat of the inter-war depression.[12] The left was not to know that the Conservatives would also accept the need for full employment and that, dubbed 'Butskellism', this economic priority would become a key feature of the political 'consensus'. In the late 1940s Keynesianism seemed radical.

Labour's moment of harmony as a governing party seems thus to have rested on the modesty of the left's aspirations, which can in turn be attributed in part to its intellectual limitations. As soon, however, as the left realised how far the party's historic agenda of nationalisation commitments and its new ability to reduce unemployment fell short of a social transformation, it rediscovered its distinctive voice.

II

The split between right and left after 1948 became increasingly apparent over two issues: electoral tactics and rearmament. The tactic of 'consolidation' which Morrison unveiled at the 1948 party conference was justified mainly as a means of retaining the loyalty of the middle-class voter. Despite his efforts to prevent any new nationalisation commitments, the manifesto for the February 1950 election, 'Labour Believes in Britain', promised to bring cement, sugar, meat slaughtering, water, and industrial assurance (which was, however, only to be 'mutualised') into public ownership. But Morrison and his colleagues on the right had kept other and more important industries which had been discussed by the National Executive Committee (NEC) – notably chemicals, shipbuilding, motors, cotton, aircraft, and oil distribution – out of this 'shopping list'; and the overall tone of both the manifesto and the party's election campaign was consolidationist. When Labour called a second election eighteen months later, Morrison was able to omit a specific list from the manifesto, although nationalisation of industries operating against the national interest was promised.[13] Whether consolidation made sense as an electoral tactic is impossible to determine: the fact that in both these elections Labour lost middle-class votes but retained or increased its working-class support can be interpreted as showing either that it was essential damage-limitation or that it was fundamentally misconceived.

Rearmament became an issue between right and left following the North Korean invasion of South Korea in June 1950 which caused the United States to press its European allies to contribute their share to western defence. In January 1951 the Labour government decided upon a rearmament programme of £4700 million over three years, to finance which Hugh Gaitskell's April 1951 budget imposed the first NHS charges, on spectacles and dentures. Bevan resigned from the Cabinet in protest (as did Harold Wilson); and under his charismatic if erratic leadership the old 'Keep Left' group was revitalised as a force of 40 or so Bevanites.[14]

Once the loss of the October 1951 election was added to consolidation and NHS charges as a source of rank-and-file frustration, the left became a vocal minority within the party. At the 1952 conference the Bevanites won six of the seven places on the NEC which were chosen by constituency delegates; over the next three years they mounted a number of parliamentary rebellions against front-bench policy, mainly on defence-related issues (which brought Bevan to the brink of expulsion in March 1955); and at the 1954 conference they and their anti-militarist and anti-German allies came close to defeating the leadership on a major issue, that of German rearmament.[15]

But the Bevanites were never more than an irritant, and were unable to prevent Hugh Gaitskell defeating Bevan either for the treasurership in 1954 or for the leadership late the following year. They were in a minority in the PLP; but the ultimate obstacle to their success was the hostility of the trade union leadership. Admittedly, the Bevanites also suffered from the lack of a convincing programme, particularly on domestic issues. Bevan's much anticipated book *In Place of Fear*, published in 1952, was an intellectual disappointment.[16] In opposition he and his colleagues continued to press for further nationalisation, and managed to insert a pledge of some degree of public ownership in chemicals and engineering into the party's May 1955 manifesto; but the left failed to adapt to the rising prosperity and Butskellist policies which enabled the Conservatives to increase their majority at that election. As yet, however, the right was doing little better. Consolidation was a negative strategy. And its more positive 'revisionist' replacement was only beginning to be put together by Gaitskell's Hampstead set.

III

While the left remained politically and ideologically subdued during the Gaitskell and early Wilson years, the right increased its ascendancy. Four factors were of importance. The first was Bevan's willingness to compromise. Always torn between the purism advocated by his wife, ex-ILP member Jennie Lee, and the realism which he had demonstrated as architect of the NHS, he moved unsteadily back towards the latter following his near-expulsion in March 1955. In 1956 he was elected party treasurer; at the 1957 party conference he suppressed his doubts and helped the leadership defeat calls for unilateral nuclear disarmament; and in 1959 he became deputy leader. Though the left remained strong enough to commit the party to unilateralism for a year just months after his death in August 1960, its influence in the party declined.

The second factor was the completion of a 'revisionist' rationale for accepting a mixed economy. Revisionism assumed that capitalism had solved the economy's supply-side problems, subject to some government-sponsored modernisation. The task of socialists was to promote social democracy directly by improving education and social security, and not indirectly by changing the ownership of the means of production. Revisionism's most articulate statement was Anthony Crosland's *The Future of Socialism*, published in 1956. But of greater political significance was the 1961 conference document 'Signposts for the

Sixties'. Emanating from Peter Shore and the Labour Research Department, it argued:

> If the dead wood were cut out of Britain's boardrooms and replaced by the keen young executives, production engineers and scientists who are at present denied their legitimate prospects of promotion, our production and export problems would be much more manageable.[17]

Similar views had long been expounded by Wilson;[18] and as party leader he crafted a 'white heat of the technological revolution' rhetoric which projected a modernising and merito-cratic appeal to the middle class while nevertheless retaining a sufficient undertone of state intervention and hostility to the existing capitalist establishment not to offend Labour's tradi-tionalists.

The third factor was the complementary leadership skills of Gaitskell and Wilson. The incisive but divisive Gaitskell laun-ched revisionism with fervour, enjoying considerable success – apart from a commitment to renationalise steel and road haul-age, the 1959 manifesto played down both public ownership and socialism[19] – but meeting a symbolic defeat in 1960 when he was forced to abandon a constitutional revision which was intended to remove all traces of Marxism in the way that the German SPD had done at its Bad Godesberg conference in November 1959. Gaitskell's sudden death in January 1963 brought the emollient and evasive Wilson to the leadership. Elected – as a former Bevanite who had challenged Gaitskell for the leadership in 1960 – with the left's support, but in reality a revisionist with a political style influenced by President Kennedy,[20] Wilson was uniquely equipped to soothe the left's fears while ensuring the victory of revisionism in the party.

In this he was helped by the fourth factor: electoral logic. When the Conservatives not only won for a third successive time but also increased their majority again in the 1959 election, so that pundits began to wonder whether Labour could ever win again, the attractions of policies and leaders who could restore the party's position became considerable. This was particularly true after 1961 when the Conservatives themselves became sufficiently worried about their stop-go record of economic management to introduce measures (notably a National Eco-nomic Development Council, and a pay pause) which moved them towards what their 1964 manifesto was to praise as 'the democratic concept of planning by partnership'.[21]

When Labour narrowly won the 1964 election, it thus did so on a manifesto which, apart from pledges to nationalise steel and water,[22] was strongly revisionist; and its basic strategy was similar to that which the Conservatives had been pursuing since 1961.[23] Wilson's assumption was that 'indicative planning' by a new Department of Economic Affairs (DEA) under the energetic and emotional George Brown could eliminate the 'stop' phases in the stop-go cycle and ensure continuous and therefore higher growth. This larger cake would permit larger slices for all: the meritocratic middle class would prosper, thereby cementing a new allegiance to the Labour Party; and the working class would also improve its position, thanks to improved social security as well as to egalitarian reforms such as the introduction of comprehensive schools. Labour would therefore entrench itself, like the Swedish Social Democrats after 1936, as the party which combined governmental competence and humanitarian progressivism; and the Conservatives would lose their position as the normal party of government.

Unfortunately for the revisionists, the economic growth upon which their strategy depended was not achieved: in his preface to the 1964 edition of *The Future of Socialism*, Crosland acknowledged that he had been 'too optimistic – not about the *capabilities* of the western-type mixed economy . . . but about the performance of the Anglo-Saxon economies in particular'. It is unclear whether the DEA could have succeeded even in a favourable international climate: its relationship of supposed 'creative tension' with the Treasury was more tense than creative; its National Plan relied on exhortation alone in regard to industry, which set its own targets; and its wages policy would probably have brought it into confrontation with the trade unions. As it was, the DEA's strategy failed because priority was given to the maintenance of the exchange rate. To avoid devaluation, despite having inherited a major balance of payments deficit, was important to Labour's strategy of governmental competence as well as to its relationship with the United States. Although increasing its majority at a skilfully timed election in March 1966 (during which the party reaffirmed its 1964 commitments), the government was forced within months into what Tony Benn later called 'a complete reversal of engines and a return to absolutely traditional Treasury policies'[24] as the only alternative to devaluation. The DEA was rendered obsolescent: after several resignation threats George Brown was compensated, for all his lack of the appropriate skills, with the Foreign Secretaryship. Having abandoned growth, the government had no strategy. What is more, its attempts to find alternatives ran into disaster: its decision in October 1966 to apply for entry to the European Economic Community was vetoed by de Gaulle in November 1967; and its attempt to reform industrial relations, outlined in its January 1969 White Paper 'In Place of Strife' which proposed compulsory strike ballots, fines and conciliation pauses, had to be abandoned in June 1969 in the face of implacable opposition even from the right of the party. Disillusioned members left the party in droves: Patrick Seyd has claimed that 'active Constituency Party organisations shrivelled to a skeleton during the period from 1966 to 1970'.[25] Most tragically, the government's sacrifice of growth proved to be in vain: it was forced to devalue in November 1967, and to deflate further in the new year.

With his alternative strategies collapsing, Wilson was left with only one shot in his locker: as his deflationary policies took effect, he could project Labour as the party which had responsibly cured the balance of payments deficit. This strategy came close to succeeding: Labour recovered well in the opinion polls, and was denied victory in the June 1970 election only by a late movement of opinion which caught most pollsters by surprise. But a strategy of governmental competence is always a gamble for the Labour right: failure guarantees that the backlash from the left will be even more bitter.

IV

The revival of the left had begun as early as 1966. In that year relaxation of discipline in the PLP led to the formation of the Tribune Group, which initially consisted of 41 MPs.[26] More significant was a new rebelliousness at party conferences: from 1966 to 1969 the leadership was defeated 13 times,[27] reflecting a diminished readiness by the trade unions to use their block votes in the loyalist cause. In part this change in trade union behaviour reflected generational turnover: bosses whose attitudes had been shaped by the need to remain vigilant against Communist infiltration of their unions were being replaced by others more sympathetic to the left, such as Hugh Scanlon, who became president of the engineering workers in 1967. But it also reflected a hostility towards incomes policy which trade unionists of all generations would have understood: union acquiescence in the Attlee government's policies of wage restraint had reflected a mood of euphoria and post-war sacrifice which could only be temporary. And the tension between the political and industrial wings of the Labour movement had been further increased by 'In Place of Strife'.

Nevertheless Labour's 1970 defeat was an important watershed. A dramatic illustration was the metamorphosis, which according to Kenneth Morgan took place 'during late 1970',[28] of Anthony Wedgwood Benn, enthusiast for Wilson's white-hot technological revolution, into Tony Benn, latter-day Bevan. The policies of the Heath government continued this process of radicalisation: its Housing Finance Act provoked some Labour-controlled local authorities, notably Clay Cross, to defy the law; and its Industrial Relations Act had a similar effect on the trade union movement.

These developments helped the left to gain control for the first time of the NEC and therefore of party policy. Although the convention of life tenure for members of the trade union section meant that it was not until the mid-1970s that the left had a clear overall majority,[29] it captured the Home Policy Committee and was able to secure support for its policies at party conferences. Between 1971 and 1973 the latter endorsed the public ownership of banking, insurance and building societies, the building industry, finance houses, road haulage, shipbuilding and repairing. *Labour's Programme 1973* made it clear that these extensions would be achieved by the purchase of majority shareholdings by a National Enterprise Board, although Wilson controversially refused to accept its proposal to nationalise 25 major companies.[30]

The left's ascendancy was taken so much for granted that conference majorities for unilateral nuclear disarmament in 1972 and 1973 created a negligible stir compared with 1960. Former Gaitskellites were for the most part more worried about the left's attack on the European Economic Community now that Heath had secured British entry. Labour MPs were instructed to vote against the principle of entry in October 1971, although 69 rebelled, one of whom, Dick Taverne, the member for Lincoln, became in 1972 the first Labour member for nine years to be de-selected by his constituency party. In an ironic reversal of positions the left now called for party policy to be binding on all

MPs (as Hugh Scanlon did in 1971),[31] while the right pleaded the rights of individual conscience. In April 1972 the Shadow Cabinet decided to support a referendum on the European issue. It did so as the only way of preventing the party from committing itself to unconditional withdrawal; but its appeasing gesture provoked Roy Jenkins to resign as deputy leader. Other signs of appeasement were the readiness of right-wingers to endorse left-wing rhetoric: even Denis Healey promised the 1973 conference tax changes which would provoke 'howls of anguish from the . . . rich'.

The left began to realise that, with policy battles largely won, the next struggle was to bring a right-dominated PLP to book. A key weapon was constituency activism. In the early 1970s the shrivelled local parties began to recruit a new kind of member, 'relatively young, higher-educated, public-sector employees, often with working-class parents' (in Seyd's words), whom the journalist Peter Jenkins memorably described as the 'Lumpen-polytechnic'.[32] Most were 'Bennites', but some were Trotskyists, whose most successful 'entryist' faction was Militant Tendency – 'a party within a party but disguised as a periodical', in Austin Mitchell's words[33] – or, to give it its true name, the Revolutionary Socialist League.[34] The NEC helped Bennites and Trotskyists put pressure on right-wing MPs: in 1972 the left-wing chairman of the Organisation Committee, Ian Mikardo, ruled that the NEC could not interfere with de-selections provided that they were procedurally proper; the following year the NEC abolished the list of proscribed organisations which the party had maintained since 1930.

Another important weapon in the left's struggle to make the PLP accountable was the Campaign for Labour Party Democracy (CLPD), launched in June 1973, largely in anticipation of Wilson's refusal to accept the 25 companies commitment.[35] By skilful use of model resolutions, this obscure but efficient organisation coordinated the efforts of constituency and trade union activists in support of three demands: that control of the electoral manifesto be handed to the NEC alone (instead of its being shared with the PLP leadership); that all sections of the party should elect the leader (instead of the PLP doing so alone); and that MPs should be required to submit themselves to reselection by their constituency parties each parliamentary session. Though, as David Hine has pointed out, these demands were 'long accepted as normal in most European social democratic parties' and were 'extremely difficult to refute by most standards of democracy',[36] they alarmed the PLP.

The left's approach seemed to be justified by the events of 1974–9. When the Heath government was provoked by industrial militancy into a premature election in February 1974, the Labour leadership managed to water the manifesto down slightly. Admittedly full public ownership was promised for mineral rights, shipbuilding, ship repairing and marine engineering, ports, the manufacture of air frames and aero engines. But only public holding companies were promised for pharmaceuticals, road haulage, construction, machine tools, and North Sea oil and gas; there was no precise commitment regarding banking, insurance, or building societies, and arguments of efficiency rather than principle were used to justify all of these choices.[37] Moreover, the manifesto did not include any commitment to unilateral nuclear disarmament.

Even so, the leadership found it too radical, and evaded many of its commitments. How did it get away with this? One factor was that it benefited from the precariousness of Labour's parliamentary position: the February 1974 election brought Labour to power as a minority government; even after a second election, in October of the same year, it had a majority of only three seats over all other parties combined; and its loss of this majority, which necessitated an electoral pact with the Liberals from April 1977 to August 1978, provided an excuse for caution.

A second factor was the astute use made by Wilson of the June 1975 referendum on whether or not to stay in the European Economic Community. Before the referendum, the government had felt obliged to pass an Industry Act, which although specifying a more modest role for the National Enterprise Board than the left had wished, nevertheless gave the government unprecedented scope for economic intervention, which moreover the Secretary of State for Industry, Tony Benn, fully intended to exploit. But Wilson widened the referendum on Europe into a general vote of confidence: did the public trust the judgement of the three party leaderships, who favoured the EEC, or that of the motley collection of right- and left-wingers (including Benn), who wished to withdraw? Wilson's two-to-one victory enabled him to move Benn from the Industry Department and thereby reduce the NEB's role to one of rescuing troubled companies. The left's view of this manoeuvre has been summed up by Chris Mullin:

The National Enterprise Board, which was supposed to take public ownership into potentially profit-making areas was saddled with the greatest lame duck in our country's history – British Leyland – so it was clear that the industrial strategy which formed the basis of the 1974 manifesto was being jettisoned, and very quickly.[38]

A third factor enabling the government to avoid implementing its manifesto in full was its ability to plead economic constraints. An inflation rate of 26 per cent by July 1975 brought the trade unions to accept an incomes policy of their own devising. And a sterling crisis in 1976 forced the government, by now under James Callaghan's prime ministership, to cut public expenditure as the price of a loan from the IMF and thereby – as the head of Callaghan's Policy Unit has admitted – launch Thatcherism.[39]

A fourth factor was that the lack of a radical economic programme was partially concealed by other legislative activity. 'Social Contract' concessions were made to the trade unions in the field of employment law; and much parliamentary time was taken up by devolution for Scotland and Wales, the 'incidental advantages' of which as a distraction from economic issues were later admitted by Callaghan.[40]

In the 'winter of discontent' of 1978–9 the government's incomes policy collapsed, as Heath's had done five years before; and in March 1979 it lost a vote of confidence in the House of Commons. For the ensuing election Callaghan insisted on a 'short, punchy and sexy' manifesto,[41] and used a characteristic blend of cajolery and resignation threats to veto many of the demands which the left had inserted into the party programme. Admittedly, the manifesto included many left-wing proposals, including a wealth tax. But, as in 1970, Labour's basic strategy was to project itself as a responsible party of government and, as in 1970, the right was to pay a high price when this failed to win the election.

Between 1974 and 1979 there were in effect, to quote David Butler and Dennis Kavanagh, 'two Labour parties, one with the voice of the NEC and Conference and the other with that of the parliamentary leadership'.[42] Only 10 of the NEC's 29 members reliably supported the Labour government of March 1974 to June 1979; and NEC documents such as *Labour's Programme 1976* called for nationalisation of the banks and insurance companies and compulsory planning agreements. Yet the government largely ignored the NEC; and the frustration felt by the left helps to explain the intensity of the effort put in to the de-selection in 1975 of a Cabinet Minister, Reg Prentice (who in October 1977 diminished the right's credibility by defecting to the Tories), and in the blind eye turned to the expanded activities of Militant Tendency.

V

Removed from office by the 1979 election, the parliamentary leadership lost control to the other Labour party. Especially during the years 1979–81, the NEC and party conference moved policy further to the left, endorsing an alternative economic strategy and both unilateral nuclear disarmament and the with-drawal of American nuclear bases. More important, two of the CLPD's aims were achieved. The election of the party leader was handed to an electoral college in which trade unions had 40 per cent and constituency parties 30 per cent of the votes, a decision which proved the final straw for many of those who broke away in 1981 to form the Social Democratic Party (SDP). Mandatory reselection of MPs led to eight of them being de-selected by 1983 and to several others joining the SDP. More significantly, it caused many more MPs to change their behaviour[43] – hence the choice by the PLP of former Bevanite Michael Foot, rather than Denis Healey, as party leader in November 1980 when Cal-laghan resigned suddenly before the new electoral college had been finalised.

    With hindsight Foot's election can be seen to have weakened the left by detaching a 'soft left' loyal to the new party leader. The 'hard left' was led by Tony Benn, backed after May 1980 by the newly formed Rank and File Mobilising Committee on which not only the CLPD but Militant Tendency were represented. This body backed Benn when in 1981 he used the new system to challenge and almost defeat Denis Healey for the deputy leader-ship. The refusal to support Benn by some members of the Tribune Group, the ranks of which had been swelled by MPs seeking to acquire left-wing credentials so as to avoid de-selection, caused the creation in 1982 of a hard-left alternative, the Campaign Group. As trade union leaders started to become unhappy with such divisiveness, the leadership regained a fragile

hold on the NEC at the 1981 conference, which they strengthened the following year. In December 1982, the right and soft left
were therefore able to proscribe Militant Tendency. But they were
unable to expel more than a handful of Militant members. And
they failed to secure more than minor changes to the left's
policies when the June 1983 election was called. Peter Shore
described Labour's resulting manifesto as 'the longest suicide
note in history'; and John Silkin complained that its organisation
during that campaign 'would have been disowned by the organ-
isers of a village fête.'[44] These problems were compounded by
Foot's dishevelled leadership; and Labour received only 27.6 per
cent of the vote – its lowest share since 1918 and only 2.2 per cent
more than the SDP-Liberal Alliance.

The continuing weakness of the right was demonstrated by the
electoral college's choice at the 1983 conference of Neil Kinnock,
a long-standing member of the Tribune Group and a unilateral-
ist. Nevertheless, at only 41 and with a young family, he projected an attractively modern image to the floating voter as well
as a reassuringly Bevanite one to party traditionalists. And,
having refused to vote for Benn in 1981, he offered the prospect of
further detaching the soft from the hard left. Although his work
was made more difficult by the 1984–5 miners' strike, the
controversy over Militant control of Liverpool, the 'loony left'
image projected by local Labour parties (particularly in London), and the intransigence of the hard left minority on the NEC,
he recruited a team of media-wise advisers (notably Peter
Mandelson as the party's head of Campaigns and Communications), put on a dark suit, and worked hard to make the party
electable. He failed, however, to prevent the de-selection of six
MPs during the 1983–7 Parliament, or to persuade the 1985
conference to adopt a one-member, one-vote system for selecting
parliamentary candidates. And, although he moderated left-wing
policies in a number of respects and kept the manifesto as short
as possible to minimise criticism, the party remained committed in
the June 1987 election to unilateralism, a wealth tax, and social
ownership of British Gas and British Telecom.[45] Despite a slick
campaign in which the left was hidden from view in order to highlight the personalities of Neil and Glenys Kinnock and campaign
coordinator Bryan Gould, Labour recovered only to 30.8 per cent.
When allowance is made for the number of seats it contested, this
was below the level achieved in its nightmare year of 1931.

VI

This third consecutive defeat did not at once cause the party to change its approach. Its campaigning style was criticised; the Campaign Group, though now divided, provoked a contest for leader and deputy leader in 1987; its defence policy remained a source of controversy; and as late as the last months of 1988 Kinnock was depressed about the party's prospects.[46] But the SDP-Liberal Alliance, after polling 22.6 per cent, succumbed to internal strife. And Kinnock's two-year policy review reached a triumphant conclusion at the 1989 conference when, as the journalist Peter Kellner observed, 'the left lost its residual power to rock Mr Kinnock's sleek new social democratic boat'.[47] Changes to the party's structure had yet to be introduced; but as the 1990s began it seemed that Kinnock had achieved a Wilson-style modernisation of the party; and the soft left had become the new right.

VII

To sum up the six phases: the opening three years of the Attlee government turned out to be a unique time of consensus between right and left; Attlee's remaining time as leader was a period in which the right maintained control but lacked a clear policy and was continually harassed by a strong and truculent left; the period from 1955 to the 1970 election was one in which the right discovered a policy and the left lost confidence; the 1970s proved to be a decade in which the left revived sufficiently to win the policy battles but without bringing the party leadership to book; between 1979 and 1987 the left not only controlled policy but also made the leadership accountable for the first time; and since 1987 the right appears to have regained control.

What lessons can be learned from the above? To satisfy right and left equally, as from 1945–8, requires exceptional conditions. Normally Labour can hope to satisfy only one of its wings. Opting for right-wing policies does not guarantee electoral success (as the examples of 1951, 1970 and 1979 show); opting for left-wing policies can sometimes pay off (as in February and October 1974). But in general Labour has done better when offending the left (as in 1964 and 1966) rather than offending the right (as in 1983 and 1987). Of course, electoral considerations have to be weighed against the drive and commitment which the left brings to the party. In a two-party system Labour has to be both an effective competitor with the Conservatives and the major outlet for popular grievances in a socially divided and economically vulnerable country. Its history since 1945 illustrates the difficulties of balancing these two roles.

13. Britain and the Two Irelands since 1945

ALAN O'DAY

1. – (1) It is hereby recognized and declared that the part of Ireland heretofore known as Eire ceased, as from the eighteenth day of April nineteen hundred and forty-nine to be part of His Majesty's dominions.
   (2) It is hereby declared that Northern Ireland remains part of His Majesty's dominions and of the United Kingdom and it is hereby affirmed that in no event will Northern Ireland or any part thereof cease to be part of His Majesty's Dominions and of the United Kingdom without the consent of the Parliament of Northern Ireland.
   (Ireland Act, 1949)

THAT the post-1945 Irish problem has ancient origins at times obscures the relatively recent character of the contemporary situation. Historically, the Irish question revolved around an interaction of the colonial relationship between England and Ireland, and the conflicting interest of Catholic and Protestant within the island. The two Irelands of the past were religious and psychological more than territorial. After 1945 the problem, of course, contained older ingredients but two crucial modern features – post-colonialism in the area of the present-day Republic and the partition of the island – have been at the forefront.

Territorial division of the country was a comparatively new phenomenon. As a consequence of the medieval English conquest it had been united, with Dublin serving as the administrative centre. Provinces or regions had little tangible substance. Devolved powers in State and Church had been conferred on counties, baronies, poor law unions, municipalities, urban districts, dioceses and parishes. Ulster had never been an area enjoying legal or informal semi-autonomy; Belfast could posit no claim to recognition as a capital. Establishment of two separate regimes in the country had only taken place between 1920 and 1922 and then as a pragmatic response to the demands of Northern loyalists. While the idea of two Irelands had earlier antecedents, it only gradually gained credence after 1886, flowering into a full-fledged demand between 1912 and 1914. Nevertheless, the creation of two nations had never been uncontested and seemed in the initial phases to be vulnerable and temporary.

Foundation of two Irelands was a direct consequence of the island's religious demography. In the nineteenth and early twentieth centuries approximately three-quarters of the Irish population was Catholic and nowhere in the area of the modern Republic did Protestants constitute more than very localised pluralities. In Ulster, however, Protestants held a narrow majority in the province as a whole and depending on the political unit used as a measure, had a preponderance of up to two-thirds of the total population. Thus, unlike in the south, the local majority covered extensive territory. Clearly, a basis for two territorial nations existed though the problem was complicated by a large Ulster Catholic minority. Again, depending on the precise division employed, the size and density of the local minority increased or declined with Catholics being in the highest proportions, often constituting local majorities, in the southern and western portions of the province. Yet, no matter what yardstick was used, the second Ireland necessarily had a considerable Catholic minority – indeed, a much higher proportion than was the case for Protestants in what became the Republic.

Claims to a second Ireland were hotly denied by nationalists who insisted upon the integrity of the historic nation, and were also deeply resented by Catholics north and south, who rejected the legitimacy of a Protestant-dominated Northern Ireland. Few British politicians before or after 1920 showed enthusiasm for two Irelands. Northern Ireland's existence was a fact but its future was clouded. Essentially, British parties wished the question away and ensured that the problem remained shelved during the inter-war period. The position took on a fresh turn, though, between 1939 and 1945 when Northern Ireland gave the war effort crucial support while the Irish Free State clung to neutrality. Winston Churchill had wanted to lure the Free State into the conflict and intimated that partition would be brought to an end but Eamon de Valera's refusal to budge strengthened the sense of two Irelands – one loyal, the other indifferent even to freedom's survival. Ulster's participation in the common sacrifice received frequent acknowledgement, not least in Churchill's victory broadcast at the conclusion of European hostilities. He contrasted the steadfastness and bravery of its people and that of ordinary citizens of the Free State with the actions of Eire's government, stating:

> owing to the action of Mr de Valera, so much at variance with the temper and instinct of thousands of southern Irishmen, who hastened to the battlefront to prove their ancient valour, the approaches which the southern Irish ports and airfields could so easily have guarded were closed by the hostile aircraft and U-boats.
>
> This was indeed a deadly moment in our life, and if it had not been for the loyalty and friendship of Northern Ireland, we should have been forced to come to close quarters with Mr de Valera, or perish for ever from the earth.
>
> However, with a restraint and poise, to which I venture to say history will find few parallels, H.M. Government never laid a violent hand upon them, though at times it would have been quite easy and quite natural, and we left the de Valera Government to frolic with the German and later with the Japanese representatives to their heart's content.[1]

It might have been expected, therefore, that the future of Northern Ireland had been consolidated by the Second World War much as the conflagration of the First World War in no small way had made its creation possible.

British governments from 1945 were confronted by a succession of usually unwelcome Irish issues. None has proved more absorbing than the difficulties of legitimising the continuation of two Irelands and securing the stability of the Northern State. Irish problems have prompted numerous shifts of outlook and policy – ranging from schemes aimed at enforcing resolution of differences within Ireland, bilateral arrangements between Belfast and Westminster, London direction of the province's affairs, and a British–Dublin axis largely by-passing Ulster. Perhaps the outstanding aspect of what have been significant changes has been the comparative absence of controversy, of partisanship over Irish matters in Britain despite the differences of opinion resulting from these policies in both Irelands. The apparent harmony over Irish questions is remarkable for two reasons – the seemingly high level of political partisanship in the 1980s on so many matters, and the long tradition of Ireland's being central to party warfare. Prior to 1922 Irish questions were subject to the full blast of partisan conflict and this decline during the inter-war years was not reflective so much of a change of heart as of the irrelevance of Ireland. Examination of the post-war Irish problem, then, offers vital clues to the political parameters of discussion and policy formation in Britain.

Although military victory enduced feelings of affection and gratitude in Britain, the spirit of comradeship was put under strain immediately by the Labour landslide at the 1945 general election. Unlike Churchill and the Conservatives who had political ties with the Ulster Unionist Party, Labour had a tradition of suspicion of the Northern Ireland regime and some of its MPs were less than enthusiastic about the existence of the State at all. In Ulster an Anti-Partition League was founded for the purpose of bringing the second Ireland to an end while at Westminster Hugh Delargy formed a Friends of Ireland group of Labour MPs who cooperated with and generally supported the mainly Catholic League.[2] In Dublin de Valera sought to reopen the issue of the continuation of partition of the country, perhaps hoping for a gesture from the Labour Party. As frequently happened, though, his public statements had counter-productive effects in London. De Valera's insistence in June and July 1945 that Eire was an independent Republic was not calculated to win over British leaders though his view that the two neighbours had much in common which might be pursued together if partition were ended struck a more congenial note.[3] With the border appearing potentially fragile, the Northern Ireland general election to Stormont was employed by Unionists as a plebiscite to demonstrate majority support for remaining part of the United Kingdom.[4]

Not surprisingly, as election results on the border were a foregone outcome, the verdict of Ulster voters for the Union in 1945 did not end the debate. Even Conservatives were cautious about the future of the Northern Ireland regime. In August 1946 Churchill revealed some of his own equivocation when writing to Bernard Shaw, to whom he postulated, 'ought we not to try to settle the Irish question? Could we not call it quits in the long tragedy? We succeeded in exercising remarkable forebearance about the Irish ports.'[5] During 1947 the Anti-Partition League made headway in Britain while the Friends of Ireland at West-minster exposed the Northern Ireland regime to relentless criticism.[6] Pressure on the second Ireland continued to gain momentum in the following year. There was increasing concern, for example, at the slow implementation of the post-war social welfare measures in Northern Ireland. Meanwhile the anti-partition movement received growing support in the Free State as well.

In the autumn of 1948, however, Ulster Unionists had their position retrieved by the declaration from de Valera's successor that the Free State intended to repeal the External Relations Act of 1936 and become a Republic. A Republic had been the goal of nationalists since 1916. It was generally recognised that the Free State meant to take the step at some point; de Valera on several occasions had all but declared the country a Republic. Also the move enjoyed overwhelming support in the Free State. Neverthe-less, conversion of Eire into a Republic was unwelcome to a British government preoccupied with reconstruction, financial difficulties, the growing Soviet menace in Europe and the prob-lems of de-colonialisation. Ireland's decision to withdraw from the Commonwealth came at a time when Britain was grappling with the Indian subcontinent and Palestine. Attlee's Cabinet was concerned to retain India within the Commonwealth and anxious to avoid any appearance of imperial disintegration. On 28 October the moment was seized to affirm in the House of Commons, 'the view of His Majesty's Government in the United Kingdom has always been that no change should be made in the constitutional status of Northern Ireland without Northern Ireland's free agreement'.[7] A month later Attlee repeated this position and also insisted that Britain would legislate to ensure that Eire would not be treated as a foreign country 'nor the citizens of Eire [placed] in the position of foreigners'.[8]

During the early months of 1949 it was plain that the Dublin government would not postpone its step. Meanwhile, the regime in Northern Ireland called a general election and to no one's amazement it demonstrated that the province continued to opt for membership of the United Kingdom.[9] On 18 April 1949, Easter Monday, a date chosen for symbolic effect, the Free State became a Republic. In May the British government introduced legislation recognising the change of status, providing for the position of Irish citizens along lines outlined by Attlee the previous autumn, and reaffirming the future of Northern Ireland.

Labour's measure met with considerable criticism in Dublin and in its own ranks at Westminster. The main point of contention was the apparently unequivocal guarantee of Northern Ireland's existence and especially the granting of the ultimate decision on its future, even on the controversial boundaries, to the Parliament of the province. Leaders in Dublin denounced the bill as a permanent sanction of partition. Attlee attempted to deflect criticism by putting the blame for the situation on the Dublin government. He stated:

> it seems to be suggested that this is a new declaration by His Majesty's Government affirming the permanence of partition, but actually the initiative did not come from this side. It is the action of the Eire Government itself in deciding to leave the Commonwealth that has made it quite inevitable that a declaration as to the position of that part of Ireland which is continuing in the Commonwealth should be made.
>
> Eire Ministers in speeches have declared the unity of Ireland. There may be something of a spiritual unity, but we have to deal with facts as they are. The adoption of the title 'Republic of Ireland' as I have said, seems to many people to be an assertion of this claim, but this Bill deals with the actual facts of the situation. It recognises, therefore, that the part of Ireland heretofore known as Eire ceases to be part of the Commonwealth, but it is a natural corollary to declare that Northern Ireland remains part of the Commonwealth and of the United Kingdom, and will not cease to be so without the consent of the Parliament of Northern Ireland.[10]

Anthony Eden, responding for the Opposition, supported the bill, albeit with a vital qualification. Eden indicated a wish to avoid partisanship on Irish matters and expressed a hope for future peaceful relations, even unity of the people of Ireland. He pointed out that although he was applauding the pledge given by the government it 'cannot bind a future Parliament, or indeed this Parliament'.[11] He hastened to state:

> it is perhaps desirable that the Conservative Party should once again make clear its attitude towards the issue. If union between North and South Ireland is to come about, it must do so not by force or by threats of force but by agreement and by Parliamentary and democratic means. It would really be

fantastic that anyone could suppose that we should invite Northern Ireland to leave the British Commonwealth against her will, or even that we should wish her to do so.

Eden's response exposed an irony that a Labour administration had adopted a more extreme guarantee than Conservative spokesmen demanded, or possibly desired.

Hugh Delargy took exception to his own government's view. He argued that the legislation would make partition permanent. Delargy accepted that at present there was a majority within Northern Ireland opposed to unification with the South. He was prepared to accept that the future status of the territory should rest on the votes of its people but was adamant that the power to reject unity must not be delegated to the Parliament of Northern Ireland. He maintained:

> the boundaries of the Northern Ireland State, which is a quite arbitrary and artificial State, were most skilfully drawn with the one purpose in view, that there should always be in the enclosed area a guaranteed Unionist majority. No one will dispute that. It is to that party and that Parliament we are leaving the decision; it is to that party with its guaranteed permanent majority, to those men whose main purpose in politics is to maintain that division of their own country.
>
> We are now in this Parliament forsaking a large part of our own responsibility since we are leaving the decision about Irish unity completely in the hands of men who are, we know, already pledged to maintain the division of their country.[12]

Disquiet about the measure was substantial and a considerable backbench Labour revolt tried to modify it. But, in the end, the government triumphed.

Declaration of the Republic effectively scuttled the partition agitation. The Friends of Ireland swiftly disintegrated; neither the Parliamentary Labour Party nor constituency organisation gave much heed to the issue. In general electors in mainland Britain of Irish stock voted Labour and attempts in 1950 and 1951 to marshal them against Attlee's party failed ludicrously.[13] Yet the situation and arguments of the late 1940s continued to be relevant into the 1990s. Discussion of Northern Ireland's future, the differing positions of London, Dublin and Belfast, and the assertion or limitation of the 'guarantee' never ceased to be pertinent. Also it seemed that the generation of politicians in charge in Dublin were either incapable of exploiting opportunities on the border question or indifferent to a resolution – certainly many displayed little agility in dealings with British leaders.

Labour's defeat in 1951 and the long Conservative ascendancy lasting until 1964 were not conducive to revival of the partition question. Like their Labour predecessors, Conservatives wished only to avoid Irish entanglements. They were normally happy to apply the convention of non-interference in the domestic affairs of Ulster. Tory ministers had other more pressing preoccupations throughout the 1950s. One problem which could not be ignored, however, was the resumption of Irish Republican Army (IRA) attacks in 1954. The assaults drew a hostile response in Ireland with the government, Opposition and Church leaders joining in condemnation of the campaign. In October the Irish Prime Minister, Costello, told the Dáil, 'if it lay in our power to achieve the unity of our country by force of arms and by beating into sullen submission the recalcitrant minority in the north-east, it would in my judgment still be the course of wisdom to pursue a policy of peace and reconciliation'.[14] In 1955 the Republic, after a lapse of seven years, restored the Offences Against the State Act passed in 1939.[15] Clearly, by the mid-1950s the Republic's leaders gave priority to internal stability and good relations with London. In December 1955 Ireland, with British support, was admitted to the United Nations.

IRA attacks persisted in 1956 and 1957. Late in 1956 the Special Powers Act was invoked by the regime in Northern Ireland. During the following year there were several hundred mainly trivial incidents.[16] Their prime impact was to burden the public purse by over £1 million. de Valera's return to power in the Republic in March 1957 led to a more vigorous suppression of IRA activity and by the close of the year approximately 100 people had been interned.[17] In the late 1950s incidents declined and finally in February 1962 the IRA announced a formal suspension of its campaign of violence. In April the government of the Republic released Republicans held in Irish jails and Northern Ireland also opened the prison doors for those incarcerated for belonging to illegal organisations.[18] In the early 1960s Irish matters were scarcely of importance in Britain and the issue of the two Irelands was quiescent. Dublin continued to raise ritualistic objections to partition but did little to poison day-today relations with Britain. Partition was cited by the government of the Republic as the reason for declining to join the North Atlantic Treaty Organisation but its participation was anyway never more than a minor British objective.

Between 1963 and 1968 there were encouraging signs that the enmity between the rival regimes in Ireland was fading. In the North, Captain Terence O'Neill became Prime Minister. Though a good Unionist on the border question, O'Neill foresaw that internal stability and the external position demanded reconciliation of the Ulster minority and improved relations with the Republic. He set out to reform the province, to make its future secure for loyalism. He was neither the first nor the last statesman who, when attempting to moderate existing repression, found that once a tiger was unleashed it had a voracious appetite. However, between 1965 and the autumn of 1968 O'Neill enjoyed considerable success. He also then stood well in the esteem of Harold Wilson, who had become Prime Minister in 1964. In early 1965 O'Neill and Sean Lemass, the Republic's Prime Minister, met initially in Belfast and followed with a second session in Dublin.[19] This spirit of rapprochement was rapturously received by Wilson. On 17 March the British leader applauded the spirit of reconciliation and stated that he looked forward to a further meeting between Irish leaders, 'not in Dublin, not in Belfast, but in No. 10 Downing Street'.[20] Wilson had little personal interest in Ireland and his government had more urgent concerns. He had no concrete objectives in closer North–South contacts but the Prime Minister was conscious that these were useful if only because they would help curb Labour Party complaints about the pace of reform in Northern Ireland. O'Neill's policy scored a further success when the Nationalists at Stormont agreed for the first time since 1920 to act as the Official Opposition.[21]

O'Neill's approach did not go uncriticised. In 1965 the Labour MP Paul Rose founded the Campaign for Democracy in Ulster which pointed to the inequities in the province and pressed for quicker and more extensive reform. During 1966 it was evident that within loyalist ranks many had reservations about over-fast changes. Republican celebrations of the 50th anniversary of the 1916 rising brought a sharp loyalist backlash while the views of the Reverend Ian Paisley attracted a considerable following.[22] Still, O'Neill was able to weather these protests and found that Wilson and the Labour government were non-interventionist in

Northern Ireland. There was nothing about the opening of 1968 to suggest that the gradualism of O'Neill might be swept aside. The Prime Ministers of both Irelands (now Jack Lynch in Dublin) met in the Republic's capital in sessions which had become almost routine.

Beneath the calm in Northern Ireland there were many Catholic grievances centred on an apparatus of discrimination in the local government franchise, housing, employment, policing and numerous other matters. Feeling was particularly acute in Derry where due to blatant gerrymandering Protestants retained firm control over the municipality despite the substantial Catholic majority there. A campaign of civil protest against discrimination drew support and sympathy. Also, although the civil rights agitation in Northern Ireland was driven by local grievances it was inspired by similar movements elsewhere, particularly in the United States. In Northern Ireland, too, 1968 was a climacteric year.

The situation reached a head in October and November. A protest demonstration scheduled for 5 October in Derry was banned by William Craig, one of the Stormont Ministers least sympathetic to O'Neill's reformism.[23] The order was defied and a violent clash took place between demonstrators on one side and police and loyalists on the other. International attention was focused on the event and its handling by the police. In the aftermath Edward McAteer, the Nationalist leader at Stormont, withdrew as the Official Opposition. Unrest continued throughout the month. Lynch, when in London, responded by advocating an end to partition in a statement which seemed to portend a collapse of the emergent rapprochement between North and South.[24] On 4 November O'Neill visited Wilson in London and came away with assurances that the British government held to the pledges of 1949.[25] Wilson was now eager that the reform programme should be advanced swiftly. On 22 November the Northern Ireland regime announced a package of measures including a housing ombudsman, a development committee to take over Derry, and a promise to abolish the Special Powers Act, aimed at taking the sting out of the civil rights protests and mounting criticism of discriminatory practices.[26]

O'Neill's standing in his party slumped, particularly when he appeared increasingly to be a pawn of London. He tried to recoup his sagging political fortunes with an electoral mandate. In the balloting in February for a new Northern Ireland Parliament O'Neill staked his hopes on winning sufficient Catholic support to offset defecting Unionists. His gamble failed. By April O'Neill's position was exposed on several fronts. IRA attacks on utilities revealed the deficiencies of locally based security arrangements. The army assumed responsibility for protecting key installations.[27] In the mid-Ulster parliamentary by-election a civil rights activist, Bernadette Devlin, emerged victorious. She instantly caught the attention of the British and world media. Her maiden speech in the House of Commons on 22 April focused on British neglect, the role of the Dublin government, and misrule in Ulster.[28] When on the following day the Northern Ireland Cabinet agreed to universal adult suffrage in local elections, the announcement seemed a further concession to British and civil rights pressure.[29] O'Neill's reputation was tarnished fatally and he resigned a few days later.

The departure of O'Neill marked a turning point in Northern Ireland's affairs. No subsequent leader was as much respected or trusted in London and by the liberally inclined media.[30] His downfall exposed the weakness of gradualism and destroyed expectations that moderate reforms were sufficient for achieving the reconciliation of communities. Moreover, until near the end O'Neill had been able to avert British interference and maintained the autonomy of the regime.

After O'Neill the British government under successive Labour and Tory ministries took more direct responsibility for change in the province while attempting to uphold the fiction of devolved power. This formula did not lead to a restoration of stability or legitimacy, indeed it ultimately contributed to the collapse of public order. The difficulties were both personal and institutional. Wilson had staked his hopes on O'Neill and after he resigned the British leader did not trust his successors, while tending to blame Unionists for the current debacle. James Callaghan, who as Home Secretary was instrumental in framing policy, shared Wilson's outlook. Edward Heath, who became Prime Minister in mid-1970, had if anything, less regard for Ulster leaders. By 1972 Brian Faulkner complained that Northern Ireland was ruled like 'a coconut colony'.[31] Certainly, the institutional limits of the new arrangements were defective and caused a vacuum of authority on vital occasions.

O'Neill's departure did not signal a halt to the protests. In July and August 1969 serious sectarian rioting in Derry and Belfast made the British government decide to employ troops to maintain order. London now was engaged fully in the province. On 19 August 1969 in a joint declaration issued in London, the British and Northern Ireland governments concurred on the arrangements for the province. Britain reaffirmed the guarantee of 1949, stated that the deployment of troops was a temporary measure and welcomed progress towards reforms based on the principle of 'full equality of treatment for all citizens'.[32] Soon afterwards, following a further meeting, Callaghan announced that the police would be reconstructed, the Royal Ulster Constabulary disarmed and a Community Relations Commission established. It did not go unnoticed that major statements were made in London by British ministers. That the loci of power rested in Britain was emphasised by the appointment of the Scarman Tribunal to examine the disturbances and the imposition of two British civil servants to assist the running of departments in Northern Ireland.

In August 1969 the Labour government reiterated the whole of the pledge of 1949. That decision was meant to restore loyalist confidence but it also defined debate on possible changes in Northern Ireland. London viewed the issue from a 1960s perspective, seeing it as a consequence of social, economic and political inequalities. Indeed, point 7 of the declaration of 19 August had emphasised that 'both Governments are determined to take all possible steps to restore normality to the Northern Ireland community so that economic development can proceed at the faster rate which is vital for social stability'.[33] The permanence of the army's role appeared confirmed in April 1970 when James Callaghan told the House of Commons: 'British troops will remain in Northern Ireland as long as it is decided by Her Majesty's Government that they should remain there; that is, for as long as it is necessary for them to do the work for which they are there.'[34]

Wilson's replacement by Heath in mid-1970 did not augur a dramatic shift in policy since the Conservatives had no more interest in the province than had Labour. A round of summer riots caused the banning of all public processions until January 1971.[35] By the close of the year more than 100 bomb outrages had been reported. During 1971 the security situation declined. By February the Provisional IRA or 'Provos' had begun a guerrilla campaign and the first soldier was killed. In March the commander-in-chief of the military operation resigned when the London government refused his request for additional troops. By summer public order was at risk. In early August, under pressure from Unionist spokesmen, the government imposed internment, a decision which met with a frosty reception in Dublin. Violence in Ulster rose sharply and Catholics began to lose confidence in the even-handedness of the army. As the situation deteriorated through the year, British politicians increasingly attributed the crisis to loyalist intransigence. Wilson reacted to events in late November when he called for the ultimate reunification of the country.[36] Heath quickly endorsed this aim. The guarantee of 1949 seemed very much in jeopardy.

Rising levels of Republican violence during 1972 sealed the estrangement of the British government from the Catholic community. That process received a sharp push when on Sunday, 30 January, 13 civilians were killed by the army in Derry.[37] The incident destroyed relations between Catholics and the military, giving rise to a rash of 'Provo' attacks. Also, relations with Dublin hit a nadir when an angry mob protesting against the Derry massacre burned down the British Embassy. Understandably, the British government felt isolated and disillusioned with all Irish politicians. In March it announced the suspension of Stormont for a year, that internment would be phased out and regular plebiscites held on the border.[38] A close colleague of Heath's, William Whitelaw, was to take charge of the province. Although a tissue of local control remained, the full substance of power unquestionably rested in British hands.

As the year progressed, it was apparent that full control by London did not lessen the violence. By the autumn Britain was anxious to canvass other possible sources of support. Previously, discussions about Northern Ireland had been conducted between London and Belfast. The position of the Republic was pertinent on security but given little weight otherwise. Indeed, the Declaration of 19 August 1969 had asserted the principle of exclusive sovereignty in Northern Ireland. In the Green Paper issued at the end of October 1972, however, it was clear that Britain was determined to reassess the guarantee. It specifically recognised the 'Irish dimension'. Earlier, British administrations had tended to blame loyalists for the troubles but that belief underwent some revision as Catholics, too, were seen as perpetuators of discord. Britain's government did not acknowledge, as yet, that it contributed to the disturbance. That this message of British goodwill was confronted by a tide of local prejudice was evident, especially in Heath's speech on 16 November. He denounced the futility of parties stating dogmatic views and refusing to move from them. He insisted:

> if we are to reach a fair and effective solution there must be understanding and realism on all sides. Our fellow citizens in the rest of the United Kingdom are being asked to make immense efforts and considerable sacrifices on behalf of Northern Ireland. It is natural that they should look closely day by day in their newspapers, night by night on their television, to see why and in what circumstances this effort and these sacrifices are required of them. They see throughout Northern Ireland steadfastness, determination, and suffering nobly borne by so many people. What they do not as yet find in Northern Ireland is the will to make an effective and lasting peace.[39]

It was little wonder that loyalists as well as Catholics developed genuine doubts about, even an aversion to, London politicians.

During 1973 and the winter and spring of 1974 the government in Britain attempted to restore the mixed mode of administration. At the beginning of March 1973 the promised referendum on the border showed the predictable preference of the majority to remain in the United Kingdom.[40] Later in the month the government unveiled its proposals for the future of the province. There was to be an Assembly elected by proportional representation and a nominated Executive. However, peace-keeping, police, elections, legal appointments and some taxation were reserved to London. Elections for the new Assembly were held in June but implementation of the new regime could not be completed until some inter-party agreement was reached. In December, at Sunningdale, negotiations created the basis for power sharing, with parties being allocated ministerial posts based on their Assembly numbers. As an added ingredient, Dublin endorsed the introduction of power sharing, agreed to prosecute fugitives from the North and accepted that no change in the status of the province could take place until a majority there opted for it. Despite an occasional clamour about partition, the Republic slowly, and with some backsliding, had been moving in the direction of guaranteeing the status of Northern Ireland.

If the scheme was disingenuous, it nevertheless failed the fundamental test of persuading both republicans and hard-line loyalists. The former saw it as a sell-out on partition while the latter believed the proposal was the thin end of a wedge aimed at driving them into the arms of the Republic. Fuelling loyalist suspicions was the fact that the pact had been negotiated by Brian Faulkner, a man of opportunist inclinations, who was mistrusted in Ulster in proportion to his growing stature in London. A flaw in the Sunningdale spirit was a British preference for dealing with men who were socially agreeable or politically pliable while hoping that support for militants on both sides could be eroded. London suffered a myopia which prevented seeing or accepting the legitimacy of less compromising opinions. The new Executive enjoyed only a brief existence. In February Heath was replaced by Wilson, who again came to power without an Irish initiative. It was inevitable that the power sharing arrangement would be challenged; Labour's return ensured that that time would be sooner rather than later. In May the Ulster Workers' Council sponsored an all-out political strike against the Northern Ireland Executive.[41] Political and trade union leaders in Britain attempted to avert the crisis and urged the people of the province to ignore the strike. Wilson's Cabinet was unwilling to allow troops to be deployed for the maintenance of essential services and the strike bit deep in a matter of days, leading to the Executive's collapse. This marked an end of forms of mixed responsibility in Northern Ireland and the recognition that direct rule was not just a temporary expedient. It also crushed the optimism of many British politicians. Wilson struck a popular chord when he spoke of those in the province who 'sponged' on British democracy.[42]

From 1974 to 1979 the main thrust of policy was to contain terrorism. Concern about violence resulted from the escalation of attacks by republican groups in 1974 and the growing number of incidents on the British mainland. The most infamous, the Birmingham pub bombings in November 1974, persuaded a Labour Cabinet to pass the Prevention of Terrorism Act which abrogated certain civil rights of those suspected of terrorist activities. A particularly controversial clause allowed British citizens from Northern Ireland to be denied entry to the mainland or to be deported back to Ulster. That provision was cold comfort to loyalists in Northern Ireland, especially as it emphasised the British wish to ensure that the violence did not leak out of Ulster. Terrorism waxed and waned during the second half of the 1970s. Spectacular killings of British ambassadors to Dublin and The Hague, and of Airey Neave, the Tory spokesman on

Northern Ireland, were vivid reminders of terrorist ability to strike at the heart of the Establishment. Most bombings and assassinations, though, were directed at people in certain exposed occupations or districts of Northern Ireland. Loyalist attacks, which became a feature of the violence, were largely employed against Catholics in the province itself.

While pursuing policies aimed at maintaining security and control of violence, the Labour government, with support from the Opposition, pinned hopes on the people of the province rejecting terrorist methods. Ordinary folk, rather than Ulster politicians, were believed to hold the key to community reconciliation. That hope, especially in 1976 and 1977, was encouraged by the Peace People movement which for a spell gained remarkable support. However, internal dissension within the movement, its rejection by militants, and the absence of a political framework appropriate to transforming the spirit of the cause into concrete form, led to a swift demise which was all but complete by 1979.

Between 1969 and 1974 there had been almost continuous experiments with constitutional forms. It is perhaps not surprising that these attempts to resolve the Irish mess were greeted with enthusiasm and bipartisanship at Westminster. However, after 1974 fresh initiatives declined and the situation reached a stalemate. From then on Labour politicians became visibly more favourable to loyalists, a factor which may account for the sustained level of consensus. Earlier James Callaghan had been critical of Unionists but during his period of office (1976–9) he adopted a more sympathetic outlook. His growing attachment to loyalists was enhanced when from 1978 his government became dependent in the House of Commons on support from other parties, including the Ulster Unionists. When in early 1978 Airey Neave stated that power sharing had ceased to be practical politics, his view was seen as a departure from bipartisanship.[43] In fact, the difference was minor – Labour no longer pursued policies which would implement a restoration of power sharing and Conservatives supported the government's emphasis on security.

While in certain respects British policy became stagnant in the mid-1970s, the growing wish to include the Republic in the future arrangements for the province showed development. Recognition of the role of the Republic had emerged in the first half of the decade. That was reinforced by membership of the

European Economic Community. Britain resented the action of the Republic in referring the treatment of republican suspects in Northern Ireland to the European Human Rights Commission. When in August 1976 the Commission ruled against Britain, it reinforced a view that the Northern Ireland problem had to be treated within a wider Anglo-Irish and European context.[44] Nevertheless, the path to closer coordination between London and Dublin was bumpy. Lynch's call at the beginning of 1978 for a British troop withdrawal and unification once more showed the limits of cooperation.[45]

While changes of political leadership in Britain and Dublin in 1979 did not lead to dramatic shifts of policy, they had important ramifications. Mrs Thatcher was more sympathetic to the plight of Ulster's loyalist people than her predecessors. Her attitude from the obverse angle was matched by Charles Haughey, who replaced Lynch in December, partly as a consequence of the latter's public quivering over border security. Paradoxically, the advent of 'hardliners' in the two capitals marked a stage in the development of better cooperation. Mrs Thatcher was eager to achieve some movement, particularly on security matters, as Britain's actions in Northern Ireland began to draw increased attention and criticism in the United States. Greater cooperation with Dublin would blunt American interference. At the same time the leadership of the Republic was conscious of the de-stabilisation caused by the northern troubles., Both governments, in fact, were reacting to public opinions at home. In Britain it was clear that the general populace felt little kinship with Northern Ireland while in the Republic public feeling proved less nationalist than the leadership – many people were seemingly quite anxious to leave the province to stew in its own juice.

The theme of improved relations between Britain and the Republic received a boost in May 1980 when Haughey told the Dáil that the country had 'no wish' 'to coerce, to dominate or to take over' the six counties.[46] Later in December the two leaders confirmed the emergent cooperation when, following talks in Dublin, they issued a communique which stressed:

4. The Taoiseach and Prime Minister agreed that the economic, social and political interests of the peoples of the United Kingdom of Great Britain and Northern Ireland and the Republic are inextricably linked, but the full

development of these links has been put under strain by division and dissent in Northern Ireland. In that context they accepted the need to bring forward policies and proposals to achieve peace, reconciliation and stability; and to improve relations between the two countries.

5. They considered that the best prospect of attaining these objectives was further development of the unique relationship between the two countries.

6. They accordingly decided to devote their next meeting in London during the coming year to special consideration of the totality of relationships within these islands. For this purpose they have commissioned joint studies, covering a range of issues including possible new institutional structures, citizenship rights, security matters, economic cooperation and measures to encourage mutual understanding.[47]

Despite shifts in the leadership of the Republic and tensions over the respective actions of both countries, the essence of the understanding remained firmly intact.

Even as the leaders conferred, the London–Dublin axis was confronted with the issue of hunger strikes by republican prisoners in Northern Ireland. The tactic was not new. A hunger striker had died at Wakefield Prison as recently as 1976. The ostensible issues at stake were certain parts of prison regimen and the 'political' or 'special' category status of republican convicts; its real purpose was to retrieve the flagging fortunes of the movement. In spring and summer 1981 the crisis reached a peak.[48] On 9 April Bobby Sands, one of the hunger strikers, won the parliamentary by-election in South Tyrone. His death on 5 May, followed by those of 9 other prisoners, the last on 20 August, poisoned the political and sectarian atmosphere in Northern Ireland and created a wave of republican sympathy in the Republic and the United States. In the short term it raised support for the IRA and Sinn Fein, brought in much needed American cash, and frustrated the spirit of cooperation. Yet it quickly became apparent that the growth of support for Sinn Fein on both sides of the border made political leaders in London and Dublin anxious to extend their coordination.

In November 1981 Margaret Thatcher and Garret FitzGerald, the Republic's Premier, met and announced their intention to establish an inter-government council and their agreement on wide areas of cooperation.[49] The Tory government also countered

criticism by issuing a White Paper on Devolution which proposed a new 78-member Assembly elected by proportional
representation and containing elements of power sharing.[50] Its
potential was blunted immediately by Unionists who insisted on
majority decision-making. Nevertheless, this and other British
efforts in the early 1980s showed that the position was not frozen.
During the period republican groups sacrificed their gains by a
campaign of violence which proved entirely counter-productive.
Bombings in Hyde Park and Regent's Park in London, the
destructive blast outside Harrods department store just before
Christmas in 1983 and the explosion in the Grand Hotel,
Brighton, during the Conservative Party conference in October
1984 were turned into massive propaganda victories for the
British government. After the Harrods outrage, Dr FitzGerald
stated, 'the Irish people feel this Christmas a stronger sense of
shared grief and shared outrage with the British public than at
any time that I can recall'.[51] He made a plea to 'the British
Government, political parties and the British public to join with
the Irish in a commitment against the gunmen'.

Moves towards closer London–Dublin links were solidified in
late 1985 with the joint acceptance of the Anglo-Irish Agreement
which was duly registered as an international treaty. The Agreement, like previous attempts at a resolution of the Irish problem,
had bipartisan support. It gave both countries some of the substance of their post-1945 aims – recognition of Northern Ireland's status but acceptance of the South's voice and role in the
internal affairs of the province. In Article 1:

The two Governments
(a) affirm that any change in the status of Northern Ireland
    would only come about with the consent of the majority of
    the people of Northern Ireland;
(b) recognise that the present wish of a majority of the people
    of Northern Ireland is for no change in the status of
    Northern Ireland;
(c) declare that, if in the future a majority of the people of
    Northern Ireland clearly wish for and formally consent to
    the establishment of a united Ireland, they will introduce
    and support in the respective Parliaments legislation to
    give effect to that wish.[52]

The guarantee of 1949 was modified but the acceptance of two

Irelands more secure than at any point since 1920. Unionists objected to the role of the Republic in the province but the responses of the Conservative ministry showed that in one respect the situation in the late 1980s was very different from that in the 1940s – Dublin's participation and interest was now valued. Public opinion in both countries supported the Agreement.

During the second half of the 1980s and the beginning of the 1990s it was apparent that the London–Dublin axis was paramount, despite personal differences between Mrs Thatcher and Charles Haughey. Cooperation rather than confrontation on the issue of the two Irelands was the hallmark. However, coordination between politicians did little to ensure that violence ceased or that the same spirit of conciliation permeated downwards to the peoples of Northern Ireland. Within the province old fears, hatreds and rivalries were as rampant in the 1990s as in 1945. Construction of high policies might ease tensions between the British and Dublin regimes and offer a firmer guarantee of the status of Northern Ireland but these did little towards improving the daily relations of the peoples in the province.

British attitudes towards the two Irelands developed considerably in the post-war era, though remaining constant in the aim of ensuring the status of Northern Ireland. Curiously, the onset of violence in the North made the task of inducing the Republic to shore-up the legal status of Northern Ireland easier. The divergence of outlook between London and Dublin in the 1940s and 50s narrowed in the 1960s and increasingly the positions of the two nations achieved compatibility in the 1970s and 80s. Equally unexpected was the degree of unanimity in Britain over Irish affairs. Unlike Irish troubles in the past, those after 1945 were never allowed to become the plaything of politicians for party ends. There was a general reluctance to permit Irish matters to reach the centre of the political stage and they were never to dominate it. Unrest in Northern Ireland roused no partisan debate but served to reinforce the bipartisan consensus. If Mrs Thatcher showed an eagerness to challenge many of the accepted norms of post-war Britain, her outlook on Ireland differed little from that of her opponents at Westminster. Competing factions in Northern Ireland have exerted scant influence and have been confined to the margins. Similarly, the province itself has remained on the fringe of contemporary Britain. No doubt the insignificance of Ulster has been abetted by the tiny Ulster representation in the House of Commons and the unimportance of the region to the economy of the United Kingdom. British leaders have ignored Bernadette Devlin's warning, 'the one point in common among Ulstermen is that they are not very fond of Englishmen who tell them what to do!'[53] Since the late 1960s, in fact, they have been ready to dictate to, or refuse to listen to, Ulster's people, with impunity. In contrast, the one-time pariahs of Dublin have been accorded an enlarged hearing. That attitude may be traced to political needs but it also has historic roots. Prior to 1921 most British politicians preferred dealing with southern rather than northern Irishmen. The symbiosis of the South and Britain outlived the end of the Union while the always fragile relationship between Ulster loyalists and London did not greatly improve in the intervening years.

14. Youth Culture and the Emergence of Popular Music

JOHN STREET

POPULAR music is now a familiar feature of everyday life. It is available 24 hours a day on radio and television; it accompanies advertisements and Hollywood films; it is piped into shops and arcades; and it is used to raise money for any number of humanitarian causes. Pop has not always enjoyed such prominence, and this chapter traces the story of pop's growing economic and cultural importance. By focusing on popular music, we can illustrate the changes both in a major industry and in the habits and hopes of a substantial part of British society. The rise of rock'n'roll in the 1950s cannot be separated from the growing impact of US popular culture on British life, or from the 'discovery' of the teenager, or from the development of new recording and other technologies, or even shifts in the distribution of political power. As the American critic, Greil Marcus, once wrote:

> a pop explosion is more than a change in style even if it is far less than a revolution ... at its heart, a pop explosion attaches the individual to a group – the fan to an audience, the solitary to a generation – in essence, *forms* a group and creates new loyalties – while at the same time it increases one's ability to respond to a particular pop artifact, or a thousand of them, with an intensity that verges on lunacy.[1]

I

In the beginning there was nothing but rock,
Then somebody invented the wheel,
And things just began to roll (Lieber and Stoller, 'That is Rock'n'Roll')

For many people, and certainly for the popular press, the arrival of rock'n'roll in Britain was announced in 1955 by the film *Rock Around the Clock*. The film had a rock'n'roll soundtrack which provided one of the first opportunities to hear the new music that was becoming increasingly popular in the United States. The emerging stars were Jerry Lee Lewis, Little Richard and Elvis Presley, but for the British, the vanguard was represented by the portly figure of Bill Haley and his Comets. British audiences expressed their enthusiasm for the new sound by tearing up the seats in the auditorium and causing small public disturbances. Anthony Bicat reported that:

> in Manchester, after showing *Rock Around the Clock*, ten youths were fined for insulting behaviour when they left the cinema. 'Rhythm crazed' youngsters, after they had seen the film, held up traffic for half an hour and trampled in the flower beds in the municipal garden. In Blackburn the Watch Committee banned the film . . . . In Croydon the police cleared the Davis Theatre on Sunday of jiving youngsters.[2]

From then on, the story runs, the popularity of rock'n'roll grew rapidly. US rock records began to appear in the British pop charts. These records in turn inspired British artists such as Cliff Richard and Tommy Steele. They were heard, too, by the schoolboys who ten years later would be acclaimed as the key figures of 1960s pop music: John Lennon and Paul McCartney of The Beatles, and Keith Richards and Mick Jagger of the Rolling Stones.

Another element of the history of British popular culture was the reaction it provoked among established interests – from parents, clergymen and politicians. The church warned of the moral damage which could result from the spread of rock'n'roll. One churchman announced that 'Rock'n'roll is a revival of devil dancing ... the same sort of thing that is done in black magic ritual'.[3] This response was partly inspired by the sexual explicitness of the new music, albeit disguised in the euphemisms of 'rocking and reeling'. Similar fears were echoed in Parliament, where attempts were made to ban certain records. The police were known to interpret public singing of rock'n'roll songs as 'ranting and raving' and magistrates dealt harshly with the fans who misbehaved after performances of *Rock Around the Clock*.[4]

When the story of pop is told like this, the enthusiasm of the fans and the reaction of the authorities combine to create the impression that the birth of rock'n'roll in Britain was a major cultural and political event. For the individuals involved it often was, but as an account of the history of the period it gives a false impression. At one level, the action and reaction were (or have become) mythologised. Though there were people who went on at length about the moral depravity wrought by rock, just as there were the rioters outside showings of *Rock Around the Clock*, it is wrong to allow these groups to be the only actors in this tale. When, in 1957, Bill Haley toured Britain to capitalise on the film's success, the press and certain politicians warned of social disruption. In fact, the concerts passed off without incident.[5]

The story, though, is not just distorted in the retelling of the events of the time. Neither rock'n'roll nor its audience arose, as if by magic, to discover each other. They were both the creation of more complex, and more mundane, processes. These include the creation of a popular music industry, a market and a means of mediating the two. We cannot understand either youth culture or popular music without seeing both as part of an economic arrangement whereby a product (records and stars) is found a market (fans). This arrangement depends on a third element: demand. The fans have to want the product, and this means that the product has to be given a meaning and the consumers an identity.

In the 1950s, young people became an important economic market. They had more money of their own to spend, partly a result of their parents' increasing income and partly because of their growing social and economic independence.[6] It was the market potential of youth that the pop industry rose to exploit. But the link between supply and demand is not so straightforward. The 'demand' has to be created and shaped; consumers have to acquire a need and an identity if they are to be sold new products. Such requirements led to the invention of the 'teenager'. Being a 'teenager' was not simply a feature of adolescence; it was a market category. As Simon Frith explains, 'The important thing about "teenager" as a concept was that it described a style of consumption'.[7] It provided a way of marking out a group of people and giving them an identity as consumers. Rock'n'roll both symbolically and literally was a key consumer product around which the teenager market was constructed.

The establishment reaction to rock can, then, be seen as a response to a (new) type of consumer behaviour. Teenagers were

defined as consumers without responsibilities; they had no need
to save to secure the future. They could afford to live for the
moment and to make leisure – not work – the focus of their
aspirations. Through their spending habits, they implicitly challenged the conventional values which underpinned the established view of money and the work ethic. Both the left and the
right feared for the consequences of the teenager phenomenon.
They saw youth's pursuit of pleasure as eroding their political
consciousness (the left) or their moral and religious commitments (the right).[8]

But while there was much noise of moral and political outrage,
there was also the accompanying sound of commercial success.
The British record industry managed to control and profit from
the flourishing new fashion. Despite the expanded market for
records, only two new companies – Pye and Phillips – were
added to the established companies (the 'majors') that had
controlled the 1930s music market. 'Such was the power of the
pop establishment', writes Frith, 'that even when a new market
was revealed (by the emergence of teenage culture and the
success of American rock'n'roll records) the majors were able to
meet the new demands (EMI signed Cliff Richard, Decca took
Tommy Steele) and to integrate the new styles into the existing
structures of pop production, pop promotion, pop programming'.[9]
We cannot understand the emergence of post-war youth culture
without reference to the industry that fuelled its key products.
But the explanation must not be reduced just to the machina-
tions of the industry. There is a crucial cultural dimension. How
else do we explain why rock'n'roll was the key product for the
youth market?

The rise of rock'n'roll in Britain cannot be separated from
the influence of (and interpretation of) US culture. The artists
and the images of the new popular culture were American.
'America' represented a set of ideas and values which the
young found attractive. It conjured up, among other things, a
particular idea of freedom. Individuals like James Dean and
Elvis Presley acted out pleasures and concerns of youth. More
particularly their 'Americanness' was a code for the new and the
modern.[10]

The importance of 'America' to youth culture can be seen in
the suspicion with which established culture treated America.
Once again, the political left and right joined in their fear for the
Americanisation of British (or more often, 'English') culture.

Writers from T. S. Eliot to George Orwell warned of the impact of US culture.[11] These prophets received a sympathetic hearing in the BBC. 'The BBC', according to Stephen Barnard, 'was in the front line of the defence against Americanisation.' The BBC's strategy was not to deny all access to American music but rather to present it in a new, 'safer' guise. Barnard describes the process: 'The BBC acted as a filter, recognising the qualities and the popularity of American music, its spark and charm.' British artists and records were favoured over their US equivalents – British-based skiffle (played by people like Lonnie Donnegan) was acceptable while rock'n'roll was not. Rock'n'roll was treated with particular suspicion. Many records were deemed 'unsuitable for regular broadcasting'.[12]

The BBC, though, did not have monopoly control over the consumption of popular music. Although it limited the playing of Elvis Presley's 'Heartbreak Hotel', the BBC could not prevent it from being in the British top twenty from May to September 1956. The record could be heard elsewhere – on juke boxes, on American Forces Networks, in dance halls, on ITV. And with the emergence of Radio Luxembourg's pop programming, there was a major radio rival to the BBC. Luxembourg was a vital contributor to the dissemination of pop, a process helped by the development of portable transistor radios.

British youth culture, and rock'n'roll in particular, therefore, was not the result simply of artistic creativity or popular demand; it owed as much to industrial and economic changes and to institutional interests. This general structure was overlaid by cultural and ideological values which gave meaning to the products of popular culture. 'America' symbolised the new, youthful, modern era. It was embraced by young people seeking a way of spending their new wealth and expressing their sense of freedom. The changing relations between these elements produce the history of British youth culture.

II

All you need is love / love is all you need (The Beatles)

It is almost impossible to disentangle the myth from the reality of the 1960s. And perhaps it is wrong to do so. The symbolic meaning of the 1960s – as a time of liberation, of a changing moral climate – is a crucial part of the rhetoric which influenced the way people acted and thought. But equally it is wrong to expect popular readings of the 1960s to tell the whole story. We have to be very wary of the easy generalisation which simply equates political and cultural change. One political scientist, for example, wrote that 'in its tunes and lyrics the new pop music expressed [the] spirit [of modernity] and carried it to the far reaches of society'.[13]

Popular culture and popular music *did* undergo radical changes in the decade, although the ten years do not really form a neat historical period (the *Oz* trial, an archetypal 1960s event, perhaps, took place in 1971). The early part of the decade saw the flourishing of indigenous British culture and a partial break with US cultural domination. Artists who had heard American rock'n'roll and the black music from which it borrowed, and who had learnt to play during the skiffle boom of the late 1950s, were beginning to produce their own pop. Groups like the Shadows, the Beatles and the Rolling Stones, singers like Cliff Richard and Billy Fury were signed to major record labels and found a huge new market in the USA. Talk of 'Americanisation' was replaced by wonder at the 'British invasion'.

To understand these events, we need to look more closely at two British cities, Liverpool and London. Why did Liverpool produce the artists who were to define the sound of British pop, and why was it London that determined how that sound was understood and marketed? Liverpool combined an established tradition of local music-making with access to the latest releases from the US. In his biography of the Beatles, Philip Norman explains:

While Britain listened to Adam Faith and 'Pop', Liverpool listened to Rhythm and Blues. The Cunard Yanks were bringing over new records by a new young black performer still confined by his own country to the low indecent level of negro 'race' music. His name was Chuck Berry. ... [His] songs broke like anthems on the young of a northern city still gripped by the Victorian age, which had had no truck with black people since the slave hulks set sail from Liverpool Bay. All over Merseyside each Saturday night, in ballrooms, town halls, Co-op halls, even swimming baths and ice skating rinks, there were amateur R&B groups playing Chuck Berry songs, Little Richard, Fats Domino and B. B. King songs.[14]

The Liverpool groups and their audiences, argues Norman, discovered a peculiar affinity with the sounds produced by black US artists, an affinity born of a sense of segregation: North was separated from South, and the working class from the middle class. To invest US music with such meanings was not, however, exclusive to Liverpool. In London, the young bohemians of the art schools (people like Pete Townshend, Eric Clapton and Keith Richards) were exhilarated too by the sound of urban America's rhythm and blues. Whatever the political or sociological backdrop to the music, the sound itself generated an excitement, a sense of the forbidden, which made much existing pop seem bland and safe by comparison.

While Liverpool learned to produce artistic capital, it was London that monopolised cultural and financial capital. It was there where 'success' was defined and found, and it was from there that the transition to the larger US markets was made. The paradigm of this particular tale of two cities was, of course, the Beatles.

The Beatles' success demonstrated the new form and character of both popular music and youth culture. Their talents as writers and performers are only part of the explanation. Their skills as performers were developed through a tough apprenticeship in the Hamburg nightclubs in 1961–2. Their songwriting and harmonies were developed through assiduous listening to US pop (especially the vocal groups being pioneered by Tamla Motown). All of this was overlaid by the sensibilities acquired by Lennon at art school. It is a singular feature of British pop that many of its main innovators were the product of art schools. Frith and Horne observe:

> students like Lennon were finding unexpected opportunities in art school life and were being changed by them. At the very least colleges offered even the idlest students material benefits. They provided stages and audiences for first, faltering performances.

These performances also gave musicians 'a chance to make music without having to please anyone, without having to fit into showbiz routines'. Finally, the art school provided these performers with a sense that they were artists (not just entertainers) and gave them role models drawn both from previous artists – Lennon learnt of the Impressionists as artistic rebels – and from their peers and their bohemian lifestyles.[15]

The Beatles' success was not just, though, a matter of their talents and artistic skills. Their sound owed much to a staff producer at EMI, George Martin. Martin worked with the Beatles throughout their career (until *Let it Be* and the break-up of the band in 1970). He helped with the song arrangements, and accentuated the group's distinctive harmonies. Later, he opened up the possibilities of the recording studio as an extra musical instrument, giving practical effect to the musicians' half-formed ideas. The other key person was Brian Epstein, the Beatles' manager. Epstein was the manager of a record retail business and gained firsthand knowledge of the Beatles' popularity. But it was not his business skill that was important, it was his ability to cultivate the group's image and style. By dressing them in identical suits and giving them their famous fringes, he established a show-biz, wholesome – if slightly sharp – character for the group.

These local factors combined with the emergence of new markets and customers. The commercial potential of pop was fast being realised as a new generation of entrepreneurs found fresh ways to sell the music and other youth artefacts. The mid-1960s saw the linking of consumption with self-expression. The idea was that you could purchase a life-style (itself a 1960s word). Dress designers (Barbara Halinuki and her Biba stores) and cosmetics companies (Mary Quant), and their models (Jean Shrimpton and Twiggy) and photographers (David Bailey and Terence Donovan), all contributed to the images and products which defined 1960s youth. The physical embodiment of the fashion was London's Carnaby Street where shops like Lord John and Chelsea Girl sold the style to eager young shoppers. Pop musicians were central icons of this new culture, providing both its soundtrack and its stylists. They were crucial to the marketing of it. When the Beatles received their MBEs in 1965 from Prime Minister Harold Wilson, this was less a tribute to their musical ability than to their economic success (the annual turnover of the British record industry was £100 million) and their capacity to attract a huge youth audience (or a future electorate, as Wilson perhaps thought of it). Iain Chambers sums up these mid-1960s developments:

> With television exposure and the world-wide success of its music, British youth culture went public. The Carnaby Street mod became Saturday-afternoon youth in any of Britain's major cities. . . . More obvious class and cultural lines, such as

those that had excluded the Teds and rock'n'roll music in the 1950s, were blurred in an expanding taste for the catchy songs of the Beatles and the more fashionable icons of the moment: mini-skirts, Biba, Mary Quant, Twiggy.[16]

The mass market pop and youth culture of the mid-1960s was only one form. According to sociological observers, there were also sub- and counter-cultures.[17] There were the mods and rockers of the mid-1960s who defined themselves through their clothes and their music. These constituted subcultures which identified common forms of life and attitudes but which lacked any explicit political character. But the 'hippy' and the 'flower children' changed this. This time the label 'counter-culture' was intended to designate its political pretensions. The rhetoric portrayed musicians and audiences as joined together in a collective endeavour to establish an alternative society. A key ingredient to the experience was drugs, particularly the halluci-nogen LSD ('acid'). A participant recalled events at one of the new venues: 'UFO, down in this cellar, was a disgusting-looking place in daylight but transformed by the light works ... Man-fred, the German acid dealer, attended and distributed the product on a handsome level. At the third UFO he gave out 400 trips'. 'It was like a trippy adventure playground really', recalled Paul McCartney.[18] A press was founded to articulate these ideas. Known as the underground press, it included such titles as *Oz*, *International Times,* and *Rolling Stone.* The pop happenings at the UFO and the Roundhouse in Camden were the basis of the later rock festivals at the Isle of Wight, Hyde Park and elsewhere. At these events, the excesses of the rhetoric were matched only by the discomforts of the facilities. Mick Jagger wrote 'Streetfighting Man' for the Rolling Stones. The former Trotskyist Tariq Ali recalls how he used to receive phone calls from John Lennon: 'He would ring me once or twice a month and talk about the state of the world'.[19] Ali was subsequently to interview Lennon for *Red Mole* and Lennon wrote the song 'Power to the People' as a direct result of their conversation.

The actual number of people involved in these ventures was relatively small and often elitist. The disc jockey John Peel remembered:

The underground was terribly small, and very very localised. I could never understand, for example, why it was that that

Country Joe and the Fish LP never got into the charts. I said to the record company, 'Why isn't this in the charts? Everybody I know has got a copy.' But what I didn't realise was that it was the other way round: I knew everybody who'd got a copy.[20]

While the key group was small, they received disproportionate attention. More importantly, they provided the ideas and styles that opened up a new way of marketing music and other products. Record companies were quick to spot the commercial potential of the counter-culture. They formed labels dedicated to selling 'alternative' records. EMI created Harvest; Polydor established Vertigo; John Peel had his own label, Dandelion. The marketing departments followed. CBS announced that 'The Revolution is on CBS'.

Audiences and artists combined to sustain the counter-culture packaging. Each made grand claims for the artistic and social importance of the music. Such claims were given further validation by writers in the quality press who began to take pop seriously. William Mann in *The Times* and Tony Palmer in *The Observer* wrote about the Beatles and others in the same terms as had traditionally been reserved for classical music. This change was important. As Robert Hewison explains:

rock'n'roll has managed a transition in cultural status from that of a minority entertainment limited to one age-group and excluded from serious consideration as an expressive medium, to one where it holds an equal place with other arts of the avant-garde. Rock reveals the extent – and the limits – of the cultural shift that followed the upheavals of 1968.[21]

In the 1980s, John Peel was awarded an honorary degree and rock music acquired equal status with the other arts in the review pages of the quality papers.

It would be wrong, however, to see 1960s culture as exclusively the product of the pop avant-garde. While students and workers were on the streets of Paris in 1968 and there were large demonstrations in London against the American military presence in Vietnam, the British public's favourite record was 'Wonderful World' sung by Louis Armstrong. Record companies were not replaced by worker cooperatives; instead they learnt new techniques for selling their product, for investing a song with meaning and significance. Two years later the Conservative government of Edward Heath was elected by voters who were disillusioned by Wilson's attempt to control trade unionism. Talk of revolution faded to the quietest of whispers.

It would be equally wrong to see the cultural politics of the late 1960s as nothing more than a passing fad. They were instrumental in giving strength to two of the most significant political developments of the following years: the women's and the green movements. They could be detected, too, in the more mixed achievements of Ken Livingstone's Greater London Council in the early 1980s. What each of these political forces learnt from the 1960s experience was the manner in which politics and culture are linked through style and image, how the way people feel and imagine things is connected to the way they act.

III

I wanna riot of my own ('White Riot', The Clash)

Conventional wisdom holds that disillusionment with the 1960s alternative society presaged the collapse of youth culture as a serious oppositional force. Young people had been turned by the record and other cultural industries into a bland exploitable market which could be sold anything. The conventional view also holds that this arrangement was briefly disrupted by the appearance of punk rock in 1976–8, when once again youth culture emerged as a counter-culture. As with all such established interpretations, there is some element of truth in this version, but its distortions tend to outstrip its accuracies.

Popular music in the period to 1976 was marked by an increasing diversification of its forms and markets. There was 'glam rock' in the shape of Roxy Music and David Bowie which made a virtue of showbiz artificiality and camp style and which ironically parodied rock's earlier, 1950s incarnation. There was the reggae music of Jamaica, epitomised by stars like Bob Marley and the Wailers, which was sold as the authentic sound of political pop. For the young fan, there were the teeny-bop sounds of the Bay City Rollers. For the serious, older rock fan there were the virtuoso guitarists such as Jimmy Page of Led Zeppelin or the introspective folk-rock of Joni Mitchell or James Taylor. Perhaps the most popular, but most derided music, was disco. Sociologists, themselves responding to the new importance that the

1960s gave to popular culture, began to analyse the different audiences attached to the various musical styles. But, at the same time, they challenged the claims that had been made for popular culture in the 1960s. They began to question the idea that 'youth' constituted a distinct social category or that musical taste was unaffected by social class. While middle-class children listened to the self-conscious 'progressive' music of Pink Floyd, the sociologists suggested, working-class children preferred Slade's injunction to 'Cum Feel the Noize'.[22] It was a form of categorisation that did not always work – what, after all, counted as 'working-class music'? did not some artists' appeal (David Bowie's, for example) cross class boundaries?[23]

The general weakness of the theory was that it tended to see popular culture merely as an external sign of a 'real' material base. It treated young people as the dupes of a manipulative and all-powerful record industry and of economic forces in general which determined their lives and attitudes. In doing so, the thesis only gave a superficial glance towards the music, and missed the politics contained within it. While the music of the pre-punk era, apart from reggae and some soul, made few explicit political points, it nonetheless addressed issues of sexual identity which arguably were more profoundly radical than all the chanting of 'revolution' in 1968. David Bowie and Mick Jagger, in their songs and images, played with different ideas of pleasure, cross-dressing and making-up. These stars provided a language and an excuse for exploring desire and challenging the roles that society sought to impose on the young. There may have been no political programme or outburst of mass hedonism, but neither could pop culture be written off an as exercise in marketing.

Besides, and this is another reason for questioning the dominant sociological view, the British record industry was not as successful as the thesis supposed. After the 1960s boom, the industry was suffering a fall in sales and profits. While pop music had won the respectability of a regular programme on BBC2, this new status was no guarantee of profits. In the period 1974–7, the British record industry's turn over fell by 17 per cent – from £450.8 million to £376.5 million (1984 prices). In 1974, 0.4 per cent of all consumer spending went on records; by 1976, the figure had dropped to 0.34 per cent.[24] The shrinkage in the market led to loss of jobs and a concentration of ownership among a few major companies, which themselves were diversifying to remain afloat. It was not just the record industry that was suffering. Unemployment rose to a million in 1975. It was into these uncertain conditions that punk emerged.

Punk made much, rhetorically, of its radical, oppositional politics. The music revived the language of revolt and oppression, but ironically it also revived the record industry. Punk reinvigorated popular music, giving record companies the excuse to market it extravagantly. The music and the popular press helped to inflate the music's social significance. The music, with its angry, fast tempo, together with the deliberately provocative style of its performers and followers, made it easy to think of punk as a direct expression of a general social malaise or the particular consequences of unemployment.[25] The song titles encouraged this view: 'Anarchy in the UK', 'White Riot'; and then there were the bondage clothes and the swastikas and the cheeks pierced with safety pins. And finally, to ensure punk's rebellious image, the leading punk band, the Sex Pistols, were banned by the BBC and dropped by their record company EMI.

The ethos of punk was 'do it yourself'. Enthusiasm counted for as much as musical skill. Recordings were made for a few hundred pounds and distributed for not much more. A profusion of independent labels and distribution networks were set up, accompanied by hastily assembled magazines and new clubs. This structure was a direct contrast to the business practices of the previous years when records were costing millions to make and stage shows were exercises in conspicuous consumption. The major labels were, temporarily, caught out by the punk boom. The initiative slipped from them to pop journalists, to punk musicians and their enterprising managers, and even to the audiences. Together these people gave punk its political rhetoric and helped to shape its social significance.

One of the most adept PR agents for punk was Malcolm Mclaren, manager of the Sex Pistols. With his art school theory and his entrepreneurial skills, he rediscovered pop's capacity to shock. The brutal energy of the music was allied to a shrewd grasp of how the popular media operated. When the Sex Pistols swore profusely on a prime-time TV show, they captured the front pages of the tabloid press. In becoming a source of moral outrage, punk became 'news' – everyone from Mary Whitehouse to MPs was driven to comment – and the Sex Pistols became a highly marketable product.

After falling out (while collecting substantial advances) with EMI and A&M, the Sex Pistols signed with Virgin records. In this alliance a symbolic connection with the 1960s was made. But the connection was stronger than mere symbolism. Punk revived the myth that music could change the world, and many of the revivalists were people who had been active in the era of flower power. Caroline Coon, who managed the punk band The Clash and who wrote *Melody Maker*'s first piece on punk, had founded the drug help clinic Release in the 1960s.

It is easy to see punk as just another passing fad in youth culture's ever faster turnover of new ideas and gimmicks. Certainly, the reaction of the tabloid press is not a good basis for sociological or historical generalisations. And it is also true that, as with the hippies, the number of people actually caught up was relatively small. Furthermore, whatever the claims of punk's various spokespeople, the bands were not simply direct representatives of the alienated and unemployed working class. Many of the musicians were graduates of art schools, equipped with theories of art, while the entrepreneurs were often the products of the British higher education system. Doubts about punk's social authenticity are overlaid by the brevity of the fad, a mere three years. Looked at this way, it is easy to be dismissive of punk's importance. It can be argued that, despite its brevity, punk was a highly significant cultural movement.[26]

Punk was instrumental in altering ideas about design and style. It not only changed a whole set of aesthetic values but also helped to forge a more general change in the way ideas and images were connected. Punk gave scope to a new group of design artists (as had pop culture in the 1960s), people such as Neville Brody and Jamie Reid who as graphic artists worked on record sleeves and magazines, and Vivienne Westwood and Jasper Conran who as fashion designers shaped the way people looked. Punk also helped to pioneer the use of video and to introduce new techniques. The impact of all these is now visible everywhere, in the layout of magazines, in the style of adverts, in the organisation of shops and in the design of whole ranges of consumer products. These particular artefacts also gave practical form to an underlying thesis which is equally pervasive today, and which establishes the political and social importance of popular culture. The design of magazines like *The Face* and *ZG* demonstrated that layout and content were linked. What the words said was only part of the meaning conveyed. Punk showed how signs and gestures carried political messages: why else were people shocked by the way punks dressed? Finally, punk's importance was established by the part it played in making possible the most significant popular cultural event of the 1980s: Live Aid.

IV

We are the World (USA for Africa)

On 13 July 1985, a vast TV audience of over 100 million watched the best known figures in popular music perform in Wembley Stadium in London and JFK Stadium in Philadelphia. The concerts were given to raise money for the people of Ethiopia who were starving as a result of widespread drought and political intransigence. The simultaneous concerts, which went under the collective title of Live Aid, were a huge success; £100 million was raised, as was public awareness.

Live Aid was largely the brainchild of a single man, Bob Geldof.[27] In the late 1970s and early 1980s, Geldof had achieved modest success as the leader of the punk-influenced Boomtown Rats. Watching a film report from Ethiopia, Geldof felt compelled to do something. He drew on his circle of pop friends to organise a recording session one Sunday in November 1984. The song was 'Do they know it's Christmas?'. The stars sang for free and record shops waived their profits. The song was a hit and the proceeds went into a Band Aid trust. Soon there was a rash of similar records from all over the world. The Live Aid concert was the culmination of these developments. Subsequently there have been Comic Aid and Sports Aid for the victims of famine, and a host of records and concerts for other causes. Rock stars have toured for Amnesty International, performed for the release of Nelson Mandela, and made records for Greenpeace.

Before Geldof dreamt up Band Aid, there had been relatively few precedents for such pop ventures. In the 1950s, pop stars had performed together to help Hungary, following the Soviet invasion; in 1971, John and Yoko released 'Happy Christmas (War is Over); and in the same year, George Harrison organised The Concert for Bangladesh. None of these matched Live Aid or Band Aid in financial or political terms. They were marginal, 'pop' events, whereas Bob Geldof won himself a place on the international stage. He argued with heads of government and was recommended for all manner of national honours.

Geldof's elevation cannot be explained just by reference to his personal charm and determination, although he lacked for neither. His role was dependent on the changing status of popular music and the culture attached to it. Pop was no longer part of an exclusive youth-culture, nor could it properly be described as subcultural. It was now part of mainstream mass entertainment. Pop music could no longer automatically provoke shock or moral outrage. Two days after Live Aid, the Prime Minister wrote to Bob Geldof. She said: 'Your efforts have been an example to young people in this country and throughout the world'.[28] When a priest wrote in 1987 that 'rock'n'roll and fearful immorality go hand-in-hand', he was greeted with derision; had he written the same thing 30 years earlier, he would have been taken seriously.[29] Pop stars had not, of course, become saints. The tabloid press still delighted in humiliating stars like Boy George (for his drug habit) or Elton John. What distinguished this type of abuse from that which greeted pop's first years were the expectations that accompanied it. The earlier teen idols were not seen as an inescapably degenerate danger because they were pop stars. It was pop that was immoral. After Live Aid, pop was identified as capable of acts of moral leadership, and pop stars as capable of representing moral orthodoxy. It was the individuals who failed to live up to these standards that were castigated. Pop performers were now part of the mainstream of popular culture, and so their failings (like those of film and TV stars before them) were ideal fare for selling tabloid papers.

The economics and demography of pop had changed too, giving added impetus to these other trends. The audience for pop was getting larger. It included not only the young but also the middle-aged who had grown up to the sound of rock. For these latter generations, pop music was the cultural norm, and with their spending power they represented an important market, indeed one whose importance grew with the decline in the number of younger fans. The opportunity to exploit the older generation came with the development of Compact Disc technology. The CD helped to salvage the record industry from another slump by providing a new customer 'need' (extra high fidelity) and a new consumer (the 1960s generation who could replace their worn-out record collection with reissued CDs).[30]

These old sounds have not just boosted the record industry's fortunes, they have also played an increasingly important part in selling other products. The songs that shocked parents and were the excuse for youthful rebellion now sell all manner of consumer goods to the whole family. Edam cheese has been sold to the sound of Jerry Lee Lewis's 'Great Balls of Fire'; Roger Daltrey of The Who has advertised American Express; and Marvin Gaye's 'I heard it through the grapevine' accompanied the Levi jeans' advertisements. Pop songs have also sold Hollywood films, a top ten hit from the soundtrack guaranteeing queues at the box office.

These developments did not just mark a change in marketing aesthetics or cultural values, nor did they just mark a social change in pop's audience. What changed was the whole edifice of mass media, and with this there was a major shift in the character of popular culture.[31] Increasingly, different media are becoming linked and interdependent. The pattern of ownership illustrates this. Robert Maxwell has commercial interests in television, newspapers, and book publishing; Rupert Murdoch has bought into the press and satellite TV (and film studios in the US). Richard Branson, however, best exemplifies the trend. In the late 1960s he founded a magazine, *Student*, for an upwardly mobile youth market. Though this venture ultimately failed, he survived to found a retail record chain, subsequently adding a record label, a recording studio, an airline company and a film company, as well as commercial TV and radio interests. These diversifications were not simple decisions about profitability and wealth, but also a reflection of the way in which the character of popular culture and its marketing has changed. The spread of interests made explicit the connection between culture and consumption. Popular culture is the means by which consumption acquires meaning.

Without these developments, the attempt at, and the success of, Live Aid would have been inconceivable. It was a venture that traded upon pop's popular and commercial potential. Pop could reach vast audiences and generate immense resources. When a Greenpeace benefit record was released in Britain in 1989, the accompanying advertisement announced, 'If you care about the world, you'll buy this album'. Just as individual identity was constructed through a series of consumption choices, mediated by the culture that invested the meaning, so too was social conscience. Each year charities and political pressure groups extend the range of T-shirts and filofaxes that the concerned citizen can buy. Popular music, by providing a public platform for individual conscience, has played a central role in the commercialisation of concern.

As popular music becomes an increasingly central part of mainstream culture, so pop stars establish themselves as speakers for general public anxieties. No longer do those stars pretend to speak only for the young; instead they claim to speak for the people. The spirit of social revolt against parents or school has become the spirit of social concern. It makes sense in these circumstances for causes and stars to exploit their mutual interests and advantage. While popular music still finds room for the rebel and the eccentric, these ambitions are not represented by social criticism; this is, after all, the convention. The rebel is now the musician who does not care, who makes a noise for the hell of it, who disclaims any meaning for his or her art.

v

Rockin' in the Free World (Neil Young)

What began in the 1950s as a fairly exclusive, and much reviled, youth culture became, in the late 1980s, mainstream popular culture. Organised around pop music, this culture is now so pervasive, so familiar, that its very ubiquity can make it almost invisible, although moral panics (over Acid House parties, for example) refocus attention on it. Pop music is to be heard on advertisements for all manner of products, on 24-hour radio stations and cable TV channels, on the soundtrack of almost all big budget films, and in supermarkets and shopping malls. Pop music is not confined, though, to the worlds of commerce and mass entertainment. Politicians and political parties have used pop to enhance their image and to win over voters, just as pop musicians have turned themselves into politicians, speaking up for an ever-increasing number of causes.

There is no reason to suppose that this trend will end. Pop music, together with television and cinema, reaches a huge audience and generates a great deal of money, directly and through the consumers it brings to other markets. It represents, therefore, an important economic resource. But its significance is not purely economic. It is also part of a living culture, and in this capacity, it is a means by which people construct a meaning for their lives. It is impossible to explain or understand the major political movements of recent years, the women's movement and the green movement, without reference to the cultural ideas and practices of youth popular culture of the past 30 years. Both the new social movements and the popular culture gave life to the idea that the personal was political.

Bibliography

(Place of publication here and in Notes and References is London unless otherwise stated.)

2. THE ECONOMIC RECORD SINCE 1945

The literature on the British economy since 1945 is vast and much of it is technical, requiring some knowledge of economic theory and concepts. The following works have been selected, as far as possible, for their jargon-free approach to the subject. Good general surveys of the period are contained in Sidney Pollard, *The Development of the British Economy 1914–1980* (1983), J. F. Wright, *Britain in the Age of Economic Management* (Oxford, 1979) and B. W. E. Alford, *British Economic Performance 1945–1975* (1988). Keith Smith, *The British Economic Crisis: Its Past and Future* (1989) and M. W. Kirby, *The Decline of British Economic Power Since 1870* (1981) set the period in its historical context, while N. F. R. Crafts, B. Duckham and N. Woodward (eds), *The British Economy Since 1945* (Oxford, 1991), contains up-to-date analyses of many of the themes covered in the chapter. Derek Morris (ed.), *The Economic System in the UK* (Oxford, 1985) is also of use at the general level. Excellent contemporary surveys of a wide range of issues pertaining to economic performance are contained in G. D. N. Worswick and P. H. Ady, *The British Eeonomy 1945–50* (Oxford, 1952) and, by the same authors, *The British Economy in the 1950s* (Oxford, 1962). The record of government economic management has been subject to intense scrutiny. The seminal works are J. C. R. Dow, *The Management of the British Economy 1945–60* (Cambridge, 1964), and F. T. Blackaby (ed.), *British Economic Policy 1960–74* (Cambridge, 1978). Also of use are Andrew Shonfield, *British Economic Policy Since the War* (1959) and (particularly on the 'stop-go' phenomenon), S. Brittan, *Steering the Economy* (3rd edn, 1971). W. Beckerman (ed.), *Slow Growth in Britain: Causes and Consequences* (1979) contains several penetrating essays on Britain's lagging growth performance. A valuable American perspective is provided by R. Caves (ed.), *Britain's Economic Prospects* (Washington, DC, 1968), and R. Caves and L. Krause (eds), *Britain's Economic Performance* (Washington, DC, 1980).

There are two key works on the analysis of de-industrialisation: Robert Bacon and Walter Eltis, *Britain's Economic Problem: Too Few Producers?* (1976), and F. T. Blackaby (ed.), *De-industrialisation* (1979). These should be supplemented by Ajit Singh, 'UK Industry and the World Economy: A Case of De-industrialisation?', *Cambridge Journal of Economics*, I, no. 2 (1977) and A. P. Thirlwall, 'De-industrialisation in the United Kingdom', *Lloyds Bank Review*, no. 144 (April 1982). Excellent analyses of Britain's lagging technological progress are to be found in K. Pavitt (ed.), *Technical Innovation and British Economic Performance* (1980) and Charles Carter (ed.), *Industrial Policy and Innovation* (1981). The reasons for Britain's relatively poor investment record are examined passionately in Sidney Pollard, *The Wasting of the British Economy* (1982), while the article by F. E. Jones, 'Our Manufacturing Industry – The Missing £100,000 Million' in *National Westminster Bank Quarterly Review* (May 1978) is particularly revealing.

The alleged retarding influence of British institutions – management, trade unions, the City of London and the Treasury – have attracted much interest recently. The key works are Bernard Elbaum and William Lazonick (eds), *The Decline of the British Economy* (Cambridge, 1986), Geoffrey Ingham, *Capitalism Divided? The City and Industry in British Social Development* (1984), and S. Newton and D. Porter, *Modernisation Frustrated: the politics of industrial decline in Britain since 1900* (1988). Also of use in this respect are G. C. Allen, *The British Disease: A Short Essay on the Nature and Causes of the Nation's Lagging Wealth* (1976), and Sir Henry Phelps Brown, 'What is the British Predicament?', *Three Banks Review*, no. 145 (July 1982). Objective critiques of the economic achievements of the Thatcher government since 1979 are rare but Graham Thompson, *The Conservatives' Economic Policy* (1986), Bruce Bartlect, 'Supply-Side Economics: Theory and Evidence', *National Westminster Bank Quarterly Review* (February 1985) and David F. Lomax, 'Supply-Side Economics: The British Experience', *National Westminster Bank Quarterly Review* (August 1982) are useful. For a more biased and favourable interpretation see A. A. Walters, *Britain's Economic Renaissance: Margaret Thatcher's Reforms* (New York, 1986). Opposing interpretations of the achievements of Thatcherism by Ken Coutts and Wynne Godley (anti), and Geoffrey Maynard (pro), are contained in *The Political Quarterly* LX, no. 2 (April–June 1989). Finally, the various editions of A. R. Prest and D. J. Coppock (eds), *The UK Economy: A Manual of Applied Economics* (first published in 1966) are an invaluable source on the nature and performance of the British economy since the 1960s.

3. ENTERPRISE AND THE WELFARE STATE: A COMPARATIVE PERSPECTIVE

Much of this chapter centres upon a comparison of the argument of Correlli Barnett, *The Audit of War* (1986) and the data published in

Peter Flora, *State, Economy and Society in Western Europe 1815–1975*, vols I and II (1983 and 1987), and Peter Flora (ed.), *Growth to Limits. The Western European Welfare States Since World War II*, vols I, II and IV (1987–8). The subject may be further studied in these volumes, and in Peter Flora and Arnold J. Heidenheimer (eds), *The Development of Welfare States in Europe and America* (1981).

4. TRADE UNIONS, THE GOVERNMENT AND THE ECONOMY

There are good general surveys in B. Pimlott and C. Cook (eds), *Trade Unions in British Politics* (2nd edn, 1991) and by H. Pelling, *A History of British Trade Unionism* (4th edn, 1987). For the theme of governments and incomes policies see L. Panitch, *Social Democracy and Industrial Militancy* (Cambridge, 1976), G. Dorfman, *Government versus Trade Unionism in British Politics Since 1968* (Stanford, 1979) and W. J. Fishbein, *Wage Restraint By Consensus* (1984). The British experience is considered alongside those of other Western European countries in R. Flanagan, D. W. Soskice and L. Ulman, *Unionism, Economic Stability and Incomes Policies* (Washington, DC 1983). For more theoretical discussions see R. E. Chater, A. Dean and R. E. Elliott (eds), *Incomes Policies* (Oxford, 1981) and J. L. Fallick and R. E. Elliott (eds), *Incomes Policies, Inflation and Relative Pay* (1981).

For an analysis of strikes in the long term (1889–1974) see J. E. Cronin, *Industrial Conflict in Modern Britain* (1979) and for a detailed analysis of the years 1946–73 see J. W. Durcan, W. E. J. McCarthy and G. P. Redman, *Strikes in Post-War Britain* (1983). Two very good surveys of industrial relations, especially for the period since 1970, are G. S. Bain (ed.), *Industrial Relations in Britain* (Oxford, 1983) and J. MacInnes, *Thatcherism at Work* (Milton Keynes, 1987). For surveys of the labour market and the wider economy see M. J. Artis (ed.), *Prest and Coppock's The UK Economy: A Manual of Applied Economics* (12th edn, 1989), C. H. Lee, *The British Economy Since 1700: A Macroeconomic Survey* (Cambridge, 1986) and B. W. Alford, *British Economic Performance 1945–1975* (1988).

5. THE JERUSALEM THAT FAILED? THE REBUILDING OF POST-WAR BRITAIN

J. Burnett, *A Social History of Housing, 1815–1970* (1978) is an essential starting point on the details of housing development. The best overview of the architectural debates influencing post-war planning is L. Esher, *A Broken Wave: the Rebuilding of England, 1940–1980* (1981) while P. Hall, *Urban and Regional Planning* (1975) provides a succinct account of the growth of the planning movement. Early developments are considered in M. Swenarton, *Homes fit for Heroes: the Politics and*

Architecture of Early State Housing in Britain (1981); see also J. Stevenson, *British Society, 1914–1945* (1984). Two excellent examples of the growth of interest in redevelopment are E. D. Simon, *Rebuilding Britain: A Twenty Year Plan* (1945) and T. Sharp, *Town Planning* (1940). London's particular problems were considered in P. Hall, *London 2000* (1964), an issue recently revisited in P. Hall, *London 2001* (1989). Further debate on the issues of the responsibility of architects and planners can be found in A. Coleman, *Utopia on Trial: Vision and Reality in Planned Housing* (1985), R. Glass, *Clichés of Urban Doom* (Oxford, 1989) and P. Hall, *Cities of Tomorrow* (Oxford, 1989). Current discussions of architectural styles can be found in C. Jencks, *Modern Movements in Architecture* (2nd edn, 1985) and *The Prince, the Architects and new wave monarchy* (1988).

6. THE RISE (AND FALL?) OF STATE-OWNED ENTERPRISE

As with so many themes in the post-1945 period, the literature on nationalised industries is immense, and what follows is very much a personal choice. Not only this, but the emphasis and concerns of writers have changed considerably in each decade since the 1940s. Students should *not* assume that only recently published material is relevant. One of the best general and internationally comparative studies is Yair Aharoni, *The Evolution and Management of State-Owned Enterprises* (Cambridge, Mass., 1986). Useful assessments of UK experience include: A. A. Rogow and Peter Shore, *The Labour Government and British Industry, 1945–1951* (Oxford, 1955); D. L. Munby, 'The Nationalized Industries', in G. D. N. Worswick and P. H. Ady (eds), *The British Economy in the Nineteen-Fifties* (Oxford, 1962); E. Eldon Barry, *Nationalisation in British Politics* (1965); R. Kelf-Cohen, *Twenty Years of Nationalisation. The British Experience* (1971 edn); David Coombes, *State Enterprise – Business or Politics?* (1971); and Leonard Tivey, *Nationalisation in British Industry* (1973 edn). For the origins and establishment of state industries in the late 1940s, the most authoritative work is Sir Norman Chester, *The Nationalisation of British Industry 1945–51* (1975), though for a broader economic perspective see also Sir Alec Cairncross, *Years of Recovery. British Economic Policy 1945–51* (1985).

More considered evaluations of performance begin with the path-breaking Richard Pryke, *Public Enterprise in Practice. The British Experience of Nationalisation over Two Decades* (1971), which should be read in conjunction with his bleaker assessment in *The Nationalised Industries. Politics and Performance since 1968* (Oxford, 1981) and with more recent studies, including Richard Molyneux and David Thompson, 'Nationalised Industry Performance: still third rate?', *Fiscal*

Studies, VIII, No. 1 (1987). The more critical climate since 1979 is reflected in John Redwood, *Public Enterprise in Crisis. The Future of the Nationalised Industries* (Oxford, 1980), and John Redwood and John Hatch, *Controlling Public Industries* (Oxford, 1983). More detached assessments include Peter Curwen's *Public Enterprise: A Modern Approach* (Brighton, 1986) and the specialised contributions of John Grieve Smith (ed.), *Strategic Planning in Nationalised Industries* (1984), and Tony Prosser, *Nationalised Industries and Public Control* (Oxford, 1986). Case studies include Leslie Hannah, *Engineers, Managers and Politicians. The First Fifteen Years of Nationalised Electricity Supply in Britain* (1982); William Ashworth, *The History of the British Coal Industry, vol. 5. 1946–82. The Nationalized Industry* (Oxford, 1986); and T. R. Gourvish, *British Railways 1948–73. A Business History* (Cambridge, 1986). For gas there is the more modest Trevor I. Williams, *History of the British Gas Industry* (Oxford, 1981), and on steel denationalisation in 1953, Kathleen Burk, *The First Privatization. The Politicians, The City, and the Denationalisation of Steel* (1988).

Privatisation has also attracted a substantial amount of recent literature. The best accounts are (for the build-up of policy) John Kay, Colin Mayer and David Thompson (eds), *Privatisation and Regulation – the UK Experience* (Oxford, 1986), and John Vickers and George Yarrow, *Privatization. An Economic Analysis* (Cambridge, Mass., 1988). Many general economic assessments of the post-1945 period contain useful insights into the role of the public sector generally and state industries in particular. See, for example, F. T. Blackaby (ed), *British Economic Policy 1960–74* (Cambridge, 1978); Sidney Pollard, *The Wasting of the British Economy* (1982); G. C. Peden, *British Economic and Social Policy. Lloyd George to Margaret Thatcher* (1985); and Jim Tomlinson, *British Macroeconomic Policy since 1940* (1985).

7. THE DEFENCE OF THE REALM: BRITAIN IN THE NUCLEAR AGE

The best introduction to this subject is John Baylis's edited *British Defence Policy in a Changing World* (1977), which contains a number of articles on both the historical and contemporary aspects of British defence policy. There is also a general survey by M. L. Dockrill, *British Defence since 1945* (Oxford, 1989). Philip Darby, *British Defence Policy East of Suez 1947–1968* (Oxford, 1973) is an excellent account of Britain's gradual abandonment of its imperial role while C. J. Bartlett's *The Long Retreat: a Short History of British Defence Policy 1945–1970* (1972) is a clear overview of a long process of retrenchment. Michael Chichester and John Wilkinson, *The Uncertain Ally* (1982) is a more recent work by two writers who believe that the history of British defence since 1945 has been one of continuous decline. The rising curve of Britain's defence spending, despite frequent efforts by Britain's politicians to slow the process down, is examined in Malcolm Chalmer's *Paying for Defence: Military Spending and British Decline* (1985).

Anglo-American defence relations, particularly in the nuclear field, have been discussed in a number of studies, the most recent of which are John Simpson, *The Independent Nuclear State: the United States, Britain and the Military Atom* (2nd edn, 1986) and John Baylis, *Anglo-American Defence Relations 1939–1980* (1980). The official history of the early years of Britain's nuclear deterrent, Margaret Gowing's *Independence and Deterrence: Britain and Atomic Energy 1945–1952* (2 vols, 1974) is essential reading since Professor Gowing had access to official documents which are still not open to researchers. Lawrence Freedman, *Britain and Nuclear Weapons* (1980), is a useful general account of the subject.

Speculative accounts about the future of Britain's defences – which, given the recent revolution in East–West relations, are likely to proliferate in the future – include John Baylis's *British Defence Policy: Striking the Right Balance* (1989), John Baylis (ed), *Alternative Approaches to British Defence Policy* (1983) and Dan Smith *The Defence of the Realm in the 1980s* (1980), a controversial and stimulating discussion of the unpleasant choices likely to be faced by British defence planners if defence expenditure is not to increase to unacceptable levels.

On specific issues, David Devereux's forthcoming monograph *British Defence Policy towards the Middle East 1948–1956* is an important contribution to our knowledge of an area which has hitherto received little scholarly attention while Britain's relations with Europe and NATO during the early 1950s are thoroughly examined in Saki Dockrill's *Britain's Policy for West European Rearmament 1950–1955* (Cambridge, 1990). The recent opening of the British archives for 1956 is resulting in an avalanche of works on the Suez crisis. The best introduction to this subject is David Carlton's *The Suez Crisis* (Oxford, 1989). The Suez crisis was followed by a major review of British defence policy in 1957 and this is dealt with in detail in Martin Navias's forthcoming *The British 'New Look': Nuclear Weapons and Strategic Planning 1955–1958* (Oxford, 1991). The Falklands War has also been the subject of a large number of monographs. The best introduction to this subject is Lawrence Freedman's *Britain and the Falklands War* (Oxford, 1983).

8. SOCIAL EQUITY AND INDUSTRIAL NEED, A DILEMMA OF ENGLISH EDUCATION

A valuable overall survey of part of the period is Roy Lowe, *Education in the Postwar Years, a Social History* (1988) which covers up to the 1960s. Michael Sanderson, *Educational Opportunity and Social Change in*

England 1900–1980s (1987) deals with widening access to different
levels of education in the post-war years and raises some of the issues
discussed here.

Deborah Thom, 'The 1944 Education Act, the art of the possible?'
in H. L. Smith (ed.), *War and Social Change, British Society in the Second
World War* (1986) takes the view that the Butler Act created little new
but merely refined the existing meritocratic system. Rene Saran, *Policy
Making in Secondary Education* (1973) is an absorbing account of a local
authority grappling with the implementation of the tripartite system
and neglecting the technical school strand. The technical schools have
been as neglected by writers as they were by administrators. Exceptions
are Reese Edwards, *The Secondary Technical School* (1960) and Thelma
Veness, *School Leavers* (1962). The latter is especially good on the
excellent ethos of the secondary technical schools.

The supersession of tripartism by the comprehensive school is re-
counted in David Rubinstein and Brian Simon, *The Evolution of the
Comprehensive School 1926–1972* (1973) and J. G. K. Fenwick, *The
Comprehensive School 1944–1970* (1976). To some extent this change in
policy was underlain by changing attitudes deriving from some of the
influential empirical sociological studies of the period. Major landmarks
were J. E. Floud, A. H. Halsey and F. Martin, *Social Class and
Educational Opportunity* (1956), J. W. B. Douglas, *The Home and the
School* (1964) and *All Our Future* (1968), A. H. Halsey, A. F. Heath and
J. M. Ridge, *Origins and Destinations* (1980). Some of these themes were
popularised in B. Jackson and D. Marsden, *Education and the Working
Class* (1962, 1966).

On higher education W. A. C. Stewart, *Higher Education in Postwar
Britain* (1989) is the only up-to-date survey of the whole field. The
Robbins Report *Higher Education* (Cmnd 2154, 1963), is indispensable.
Michael Sanderson, *The Universities and British Industry 1850–1970*
(1972) deals with causes of expansion in the 1960s and its relation to
industry. Harold Perkin, *New Universities in the United Kingdom* (1969)
is good and critical on the 'new' universities while Michael Beloff, *The
Plateglass Universities* (1968) is a first-hand journalistic account, aware
of their dilemmas. Sir Peter Venables, *Higher Education Developments,
the Technological Universities* (1978) deals with the other new universities coming from an earlier technical tradition.

The polytechnics are discussed in E. E. Robinson, *The New Polytech-
nics* (1968) an early account by an enthusiast. Greater unease about
their directions from the mid-1970s is expressed in J. Pratt and T.
Burgess, *Polytechnics, a Report* (1974), Lex Donaldson, *Policy and the
Polytechnics* (1975), J. Whitburn, M. Mealing and C. Cox, *People in
Polytechnics* (1976).

Insights into the attitudes of some of the key actors may be gained
from the memoirs of Lord Butler, *The Art of the Possible* (1971), Susan
Crosland's vivid biography of her husband *Tony Crosland* (1982) and

Maurice Kogan's conversations with Edward Boyle and Antony Crosland in *The Politics of Education* (1971). A perceptive overview, agreeing
at many points with this present analysis, is D. H. Aldcroft, 'Education
and Britain's Growth Failure 1950–1980' in G. Tortella and L. Sand-
berg, *Education and Economic Development*, Session A-5 of the X
International Economic History Congress (Valencia, 1990).

9. TOWARDS EQUAL OPPORTUNITIES? WOMEN IN BRITAIN SINCE 1945

Good analysis and commentary on this very recent period are only now
beginning to emerge and currently are few. The most useful works are
referred to in the 'Notes and References'. Penny Summerfield, *Women
Workers in the Second World War* (1984) provides useful background on
the immediately preceding period. Elizabeth Meehan, *Women's Rights
at Work* (1985) is an excellent study of the background to the Equal Pay
Act and provides comparison with the American experience. Her essay,
'British feminism from the 1960s to the 1980s', in H. L. Smith (ed.),
British Feminism in the Twentieth Century (Aldershot, 1990) is a stimulating overview. Other essays in this collection will also provide useful
background reading. April Carter, *The Politics of Women's Rights* (1988)
also provides a longer, and also very useful, overview of the period since
1945, though her introductory comments on the history of women before 1945 should be avoided. H. L. Smith's 'The Politics of Conservative
Reform: The Equal Pay for Equal Work Issue, 1945–1955', *Historical
Journal* (1991) appeared too late to be taken into account here.

10. IMMIGRATION

Much of the early work on the immigration of blacks and Asians from
the Indian subcontinent is associated with 'the Edinburgh school', a
subject which itself is worth an extended consideration. Important
items include K. Little, *Negroes in Britain, A Study of Racial Relations in
English Society* (1948, new edn, 1972) and M. Banton, *The Coloured
Quarter. Negro Immigrants in an English City* (1955). S. Collins,
*Coloured Minorities in Britain. Studies in British Race Relations based on
African, West Indian and Asiatic Immigrants* (1957) is also useful.
Another important early study with a different provenance is R. Glass,
Newcomers. West Indians in London (1960).
  A massive increase in literature occurred in the course of the 1960s.
C. Peach, *West Indian Migration to Britain: A Social Geography* (1968) is
valuable for an understanding of the migration process. Two well-
known publications of this period are J. Rex and R. Moore, *Race,
Community and Conflict. A Study of Sparkbrook* (1967) and E. J. B. Rose
(ed.), *Colour and Citizenship. A Report on British Race Relations* (1969).
  The 1970s and 1980s have seen no diminution of interest in blacks

and Asians. Legislative developments are usefully summarised in V. Bevan, *The Development of British Immigration Law* (1987). Two specific comparative studies, rare commodities indeed, can be found in I. Katznelson, *Black Men: White Cities: Race, Politics and Migration in the United States 1900–1930 and Britain 1948–68* (1973) and G. P. Freeman, *Immigrant Labor and Racial Conflict in Industrial Societies. The French and British Experience 1945–1975* (Princeton, 1979). Other studies concentrate exclusively on locations or groups in Britain. D. Lawrence, *Black Migrants, White Natives. A Study of Race Relations in Nottingham* (1974) is a good, yet neglected work. J. Rex and S. Tomlinson, *Colonial Immigrants in a British City: A Class Analysis* (1979), is a well-known analysis of Handsworth, Birmingham. M. Anwar, *The Myth of Return. Pakistanis in Britain* (1979) is an important contribution to our understanding of this Asian group. Useful works of a later vintage include Z. Layton-Henry and P. B. Rich (eds), *Race, Government and Politics in Britain* (1986) and P. Gilroy, *'There ain't no black in the union jack': the Cultural Politics of Race and Nation* (1987). P. Fryer, *Staying Power. The History of Black People in Britain* (1984), is a major study, acutely aware of the historical dimension to post-war developments.

European groups have been less well researched. The Poles are discussed in J. Zubrzycki, *Polish Immigrants in Britain. A Study of Adjustment* (The Hague, 1956) and, more recently, in K. Sword with N. Davies and J. Ciechanowski, *The Foundation of the Polish Community in Great Britain 1939–1950* (1989). The fullest account of the EVWs remains J. A. Tannahill, *The European Volunteer Workers in Britain* (Manchester, 1958). The neglected Italians are touched upon briefly by R. Palmer, 'The Italians: Patterns of Migration to London', in J. L. Watson (ed.), *Between Two Cultures* (Oxford, 1977). Even the Irish have attracted little attention. The fullest general surveys are J. A. Jackson, *The Irish in Britain* (1963) and the more popular study K. O'Connor, *The Irish in Britain* (Dublin, 1974). There are some sharp insights into alien immigration in P. Foot, *Immigration and Race in British Politics* (1965). The concluding sections of C. Holmes, *John Bull's Island. Immigration and British Society 1871–1971* (1988), survey the whole field of post-war immigration.

Groups from beyond Europe, other than blacks, and Asians from the Indian subcontinent, have received little attention. Ng Kwee Choo, *The Chinese in London* (1968), is a preliminary study of the Chinese in the capital. J. L. Watson, 'The Chinese', in his *Between Two Cultures* (Oxford, 1977), also draws on the community in London. P. R. Jones, *Vietnamese Refugees. A Study of their Reception and Settlement in the United Kingdom* (1982), considers a particularly neglected Asian group. Mediterranean groups are likewise ignored. However, on the Maltese there is G. Dench, *The Maltese in London: A Case Study of the Erosion of Ethnic Consciousness* (1975). The fullest studies of the Cypriot minority remain unpublished.

The history of post-war immigration into Britain benefits from being viewed as part of a widespread European development. Books which take a broad European perspective include S. Castles and G. Kosack, *Immigrant Workers and Class Structure in Western Europe* (1973, new edn, 1985) and S. Castles *et al.*, *Here for Good. Western Europe's New Ethnic Minorities* (1984). The history of refugees in Britain finds its wider context in M. R. Marrus, *The Unwanted. European Refugees in the Twentieth Century* (Oxford, 1985).

11. THE CONSERVATIVE PARTY SINCE 1945.

There are no detailed studies of the Conservative Party in the post-war period. The best short commentary is John Ramsden, 'Conservatives since 1945', *Contemporary Record* 2 (spring 1988). This is reprinted in extended form as 'The Conservative Party since 1945' in Anthony Seldon (ed.), *U.K. Political Parties since 1945* (1989). Robert Blake, *The Conservative Party from Peel to Thatcher* (1985), is useful but general. See, also John Ramsden, *The Making of Conservative Policy: The Conservative Research Department since 1929* (1980); T. F. Lindsay and M. Harrington, *The Conservative Party 1918–79* (2nd edn 1979); Zig Layton Henry (ed.), *Conservative Party Politics* (1980); and Andrew Gamble, *The Conservative Nation* (1974). Most areas of the Conservative Party after 1945 are in need of detailed examination, especially its organisation at central and local level, recruitment and the social class of the membership. Some valuable, more exhaustive studies, however, have appeared. For the years 1945–51 see J. D. Hoffman, *The Conservative Party in Opposition 1945–51* (1964) and note, also, John Ramsden, 'A Party of Owners or a Party for Earners? How far did the British Conservative Party Really Change after 1945?', *Transactions of the Royal Historical Society*, 37 (1987). Conservative ideology can be approached through Noel O'Sullivan, *Conservatism* (1976), Ian Gilmour, *Inside Right* (1977), Philip Norton and Arthur Aughey, *Conservatives and Conservatism* (1981), Robert Nisbet, *Conservatism* (1986), Frank O'Gorman, *British Conservatism* (1986), and Martin Durham, 'The Right; The Conservative Party and Conservatism', in Leonard Tivey and Anthony Wright (eds), *Party Ideology in Britain* (1989). The Conservative Party in the 1950s and 1960s has not been covered well, but Nigel Harris, *Competition and the Corporate Society* (1972), and Andrew Gamble, cited above, contain good material. A number of sound texts on the party in the 1970s and 80s can be found in the Notes for this chapter.

12. LABOUR AS A GOVERNING PARTY: BALANCING RIGHT AND LEFT

Among the enormous literature on this topic are some works of quality. The most thoughtful introduction to Labour's approach to governing is

David Howell, *British Social Democracy* (1980). More recent events are covered well in David Kogan and Maurice Kogan, *The Battle for the Labour Party* (1983 edn), Philip Williams, 'The Labour Party: the rise of the left' in Hugh Berrington (ed.), *Change in British Politics* (1984), and Patrick Seyd, *The Rise and Fall of the Labour Left* (1987), and disappointingly in Colin Hughes and Patrick Wintour, *Labour Rebuilt: the new model party* (1990). This last book compares unfavourably as instant history with *The British General Election* series, sponsored by Nuffield College, Oxford, written since 1951 by David Butler and various collaborators, and published by Macmillan. Neither Lewis Minkin, *The Labour Party Conference* (1978) nor Eric Shaw, *Discipline and Discord in the Labour Party* (Manchester 1988) is light reading; but both are authoritative and deserve to become classics. Britain's two leading political historians have both produced major studies of the Attlee government: Kenneth O. Morgan, *Labour in Power 1945–51* (Oxford, 1984), and Henry Pelling, *The Labour Governments, 1945–51* (1984).

13. BRITAIN AND THE TWO IRELANDS SINCE 1945

If the hostilities in Northern Ireland have been unpleasant for the province's peoples, they have ensured that virtually every aspect of life there has been placed under a microscope. Although much of the literature has a political coloration, there are many commendable studies also. Good overviews are David W. Miller, *Queen's Rebels* (1978) and A. T. Q. Stewart, *The Narrow Ground* (1977). Likewise, Patrick Buckland, *A History of Northern Ireland* (1981) and David Harkness, *Northern Ireland since 1920* (1983) are valuable. Other important accounts include Richard Rose, *Governing Without Consensus* (1971) and *Northern Ireland: A Time of Choice* (1976), Ian Budge and Cornelius O'Leary, *Belfast: Approach to Crisis* (1973), John Darby, *Intimidation and the Control of Conflict in Northern Ireland* (1986) and his (ed.), *Northern Ireland: The Background to the Conflict* (1983). Ed Cairns, *Caught in Crossfire* (1987), Michael MacDonald, *Children of Wrath* (1986), Gerald Hogan and Clive Walker, *Political Violence and the Law* (1986), Tom Wilson, *Ulster: Conflict and Consent* (1989), Richard Jenkins (ed.), *Northern Ireland, Studies in Economic and Social Life* (1989), Charles Townshend (ed.), *Consensus in Ireland* (1988), Yonah Alexander and Alan O'Day (eds), *Ireland's Terrorist Trauma* (1989), *The Irish Terrorism Experience* (1991) along with Gerald McElroy, *The Catholic Church and the Northern Ireland Crisis 1968–86* (1991) add various insights. Not to be missed though is Paul Arthur and Keith Jeffery, *Northern Ireland since 1968* (1988). Rosemary Harris, *Prejudice and Tolerance in Ulster* (1972) is a classic study while Steve Bruce, *God Save Ireland* (1986) and Clifford Smyth, *Ian Paisley* (1987) consider the key Protestant figure. Writings on the Left include Geoffrey Bell, *The Protestants of Ulster* (1977), Michael Farrell, *Northern Ireland, The Orange State* (2nd edn, 1980), Liz Curtis, *Ireland and the Propaganda War* (1984) and Bob Rowthorn and Naomi Wayne, *Northern Ireland, The Political Economy of Conflict* (1988), although pride of place goes to the voluminous studies by Paul Bew and Henry Patterson, the most recent being Patterson's *The Politics of Illusion* (1989) and their combined study, *The State in Northern Ireland* (1979). This list is not exhaustive.

Less troubled and the subject of a smaller literature is the Republic of Ireland. General accounts of developments there can be found in Ronan Fanning, *Independent Ireland* (1983) and J. J. Lee, *Ireland 1912–1985* (1989), a long book which should be approached with caution. Other useful volumes include Neil Collins and Frank McCann, *Irish Politics Today* (1989), John Bowman, *De Valera and the Ulster Question* (1982), Paul Bew and Henry Patterson, *Sean Lemass* (1982) and their joint effort with Ellen Hazelkorn, *The Dynamics of Irish Politics* (1989). Surprisingly, there is no authoritative analysis of the Republic's policy towards post-war Northern Ireland, a notable omission in view of the accusations made against it in the years since 1968.

British policies towards Northern Ireland and the Republic have not been examined in detail. The essay by David Carlton in *Contemporary Terror* (1981) edited by him and Carlo Schaerf remains compulsive reading. The various writings of Paul Wilkinson, especially *Terrorism and the Liberal State* (1986 edn) and his contribution to *The Threat of Terrorism* (1988), edited by Juliet Lodge, form significant reading. References to the problem in diaries and accounts by Richard Crossman, Tony Benn, Harold Wilson, James Callagham and others provide interesting opinions, though often revealing the unimportance in which all parts of Ireland were held by contemporary leaders. Clearly, the topic merits further inquiry.

Finally, aside from newspapers and journals, the *Annual Register* is a good source while Terence O'Neill, *Ulster at the Crossroads* (1969) and his *Autobiography* (1972) along with Brian Faulkner, *Memoirs of a Statesman* (1978) must remain indispensable.

14. YOUTH CULTURE AND THE EMERGENCE OF POPULAR MUSIC

The fullest account of post-war British cultural history is to be found in two elegantly written volumes by Robert Hewison, *In Anger: Culture in the Cold War 1945–60* (1981) and *Too Much: Art and Society in the Sixties 1960–75* (1986). However, these books tend to say more about drama and literature than popular music. For the history of the early days of rock'n'roll, it is worth reading Charlie Gillett, *The Sound of the City: The Rise of Rock and Roll* (1983). Although the focus is primarily on the USA, this is the best historical account of rock music. Two books on the 1960s which were written then and contain a flavour of the time are Nik Cohn's *AWopBopaLooBop AlopBamBoom* (1969) and George Melly's *Revolt into Style: The Pop Arts in Britain* (1970). Other books are rather more dispassionate. Iain Chambers, *Urban Rhythms: pop music and popular culture* (1985) provides a sophisticated, well-informed account of the changing styles of post-war popular culture. Bernice Martin adds a sociological perspective to a similar story in her *A Sociology of Contemporary Cultural Change* (Oxford, 1981). Simon Jones, in his *Black Culture, White Youth* (1988), focuses on the important area of black music in Britain. For a discussion of the political economy of popular music and its potential significance, Simon Frith's *Sound Effects* (1983) is the best book on the subject. His collection of essays, *Music for Pleasure* (Oxford, 1988), contains analysis both of the history of popular music and of its current state. For a detailed account of the background to, and importance of, punk, there is Dave Laing's *One Chord Wonders* (Milton Keynes, 1985). Dick Hebdige's *Subculture: The Meaning of Style* (1979) and his later book *Hiding in the Light* (1988) also discuss punk, setting it in its cultural and historical context. Some pop biographies contain useful historical insights, in particular two volumes by Philip Norman, *Shout: The True Story of the Beatles* (1981) and *The Stones* (1984). Relatively little has been written about Live Aid and after. There is Bob Geldof's autobiography *Is that it?* (1986) and Robin Denselow's *When the music's over* (1989).

Notes and References

2. THE ECONOMIC RECORD SINCE 1945 *M. W. Kirby*

1. Sir Henry Phelps Brown, 'What is the British Predicament?', *Three Banks Review*, 145 (July 1982) 249.

2. Christopher Allsopp, 'The Management of the World Economy', in Wilfred Beckerman (ed.), *Slow Growth in Britain: Causes and Consequences* (Oxford, 1979) p. 147.

3. R. C. O. Matthews, 'Why has Britain had Full Employment since the War?' *Economic Journal*, LCCVIII, 3 (September 1968) 555–69.

4. Robert Bacon and Walter Eltis, *Britain's Economic Problem: Too Few Producers* (2nd edn, 1978); Frank Blackaby (ed.), *De-Industrialisation* (1978); Keith Smith, *The British Economic Crisis: Its Past and Future* (1989); B. W. E. Alford, *British Economic Performance 1945–1975* (1988).

5. C. J. F. Brown and T. D. Sheriff, 'De-industrialisation: a background paper', in Blackaby, *De-industrialisation*, p. 236.

6. Colin Clark, *The Conditions of Economic Progress* (1940); Daniel Bell, *The Coming of the Post-Industrial Society* (1974).

7. Robert Bacon and Walter Eltis, 'The Non-Market Sector and the Balance of Payments', *National Westminster Bank Quarterly Review* (1978) 65–9.

8. J. R. Sargent, 'UK Performance in Services', in Blackaby, *De-Industrialisation*, p. 508; Ajit Singh, 'UK Industry and the World Economy: A Case of De-industrialisation?', *Cambridge Journal of Economics*, I, 2 (1977) 121–2.

9. Alford, *British Economic Performance*, p. 57.

10. Bacon and Eltis, *Britain's Economic Problem*.

11. Central Policy Review Staff, *The Future of the British Car Industry* (1975); C. F. Pratten and A. C. Atkinson, 'The Use of Manpower in British Manufacturing Industry', *Department of Employment Gazette* (June, 1976); D. K. Stout, 'De-industrialisation and Industrial Policy', in Blackaby, *De-industrialisation*, pp. 171–96.

12. Stanislaw Gomulka, 'Britain's Slow Industrial Growth – Increasing Inefficiency Versus Low Rate of Technical Change', in Beckerman (ed.), *Slow Growth*, pp. 179–80.

13. A. R. Thatcher, 'Labour Supply and Employment Trends', in Blackaby, *De-Industrialisation*, p. 31.

14. HM Treasury, *Evidence on the Financing of Trade and Industry to the Committee to Review the Functioning of Financial Institutions*, vol. I (1977).

15. D. Savage, 'The Channels of Monetary Influence: A Survey of the Empirical Evidence', *National Institute Economic Review* (February 1978) 73–89.

16. B. Moore and J. Rhodes, 'The Relative Decline of the UK Manufacturing Sector', *Economic Policy Review*, no. 2 (Cambridge, 1976) 40.

17. M. A. King, 'The United Kingdom Profits Crisis: Myth or Reality?', *Economic Journal*, LXXXV, 2 (1975) 33–54.

18. D. K. Stout, 'De-industrialisation and Industrial Policy', in Blackaby, *De-industrialisation*, p. 174.

19. For a good discussion of the impact of North Sea oil on the economy see J. C. Whiteman, 'North Sea Oil', in Derek Morris (ed.), *The Economic System in the UK* (3rd edn, Oxford, 1985) pp. 829–50.

20. Singh, 'UK Industry', p. 128.

21. Ibid., p. 129.

22. H. S. Houthakker and S. P. Magee, 'Income and Price Elasticities in World Trade', *Review of Economics and Statistics*, LX (1978) 275–86.

23. C. F. Freeman, 'Technical Innovation and British Trade Performance', in Blackaby, *De-industrialisation*, pp. 65–72. David C. Mowery, 'Industrial Research 1900–1950', in Bernard Elbaum and William Lazonick (eds), *The Decline of the British Economy* (Oxford, 1986) pp. 189–222.

24. P. D. Henderson, 'Two British Errors: Their Probable Size and Some Possible Lessons', *Oxford Economic Papers*, XXIX (1977) 186–94; D. Burn, *Nuclear Power and the Energy Crisis: Politics and the Atomic Industry*, Trade Policy Research Centre (1978).

25. S. B. Saul, 'Research and Development in British Industry from the End of the Nineteenth Century to the 1960s', in T. C. Smout (ed.), *The Search for Wealth and Stability: Essays in Economic and Social History Presented to M. W. Flinn* (1979) pp. 114–38.

26. Merton J. Peck, 'Science and Technology', in Richard E. Caves and associates, *Britain's Economic Prospects* (1968) pp. 448–84; Freeman, 'Technical Innovation', pp. 65–72.

27. Sidney Pollard, *The Wasting of the British Economy: British Economic Policy 1945 to the Present* (1982).

28. Ibid., p. 16.

29. For further commentary on 'stop-go' see Samuel Brittan, *Steering the Economy. The Role of the Treasury* (Harmondsworth, 1971) pp. 448–56; Richard A. and Peggy B. Musgrave, 'Fiscal Policy', in Caves and associates, *Britain's Economic Prospects*, pp. 42–3; Sidney Pollard, *The Development of the British Economy 1914–1980* (3rd edn, 1983) pp. 408–30;

A. Whiting, 'An International Comparison of the Instability of Economic Growth', *Three Banks Review*, LCVI (1976) 26–46.

30. Pollard, *Wasting of the British Economy*, pp. 71–98.

31. Frank Blackaby (ed.), *British Economic Policy 1960–74; Demand Management* (Cambridge, 1979) p. 421.

32. Scott Newton and Dilwyn Porter, *Modernization Frustrated: The Politics of Industrial Decline in Britain since 1900* (1988).

33. M. W. Kirby, 'Supply Side Management', in N. F. R. Crafts, B. F. Duckham and N. W. C. Woodward (eds), *The British Economy Since 1945* (Oxford, 1991) pp. 236–60.

34. Andrew Kilpatrick and Tony Lawson, 'On the Nature of Industrial Decline in the UK', *Cambridge Journal of Economics*, IV, I (1980) 87.

35. Bernard Elbaum and William Lazonick, 'An Institutional Perspective on British Decline', in Elbaum and Lazonick, *Decline of the British Economy*, p. 4.

36. Martin Weiner, *English Culture and the Decline of the Industrial Spirit* (Cambridge, 1981).

37. James Raven, 'British History and the Enterprise Culture', *Past and Present*, 123 (May 1989) 178–204.

38. D. C. Coleman, 'Failings and Achievements: Some British Businesses 1910–80', in R. P. T. Davenport-Hines and Geoffrey Jones (eds), *Enterprise, Management and Innovation in British Business, 1914–1980* (1988) pp. 1–17; T. R. Gourvish, 'British Business and the Transition to a Corporate Economy: Entrepreneurship and Management Structures', in ibid., pp. 18–45.

39. W. B. Walker, 'Britain's Industrial Performance 1850–1950: A Failure to Adjust', in K. Pavitt (ed.), *Technical Innovation and British Economic Performance* (1980) pp. 19–37.

40. Mancur Olson, *The Rise and Decline of Nations: Economic Growth, Stagflation and Social Rigidities* (New Haven, Ct. and London, 1982).

41. M. W. Kirby, 'Industrial Policy', in Paul Hare and Maurice Kirby (eds), *An Introduction to British Economic Policy* (Brighton, 1984) pp. 93–109.

42. Charles Carter (ed.), *Industrial Policy and Innovation* (1981).

43. Francis Cripps and Wynne Godley, 'Control of Imports as a Means to Full Employment and the Expansion of World Trade', *Cambridge Journal of Economics*, II, 3 (1978) 327–34; Wynne Godley, 'Britain's Chronic Recession: Can Anything be Done?' in Beckerman (ed.), *Slow Growth*, pp. 226–33.

44. David F. Lomax, 'Supply-side Economics: The British Experience', *National Westminster Bank Quarterly Review* (August 1982) 2–15; A. A. Walters, *Britain's Economic Renaissance: Margaret Thatcher's Reforms, 1979–1984* (New York, 1986).

45. Milton Friedman, *Money and Economic Development* (1973); F. A. Hayek, *The Road to Serfdom* (1976).

46. Kirby, 'Industrial Policy', p. 104.

47. Clare Group, 'Problems of Industrial Recovery', *Midland Bank Review* (spring 1982) 9–16.

48. Ken Coutts and Wynne Godley, 'The British Economy under Mrs Thatcher', *The Political Quarterly*, LX, 2 (April–June 1989) 137–51.

49. Geoffrey Maynard, 'Britain's Economic Revival and the Balance of Payments', *The Political Quarterly*, LX, 2 (April–June 1989) 152–63; Samuel Brittan, *The Thatcher Government's Economic Policy* (Esmé Fairbairn Lecture, University of Lancaster, 1989).

50. Maynard, 'Britain's Economic Revival', pp. 159–60.

51. A. P. Thirlwall, 'Deindustrialisation in the United Kingdom', *Lloyds Bank Review*, 144 (April 1982) 31.

52. *Report from the Select Committee on Overseas Trade: House of Lords: Session 1984/85* (1985).

3. ENTERPRISE AND THE WELFARE STATE   *Jose Harris*

An earlier version of this chapter was published in the *Transactions of the Royal Historical Society*, 5th Series, 40 (1990). I wish to thank the Society for allowing republication of this article.

1. On the evolution of such dichotomies, see Istvan Hont and Michael Ignatieff (eds), *Wealth and Virtue. The Shaping of Political Economy in the Scottish Enlightenment* (Cambridge, 1983) ch. 1; Gertrude Himmelfarb, *The Idea of Poverty: England in the Early Industrial Age* (1984) chs 1 and 2; E. P. Thompson, 'The Moral Economy of the English Crowd in the Eighteenth Century', *Past and Present*, 50 (February 1971) 76–136; A. W. Coats, 'Contrary Moralities: Plebs, Paternalists and Political Economists', *Past and Present*, 54 (February 1972) 130–3.

2. M. A. Crowther, *The Workhouse System, 1834–1929. The history of an English Social Institution* (1981) esp. ch. 9; David Thomson. 'Welfare and the Historians', in Lloyd Bonfield, Richard M. Smith and Keith Wrightson, *The World We Have Gained. Histories of Population and Social Structure* (Oxford, 1986) p. 355–78.

3. Michael Freeden, *The New Liberalism. An Ideology of Social Reform* (Oxford, 1978); Geoffrey Searle, *The Quest for National Efficiency. A Study in British Politics and British Political Thought 1899–1914* (Oxford, 1971) esp. pp. 171–204.

4. M. Ginsberg (ed.), *Law and Opinion in England in the Twentieth Century* (1959); S. Finer, *The Life and Times of Sir Edwin Chadwick* (1952); Royston Lambert, *Sir John Simon 1818–1904 and English Social Administration* (1963).

5. Gareth Stedman Jones, *Outcast London. A Study in Relations between the Classes* (Oxford, 1971); J. R. Hay, 'Employers' Attitudes to Social Policy and the Concept of Social Control, 1900–1920', in P. M.

Thane (ed.), *The Origins of British Social Policy* (1978) pp. 107–25; Roger Davidson, *Whitehall and the Labour Problem in late-Victorian and Edwardian Britain* (1985).

6. Arthur Seldon, *Taxation and Welfare. A Report on Private Opinion and Public Policy* (1969); Hermione Parker, *The Moral Hazard of Social Benefits. A Study of the Impact of Social Benefits and Income Tax on Incentives to Work* (1982).

7. Correlli Barnett, *The Audit of War. The Illusion and Reality of Britain as a Great Nation* (1986).

8. BBC, Radio Four, 'Any Questions' programme, March 1987.

9. Barnett, *Audit of War*, p. 304.

10. Ibid.

11. Ibid., pp. 278–91.

12. Ibid., pp. 13–19, 36–7, 279–304.

13. Ibid., pp. 12–15, 213–33.

14. Ibid., pp. 62, 93, 145–51.

15. OECD Social Policy Studies, *Social Expenditure 1960–1990. Problems of Growth and Control* (Paris, 1985); Gaston Rimlinger, *Welfare Policy and Industrialization in Europe, America and Russia* (New York, 1971); P. R. Kaim-Caudle, *Comparative Social Policy and Social Security. A Ten Country Study* (1973); B. R. Mitchell, *European Historical Statistics 1750–1975* (2nd revd edn, 1981); Peter Flora *et al.*, *State, Economy and Society in Western Europe, 1815–1975.* vol. 1, *The Growth of Mass Democracies and Welfare States*; vol. II, *The Growth of Industrial Societies and Capitalist Economies* (Frankfurt and London, 1983 and 1987); Peter Flora (ed.), *Growth to Limits. The Western European Welfare States since World War Two*, vols I, II and IV (New York and Berlin, 1987–8).

16. Flora, *State, Economy and Society*, vol. I, p. 456; Edward James and Andre Laurent, 'Social Security: the European Experiment', *Social Trends*, 5 (1974) 26–34.

17. Brian Abel-Smith, *An International Study of Health Expenditure*, WHO Public Paper No. 32 (Geneva, 1967); *Report of the Committee of Enquiry into the Cost of the National Health Service* (Cmnd. 9663, 1956) pp. 286–9.

18. Flora, *State, Economy and Society*, vol. I, pp. 456–7; Brian Abel-Smith and Alan Maynard, *The Organization, Financing and Cost of Health Care in the European Community* (Commission of the European Communities, Social Policy Series, No. 36, Brussels, 1978) esp. pp. 108–12.

19. Jurgen Kohl, 'Trends and Problems in Postwar Public Expenditure Development in Western Europe and North America', in Peter Flora and Arnold J. Heidenheimer (eds), *The Development of Welfare States in Europe and America* (New Brunswick and London, 1981) pp. 307–44, esp. Table 9.4 on p. 317.

20. Statistical Office of the European Communities (Eurostat), *Social*

Indicators for the European Community 1960–1975 (Brussels, 1977) Table V/1, pp. 184–5, and Table V/4, pp. 190–1.

21. OECD, *Social Expenditure 1960–1990*, p. 21. See also Jurgen Kohl, 'Trends and Problems', p. 319.

22. Harold L. Wilensky, 'Democratic Corporatism, Consensus, and Social Policy', in *The Welfare State in Crisis. An account of the Conference on Social Policies in the 1980s*, 20–23 October 1980, pp. 191–2 (Paris, 1981).

23. Flora, *State, Economy and Society*, vol. I, pp. 459, 462–551; Edward James and Andre Laurent, 'Social Security', pp. 27–8.

24. Flora, *State, Economy and Society*, pp. 462–3, 476–7, 483–4, 490–1, 504–5, 518–19, 525–6, 532–3, 539–40, 546–7. One major cause of the growth of Britain's public assistance sector was that its social insurance benefits were so much lower than in most other Western European countries; hence the phenomenon of 'supplementary benefit'.

25. The story of the gradual dismantling and transformation of the Poor Law remains to be told. For analysis of some of the later stages of that process, see Alan Deacon, 'An End to the Means Test? Social Security and the Attlee Government', *Journal of Social Policy*, 11, Part 3 (July 1982) 289–306, and Phoebe Hall, Hilary Land, Roy Parker and Adrian Webb, *Change, Choice and Conflict in Social Policy* (1975) pp. 410–71.

26. Edward James and Andre Laurent, 'Social Security', pp. 31–2.

27. Apart from Britain, only Denmark had a tax-financed health service with 100 per cent coverage (Abel-Smith and Maynard, *Health Care in the European Community*, pp. 9–102, and Table 4, p. 116).

28. The Guillebaud committee in 1956, for example, found that most NHS patients firmly believed that they had paid for their treatment through contributory national insurance.

29. Barnett, *Audit of War*, pp. 26–31, 45–9.

30. Ibid., pp. 26–31, 45–7.

31. Correlli Barnett, 'Decline and Fall of Beveridge's New Jerusalem', *Daily Telegraph*, 1 December 1986.

32. Barnett, *Audit of War*, pp. 19, 25.

33. Ibid., pp. 30–2.

34. Ibid., pp. 276–91.

35. Harriet Martineau, Joseph Chamberlain, Charles Booth and Helen Bosanquet spring to mind as prominent examples. The phrase 'state sternness' comes from a famous letter written by Joseph Chamberlain to Beatrice Webb, in which he stressed the need to legitimise the state's 'power of being very strict with the loafer and the confirmed pauper', quoted in Peter Fraser, *Joseph Chamberlain: Radicalism and Empire* (1966) p. 125.

36. Jose Harris, *William Beveridge. A Biography* (Oxford, 1977) pp. 271–2. Barnett, *Audit of War*, pp. 228–30. On Beveridge's early admiration for Bismarckian welfare institutions, an admiration that

inspired his whole subsequent career as a social reformer, see the series of articles on 'Social Reform: How Germany deals with it', *Morning Post*, September 1907.

37. Harris, *Beveridge*, pp. 100–57.

38. Ibid., pp. 99–100, 171–6, 323, 353, 355–6.

39. Beveridge Papers, VIII, 45, Advisory Panel on Home Affairs, minutes, 9 July 1942.

40. Harris, *Beveridge*, p. 396–9; John McNicol, *The Movement for Family Allowances 1918–45. A Study in Social Policy Development* (1980) pp. 185–7.

41. Beveridge Papers, IXa, 37(2), 'Social Insurance – General Considerations', by W. H. Beveridge, July 1941; PRO, CAB 87/76, 'Basic Problems of Social Security with Heads of a Scheme', by W. H. Beveridge, 11 December 1941, and PRO, CAB 87/76, 'Finance of Social Insurance. Some Statistical Short Cuts', by W. H. Beveridge, 19 December 1941.

42. Harris, *Beveridge*, pp. 407–12. Beveridge agreed with the Treasury to keep the proposed public costs of his scheme to within £100 million p.a. during the first five years of its operation. The total sum expended by public authorities on all social services (not just social insurance) in 1938 was £596.3 million.

43. Beveridge Papers VIII, files 28 and 37. The whole question of the benefit levels envisaged in the Beveridge Report has recently been analysed in detail by Professor John Veit-Wilson, who concludes that, beneath Beveridge's somewhat ambiguous utterances on this issue, there was no intention on Beveridge's part to accept the more broadly-based and relativistic definition of need currently being propounded by Seebohm Rowntree (John Veit-Wilson, 'Genesis of Confusion: the Beveridge Committee's Poverty Line for Social Security', paper for the seminar at the Suntory Toyota International Centre for Economics and Related Disciplines, London School of Economics, 1 November 1989). I am grateful to Professor Veit-Wilson for letting me see his paper.

44. *Social Insurance and Allied Services*, Cmd. 6404 (1942) pp. 92–5.

45. Ibid., para. 292.

46. PRO, CAB 87/78, Social Insurance Committee minutes, 17 June 1942, QQ. 4720, 4726; Barnett, *Audit of War*, p. 30.

47. *Social Insurance and Allied Services*, p. 11.

48. W. H. Beveridge, *Unemployment: a Problem of Industry* (1930 edn) pp. 288–94.

49. *Social Insurance and Allied Services*, paras 369, 440; *W. H. Beveridge, Full Employment in a Free Society* (1944) p. 173.

50. Hubert Henderson Papers, memorandum on 'The Beveridge Proposals', by J. M. Keynes, 20 July 1942; Norman Chester Papers, 'Finance of the Proposals in the Beveridge Report', by D. N. Chester, 18 November 1942.

51. Cherwell Papers, H256, memorandum by an unnamed economist to Lord Cherwell, 22 January 1943. I am most grateful to Dr Derek Fraser, who has been working for some years on the making and impact of the Beveridge Report, for drawing my attention to this paper.

52. Brian Abel-Smith, 'Public Expenditure on the Social Services', *Social Trends*, 1 (1970) p. 19; Edward James and Andre Laurent, 'Social Security', pp. 26–34; Jurgen Kohl, 'Trends and Problems', pp. 307–44.

53. T. H. Marshall, *Sociology at the Crossroads and other Essays* (1953) pp. 267–308.

54. Harold L. Wilensky, 'Leftism, Catholicism and Democratic Corporatism: the Role of Political Parties in Recent Welfare State Development', in Flora and Heidenheimer (eds), *Development of Welfare States*, pp. 345–82, and esp. 356–62.

55. Barnett, *Audit of War*, pp. 13–18, 25, 243, 250.

56. Ibid., pp. 14–15.

57. Dalton, an atheist, had 'abandoned Christianity on the playing fields of Eton', Ben Pimlott, *Hugh Dalton* (1985) p. 35.

58. Barnett, *Audit of War*, pp. 15, 253.

59. Conservative Party archives, CRD 600/02, Geoffrey Faber to Walter Oakeshott, 27 August 1942; and CRD 600/05, 'The Ultimate Religious Field and the State', n.d.; CRD 058, 'Planning for Freedom: Some Remarks on the Necessity for Creating a Body which could Co-ordinate Theory and Practice in our Future Policy', by Karl Mannheim. On the curious vogue for Mannheim's ideas among certain sections of the Conservative intelligentsia in this period, see Colin Loader, *The Intellectual Development of Karl Mannheim, Culture, Politics and Planning* (Cambridge, 1985) pp. 149–77.

60. CRD, 600/05, press cuttings, 1942.

61. Flora and Heidenheimer (eds), *Development of Welfare States*, p. 19.

62. This point applies to the financing of social security rather than to its organisation. One respect in which the British system is indubitably 'Beveridgean' (or at least stems from the tradition of administrative reform of which Beveridge was an exemplar) is that it is nationally uniform, centralised and bureaucratic, whereas most continental systems allow much more scope for pluralism, localism and democratic self-government. An observer writing a century ago would surely have predicted the exact opposite. The role played by social policy in bringing about this kind of transformation of political culture in Britain and elsewhere deserves further analysis.

63. See e.g. Harold L. Smith (ed.), *War and Social Change. British Society in the Second World War* (Manchester, 1986); H. Kopsch, 'The Approach of the Conservative Party to Social Policy during World War Two', London Ph.D. thesis, 1970; Kevin Jeffreys, 'British Politics and Social Policy during the Second World War', *Historical Journal*, 30, 1 (1987) 123–44.

4. TRADE UNIONS, THE GOVERNMENT AND THE ECONOMY   *Chris Wrigley*

1. Lord Birkenhead, *Walter Monkton* (1969) p. 276.
2. *This is the Road: The Conservative and Unionist Party's Policy* (1950).
3. H. A. Clegg and R. Adams, *The Employers' Challenge* (Oxford, 1957) especially pp. 45–82.
4. D. Metcalf and R. Richardson, 'Labour', in M. J. Artis (ed.), *Prest and Coppock's The UK Economy: A Manual of Applied Economics* (11th edn, 1986) p. 272.
5. It can be expressed numerically:

| Unemployment rate | 1.0 | 2.0 | 3.0 | 4.0 | 5.0 |
| Percentage change in wage rates | 8.7 | 2.8 | 1.2 | 0.5 | 0.1 |

A. W. Phillips, 'The Relation between Unemployment and the Rate of Change of Money Wage Rates in the United Kingdom, 1861–1957, *Economica* (1958) 283–99.
6. R. J. Davies, 'Incomes and Anti-Inflation Policy' in G. S. Bain (ed.), *Industrial Relations in Britain* (Oxford, 1963) pp. 419–55; M. C. Kennedy, 'The Economy as a Whole' in Artis (ed.), *The UK Economy* (12th edn, 1989) pp. 1–65; J. L. Fallick and R. E. Elliott (eds), *Incomes Policies, Inflation and Relative Pay* (1981).
7. Historical accounts of incomes policies include K. Hawkins, *British Industrial Relations 1945–1975* (1976); L. Panitch, *Social Democracy and Industrial Militancy* (Cambridge, 1976); G. A. Dorfman, *Government versus Trade Unionism in British Politics since 1968* (Stanford, 1979); B. Towers, *British Incomes Policies* (1981); W. H. Fishbein, *Wage Restraint By Consensus* (1984); and R. J. Flanagan, D. W. Soskice and L. Ulman, *Unionism, Economic Stability and Incomes Policies* (Washington, DC 1983).
8. Fishbein, *Wage Restraint*, pp. 136–7, Flanagan *et al.*, *Unionism*, pp. 407–10.
9. D. Healey, *The Time of My Life* (1989) p. 394.
10. D. Jackson, H. A. Turner and F. Wilkinson, *Do Trade Unions Cause Inflation?* (Cambridge, 1973).
11. Fishbein, *Wage Restraint*, p. 186.
12. R. Maudling, *Memoirs* (1978) p. 112.
13. C. D. Cohen, *British Economic Policy 1960–1969* (1971) pp. 256–8; Davies, 'Incomes', pp. 441–3; Fishbein, *Wage Restraint*, pp. 173–8.
14. Davies, 'Incomes', pp. 435 and 442–4; Flanagan *et al.*, *Unionism*, pp. 415–16; W. Brown, 'Incomes Policy and Pay Differentials', *Oxford Bulletin of Economics and Statistics*, 38 (1976) 27–49.
15. Flanagan, *et al.*, *Unionism*, pp. 395–6; T. R. Gourvish, *British Railways 1948–1973* (Cambridge, 1986) pp. 233, 529–30, 557; W. Ashworth, *The History of the British Coal Industry*, vol. 5 (Oxford, 1986) especially p. 304.
16. Hawkins, *British Industrial Relations*, p. 40. Davies, 'Incomes', pp. 442, 444.

17. C. Mulvey, *The Economic Analysis of Trade Unions* (Oxford, 1978) p. 143.

18. K. Middlemas, *Politics In Industrial Society* (1979) pp. 450, 458.

19. *Financial Times*, 3 June 1987; cited in J. MacInnes, *Thatcherism At Work* (Milton Keynes, 1987) p. xii.

20. J. W. Durcan, W. E. J. McCarthy and G. P. Redman, *Strikes in Post-War Britain* (1983) pp. 26–57; K. Jeffrey and P. Hennessy, *States of Emergency* (1983) pp. 150–221. See Table 4.1.

21. J. E. Cronin, *Industrial Conflict in Modern Britain* (1979) pp. 140–1; C. T. B. Smith, R. Clifton, P. Makeham, S. W. Creigh and R. V. Burn, *Strikes in Britain* (1978) p. 12.

22. Dorfman, *Government vs* Trade Unionism, pp. 8–49; P. Jenkins, *The Battle of Downing Street* (1970); R. Crossman, *The Diaries of a Cabinet Minister*, vol. 3 (1977) p. 299.

23. Hawkins, *British Industrial Relations*, pp. 106–20; H. Pelling, *A History of British Trade Unionism* (4th edn, 1987) pp. 266–8, 280–3. See Table 4.1.

24. Smith *et al.*, *Strikes in Britain*, p. 56; Durcan *et al.*, *Strikes in Post-War Britain*, pp. 426–7.

25. Smith *et al.*, *Strikes in Britain*, p. 63; Royal Commission on Trade Unions and Employers' Associations, *Report*, Cmnd 3623 (1968) pp. 94–121; S. J. Prais, 'The Strike-proneness of Large Plants in Britain', *Journal of the Royal Statistical Society*, 141 (1978) 368–84.

26. Durcan *et al.*, *Strikes in Post-War Britain*, pp. 39–42; Smith *et al.*, *Strikes in Britain*, p. 24.

27. Durcan *et al.*, *Strikes in Post-War Britain*, pp. 407–12.

28. *The Times*, 8 August 1985.

29. R. Taylor, *Workers and the New Depression* (1982) pp. 150–6.

30. G. S. Bain and R. Price, *Profiles of Union Growth* (Oxford, 1980) pp. 40, 51, 67.

31. Ibid., pp. 40 and 42; G. S. Bain and R. Price, 'Union Growth and Employment Trends in the United Kingdom 1964–70', *British Journal of Industrial Relations*, X (1972) 366–81; R. Price and G. S. Bain, 'Union Growth Revisited 1948–1974 in Perspective', *British Journal of Industrial Relations*, XIV (1976) 339–55.

32. Figures drawn from, or calculated from, Bain and Price, *Profiles*, pp. 40, 42; Price and Bain, 'Union Growth Revisited', p. 347; and R. Price and G. S. Bain, 'Union Growth: Retrospect and Prospect', *British Journal of Industrial Relations*, XXI (1983) Table 4.

33. J. Cable, 'Industry' in Artis (ed.), *The UK Economy* (11th edn) pp. 205–7; *Department of Employment Gazette* (December 1989).

34. N. Millward and M. Stevens, *British Workplace Industrial Relations 1980–1984* (Aldershot, 1986) pp. 52–61.

35. F. Elsheikh and G. S. Bain, 'Unionisation in Britain: an Inter-Establishment Analysis Based on Survey Data', *British Journal of Industrial Relations*, XVIII (1980) 169–78; G. S. Bain and P. Elias,

'Trade Union Membership in Great Britain: An Individual-Level Analysis', Institute for Employment Research Discussion Paper 28 (1984); N. Millward and M. Stevens, 'Union Density in the Regions', *Employment Gazette* (May 1988); Fogarty with Brooks, *Trade Unions and British Industrial Development* (2nd edn, 1989) p. xxii.

36. Calculated from Table 4.2 and Bain and Price, *Profiles*, pp. 37–8. For the inter-war pattern of trade union growth see C. Wrigley, 'The Trade Unions Between the Wars' in C. Wrigley (ed.), *A History of British Industrial Relations, vol. 2: 1914–1939* (Brighton, 1986) pp. 71–128.

37. G. S. Bain and F. Elsheikh, *Union Growth and the Business Cycle* (Oxford, 1976) pp. 26–58, 62–70; G. S. Bain, 'Trade Unions', in Bain (ed.), *Industrial Relations*, pp. 16–18; Flanagan *et al.*, *Unionism*, p. 373.

38. ACAS, *Labour Flexibility in Britain: The 1987 ACAS Survey* (1988) pp. 7–13; S. Hill, P. Blyton, A. Gorham, 'The Economics of Manpower Flexibility', *Royal Bank of Scotland Review*, 163 (1989) 15–26; C. Hakim, 'Trends in the flexible workforce', *Employment Gazette* (November 1987) 549–60.

39. O. Robinson and J. Wallace, 'Growth and Utilisation of Part-time Labour in Great Britain', *Employment Gazette* (September 1984) 391–7; O. Robinson, 'The Changing Labour Market: The Phenomenon of Part-time Employment in Britain', *National Westminster Bank Quarterly Review* (November 1985) 19–29. See Table 4.3.

40. ACAS, *Labour Flexibility*, pp. 8, 10.

41. Early critiques of privatisation of local government services include S. Hastings and H. Levie (eds), *Privatisation?* (1983) and D. Whitfield, *Making It Public* (1983).

42. Bain, 'Trade Unions', pp. 24–5.

43. Figures from *Employment Gazette* (November 1989); C. Hakim, 'New Recruits to Self-Employment in the 1980s', *Employment Gazette* (June 1987) 286–97.

44. ACAS, *Labour Flexibility*, pp. 14–34. For 1959–77 data on the growth of female part-time shift work, mainly 'twilight', see P. Dawkins and D. Bosworth, 'Shiftworking and unsocial hours', *Industrial Relations Journal*, 11 (1980) 32–40; Hakim, 'Trends', p. 559.

45. A point argued by A. J. Taylor, *Trade Unions and Politics* (1989) p. 123.

46. P. Bassett, *Strike Free* (1986).

47. P. Ingham and J. Cahill, 'Pay determination in private manufacturing', *Department of Employment Gazette* (June 1989) 281–5. The Workplace Industrial Relations Surveys of 1980 and 1984 found the same; Millward and Stevens, 'Union Density', pp. 66–9.

48. Ingham and Cahill, 'Pay determination', p. 285.

49. MacInnes, *Thatcherism*, pp. 104, 143–4, 150.

50. C. H. Lee, *The British Economy Since 1700: A Macroeconomic*

Perspective (Cambridge, 1986) pp. 243–8; Kennedy, 'The Economy', pp. 35–8, 46–7.

51. Davies, 'Incomes', p. 447; MacInnes, *Thatcherism*, pp. 133–4.

5. THE JERUSALEM THAT FAILED? THE REBUILDING OF POST-WAR BRITAIN   *John Stevenson*

1. For the fullest account see M. Swenarton, *Homes fit for Heroes: the Politics and Architecture of Early State Housing in Britain* (1981).

2. On Wythenshawe as a prototype see E. D. Simon, *Rebuilding Britain: A Twenty Year Plan* (1945) pp. 194–211.

3. R. Roberts, *The Classic Slum: Salford Life in the First Quarter of the Century* (1971); R. Hoggart, *The Uses of Literacy: Aspects of working-class life with special reference to publications and entertainments* (1957); P. Willmot and M. Young, *Family and Kinship in East London* (Penguin edn., 1962); G. C. M. M'Gonigle and J. Kirby, *Poverty and Public Health* (1937).

4. See the comments by B. Seebohm Rowntree on York and Ernest Simon on Manchester cited in J. Stevenson, *Social Conditions in Britain between the Wars* (1976) pp. 213–15, 218–21.

5. See J. Stevenson, 'Planners' Moon? The Second World War and the Planning Movement' in H. L. Smith (ed.), *War and Social Change: British Society in the Second World War* (Manchester, 1986) pp. 58–66.

6. Ibid., pp. 66–74; see also P. Addison, *The Road to 1945: British Politics and the Second World War* (1975), ch. IV.

7. K. Richardson, *Twentieth Century Coventry* (Coventry, 1972) pp. 281–90.

8. *Picture Post*, 4 January 1941, pp. 16–20.

9. J. B. Cullingworth, *Town and Country Planning in England and Wales: An Introduction* (rev. edn, 1967) pp. 223–40.

10. *Liverpool Daily Post*, 13 September 1944; *Liverpool Daily Post*, 21 July 1945. I am grateful for these references to Mr R. J. M. Horrocks.

11. J. Burnett, *A Social History of Housing, 1815–1970* (1978) p. 272.

12. Ibid., p. 279.

13. L. Esher, *A Broken Wave: the Rebuilding of England, 1940–1980* (1981) pp. 46–8 describes it as a 'serviceable brick-and-tile vernacular'; for more hostile responses see C. Jencks, *Modern Movements in Architecture* (1973) pp. 245–7.

14. Esher, *A Broken Wave*, pp. 246–71.

15. Ibid., pp. 249–50; a recent decision (1989) has been taken to demolish some of the Runcorn new town.

16. Jencks, *Modern Movements*, pp. 248–9; Esher, *A Broken Wave*, pp. 204–8. It was decided to demolish the central Hyde Park complex after its use as accommodation for the World Student Games in 1991.

17. R. Bradbury, 'Post-War Housing in Liverpool', *Town Planning Review*, v, 27 (1956/7) 150; Esher, *A Broken Wave*, p. 227.

18. Burnett, *Social History of Housing*, p. 286.

19. See A. Coleman, *Utopia on Trial: Vision and Reality in Planned Housing* (1985) pp. 121, 180–4.

20. For the so-called 'New Brutalism' see Esher, *A Broken Wave*, pp. 59–61; Jencks, *Modern Movements*, pp. 256–9.

21. The Byker project was completed in 1972–6, see Esher, *A Broken Wave*, pp. 185–8.

22. See C. Jencks, *The Prince, the Architects and the New Wave Monarchy* (1988) which contains extracts from his most important speeches and a critique of his position.

23. These figures are contained in a recent article on homelessness by S. Platt, *New Statesman and Society*, 3 November 1989, p. 13.

6. THE RISE (AND FALL?) OF STATE-OWNED ENTERPRISE   *Terry Gourvish*

1. Cf. David and Gareth Butler, *British Political Facts 1900–1985* (1986) p. 397, and Richard Pryke, *Public Enterprise in Practice. The British Experience of Nationalization over Two Decades* (1971) pp. 9–12.

2. Herbert Morrison, *Socialisation and Transport* (1933) pp. 149–76; Yair Aharoni, *The Evolution and Management of State Owned Enterprises* (Cambridge, Mass., 1986) pp. 6–13.

3. Labour Party, *Let Us Face The Future* (1945).

4. The government took a minority holding in Cable & Wireless in 1938 and purchased the rest of the assets in 1946.

5. GDP at factor cost, £12,381m, workforce in employment 23,603,000: CSO, *Economic Trends. Annual Supplement 1990* (1990) pp. 10, 111. Net output, rather than turnover, would be a better indicator to compare with GDP. Pryke shows that in 1950 public enterprises (excluding iron & steel) had a combined net output equivalent to 8.2 per cent of GDP: Pryke, *Public Enterprise*, pp. 15–16.

6. W. J. Reader, *Imperial Chemical Industries. A History. Vol. II. The First Quarter Century 1926–52* (1975) p. 497.

7. CSO, *Economic Trends. Annual Supplement 1990*, p. 60.

8. A. A. Rogow and Peter Shore, *The Labour Government and British Industry, 1945–1951* (Oxford, 1955); E. Eldon Barry, *Nationalisation in British Politics* (1965); Sir Norman Chester, *The Nationalisation of British Industry 1945–51* (1975). For other important works see Bibliography.

9. Cf. Kenneth O. Morgan, *Labour in Power 1945–1951* (Oxford, 1984) p. 140, and Alec Cairncross, *Years of Recovery. British Economic Policy 1945–51* (1985) pp. 463–94.

10. Barry, *Nationalisation*, pp. 277–80, 290–300, 354–68; Leslie Hannah, *The Rise of the Corporate Economy* (1983 edn) pp. 27–40.

11. Barry, *Nationalisation*, p. 370; Peter J. Curwen, *Public Enterprise. A Modern Approach* (Brighton, 1986) pp. 28–9.

12. T. R. Gourvish, *British Railways 1948–73. A Business History* (Cambridge, 1986) pp. 1–16, and see also his 'Government, Nationalisation and Business Performance: the Nationalised Transport Enterprises in the U.K. 1830–1980', *Annali di Storia dell'impresa 3* (Milan, 1987) pp. 173–82. The summary of monographs is based upon Terence R. Gourvish, 'Die Entstehungsgeschichte der Staatsigenen Unternehmen im Vereinigten Königreich – Transport, Kohle, Elektrizität', in *Wissenschaftliche Zeitschrift der Humboldt-Universität zu Berlin, Reihe Gesellschafts Wissenschaften*, 39 (1990) I, pp. 16–25, published in English as 'The Genesis of State-Owned Enterprises in the United Kingdom – Transport, Coal and Electricity', in Manuel J. Pelaez (ed.), *Historia Economica y de las Instituciones Financieras en Europa. Trabajos en Homenaje a Ferran Valls I Taberner* (Barcelona, 1989) pp. 3607–23.

13. Barry Supple, *The History of the British Coal Industry. Vol. 4. 1913–46: The Political Economy of Decline* (Oxford, 1987) pp. 78–9, 295–306, 319–21, 330–57, 598–605. See also Barry Supple, 'Ideology or pragmatism? The nationalization of coal, 1919–46', in Neil McKendrick and R. B. Outhwaite (eds), *Business Life and Public Policy. Essays in Honour of D. C. Coleman* (Cambridge, 1986) pp. 229–40, and M. W. Kirby, *The British Coalmining Industry, 1870–1946* (1977) pp. 108–68.

14. William Ashworth, *The History of the British Coal Industry. Vol. 5. 1946–1982: The Nationalized Industry* (Oxford, 1986) pp. 5–7.

15. Supple, *British Coal Industry*, pp. 357–8, 423–4, 590–1, 605–27, 694; Supple, 'Ideology', pp. 228–9, 240–3, 246–8; W. H. B. Court, *Coal* (1951) pp. 17–28, 163–77, 249–50.

16. Leslie Hannah, *Electricity before Nationalisation. A Study of the Development of the Electricity Supply Industry in Britain to 1948* (1979) pp. 5–9, 22–3, 214; Leslie Hannah, *Engineers, Managers and Politicians. The First Fifteen Years of Nationalised Electricity Supply in Britain* (1982) pp. 1–3. See also I. C. R. Byatt, *The British Electrical Industry, 1875–1914* (Oxford, 1979).

17. Hannah, *Electricity before Nationalisation*, pp. 73–8, 100–7, 146–9, 180, 213, 238–40, 249–56, 334–6. In addition to the North of Scotland Board an Electricity Board for Northern Ireland had been created (in 1931).

18. Hannah, *Engineers*, pp. 2–3; Gourvish, *British Railways*, pp. 571, 577.

19. Trevor I. Williams, *A History of the British Gas Industry* (Oxford, 1981) pp. 68–99; Malcolm Falkus, *Always Under Pressure. A History of North Thames Gas since 1949* (1988) pp. 16–17.

20. Cf. A. W. J. Thomson and L. C. Hunter, *The Nationalized Transport Industries* (1973) pp. 10–13.

21. See Kathleen Burk, *The First Privatisation. The Politicians, the City and the Denationalisation of Steel* (1988), who argues that both

Labour and Conservative governments were more equivocal about steel than party dogma implied. On road haulage see Gourvish, *British Railways*, pp. 137–9.

22. E. Shinwell, *Conflict Without Malice* (1955) p. 172, cited *inter alia*, in Thomson and Hunter, *Nationalized Transport*, p. 6.

23. Supple, *British Coal Industry*, pp. 629–31. Dalton, author of *Practical Socialism for Britain* (1935), was President of the Board of Trade, 1942–5 and Chancellor of the Exchequer, 1945–7; Morrison was Minister of Transport, 1929–31, Home Secretary, 1940–5, and Lord President of the Council, 1945–51 (and see above, p. 112); Durbin, author of *Democratic Socialism* (1940), was an LSE economist, Attlee's personal assistant, 1942–5, and a junior minister in the Ministry of Works, 1947–8. See Ben Pimlott, *Hugh Dalton* (1985) pp. 218–19, 396–7; Thomson and Hunter, *Nationalized Transport*, p. 6.

24. J. R. Bellerby, *Economic Reconstruction. A Study of Post-war Problems. Vol. I: National, Industrial and Regional Planning* (1943).

25. Cf. G. W. Crompton, ' "Good Business for the Nation". The Railway Nationalisation Question, 1921–47', unpublished Business History Unit seminar paper, 1990.

26. Supple, *British Coal Industry*, pp. 596–8, 611–15, 619, 673; Supple, 'Ideology', pp. 241–6. Gowers had been Permanent Under Secretary in the Mines Department, 1920–7, and Chairman of the Coal Mines Reorganisation Committee, 1930–8, while Hyndley had been Commercial Adviser to the Mines Department throughout the inter-war years.

27. Gourvish, *British Railways*, pp. 16–20, 24, 31; Hannah, *Electricity before Nationalisation*, pp. 290–1, 337–9; M. R. Bonavia, *The Nationalisation of British Transport. The Early History of the British Transport Commission, 1948–53* (1987) pp. 5–6.

28. Supple, *British Coal Industry*, p. 675. Ashworth, however, is more critical of Reid's position: *Coal Industry*, pp. 123, 184–6.

29. Supple, *British Coal Industry*, pp. 646–8, 675–7; Ashworth, *Coal Industry*, pp. 5–8, 31–3, 121–3, 129, 138–42, 171, 184–6, 191–7, 612–29; Chester, *Nationalisation*, pp. 550–8, 1032–4.

30. Gourvish, *British Railways*, pp. 24–5, 31–67. Electricity, too, had problems with an over-centralised British Electricity Authority before decentralisation in the mid–late 1950s: Hannah, *Electricity before Nationalisation*, pp. 338–40.

31. Gourvish, *British Railways*, pp. 68–90, 173–203; Ashworth, *Coal Industry*, pp. 164–5, 228–38; and see also D. L. Munby, 'The Nationalized Industries', in G. D. N. Worswick and P. H. Ady, *The British Economy in the Nineteen-Fifties* (Oxford, 1962) pp. 378–80.

32. Acton Society Trust, *Extent of Decentralisation* (1951) and *Patterns of Organisation* (1951), and H. A. Clegg and T. E. Chester, *The Future of Nationalization* (Oxford, 1953), esp. p. 131ff., cited in Leonard Tivey, *Nationalization in British Industry* (1973 edn) p. 111.

33. However, decentralisation was essentially a failure, and the Commission took up most of the functions of the Railway Executive. Gourvish, *British Railways*, pp. 137–58.

34. The Herbert Committee had recommended that the Electricity Council be staffed by outsiders; in fact, it was dominated by the Area Board chairman and representatives of the CEGB. The separation of generation and distribution was also provoked by support for a nuclear power programme. See Hannah, *Engineers*, pp. 2–4, 7–22, 60–3, 161–7, 183–4; R. Kelf-Cohen, *Twenty Years of Nationalisation. The British Experience* (1971 edn) pp. 109–11.

35. Ashworth, *Coal Industry*, pp. 193–7, 618–21.

36. Transport Act, 1947, Section 3(1), 3(4). It is difficult to see how the Commission could have succeeded in fulfilling the twin goals of integration and profitability with the resources at its disposal in 1948.

37. Gourvish, *British Railways*, pp. 308–30. The Stedeford Advisory Group was appointed to advise (in secret) the then Minister of Transport, Ernest Marples.

38. White Papers: P. P. 1960–1, XXVII, Cmnd. 1337; P.P. 1967–8, XXXIX, Cmnd. 3437. See also Gourvish, *British Railways*, p. 307. The 1967 White Paper also stipulated pricing according to long-run marginal cost, as well as setting investment returns and overall financial targets. It has been pointed out that this was to introduce inconsistent or contradictory requirements, since if the pricing and investment rules were followed, they would automatically set the return. Cf. Michael Posner, 'Policy towards nationalized industries', in Wilfrid Beckerman (ed.), *The Labour Government's Economic Record* (1972) p. 251.

39. From January 1973 the industry was run by the British Gas Corporation. North Sea discoveries also prompted the establishment of the British National Oil Corporation in 1976. K. Jones, 'Policy Towards the Nationalised Industries', in F. T. Blackaby (ed.), *British Economic Policy 1960–74* (Cambridge, 1978) p. 485; John Redwood, *Public Enterprise in Crisis. The Future of the Nationalized Industries* (Oxford, 1980) pp. 35, 78; John Vickers and George Yarrow, *Privatization. An Economic Analysis* (Cambridge, Mass., 1988) pp. 318–19.

40. Martin Holmes, *The Labour Government, 1974–79* (1985) pp. 40–57; Redwood, *Public Enterprise in Crisis*, pp. 54, 56, 81, 108–9.

41. Gourvish, *British Railways*, pp. 352–9, 451ff.

42. Ibid., pp. 369–72, 478–9, 547–8, 569–70.

43. Cf. Jones, 'Policy', pp. 502–3.

44. Cf. Nevil Johnson, 'The Public Corporation: An Ambiguous Species', and Aubrey Silberston, 'Nationalised Industries: Government Intervention and Industrial Efficiency', in David Butler and A. H. Halsey (eds), *Policy and Politics. Essays in honour of Norman Chester* (1978) pp. 126–7, 146–9; Aubrey Silberston, 'Steel in a Mixed Economy', in Lord Roll (ed.), *The Mixed Economy* (1982) pp. 98–103.

45. See the case studies of electricity, coal and the railways by

Hannah, Ashworth and Gourvish, and cf. Vickers and Yarrow, *Privatization*, pp. 39–43.

46. Pryke, *Public Enterprise*, pp. 58–77, 433–7, 444; Richard Pryke, *The Nationalised Industries. Policies and Performance since 1968* (Oxford, 1981); 'The Comparative Performance of Public and Private Enterprise', *Fiscal Studies*, III, No. 2 (1982) 68–81; 'Strategies for Coal and Electricity', in John Grieve Smith (ed.), *Strategic Planning in Nationalised Industries* (1984) pp. 240, 250–1. For a critique of Pryke (1971) see Redwood, *Public Enterprise in Crisis*, p. 19ff.

47. For example, industrial production growth was 3.0 per cent p.a., 1960–73, but only 0.6 per cent p.a., 1973–85. Kirby, above, p. 13.

48. Robert Millward, 'The Comparative Performance of Public and Private Ownership', in Roll, *Mixed Economy*, pp. 58–65, 82–5. For a criticism of Millward see Vickers and Yarrow, *Privatization*, pp. 40–3.

49. See Gourvish, *British Railways*, pp. 460–8.

50. Pryke, *Public Enterprise*, pp. 434–5. My estimates of railway productivity reveal an average annual growth of 3.8 per cent for labour (output per head) and 2.1 per cent for total factor, 1948–73; Gourvish, *British Railways*, p. 563.

51. Philip S. Bagwell, *End of the Line? The Fate of British Railways Under Thatcher* (1984) pp. 47–8.

52. Investment appraisal in the private sector often left a lot to be desired, as the Radcliffe Committee of 1958 discovered: Gourvish, *British Railways*, pp. 304, 379–80, 517–20, and see also Tony Prosser, *Nationalised Industries and Public Control. Legal, Constitutional and Political Issues* (Oxford, 1986) pp. 113–14.

53. British Railways Board, *Annual Report and Accounts*, 1984/5, 1988/9.

54. The PSBR fell from £10,161m in 1975 to £5419m in 1977, then rose to £12,531m in 1979 (current prices); the element represented by public corporations was: 1975, £2424m; 1977, £1445m; 1979, £3563m. CSO, *Economic Trends. Annual Supplement 1990* (1990) Tables 34 and 36.

55. Richard Molyneux and David Thompson, 'Nationalised Industry Performance: still third-rate?', *Fiscal Studies*, VIII, No. 1 (1987) 51–2.

56. Sir Geoffrey Howe, *Parliamentary Debates (Commons)*, 5th ser. (Session 1979–80), vol. 968, 12 June 1979, c. 246. See also John Kay, Colin Mayer and David Thompson (eds), *Privatisation and Regulation – the UK Experience* (Oxford, 1986).

57. The figure of £25,250m is for the period 1979/80–8/9 and includes revenue from North Sea Licence premiums and the proceeds from the sale of subsidiaries (these were retained by the businesses, but reduced the call on the Exchequer by these businesses). Treasury, *Government Expenditure Plans 1990–91 to 1992–93*, January 1990, P.P. 1989–90, Cm. 1021, Table 21.5.13.

58. CSO, *Economic Trends, 1990*, Tables 34, 36.

59. Vickers and Yarrow, *Privatization*, pp. 173–80.

60. On a TFP basis steel, coal and electricity exhibited improved results, for example: Molyneux and Thompson, 'Nationalised Industry Performance', pp. 58–9.

61. British Rail, for example, converted a group loss of £0.6m in 1979 to a profit of £64m in 1983 and £226m in 1988/9 (all in constant 1982 prices). Calculated from BRB, *Report and Accounts*, 1979, 1983, 1988/9.

62. Data for 1988. The Electricity Council (now about to be privatised) was the 4th largest on this basis, and in terms of labour the rankings were: British Rail 6th, British Coal 7th, Electricity Council 9th. *The Times 1000 1989–90* (1989) pp. 6, 30.

63. Curwen, *Public Enterprise*, pp. 216–17.

7. THE DEFENCE OF THE REALM: BRITAIN IN THE NUCLEAR AGE
Michael Dockrill

1. Brian Bond, *British Military Policy between the Two World Wars* (Oxford, 1980) pp. 287ff.

2. Kenneth O. Morgan, *Labour in Power 1945–1951* (Oxford, 1984) p. 233.

3. Quoted in Alan Bullock, *Ernest Bevin: Foreign Secretary 1945–1951* (1983) p. 113.

4. Wm Roger Louis, *The British Empire in the Middle East: Arab Nationalism, the United States and Postwar Imperialism* (Oxford, 1984) pp. 27–35. For a full account of Britain's strategic dilemma in the Middle East see David Devereux, *British Defence Policy towards the Middle East 1948–1956* (1990).

5. For twelve months in 1946. It was raised to eighteen months in 1947 and to two years in 1950, as a result of the outbreak of the Korean War.

6. Antony Adamthwaite, 'Britain: the View from the Foreign Office', in Josef Becker and Franz Knipping (eds), *Power in Europe? Great Britain, France, Italy, and Germany in a Postwar World 1945–59* (Berlin, 1986) p. 13.

7. Figures in Malcolm Chalmers, *Paying for Defence: Military Spending and British Decline* (1985) p. 113.

8. Morgan, *Labour in Power*, pp. 280–4.

9. Stephen Kirby, 'Britain, NATO and European Security: The Irreducible Commitment', in John Baylis (ed.), *British Defence Policy in a Changing World* (1977) p. 100.

10. John Lewis Gaddis, *Strategies of Containment: A Critical Appraisal of Post War National Security Policy* (Oxford, 1982) p. 62.

11. Geoffrey Warner, 'Britain: the View from the Cabinet', in Becker and Knipping, *Power in Europe?* pp. 29–30.

12. Saki Dockrill, 'Britain and a West German Contribution to

NATO 1950–1955', Ph.D University of London (1988) pp. 20–1. To be published in Cambridge in 1990 and entitled *Britain's Policy for West German Rearmament 1950–1955.*

13. Named after the American Secretary of State, George C. Marshall.

14. For the Marshall Plan see Michael J. Hogan, *The Marshall Plan: America, Britain and the Reconstruction of Western Europe, 1947–1952* (Cambridge, 1987); Henry Pelling, *Britain and the Marshall Plan* (1988); Alan S. Milward, *The Reconstruction of Western Europe, 1947–1951* (1984).

15. Michael Dockrill, *British Defence since 1945* (Oxford, 1989) pp. 32–3; Saki Dockrill, 'Contribution to NATO', p. 23.

16. C. J. Bartlett, 'The Military Instrument in British Foreign Policy', and John Baylis, 'The Anglo-American Relationship in Defence', both in Baylis, *British Defence Policy*, pp. 35, 67, 74.

17. Burton I. Kaufman, *The Korean War: Challenges in Crisis, Credibility and Command* (Philadelphia, 1986) pp. 32, 34.

18. Ibid., p. 34; Callum MacDonald, *Britain and the Korean War* (Oxford, 1990). See also M. L. Dockrill, 'The Foreign Office, Anglo-American Relations and the Korean War, June 1950–June 1951', *International Affairs*, 62, no 3 (summer 1986).

19. See Saki Dockrill 'Contribution to NATO' for a full account of the EDC negotiations, pp. 69ff.

20. Ibid.

21. Alec Cairncross, *Years of Recovery: British Economic Policy 1945–1951* (1985) pp. 224–5.

22. Anthony Seldon, *Churchill's Indian Summer: The Conservative Government, 1951–55* (1981) p. 335; see also M. Dockrill, *British Defence*, pp. 45–7.

23. Dockrill, *British Defence*, pp. 34–9.

24. For the Suez crisis see David Carlton, *Britain and the Suez Crisis* (Oxford, 1988).

25. Alistair Horne, *Macmillan: Volume II of the Official Biography*, 2 vols (1989) II p. 50.

26. For a detailed discussion of the Sandys reforms and their effects see Martin Navias, *The British 'New Look': Nuclear Weapons and Strategic Planning, 1955–1958* (forthcoming, Oxford, 1991).

27. Chalmers, *Paying for Defence*, p. 67.

28. M. Dockrill, *British Defence*, p. 142.

29. Gavin Kennedy, *The Economics of Defence* (1975) p. 102.

30. M. Dockrill, *British Defence*, pp. 54, 63–71.

31. Horne, *Macmillan*, II, pp. 23–7, 55–7.

32. For details see John Simpson, *The Independent Nuclear State: the United States, Great Britain and the Military Atom* (1986) pp. 142–9.

33. Horne, *Macmillan*, II, p. 433.

34. Ibid., pp. 472–3.

35. Clive Ponting, *Breach of Promise: Labour in Power, 1964–70* (1989) p. 86.

36. M. Dockrill, *British Defence*, p. 79.

37. Quoted in Harold Macmillan, *At the End of the Day* (1973) p. 412, also quoted in Philip Ziegler, *Mountbatten, The Official Biography* (1986) p. 563.

38. M. Dockrill, *British Defence*, pp. 88–9.

39. Ponting, *Breach of Promise*, p. 98.

40. M. Dockrill, *British Defence*, pp. 88–9.

41. Andrew Schonfield, *British Economic Policy since the War* (rev. Penguin edn, 1959) p. 99.

42. Ponting, *Breach of Promise*, pp. 85–6.

43. M. Dockrill, *British Defence*, pp. 93–7.

44. Richard Crossman, *The Crossman Diaries: Selections from the Diaries of a Cabinet Minister 1964–1970*, Anthony Howard (1979) p. 397.

45. M. Dockrill, *British Defence*, pp. 96–7.

46. See Dan Smith, *The Defence of the Realm in the 1980s* (1980) pp. 111–50.

47. Baylis, *British Defence Policy*, pp. 23–4.

48. For the Falklands War see Lawrence Freedman, *Britain and the Falklands War* (Oxford, 1988) and Max Hastings and Simon Jenkins, *The Battle for the Falklands* (1983).

49. Quoted in Freedman, *Falklands War*, p. 92.

50. Baylis, *British Defence Policy*, p. 77.

51. For an excellent analysis of these and other defence issues see Baylis, *British Defence Policy*.

52. Lawrence Freedman, 'The strategic concept', in Philip Sabin (ed.), *The Future of United Kingdom Airpower* (1988).

53. David Greenwood, 'Defence and National Priorities since 1945', in Baylis, *British Defence Policy*, p. 189.

54. On this see Dan Smith, *The Defence of the Realm in the 1980s* (1980); Baylis, *British Defence Policy*; and Malcolm Chalmers, *Paying for Defence: Military Spending and British Decline*, (1985). For an excellent discussion of the issues see John Baylis, ' "Greenwoodery" and British Defence Policy', *International Affairs*, 62, no 3 (summer 1986) 443–57. For a magisterial survey of the effects of excessive defence expenditure on the global power position of various states throughout history, which has excited considerable controversy, see Paul Kennedy, *The Rise and Fall of the Great Powers: Economic Change and Military Conflict from 1500 to 2000* (New York, 1987).

55. Cited in Baylis, *British Defence Policy*, p. 89.

8. SOCIAL EQUITY AND INDUSTRIAL NEED: A DILEMMA OF ENGLISH
EDUCATION SINCE 1945   *Michael Sanderson*

1. Public Record Office, Education Papers ED 12/419, Interview Memorandum 2 November 1933.

2. Michael Sanderson, *Educational Opportunity and Social Change in England* (1987) ch. 4.

3. Lord Eustace Percy, *Education at the Crossroads* (1930) p. 58.

4. Deborah Thom, 'The 1944 Education Act, the art of the possible?' in Harold L. Smith (ed.), *War and Social Change, British Society in the Second World War* (Manchester, 1986) p. 107 notes that a Mass Observation survey of 1942 found 71 per cent of respondents cited 'equality of opportunity' in education as the reform they chiefly desired.

5. R. A. Butler, *The Art of the Possible* (1971) p. 94.

6. *Higher Technological Education* (Lord Eustace Percy) 1945.

7. PP. 1945–6 XIV *Scientific Manpower* (Sir Alan Barlow) 1945–6 Cmnd 6824.

8. *Report of the Consultative Committee on Secondary Education with Special Reference to Grammar Schools and Technical High Schools* (Sir Will Spens), HMSO 1938.

9. *Curriculum and Examinations in Secondary Schools* (Sir Cyril Norwood), HMSO 1943. Sir Cyril was the President of St John's College, Oxford, and the former headmaster of Harrow and Marlborough.

10. *The Nation's Schools, their Plan and Purpose*, Ministry of Education Pamphlet No. 1 (1945) pp. 17–19.

11. *The New Secondary Education*, Ministry of Education Pamphlet No. 9 (1947) pp. 49–57.

12. *Ministry of Education Annual Reports* PP. 1947–8 XI, Cmnd 7426. 1962–3 XI, Cmnd 1990.

13. Sir Peter Venables, *Technical Education, its Aims, Organisation and Future Development* (1955) p. 95.

14. Betty Vernon, *Ellen Wilkinson 1891–1947* (1982) pp. 204, 222, 217.

15. 1948–9 XIV Cmnd 7724 *Education in 1948. Report of the Ministry of Education* (1949) p. 10.

16. Fred Blackburn, *George Tomlinson* (1954). It is significant that in a newsreel (*c.* 1947/8) in *Now the War is Over – Schooldays*, BBC 2, 27 August 1990, George Tomlinson is shown in a new school telling a lad who wanted to leave school at 14 to enter the building trade that he will be better prepared by staying on until 15. The lad looks unconvinced.

17. A. J. Jenkinson, 'What is Secondary Technical Education?' *Vocational Aspect*, 3 (1951) 91.

18. A. J. Jenkinson, 'The Slow Progress of Secondary Technical Education', *Vocational Aspect*, 1 (1949) 297.

19. Stuart Maclure, *One Hundred Years of London Education 1870–1970* (1970) pp. 130, 170–5.

20. W. Jacob, 'The London Secondary Technical Schools for Girls', *Journal of Education* (August 1954).

21. Rene Saran, *Policy Making in Secondary Education* (Oxford, 1973).

22. *The Nation's Schools* (1945) p. 15.

23. 1951–2, X Cmnd 8554, *Education in 1951 Report of the Ministry of Education* (1952) p. 11.

24. *Early Leaving,* Report of the Central Advisory Council for Education, HMSO 1954.

25. 1956–7 X *Education in 1956,* Cmnd 1957, p. 10.

26. ED 147/207 Memorandum Sir David Eccles, 20 December 1954.

27. The Problems of Secondary Education, n.d. a series of questions and annotated answers by the minister.

28. Secondary Technical Education. Memorandum Sir Toby Weaver, 14 January 1955.

29. Memorandum A. R. Maxwell Hyslop, 15 January 1955.

30. Memorandum D. H. Morrell, 3 January 1955.

31. Memorandum Sir Anthony Part, 17 January 1955.

32. Memorandum HMI Mr Bray, 17 January 1955.

33. Report on the minister's meeting, 23 February 1955.

34. Memorandum Sir Toby Weaver to Sir Anthony Part, 29 November 1955, reproduces the key part of Sir David Eccles' April speech to the NUT.

35. 1962–3 XI, *Education in 1962,* Cmnd 1990 (1963) p. 5.

36. 1963–4 XI, *Education in 1963,* Cmnd 2316 (1964) p. 43.

37. G. L. Payne, *Britain's Scientific and Technological Manpower* (Stanford, 1960) pp. 121–2.

38. Thelma Veness, *School Leavers* (1962). Her study was in 1956.

39. Jean Floud, A. H. Halsey and F. Martin, *Social Class and Educational Opportunity* (1956) found a rise only from 10 per cent of working-class children who attended grammar schools in the 1930s to 12 per cent in Middlesborough and 15 per cent in south-west Herts by 1953.

40. J. W. B. Douglas, *The Home and the School* (1964).

41. P. E. Vernon, *Secondary School Selection* (1957); B. Simon, *Intelligence, Psychology and Education* (1971).

42. Anthony Crosland, *The Future of Socialism* (1956).

43. *Policies for Higher Education in the 1980s* (OECD, Paris, 1983) p. 105.

44. Hansard, Vol 71, No. 1333, Written Answer 22 January 1985, Sir Keith Joseph.

45. John MacGregor in *The Independent,* 14 June 1990.

46. E.g. S. Prais, 'What can we learn from the German system of education and vocational training?' in G. D. N. Worswick, *Education and Economic Performance* (Aldershot, 1985). Michael Sanderson, 'Education and Economic Decline 1890–1980s', *Oxford Review of Economic Policy,* 4, No. 1 (spring 1988).

47. *Daily Telegraph,* 21 March 1986.

48. *Fifteen to Eighteen, Report of the Central Advisory Council for Education* (Sir Geoffrey Crowther) (1959) pp. 226–7.

49. *The Age Group Bulge and its Possible Effects on University Policy*, Home Universities Conference 1955.

50. *Higher Education* (Lord Robbins) Cmnd 2154 (1963) p. 260.

51. A. Little and J. Westergaard, 'The Trend of Class Differentials in Educational Opportunity in England and Wales', *British Journal of Sociology* (1964).

52. Robbins, *Higher Education*, p. 50.

53. M. M. Postan, *An Economic History of Western Europe 1945–64* (1967) pp. 12, 17.

54. M. C. Kaser, 'Education and Economic Progress: Experience in Industrialised Market Economies', in E. A. G. Robinson and J. Vaizey, *The Economics of Education* (1966).

55. Robbins, *Higher Education*, p. 127.

56. Higher Education. Evidence to the Government Committee (Robbins) by the Federation of British Industries, November 1961.

57. E. P. Thompson, *Warwick University Ltd* (1970).

58. *The Independent*, 26 August 1989. UFC Appraisal Survey.

59. Walter Perry, *The Open University* (1976).

60. Michael Beloff, *The Plateglass Universities* (1968) p. 39. See also Michael Sanderson, *The Universities and British Industry 1850–1970* (1972) ch. 13; H. J. Perkin, *New Universities in the United Kingdom* (OECD, Paris, 1969).

61. *Industry, Science and the Universities, Report of a Working Party on Universities and Industrial Research* (P. Docksey) July 1970, pp. 81, 100.

62. Vera Morris, 'Investment in higher education in England and Wales: a subject analysis', in C. Baxter, P. J. O'Leary, A. Westoby (eds), *Economics and Education Policy: a Reader* (1977) p. 83. See also pp. 181, 182, 202.

63. *Enquiry into the Flow of Candidates in Science and Technology into Higher Education* (Sir Frederick Dainton) Interim 1966, Cmnd 2893. Final 1968 Cmnd 3541.

64. Report of the Vice Chancellor, University of Salford 1967/8; Sanderson, *Universities and British Industry*, p. 376.

65. *Daily Telegraph*, 30 January 1970.

66. UMIST Newscuttings *passim* for many references of this kind.

67. Sir Peter Venables, *Higher Education Developments: The Technological Universities* (1978) p. 295.

68. Ibid., p. 268.

69. *The Independent*, 26 August 1989. What we here term 'poorly rated' was defined by the UFC as 'research quality that equates to attainable levels of national excellence in none or virtually none, of the subareas of activity'.

70. Eric E. Robinson, *The New Polytechnics* (1968) p. 103.

71. A. H. Halsey in *Times Higher Education Supplement*, 26 January 1990.

72. Robinson, *New Polytechnics*, p. 108.

73. Julia Whitburn, Maurice Mealing and Caroline Cox, *People in Polytechnics* (SRHE, Guildford, 1976) p. 72.

A-level scores	Eng. and Tech.	Science	Social	Lit., Lang., Arts
0–3	56.2%	43%	11%	5%
7–9	18%	19%	41%	44%

74. E. G. Edwards, *Higher Education for Everyone* (1982) p. 52.

75. Keith Jacka, Caroline Cox, John Marks, *Rape of Reason, the Corruption of the Polytechnic of North London* (Enfield, 1975). Students and Staff of the Hornsey College of Art, *The Hornsey Affair* (1969).

76. Lex Donaldson, *Policy in the Polytechnics, Pluralistic Drift in Higher Education* (1975) p. 26.

77. Elaine Henry, *Oxford Polytechnic, Genesis to Maturity 1865–1980* (Oxford Polytechnic, 1981?).

78. *The English Polytechnics: an HMI Commentary* (HMSO, 1989) cited *The Independent*, 6 October 1989.

79. *The Independent*, 12 October 1989.

Graduate unemployment rates 1988

	Univs	Polys
English	15.2	29.7
Foreign Lang.	12.9	21.2
Humanities	16.2	30.6
Economics	10.3	22.3

80. Shirley Keeble, *University Education in Business Management from the 1890s to the 1950s, a Reluctant Relationship*, University of London, PhD (1984).

81. The city of Leicester is an interesting example where *both* the university and the polytechnic teach education, music, art history and economic history. It is also indicative that on the death of Sir Alfred Ayer, *The Independent*, 29 June 1989, noted that much of the advance in philosophy was now taking place in polytechnics.

82. It is an interesting contrast that the Technical High School at Darmstadt expanded from 6903 to 16,091 students between 1970/1 and 1988/9 yet actually *increased* its proportion studying Natural Sciences and Engineering from 85.7 to 88.8 per cent. I am grateful to Frl. Cora Diehl for these figures.

83. Adrian Wooldridge, 'The Professional Elite, Liberal Education and Economic Lag in Britain 1850–1980', Royal Historical Society Conference, Institute of Historical Research, 23 September 1989.

84. A. J. Peters, 'The Changing Idea of Technical Education', *British Journal of Educational Studies*, XI (May 1963).

85. 1959–60 XII, *Education in 1959. Report of the Ministry of Education* Cmnd 1088 (1960) p. 77.

86. Eustace Percy, *Some Memories* (1958) pp. 94–5.

87. Robinson, *New Polytechnics*, p. 13.

88. Mary Warnock, *A Common Policy for Education* (Oxford, 1988) pp. 2, 9–10.

89. Conversation with Mrs Jean Floud CBE, 25 May 1989.

90. Tyrell Burgess, *Education for Capability*, edited for the Royal Society of Arts (NFER, Nelson, 1986).

91. D. H. Aldcroft, 'Education and Britain's Growth Failure 1950–1980', in Gabriel Tortella (ed.), *Education and Economic Development since the Industrial Revolution* (Valencia, 1990) (Papers of the X International Economic History Congress, Leuven, 1990).

92. The references are of course to the key British university novels of this time, Kingsley Amis' *Lucky Jim* (1953), Malcolm Bradbury's *The History Man* (1975) and David Lodge's *Nice Work* (1988). 'Dixon', 'Kirk' and 'Penrose' are respectively university lecturers in history, sociology and English literature, hostile or indifferent to industry. 'Wilcox' is a non-university, technically trained engineering manager.

9. TOWARDS EQUAL OPPORTUNITIES? WOMEN IN BRITAIN SINCE 1945
Pat Thane

1. For an introduction to the debate on the effect of the Second World War on women, see P. Summerfield, 'Women, war and social change', in A. Marwick (ed.), *Total War and Social Change* (1988) pp. 95–118.

2. R. Croucher, *Engineers at War 1939–1945* (1982), p. 294. In ch. 5. Croucher provides a very good discussion of women in engineering during the war. See also H. L. Smith, 'The problem of "equal pay for equal work" in Great Britain during World War II', *Journal of Modern History*, 53 (December 1981).

3. *Royal Commission on Equal Pay 1944–6. Report. Parliamentary Papers 1944–6*, Vol. XI, p. 156.

4. RC Equal Pay, *Report*, p. 43.

5. Denise Riley, *War in the Nursery* (1983) pp. 163–4.

6. RC Equal Pay, *Report*, p. 75.

7. Ibid., p. 163.

8. For some discussion of this point see M. Savage, 'Trade unionism, sex segregation and the state', *Social History*, 13, No. 2 (May 1988) 209–29.

9. Ibid., Appendices, pp. 118–24.

10. Ibid., pp. 124–7.

11. Ruth Milkman, *Gender at Work. The Dynamics of Job Segregation by Sex in World War Two* (Urbana and Chicago, 1987) studies comparable processes in the US.

12. Monica Charlot, 'Women and Elections in Britain', in H. R. Penniman (ed.), *Britain at the Polls, 1979* (Washington and London, 1981) p. 244.

13. W. Crofts, 'The Attlee Government's Pursuit of Women', *History Today* (August 1986) 29–35.

14. Riley, *War in the Nursery*, p. 120.

15. Geoffrey Thomas, *Women at Work* (1944) p. 29; Geoffrey Thomas, *Women and Industry* (1948).

16. Pat Thane, 'The debate on the declining birth-rate in Britain: the "menace" of an ageing population, 1920s–1950s', *Continuity and Change*, 5, 2 (July 1990) 283–305.

17. D. W. Winnicott, *The Child, the Family and the Outside World* (1964).

18. Notably J. Bowlby, *Child Care and the Growth of Love* (1953).

19. This is well discussed in Riley, *War in the Nursery*, pp. 80ff.

20. Ibid., p. 133.

21. Thomas, *Women and Industry*.

22. J. Ermisch and R. E. Wright, *Women's Wages in Full- and Part-Time Jobs in Great Britain* (London: Centre for Economic Policy Research. Discussion Paper No. 234, 1988).

23. M. Pugh, 'Domesticity and the Decline of Feminism, 1930–1950', in H. L. Smith (ed.), *British Feminism in the Twentieth Century* (Aldershot, 1990) p. 152.

24. Michael Anderson, 'The emergence of the modern life-cycle in Britain', *Social History*, 10 (January 1985) pp. 69–87.

25. Crofts, 'Attlee ... Pursuit of Women'; Riley, *War in the Nursery*, p. 133.

26. Croucher, *Engineers at War*, p. 297; Crofts, 'Attlee ... Pursuit of Women', pp. 34–5.

27. A. Myrdal and V. Klein, *Women's Two Roles. Home and Work* (1956) p. 58.

28. Thomas, *Women at Work*, p. 27.

29. M. Spring-Rice, *Working Class Wives* (2nd edn, 1981).

30. For a discussion of the background to this book see Jane Lewis, 'Myrdal, Klein, Women's two Roles and Postwar Feminism 1945–1960', in Smith (ed.), *British Feminism*, pp. 167–88.

31. See Pat Thane, 'The women of the British Labour Party and feminism, 1906–1945', in Smith (ed.), *British Feminism*, pp. 124–43, and other essays in this volume.

32. Published in London, 1965.

33. 'Survey of the employment of women scientists and engineers', *Ministry of Labour Gazette* (September 1960) 356–7.

34. N. Seear, V. Roberts and J. Brick, *A Career for Women in Industry* (London and Edinburgh, 1964).

35. Audrey Hunt, *A Survey of Women's Employment* (1968).

36. Pearl Jephcott's surveys, *Girls Growing Up* (1942) and *Rising Twenty* (1948) had emphasised the eagerness of working-class working girls to escape permanently into marriage from the low pay and poor conditions of the jobs available to them.

37. Royal Commission on Trade Unions and Employers' Associations, 1965–1968. *Report* (1968) pp. 90–3.

38. Ibid. Research papers, 11; N. Seear, *The Position of Women in Industry* (1968).

39. E. Meehan, 'British feminism from the 1960s to the 1980s' in Smith (ed.), *British Feminism*, pp. 189–204; Riley, *War in the Nursery*, pp. 178–9.

40. Meehan, 'British feminism'; April Carter, *The Politics of Women's Rights* (London and New York, 1988).

41. Meehan, 'British feminism'; Meehan, *Women's Rights at Work* (1985).

42. A. Zabalza and Z. Tzannatos, *Women and Equal Pay: the effects of legislation on Female Employment and Wages in Great Britain* (Cambridge, 1985); R. E. Wright and J. F. Ermisch, *Gender Discrimination in the British Labour Market: a reassessment* (London: Centre for Economic Policy Research, Discussion Paper No. 278, 1988).

43. Reported in M. Fogarty, R. and R. N. Rapoport, *Sex, Career and Family* (1971).

44. Meehan, 'British feminism'.

10. IMMIGRATION   *Colin Holmes*

1. J. Clark, 'A patriot for me', *The Guardian*, 18 July 1989.

2. M. Banton, *The Coloured Quarter* (1955) and J. Rex *et al.*, *Colonial Immigrants in a British City: A Class Analysis* (1979), are two well-known sociological works.

3. P. Panayi, 'Middlesborough: A British Race Riot of the 1960s?' unpublished MS.

4. P. Fryer, *Staying Power. The History of Black People in Britain* (1984) and R. Visram, *Ayahs, Lascars and Princes. The Story of Indians in Britain 1700–1947* (1986) help to provide balance.

5. *Census 1971. Great Britain. Country of Birth Tables* (HMSO, 1974) p. 26.

6. N. Carrier and J. R. Jeffery, *External Migration. A Study of the Available Statistics* (HMSO, 1950) pp. 127–8; *Census 1951 England, Wales, General Report* (HMSO, 1958) p. 108; *Census 1951, Scotland. General Volume* (Edinburgh: HMSO, 1954), p. 55; *Census 1971 Great Britain*, p. 26.

7. R. King, 'Italian Migrants to Great Britain', *Geography*, 62, (1977) 179.

8. C. Holmes, *John Bull's Island. Immigration and British Society 1871–1971* (1988) develops the theme.

9. J. Geipel, *The Europeans. An Ethnohistorical Survey* (1969) pp. 163–4.

10. *Census 1971. Great Britain*, p. 26.

11. R. K. Kelsall, *Population* (4th edn, 1979) pp. 29–30, 115. See Office of Population Censuses and Surveys, *International Migration 1987* (HMSO, 1989) p. 1.

12. M. Lang, *An Austrian Cockney* (1980) dedication.

13. C. Holmes, *A Tolerant Country? Immigrants, Refugees and Minorities in Britain* (1991), addresses this theme.

14. B. Hepple, *Race, Jobs and the Law* (1968).

15. See Holmes, *John Bull's Island* for more detail on these themes.

16. Office of Population Censuses and Surveys to author, 3 October 1986.

17. J. L. Watson, 'The Chinese', in J. L. Watson (ed.), *Between Two Cultures* (Oxford, 1977) pp. 82–3.

18. V. G. Kiernan, 'Britons Old and New', in C. Holmes (ed.), *Immigrants and Minorities in British Society* (1978) p. 54.

19. I. McAuley, *Guide to Ethnic London* (1987).

20. J. A. Tannahill, *European Volunteer Workers in Britain* (Manchester, 1958).

21. See L. Grant and I. Martin, *Immigration Law and Practice* (1982); V. Bevan, *The Development of British Immigration Law* (1986).

22. R. Crossman, *The Diaries of a Cabinet Minister, Vol. I, Minister of Housing 1964–1966* (1975) pp. 149–50, entry for 5 February 1965.

23. The Runnymede Trust and Radical Statistics Race Group, *Britain's Black Population* (1980) p. 39.

24. R. Thurlow, *Fascism in Britain. A History, 1918–1985* (Oxford, 1987) pp. 75–7.

25. M. Supperstone and J. Cavanagh, *Immigration; The Law and Practice* (2nd edn, 1988) pp. 142–8. See also *Runnymede Trust Bulletin*, 218 (September 1988) 5.

26. *The Times*, 15 December 1989, 21 December 1989, 22 December 1989; *Sunday Telegraph*, 31 December 1989; *The Independent*, 6 January 1990.

27. *The Guardian*, 13 December 1989; *The Times*, 13 December 1989.

28. *The Guardian*, 19 December 1989, 'A chance to get out of the swamp' (Hugo Young).

29. K. O'Connor, *The Irish in Britain* (Dublin, 1974) p. 101.

30. D. Murphy, *Tales from Two Cities. Travel of another sort* (1987) p. 69.

31. C. Searle, 'Your Daily Dose: Racism and the *Sun*', *Race and Class*, XXIX (summer 1987) 55–72.

32. D. Lovibond, 'Will this be the death of England?', *Sunday Telegraph*, 13 August 1989 and 20 August 1989. See also J. Casey, 'One Nation: The Politics of Race', *Salisbury Review* (autumn 1982) pp. 23–8.

33. *Parliamentary Debates* (Commons), Vol, 138, 27 July 1988, col. 422.

34. Quoted *The Guardian*, 28 August 1989.

35. R. Jowell and C. Airey (eds), *British Social Attitudes. The 1984 Report* (Aldershot, 1984) pp. 121–5.

36. Law Society, *The Race Report* (1989).

37. Fifth Report from the Home Affairs Committee, *Racial Disadvantage*, H.C. 424–1 1981; p.lxxi.

38. *The Times* (letter) 9 February 1989.

39. Quoted in *The Times*, 17 May 1989. See Home Office, *Racial Attacks* (1981), for an earlier official assessment.

40. See generally M. Kettle and L. Hodges, *Uprising!* (1982). On Brixton see *The Brixton Disorders 10–12 April 1981*. Cmnd. 8427 (1981), better known as the Scarman Report.

41. *Runnymede Trust Bulletin*, 227 (July–August 1989) 3.

42. Racial Harassment Project, Sheffield City Council, *Because their skin is black* (Sheffield, 1989) pp. 46–7.

43. Information on Ireland, *Nothing but the Same Old Story. The Roots of Anti-Irish Racism* (1984) pp. 76ff; *The Guardian*, 18 August 1982, 'Silent Exiles in Search of a Voice'.

44. *War Crimes, Report of the War Crimes Enquiry*. Cm. 744 (1989).

45. *The Times*, 26 December 1989.

46. Bradford Heritage Recording Unit, Tape M0006/01/22.

47. J. Betjeman, *Summoned by Bells* (1976), p. 4.

48. S. Field *et al.*, *Ethnic Minorities in Britain. A Study of Trends in Their Position since 1961* (1981) is useful in this regard on blacks and Asians.

49. Quoted M. Banton, 'Social Acceptance and Rejection', in R. Hooper (ed.), *Colour in Britain* (1965) p. 115.

50. J. A. Jackson, *The Irish in Britain* (1963) p. 108.

51. *Loosen the Shackles*. First Report of the Liverpool 8 Inquiry into Race Relations in Liverpool (1989).

52. C. Husbands, 'East End Racism 1900–1980. Geographical Continuities in Vigilantist and Extreme Right Wing Political Behaviour', *London Journal*, 8 (1982) 21.

53. Stepney Trades Council, *Blood on the Streets* (1978?).

54. *The Times*, 1 April 1988.

11. THE CONSERVATIVE PARTY SINCE 1945 *Anthony Seldon*

NB Most references are to easily accessible sources, especially *Contemporary Record*. I am grateful to John Barnes, John Ramsden and William Bracken for reading and commenting on the chapter.

1. See, for example, the Bibliography to Chapter 12.

2. Publication in 1992/3 of Anthony Seldon (ed.), *The Conservative Party 1900–90* will fill some of the gaps.

3. David Butler, *British General Elections since 1945* (Oxford, 1989) pp. 9–11.

4. See H. G. Nicholas, *The British General Election of 1950* (1951).

5. Anthony Seldon, *Churchill's Indian Summer* (1981) pp. 54–5.

6. 'Had it not been for a much-reduced tally of Liberal candidates, Churchill would not have won at all.' Kenneth O. Morgan, *Labour in Power, 1945–51* (Oxford, 1984) p. 480.

7. Butler, *General Elections*, pp. 14–15.

8. Ibid., pp. 16–19.

9. Symposium, '1961–64: Did the Conservatives Lose Direction?' *Contemporary Record*, 2 (spring 1989) 26–31.

10. Butler, *General Elections*, pp. 19–23.

11. Michael Pinto-Duschinsky, 'From Macmillan to Home, 1959–64', in Peter Hennessy and Anthony Seldon (eds), *Ruling Performance* (Oxford, 1987) p. 156.

12. Butler, *General Elections*, pp. 23–5.

13. Symposium, 'Conservative Party Policy Making, 1965–70', *Contemporary Record*, 3 (spring 1990) 32–4; 3 (April 1990) 36–8.

14. John Callaghan, 'The Fragmenting Left since 1964', *Contemporary Record*, 1 (winter 1988) 14.

15. Butler, *General Elections*, pp. 32–6.

16. The widespread belief in the importance of the 'Falklands Factor' was challenged by David Sanders *et al*, 'Government Popularity and the Falklands War: a Re-assessment', *British Journal of Political Science*, 17 (1987) 281–314. It was taken up in *Contemporary Record*: see particularly Mark N. Franklin's and Lawrence Freedman's commentaries in 1 (autumn 1987) 27–9.

17. The debate is summarised in Ivor Crewe, 'Voting Patterns since 1959', *Contemporary Record*, 1 (winter 1988) 2–6. See also Anthony Heath, R. Jowell and John Curtice, *How Britain Votes* (Oxford, 1985).

18. John Ramsden, 'Conservatives since 1945', *Contemporary Record*, 2 (spring 1988) 19.

19. On the post-war consensus, see Dennis Kavanagh, *Thatcherism and British Politics* (2nd edn, Oxford, 1990) and Kavanagh and Peter Morris, *Consensus Politics* (Oxford, 1989).

20. Ben Pimlott, 'Is the Postwar Consensus a Myth?', *Contemporary Record*, 2 (summer 1989) 12–14.

21. Kenneth O. Morgan, 'Nationalisation and Privatisation', *Contemporary Record*, 1 (winter 1988) 33.

22. For a useful introduction, see Rodney Lowe, 'The Origins of the Welfare State in Britain', *Modern History Review* (September 1989) 24–5.

23. Ramsden, 'Conservatives since 1945', p. 21.

24. See Symposium, 'The Trade Unions and Fall of the Heath Government', *Contemporary Record*, 1 (spring 1988) 36–46.

25. Martin Holmes, 'Thatcherism: Scope and Limits', *Contemporary Record*, 1 (autumn 1987) 5.

26. Julian LeGrand, 'Recent History of the Welfare State = End of Consensus?', paper given at ICBH 3rd annual conference, April 1990.

27. John Curtice, 'North and South: The Growing Divide', *Contemporary Record*, 1 (winter 1988) 7–8.

28. For a useful survey, see Alan Ryan, 'Party Ideologies since 1945', *Contemporary Record*, 1 (winter 1988) 17–22.

29. Martin Durham, 'The Right: the Conservative Party and Con-

servatism', in Leonard Tivey and Anthony Wright (eds), *Party Ideology in Britain* (1989) pp. 53–4.

30. Harold Macmillan, *The Middle Way* (1938).

31. Quintin Hogg, *The Case for Conservatism* (Penguin edn, 1947) p. 32.

32. See Durham, 'The Right'.

33. Ian Gilmour, *Inside Right* (1977) p. 121.

34. See Michael Bentley, 'Is Mrs. Thatcher a Conservative?', *Contemporary Record*, 2 (summer 1989) 35–6.

35. See John Barnes' unpublished papers, 'Conservative Party Ideology since 1900', in Anthony Seldon (ed.), *The Conservative Party since 1900* (forthcoming, Oxford University Press).

36. Vincent McKee, 'Conservative Factions', *Contemporary Record*, 3 (autumn 1989) 30–2. McKee produced the chart of the factions.

37. The clearest exposition of the new right's thinking about the direction of post-war government policy can be found in Robert Skidelsky's own introductory essay in his (ed.), *Thatcherism* (1989). The two best introductions to the background to the Thatcher period are Kavanagh *Thatcherism ... Politics* and Peter Jenkins, *Mrs Thatcher's Revolution* (1987).

38. Arthur Seldon quoted in Kavanagh, *Thatcherism ... Politics*, p. 84.

39. See Douglas Schoen, *Enoch Powell and the Powellites* (1977), and also the short section in Durham, 'The Right' pp. 58–60.

40. John Campbell, 'Defining "Thatcherism"', *Contemporary Record*, 1 (autumn 1987) 2. For a left-wing interpretation, see Stuart Hall and Martin Jacques, *The Politics of Thatcherism* (1983).

41. For a record of these policies, see Peter Riddell, *The Thatcher Government* (Oxford, 1989), Martin Holmes, *The Thatcher Government 1979–83* (Brighton, 1985), and Holmes, *Thatcherism: Score and Limits, 1983–87* (1989). See also Bob Jessop *et al*, *Thatcherism* (Oxford, 1988), and Dennis Kavanagh and Anthony Seldon (eds), *The Thatcher Effect* (Oxford, 1989). The last tome contains 25 essays examining the impact of Mrs Thatcher on different areas over her first ten years in office.

42. Campbell, 'Defining "Thatcherism"', pp. 2–5.

43. See, for example, Arthur Seldon (ed.), *The New Right Enlightenment* (1985).

44. Ben Pimlott, 'The Unimportance of "Thatcherism"', *Contemporary Record*, 3 (autumn 1989) 15.

45. See Ivor Crewe, 'The Policy Agenda', *Contemporary Record*, 3 (February 1990) 2–6.

46. Dennis Kavanagh strongly rejects claims about the alleged unimportance of Thatcherism. See Kavanagh and Morris, *Consensus Politics*.

47. Robert T. McKenzie, *British Political Parties* (1955).

48. McKenzie's arguments are discussed critically in Richard Kelly

and Steve Foster, 'Power in the Parties. McKenzie Re-visited', *Contemporary Record*, 3 (February 1990) 18–20.

49. Seldon, *Churchill's Indian Summer*, pp. 38–54.

50. Norton's views are neatly summarised in his article 'The Changing Face of Parliament', *Contemporary Record*, 1 (autumn 1988) 2–6.

51. See Peter Hennessy, Cabinet (1986). See also George W. Jones, 'Mrs Thatcher and the Power of the PM', *Contemporary Record*, 3 (April 1990) 2–6.

52. Ramsden, 'Conservatives since 1945', p. 23.

53. Kevin Swaddle, 'Hi-Tech Elections', *Contemporary Record*, 1 (spring 1988) 33.

54. Gillian Peele, 'British Political Parties in the 1980s', in Anthony Seldon (ed.), *UK Political Parties since 1945* (1990) p. 148.

55. Ramsden, 'Conservatives since 1945', p. 26.

56. Michael Pinto-Duschinsky, 'Party Finance. Funding of Political Parties since 1945', *Contemporary Record*, 1 (winter 1988) 21.

57. Keith Ewing, *The Funding of Political Parties in Britain* (Cambridge, 1987) p. 177.

58. Pinto-Duschinsky, 'Party Finance', p. 20.

59. It is of course a subject of debate as to whether parties in power change the course of policy. See Richard Rose, *Do Parties Make a Difference?* (1980). See also, Peter Pulzer, 'Do Parties Matter', *Contemporary Record*, 1 (winter 1988) 23–4.

60. Each government is assessed in turn in Hennessy and Seldon, *Ruling Performance*.

12. LABOUR AS A GOVERNING PARTY: BALANCING RIGHT AND LEFT
Martin Ceadel

1. Vernon Bogdanor, *The People and the Party System* (Cambridge, 1981) p. 1.

2. Harold Macmillan, *Tides of Fortune* (1969) p. 278.

3. The best account of this process, and indeed of Labour's approach to government throughout its history, is David Howell, *British Social Democracy* (1980 edn).

4. Jose Harris, *William Beveridge: a Biography* (Oxford, 1977) p. 413.

5. Jonathan Schneer, *Labour's Conscience: The Labour Left 1945–51* (Boston, 1988) p. 26.

6. Howell, *British Social Democracy*, p. 79. This had been identified as an ultimate goal as early as the 1908 party conference. By 1914 there were specific commitments in regard to the mines, railways and canals, to which in 1918 'Labour and the New Social Order' had added electricity, roads, shipping and harbours, industrial assurance and brewing.

7. Kenneth O. Morgan, *Labour in Power 1945–1951* (Oxford, 1984) pp. 16, 26.

8. Ibid., pp. 110–19.

9. Ibid., p. 135 (see also pp. 130–6, 366–9); and Henry Pelling, *The Labour Governments, 1945–51* (1984) p. 171.

10. See Martin Ceadel, 'British Political Parties and the European Crisis of the late 1940s', in Josef Becker and Franz Knipping (eds), *Power in Europe? Great Britain, France, Italy and Germany in a Postwar World* (Berlin and New York, 1986).

11. Edwin Plowden, *An Industrialist in the Treasury: the post-war years* (1989) p. 153.

12. *Labour Party Conference Report 1944*, pp. 165–7.

13. Howell, *British Social Democracy*, pp. 168–71.

14. Hugh Berrington, *Backbench Opinion in the House of Commons 1945–55* (Oxford, 1973) pp. 92–3; Mark Jenkins, *Bevanism: Labour's High Tide* (Nottingham, 1979) pp. 152–3.

15. For details see Martin Ceadel, 'British parties and the European situation 1950–57', *Storia delle relazioni internazionali*, IV(i) (1988) 174–5, 191–3.

16. For a devastating critique see John Campbell, *Nye Bevan and the Mirage of British Socialism* (1987), ch. 18.

17. Cited in Howell, *British Social Democracy*, p. 222.

18. A point made by Robert Rhodes James, *Ambitions and Realities* (1972) p. 15.

19. D. E. Butler and Richard Rose, *The British General Election of 1959* (1960) pp. 132, 273–4.

20. Paul Foot, *The Politics of Harold Wilson* (Penguin edn, 1968) pp. 9–16.

21. D. E. Butler and Anthony King, *The British General Election of 1966* (1966) p. 64.

22. D. E. Butler and Anthony King, *The British General Election of 1964* (1965) p. 135.

23. Samuel Brittan, *Left or Right: the Bogus Dilemma* (1968) p. 115.

24. Martin Jacques and Francis Mulhern (eds), *The Forward March of Labour Halted?* (1981) p. 83.

25. Lewis Minkin, *The Labour Party Conference* (1978) p. 87.

26. Patrick Seyd, *The Rise and Fall of the Labour Left* (1987) pp. 77–8.

27. Howell, *British Social Democracy*, p. 246.

28. Kenneth O. Morgan, *Labour People* (Oxford, 1988) pp. 302–5.

29. Eric Shaw, *Discipline and Discord in the Labour Party* (Manchester, 1988) pp. 182–3. See also Michael Hatfield, *The House The Left Built: Inside Labour Policy-Making 1970–75* (1978) pp. 191–2; Minkin, *Labour Party Conference*, p. 336.

30. Howell, *British Social Democracy*, p. 288–9; David Coates, *Labour in Power?* (1980) p. 89.

31. Minkin, *Labour Party Conference*, p. 329.

32. Seyd, *Rise and Fall*, pp. 44–6.

33. Austin Mitchell, *Four Years in the Death of the Labour Party* (1983) p. 20.

34. Michael Crick, *Militant* (1984) p. 42.

35. David Kogan and Maurice Kogan, *The Battle for the Labour Party* (1983 edn) p. 29.

36. D. Hine, 'Leaders and Followers', in William E. Paterson and Alastair H. Thomas (eds), *The Future of Social Democracy* (Oxford, 1986) p. 279.

37. Howell, *British Social Democracy*, p. 291.

38. Cited in Kogan and Kogan, *Battle*, p. 61.

39. Bernard Donoughue, *Prime Minister: the Conduct of Policy under Harold Wilson and James Callaghan* (1987) p. 94.

40. James Callaghan, *Time and Chance* (1987) p. 509.

41. Cited in David Butler and Dennis Kavanagh, *The British General Election of 1979* (1980) p. 148.

42. Ibid., p. 46; see also pp. 50–6.

43. Philip Williams, 'The Labour Party: the rise of the left', in Hugh Berrington (ed.), *Change in British Politics* (1984) p. 43.

44. David Butler and Dennis Kavanagh, *The British General Election of 1983* (1984) p. 62; J. Silkin, *Changing Battlefields* (1987) p. 14.

45. David Butler and Dennis Kavanagh, *The British General Election of 1987* (1988) p. 71.

46. Colin Hughes and Patrick Wintour, *Labour Rebuilt: the New Model Party* (1990) ch. 13.

47. Peter Kellner, 'The week Labour's left was routed', *Independent*, 6 October 1989, p. 19.

13. BRITAIN AND THE TWO IRELANDS SINCE 1945   *Alan O'Day*

D. G. Boyce, Michael Bromley, Dennis Dean and John Hutchinson made valuable suggestions for the revision of this chapter.

1. Quoted in Martin Gilbert, *Winston Churchill 1945–1965*, VIII (1988) p. 12.

2. Bob Purdie, 'The Friends of Ireland: British Labour and Irish Nationalism, 1945–49', in *Contemporary Irish Studies*, ed. Tom Gallagher and James O'Connell (Manchester, 1983) pp. 81–94.

3. *Annual Register* (1948) p. 113. Hereafter cited as *AR*.

4. Ibid., p. 108.

5. Quoted in Gilbert, *Winston Churchill*, VIII, p. 254 n. 2.

6. Purdie, 'The Friends of Ireland', pp. 86–7.

7. *Parliamentary Debates*, 5th Series, Vol. 257 (1948) 239. Hereafter cited as *PD*.

8. *AR* (1948) p. 129.

9. Ibid. (1949) p. 72.

10. *PD*, Vol. 264 (1948–9) 1856.
11. Ibid., 1863–67.
12. Ibid., 1885–86.
13. Purdie, 'The Friends of Ireland', p. 92.
14. *AR* (1954) p. 209.
15. Ibid. (1955) p. 210.
16. Ibid. (1956) p. 70.
17. Ibid. (1957) pp. 71, 231, 233.
18. Ibid. (1962) p. 60.
19. Ibid. (1965) p. 57.
20. *The Times*, 18 March 1965.
21. *AR* (1968) p. 52.
22. Ibid. (1965) p. 50.
23. Ibid. (1968) p. 51.
24. *The Times*, 30 October 1968.
25. Ibid., 5 November 1968.
26. Ibid., 23 November 1968.
27. Ibid., 22 April 1969.
28. *PD*, Vol. 782 (1968–9) 287; see Richard Crossman, *The Diaries of a Cabinet Minister 1968–70*, III (1977) pp. 450–1.
29. *The Times*, 24 April 1969.
30. See O'Neill's obituaries: *Guardian, Times, Independent*, 14 June 1990.
31. *AR* (1972) p. 43.
32. *The Times*, 20 August 1969; see Brian Faulkner, *Memoirs of a Statesman* (1978) pp. 64–71.
33. *The Times*, 30 August 1969.
34. *PD*, Vol 799 (1969–70) 319.
35. *The Times*, 24 July 1970.
36. *PD*, Vol. 826 (1971–2) 1586–90.
37. *The Times*, 31 January 1972.
38. *AR* (1972), pp. 42–7, 165.
39. *The Times*, 17 November 1972.
40. Ibid., 9 March 1973.
41. *AR* (1974) p. 66.
42. *The Times*, 27 May 1974.
43. Ibid., 2 February 1978.
44. *AR* (1976) p. 37.
45. *The Times*, 9 January 1978.
46. Ibid., 30 May 1980.
47. Ibid., 9 December 1980.
48. *AR* (1981) pp. 52–3.
49. *The Times*, 7 November 1981.
50. See Cornelius O'Leary, Sidney Elliott and R. A. Wilford, *The Northern Ireland Assembly, 1982–1986* (1988).

51. *The Times*, 23 December 1983.

52. Ibid., 16 November 1985.

53. *PD*, Vol. 782 (1968–9), 287.

14. YOUTH CULTURE AND THE EMERGENCE OF POPULAR MUSIC   *John Street*

Acknowledgements: I owe thanks to Terry Gourvish for helping me to improve an earlier version of this chapter.

1. G. Marcus, 'The Beatles' in J. Miller (ed.), *The Rolling Stone Illustrated History of Rock and Roll* (New York, 1976) p. 175.

2. A. Bicat, 'Fifties Children: Sixties People', in V. Bogdanor and R. Skidelsky (eds), *The Age of Affluence 1951–1964* (1970).

3. *Melody Maker*, 30 June 1956, p. 4.

4. L. Martin and K. Segrave, *Anti-Rock: the Opposition to Rock'n'Roll* (New York, 1988) pp. 33–5.

5. N. Cohn, *Awopbopaloobop Alopbamboom: Pop from the Beginning* (1970) p. 21.

6. M. Abrams, *The Teenage Consumer* (1959).

7. S. Frith, *The Sociology of Rock* (1978) p. 19.

8. For example, on the left, the Labour MP Marcus Lipton called for the banning of certain records; on the right, there was the Moral Welfare Council of the Church of England making the same plea (*Melody Maker*, 30 June 1956, p. 4). The trend continued into the 1960s when Paul Johnson, then on the left but already moving to the right, wrote a notorious piece on 'The Menace of Beatlism', *New Statesman*, 28 February 1964, pp. 326–7.

9. S. Frith, 'The Making of the British Record Industry 1920–1964', in J. Curran *et al.* (eds), *Impacts and Influences*, (1987) p. 288.

10. D. Hebdige, 'Towards a Cartography of Taste 1935–1962', in *Hiding in the Light* (1988) pp. 45–76.

11. D. Webster, *Looka Yonder: The Imaginary America of Popular Culture* (1988) pp. 181–6.

12. S. Barnard, *On the Radio: Music Radio in Britain* (Milton Keynes, 1989) pp. 29, 37–8.

13. S. Beer, *Britain Against Itself* (1977) p. 140; for a discussion of the political significance of the 1960s, see A. Marwick, 'The 1960s: Was There a "Cultural Revolution"?' *Contemporary Record*, 2, No. 3 (autumn 1988) 18–20.

14. P. Norman, *Shout! The True Story of the Beatles* (1981) p. 56.

15. S. Frith and H. Horne, *Art into Pop* (1987) pp. 81–5.

16. I. Chambers, *Popular Culture: the Metropolitan Experience* (1986) p. 159.

17. See, for example, M. Brake, *The Sociology of Youth Culture and Youth Subcultures* (1980).

18. J. Green, *Days in the Life* (1988) pp. 135–6.

19. T. Ali, *Street Fighting Years* (1987) p. 250.

20. Green, *Days in the Life*, p. 187.

21. R. Hewison, *Too Much: Art and Society in the Sixties* (1986) p. 189.

22. G. Pearson and G. Mungham, *Working-Class Youth Culture* (1976).

23. S. Frith, *Sound Effects* (1983) ch. 9.

24. D. Laing, *One Chord Wonders* (Milton Keynes, 1985) p. 5; J. Qualen, *The Music Industry* (1985).

25. A view propagated by books such as J. Burchill and T. Parsons, *The Boy Looked at Johnny* (1978).

26. G. Marcus, *Lipstick Traces: A Secret History of the 20th Century* (Cambridge, Mass., 1989).

27. B. Geldof, *Is that it?* (1986).

28. Ibid., p. 304.

29. *Press and Journal* (Glasgow), 11 December 1987.

30. *BPI Year Book 1988/9* (1989).

31. S. Frith (ed.), *Facing the Music* (1990).

Notes on Contributors

MARTIN CEADEL, MA, DPhil (Oxford) is Official Fellow and Tutor in Politics at New College, Oxford. He was previously a Lecturer at the University of Sussex and at Imperial College. His publications include *Pacifism in Britain 1914–1945* and *Thinking about Peace and War*.

MICHAEL DOCKRILL, BSc (Econ) (London), MA (Illinois), PhD (London) is Senior Lecturer in War Studies, King's College, London. His many writings include *The Mirage of Power: British Foreign Policy 1902–1922* (with C. J. Lowe), *Peace without Promise: Britain and the Peace Conferences 1919–1923* (with J. Douglas Goold), *The Formulation of a Continental Foreign Policy by Great Britain 1908–1912*, *The Cold War 1945–1963*, *British Defence since 1945*, *The Ethics of War* (with Barrie Paskins), and (co-ed), *British Security Policy 1945–1956*.

TERRY GOURVISH, BA, PhD (London) is Director of the Business History Unit at the London School of Economics and Political Science, and formerly was Dean of the School of Economic and Social Studies, University of East Anglia. His publications include *Mark Huish and the London and North Western Railway*, *Railways and the British Economy 1830–1914*, *British Railways 1948–73: A Business History*, and *Norfolk Beers from English Barley, A History of Steward & Patteson*. He co-edited *Later Victorian Britain* in the PiF series and has been joint editor of the *Journal of Transport History*.

JOSE HARRIS, MA, PhD (Cambridge), is Reader in Modern History, University of Oxford and Fellow of St Catherine's College, Oxford. She was formerly Senior Lecturer in Social Administration, the London School of Economics and Political Science. Her publications include *Unemployment and Politics 1886–1914* and *William Beveridge: A Biography*.

COLIN HOLMES is a Professor in the Department of History at the University of Sheffield. His publications include *Immigrants and Minorities in British Society*, *Anti-Semitism in British Society 1876–1939*, *John Bull's Island. Immigration and British Society 1871–1971* and *A Tolerant Country? Immigrants, Refugees and Minorities in Britain*. He is joint-editor of the Journal *Immigrants and Minorities*.

MAURICE KIRBY, BA (Newcastle upon Tyne), PhD (Sheffield) is Reader in Economic History at the University of Lancaster. His well-known publications include *The British Coalmining Industry 1870–1946*, *The Decline of British Economic Power since 1870*, and *Men of Business and Politics: The Rise and Fall of the Quaker Pease Dynasty of North-East England*.

ALAN O'DAY, BA (Michigan), MA (Roosevelt; Northwestern), PhD (London) is Senior Lecturer in History at the Polytechnic of North London. His numerous publications include *The English Face of Irish Nationalism*, *Parnell and the First Home Rule Episode*, (ed.), *The Edwardian Age* in the PiF series, (ed.), *Reactions to Irish Nationalism 1865–1914*, *A Survey of the Irish in England (1872)*, (co.-ed.), *Terrorism in Ireland*, (co.-ed.), *Ireland's Terrorist Dilemma*, (co.-ed.), *Ireland's Terrorist Trauma*, (co.-ed.), *The Irish Terrorism Experience*, (co.-ed.), *Later Victorian Britain* in the PiF series, (co.-ed.), *Irish Historical Documents, since 1800*, and jointly edited *Governments and Non-Dominant Ethnic Groups in Europe, 1850–1940: The Rise of Social and Political Elites*.

MICHAEL SANDERSON, MA, PhD (Cambridge) is Reader in Economic and Social History at the University of East Anglia. Among his many writings are *The Universities and British Industry, 1850–1970*, *The Universities in the Nineteenth Century*, *Education, Economic Change and Society 1780–1870*, *From Irving to Olivier: A Social History of the Acting Profession in England 1880–1983*, and *Educational Opportunity and Social Change in England 1900–1980s*.

ANTHONY SELDON, MA (Oxford), PhD (London) is Director, Institute of Contemporary British History, London. He has written *Churchill's Indian Summer*, *By Word of Mouth* (with Joanna Pappworth), *Ruling Performance* (with Peter Hennessy), *The Thatcher Effect* (with Dennis Kavanagh), *Governments and Economics since 1945* (with Andrew Graham). He is editor and co-editor of three journals, *Contemporary Record*, *Modern History Review*, and *Twentieth Century British History*.

JOHN STEVENSON, MA, DPhil (Oxford) is Official Fellow and Tutor in Modern History at Worcester College, Oxford, and was formerly Reader in History, University of Sheffield. He has written, co-authored, edited and co-edited more than twenty volumes, including *The Slump*, *Popular Disturbances in England, 1700–1870*, *Popular Protest and Public Order*, *British Society 1914–45*, and *Social Conditions Between the Wars*.

JOHN STREET, BA (Warwick), DPhil (Oxford) is Lecturer in Politics at the University of East Anglia. Previously, he was a Junior Research Fellow at Nuffield College, Oxford. His publications include *Rebel Rock:*

The Politics of Popular Music and several articles. He is a member of the executive of the British section of the International Association for the Study of Popular Music.

PAT THANE, MA (Oxford), PhD (London) is Reader in Social History and Head of the Department of Social Science and Administration, Goldsmiths' College, London. Her well-known publications include *The Foundations of the Welfare State*, (ed.), *Origins of British Social Policy*, (co.-ed.), *Essays in Social History*, Vol. 2, and the chapter 'Government and Society in England and Wales, 1750–1914', in F. M. L. Thompson (ed.), *A Cambridge Social History of Britain, 1750–1950*.

CHRIS WRIGLEY, BA (East Anglia), PhD (London) is Professor of Modern British History at the University of Nottingham. His impressive list of writings includes *David Lloyd George and the British Labour Movement, Lloyd George and the Challenge of Labour, Arthur Henderson, A. J. P. Taylor: A Complete Bibliography*, (ed.), *Warfare, Diplomacy and Politics*, (ed.), *A History of British Industrial Relations, 1875–1914*, Vol. 1, *1914–1939*, Vol. 2.

Index

wages, *see* industrial relations
Wakefield prison, 300
Wales, 169, 196, 277
Wales, South, 96, 216
Weaver, Sir Toby, 167
welfare state, 5, 36, 39–58, 160, 243, 245, 247–8
Welwyn Garden City, 92
Westland crisis 1986, 241
Westwood, Vivienne, 318
Whitehouse, Mary, 317
Whitelaw, William, 256, 295
Who, The, 321
Wiener, Martin, 27–8
Wilensky, Harold, 45
Wilkinson, Ellen, 162
Wilmot, John, 266
Wilmot and Young, 92
Wilson, Harold, 60, 63, 67, 71, 119, 148, 150–1, 218, 236–40, 267, 269, 271–6, 291–5, 297, 312, 315
women, 8, 18, 81–3, 85, 178, 183–208
Women's Liberation Workshop, 204–5
Woolton, Lord, 258
Worcester, 106
workers' control, 266
working class, 41, 106–7, 169, 171, 195, 197, 201–2, 237, 269, 272, 311, 316
Wythenshawe, 92

youth culture, 305–23

Zuckerman Report, 201